*The Metaphysics
of Evolution*

SUNY Series in
Philosophy and Biology

David Edward Shaner, Editor

The Metaphysics
of Evolution

David L. Hull

State University of New York Press

PHOTOGRAPH (BACK COVER) By Larry Lapidus

Published by
State University of New York Press, Albany

© 1989   State University of New York

For information, address State University of New York
Press, State University Plaza, Albany, N.Y., 12246

Library of Congress Cataloging-in-Publication Data

Hull, David L.
     The metaphysics of evolution / David L. Hull
          p.   cm.—(SUNY series in the philosophy of biology)
     Bibliography: p.
     Includes index.
     ISBN 0-7914-0211-8.—ISBN 0-7914-0212-6 (pbk.)
     1. Evolution—Philosophy.   2. Metaphysics.   I. Title.
II. Series: SUNY series in philosophy and biology.
QH371.H85 1989   89-31776
575'.001—dc20   CIP

10 9 8 7 6 5 4 3 2 1

For Michael Ruse,
a good friend of many years.

Contents

Introduction

In his sympathetic summary of my work over the past two decades, Michael Ruse (1989) accurately perceives my overall goal as presenting an "organicist" or "holist," albeit hard-nosed, view of both nature and science. I have wanted to do more than just gesture at organization and cohesiveness, whether in the context of plants and animals or in the context of science itself. Sexual organisms reproduce by pooling their genetic material. What effect does this practice have on biological evolution? What implications does it have for those organisms that rarely, if ever, recombine their genes? Scientists actually do expose their views to serious testing, but why? Why does science work the way that it does?

To answer such questions I have striven to obtain at least a second-hand knowledge of selected area of biology (evolutionary theory and systematics) and to study scientists the way that scientists study everything else. The unity I have perceived concerns both the processes responsible for biological, social, and conceptual change, and the nature of the entities that function in these processes. In the past, philosophers and scientists have cooperated to forge a reasonably good notion of functional organization that applies to a variety of functionally organized systems from organisms to computers. For some reason, much less effort has been expended in producing a comparable general account of selection processes. We are now in the midst of working out the general features of selection processes regardless of whether the subject matter is biological evolution, the response of the immune system to antigens, the ontogenetic development of the central nervous system, or conceptual change in science. One essential element in all these processes is the ancestor-descendant relationship and its attendant notion of generations.

In my work I have shied away from the philosophical issues most intimately connected to one species out of the millions that have evolved in the past few billion years, the species to which I happen to belong. All species evolve, including *Homo sapiens*. All species are also unique, including ours. In general, my conviction has been that we have paid too much attention to the ways in which the human species differs from all other species and too little attention to the ways in which we are like all other species. This book begins with a paper in which I vent my irritation at those who propose to base ethics on "human nature," when they know little more about the human species than they have learned from their limited experience in their own tiny corner of their particular subculture. On the basis of such minimal experience, they conclude that we are all basically the same or, more bluntly, that everyone is basically like me and mine. Any departures from this immutable norm are deviations. The reasoning seems to be that I certainly have rights, and others have rights to the extent that they are similar to me.

Anyone who doubts these bald assertions can check their accuracy by reading at random in the works of such great ethicists as Kant. The principles enunciated are general enough, but when they are applied to real cases, such as male dominance and euthanasia, the results are embarrassing. Even the most thoughtful and rebellious human beings are children, if not prisoners, of their own subcultures. In my essay "On Human Nature" I take seriously the goal of basing ethics on what biologists tell us about the nature of *Homo sapiens* as a biological species. My argument is straightforward: the essence of sexual species is variability. We are a sexual species. Hence, our essence lies in our variability. Any ethical system that depends on all people being essentially the same is mistaken. If we will have rights, we must have rights even if we are not all basically the same.

Through the years, I have written on Darwin, aided tremendously by the efforts of what too often is derided as the Darwin industry. No one can do everything, and I for one have found the results of the intensive investigations conducted by Darwin scholars to be invaluable. My chief concern has been the connection between Darwin's theory and philosophical issues. Why did the leading philosophers of science in Darwin's day, John Herschel, William Whewell, and John Stuart Mill, reject his theory? The answer is that it struck at the foundations of the philosophies of science that they themselves were promulgating, in particular teleology and essentialism. Nineteenth century British philosophers interposed invariable laws between God and his creation. God did not create a slipshod universe that needed constant tinkering. From studying the book of nature, Victorian scientists thought that they could discern the face of God. Unfortunately, the God that Darwin's mechanism of chance variation and natural selection implied was anything but the nineteenth-century God of waste not, want not. More importantly, invariable laws required eternal immutable natural kinds, and one of the two most frequently cited examples of such natural kinds were biological species. Darwin's philosophically-oriented contemporaries reasoned that, if species evolve, laws of nature evolve, and if natural laws evolve, scientific knowledge is impossible. Faced with this alternative, the leading philosophers in Darwin's day had no choice but to reject Darwin's theory.

An issue that has come into some prominence recently is the relative influence on the generation and acceptance of scientific ideas of such factors internal to science as reason, argument, and evidence, and such external factors as prestige, availability of research money, social class, and the like. One of the external factors most commonly cited is age: we assume that old scientists are less creative in producing radically new views and less likely to accept those generated by their younger colleagues. After an extensive study of the reception of Darwin's hypothesis that species evolve, I was forced to conclude that age played a much smaller role than commonly thought, widespread prejudice against older scientists notwithstanding. If nothing else, this paper indicates the various claims about influences on science, no matter their sort, need careful study. A few examples are not good enough—we need statistical studies.

The final paper in part II concerns Darwin's strategy in confronting his perceived opponents. In his *Origin of Species*, he argued explicitly and extensively against such creationists as William Whewell, while ignoring such equally powerful opponents as his scientific mentor, Charles Lyell, who opted for reverent silence, and such idealists as Richard Owen. Darwin knew that his theory of evolution would cause Lyell considerable trouble. If Darwin was right about species evolving, then, as Lyell moaned, he would have to rewrite totally the second volume of his *Principles of Geology*. Once again, the issue is the implications of Darwin's theory for our understanding of science. Accepting Darwin's theory required the rejection of the views most widely held at the time about the nature of science.

In part III, I turn to evolutionary theory proper; in particular, what sorts of entities can function in the evolutionary process. I argue that an account of selection processes that is sufficiently general to handle the range of creatures living here on Earth—from slime molds and blue-green algae to blood flukes and aspens—must abandon the *traditional* hierarchy of genes, chromosomes, cells, organs, organisms, demes, species, niches, and ecosystems. Evolution *is* hierarchical, but the traditional hierarchy is not good enough. At minimum, biologists need to think in terms of replicators, interactors, and lineages. Selection processes must be defined in terms of these technical notions. The question then becomes, in any particular selection regimen, which entities play which roles? My chief metaphysical claim is that only spatiotemporally localized and cohesive entities can function as replicators and interactors. As a result, if species are to perform either of these roles, then they must be individuals of a highly organized sort. The organization exhibited by lineages is much less cohesive. Lineages can change indefinitely through time. However, because lineages are defined in terms of replication, they too are spatio-temporally localized. It may well be that species function primarily as lineages and rarely as replicators and interactors. They nevertheless count as individuals. In short, all the entities that *function in* selection processes or *result from* them are individuals in the appropriate sense. The alterations in our understanding of biological evolution that are entailed by this change in perspective are as pervasive as they are beneficial — so I claim.

The science of biological systematics has quite understandably been central to my research program, both because species have traditionally played such a central role in biological evolution, and because systematics was one of the two areas of science that I chose to study in order to understand why science works as it does. I began my research by studying a burgeoning school at the University of Kansas, a group who called themselves "numerical taxonomists" to emphasize their reliance on mathematical techniques, in particular those that allow the use of computers to make taxonomic judgments. Their opponents tended to call them "numerical pheneticists" to highlight their empirical, inductivist, operationist philosophy. While I was studying the numerical taxonomists, another group developed at the American Museum of Natural History in New York. Because the members of this group traced their views about systematics to Willi Hennig's *Grundzüge einer Theorie der Phylogenetischen Systematik* (1950), they began by calling themselves "phylogeneticists," but other systematists objected that they were just as concerned with phylogeny as were the Hennigians. Eventually, Hennig's followers became known as "cladists," after the Greek word for branch. The name was appropriate because cladists, in the early years at least, restricted themselves to discerning the order of branching in phylogenetic development.

In my first graduate school paper, I attempted to discover the sort of relationship that one could establish between phylogeny and hierarchical classifications using the principles of classification set out by G. G. Simpson (1961). Because I was totally unaware of Hennig at the time, and the dispute between cladistics and other taxonomic philosophies was a decade away, I called Simpson's views "phylogenetic," but it should be obvious that throughout this paper I am talking about Simpson's views, not those of Hennig. My conclusion was that, given Simpson's rather flexible principles of classification, any phylogeny can be classified in a variety of ways, and conversely, any classification can be based on numerous different phylogenies. As a result of this many-many relationship between phylogenies and classifications, little can be inferred from a classification about the phylogeny that gave rise to it.

Hennig took just the opposite tack, asking what can be unequivocally represented about phylogeny given the limits of the Linnean hierarchy. He selected the sister-group relation as the relation to represent in cladistic classifications. A and B are more closely related to each other than either is to C if and only if A and B branched off from each other after branching off from C. Hennig maintained that representing one aspect of phylogeny clearly and unequivocally was superior to representing several vaguely and impressionistically.

Initially Hennig's intellectual descendants pursued his general goals and philosophy, but the development of cladistics took an unexpected turn when several of his most influential descendants began to argue that no assumptions about the evolutionary process need be made in order to carry out a cladistic analysis. According to these cladists, the essence of Hennig's system is the methodology that he worked out to handle sister-group relations, and the most that this method requires is descent with modification. In fact, even this modest assumption may not be necessary. Species might exhibit hierarchical relations even if they had been specially created. At times, advocates of what came to be known as pattern cladism seemed to argue that all systematists should actually do is discern patterns. All else is unscientific speculation. At the very least, pattern is prior to any considerations of process.

The first major presentation of pattern cladism appeared in Gareth Nelson and Norman Platnick's *Systematics and Biogeography* (1981). In this book, Nelson and Platnick combine Hennig's principles of classification with Leon Croizat's views on biogeography and the philosophy of Karl Popper; in particular, his principle of falsifiability. In my paper "Karl Popper and Plato's Metaphor," I argue that Popper designed his principle of falsifiability to distinguish genuine theories about natural processes from pseudoscientific surrogates, not biological classifications. In order to apply Popper's principle of falsifiability to biological classifications, taxa would have to be natural kinds. Biological taxa can be interpreted as particulars (or individuals), possibly even numerical universals, but not natural kinds. Hence, in order to use Popper's philosophy, Nelson and Platnick had to transform it—as they had transformed the views of Hennig and Croizat.

When Nelson first began to urge Hennig's principles of biological classification on the systematics community, he insisted that no such thing as cladism as a philosophy of classification actually existed. It was an invention of his enemies. In fact, Ernst Mayr *was* instrumental in renaming Hennig's phylogenetics "cladistics," as he had successfully introduced the term "numerical phenetics" to replace "numerical taxonomy." When an unsuspecting young philosopher, John Beatty (1982a), broached the idea that perhaps some of Hennig's descendants had departed significantly from the views of their intellectual ancestor and named this emerging group "pattern cladists," he was treated quite roughly. Pattern cladism did not exist. In my "Cladistic Theory: Hypotheses that Blur and Grow," I argue that such disputes in science arise from scientists treating scientific change "essentialistically"; that is, from viewing scientific research programs as consisting of essential tenets. On this interpretation, any scientist who changes his or her mind on any of the essential tenets of a research program immediately and automatically has abandoned this program.

As we might expect, scientists are not anxious to be characterized as completely abandoning their previous views simply because they modify one of them. Thus, they spend an inordinate amount of time in textual exegesis, arguing that they always held the views they now hold. Any appearance of change results from misinterpretation. Although falsifiability may well be the hallmark of science, they are fortunate that all their essential beliefs have turned out to be correct. On occasion scientists publicly admit that positions they formerly advocated are simply false, but not often. Instead, they silently modify their views under the cover of verbal smoke screens. In part V, I show how differently science appears when viewed from an evolutionary perspective in which hypotheses blur and grow. In fact, they can grow only by blurring.

In the past, philosophers have tended to conceive of conceptual change in the same atemporal way that ideal morphologists perceive the relationships among living organisms. Just as a circle can be transformed into an ellipse, a fin can be transformed into a leg or wing. But for ideal morphologists, such transformations are first and foremost formal and only secondarily temporal. In two of the papers in this part, I show how profoundly we must restructure how we treat conceptual identity if we are to understand conceptual change as a temporal process. To be specific, we must distinguish between conceptual homologies and conceptual analogies (or homoplasies). The change in perspective is profound and disturbingly counterintuitive.

Philosophers of history have long argued against "presentism"—reconstructing the past from the vantage of the present. Although historiographers are right to condemn many of the practices that they label "presentist," at times they seem to go too far. Like it or not, anyone who tries to reconstruct the past is lodged firmly in the present. The only data available are those that have survived to the present. More importantly, historians can and must use current best estimates of how the world operates to infer the past. Perhaps in the period under investigation, people believed that eclipses of the moon result from a dragon eating this celestial body, but present-day historians think differently. To refuse to use celestial mechanics to date a particular eclipse for fear of presentism is counterproductive in the extreme. There is no justification in a present-day historian chastising a scientist in any earlier age for not knowing what we know today, but histories are not improved by our ignoring that we do hold beliefs that depart significantly from those of our subjects.

But even if historians could totally divorce themselves from the present in reconstructing the past, they would still have to reintroduce the present when it came time to write up the results of their research because historians write for their contemporaries. Ignoring the knowledge and perspective of one's readers is guaranteed to produce misunderstanding. Even if a historian is writing *about* nineteenth century British naturalists, he or she cannot possibly write *for* them. They are dead.

In part VI, I sketch a general view of the mechanisms that I take to be responsible for science working the way that it does, and use the recent history of sociobiology to illustrate my general view. Anyone who presents a theory about how theories change is involved in a self-referential activity. If others try to camouflage changes in their ideas, then so might the author making such a claim. If science proceeds by means of a complex interplay between conceptual inclusive fitness and group allegiance, then so might the science of science. Taken literally, sociobiology is the attempt to extend biological evolution to include human behavior and the social relations exhibited in human societies. If biological evolution is necessarily gene-based, then the explanations sociobiologists present for all human behavior, including their own, is necessarily gene-based. Much of the controversy which the most recent resurgence of sociobiology elicited has concerned the role of genes in human behavior and societies. The theory that I present does not depend on such a construal. Perhaps the general characteristics that make scientists behave the way they do are in some sense gene-based, but the mode of transmission central to conceptual change, including scientific change, is largely independent of genetic transmission. Instead, I assimilate both gene-based and meme-based change to the general analysis of selection processes that I set out in part III (for a fuller treatment, see Hull 1988).

Although the papers included in this volume were published over twenty-five years, the reader should not be surprised to discover that they all converge on a single, unified perspective. At least that is the way that I perceive them—as I should. If the general theory of conceptual change that I present is basically correct, then this is precisely how I must perceive my own work if I am not to falsify my own position.

Part I

On Human Nature

Chapter 1

On Human Nature*

Generations of philosophers have argued that all human beings are essentially the same, that is, they share the same nature, and that this essential similarity is extremely important. Periodically philosophers have proposed to base the essential sameness of human beings on biology. In this paper, I argue that if 'biology' is taken to refer to the technical pronouncements of professional biologists, in particular evolutionary biologists, it is simply not true that all organisms that belong to *Homo sapiens* as a biological species are essentially the same. If 'characters' is taken to refer to evolutionary homologies, then periodically a biological species might be characterized by one or more characters which are both universally distributed among and limited to the organisms belonging to that species, but such states of affairs are temporary, contingent, and relatively rare. In most cases, any character universally distributed among the organisms belonging to a particular species is also possessed by organisms belonging to other species, and conversely any character that happens to be limited to the organisms belonging to a particular species is unlikely to be possessed by all of them.

The natural move at this juncture is to argue that the properties that characterize biological species at least "cluster." Organisms belong to a particular biological species because they possess enough of the relevant properties or enough of the more important relevant properties. Such unimodal clusters do exist, and might well count as 'statistical natures,' but in most cases the distributions that characterize biological species are multimodal, depending on the properties studied. No matter how desperately one wants to construe biological species as natural kinds characterizable by some sort of "essences" or "natures," such multimodal distributions simply will not do. To complicate matters further, these clusters of properties, whether uni- or multi-modal, change through time. A character state (or allele) which is rare may become common, and one that is nearly universal may become entirely eliminated. In short, species evolve, and to the extent that they evolve through natural selection, both genetic and phenotypic variation are essential. Which particular variations a species

---

*Reprinted with permission from *PSA 1986*, Volume 2, pp. 3-13. © 1987 by the Philosophy of Science Association.

exhibits is a function of both the fundamental regularities that character-ize selection processes and numerous historical contingencies. However, variation as such is hardly an accidental characteristic of biological spe-cies. Without it, evolution would soon grind to a halt. *Which* variations characterize a particular species is to a large extent accidental; *that* varia-tion characterizes species as such is not.

The preceding characterization depends on the existence of a criter-ion for individuating species in addition to character covariation. If spe-cies are taken to be the things that evolve, then they can and must be characterized in terms of ancestor-descendant relations, and in sexual spe-cies these relations depend on mating. The organisms that comprise sex-ual species form complex networks of mating and reproduction. Any organism that is part of such a network belongs to that species even if the characters it exhibits are atypical or in some sense aberrant. Conversely, an organism that happens to exhibit precisely the same characters as an organism belonging to a particular species might not itself belong to that species. Genealogy and character covariation are not perfectly coinci-dent, and when they differ, genealogy takes precedence. The priority of genealogy to character covariation is not negated by the fact that species periodically split or bud off additional species. To the extent that speciation is punctuational, such periods will be short and will involve only a rela-tively few organisms, but inherent in species as genealogical entities is the existence of periods during which particular organisms do not belong unequivocally to one species or another. *Homo sapiens* currently is not undergoing one of these periods. The genealogical boundaries of our spe-cies are extremely sharp. The comparable boundaries in character space are a good deal fuzzier. As a result, those who view character covariation as fundamental and want our species to be clearly distinguishable from other species accordingly are forced to resort to embarrassing conceptual contortions to include retardates, dyslexics, and the like in our species while keeping bees and computers out.

The preceding observations about species in general and *Homo sapiens* in particular frequently elicit considerable consternation. Biologi-cal species cannot possibly have the characteristics that biologists claim they do. There *must* be characteristics that all and only people exhibit, or at least *potentially* exhibit, or all *normal* people exhibit—at least poten-tially. I continue to remain dismayed at the vehemence with which these views are expressed in the absence of any explicitly formulated biological foundations for these notions. In this paper, I argue that biological spe-cies, including our own, do have the character claimed by evolutionary biologists, and that attempts to argue away this state of affairs by refer-ence to "potentiality" and "normality" have little if any foundation in biology. Perhaps numerous ordinary conceptions exist in which an organism that lacks the genetic information necessary to produce a particular enzyme nevertheless possesses this enzyme potentially. I am equally sure that there are conceptions of normality according to which worker bees are abnormal. But these ordinary conceptions have no foundation in biology as a technical discipline. To make matters even worse, I do not see why the existence of human universals is all that important. Perhaps all and only people have opposable thumbs, use tools, live in true societies, or what have you. I think that such attributions are either false or vacuous, but even if they were true and significant, the distributions of these particular characters is largely a matter of evolutionary happenstance. I for one would be extremely uneasy to base something as important as human rights on such temporary contingencies. Given the character of the evolutionary process, it is extremely unlikely that all human beings are essentially the same, but even if we are, I fail to see why it matters. I fail to see, for example, why we must all be essentially the same to have rights.

To repeat, in my discussion of human nature, I am taking 'human' to refer to a particular biological species. This term has numerous other meanings which have little or nothing to do with DNA, meiosis, and what have you. Nothing that I say should be taken to imply anything about ordinary usage, commonsense conceptions, or what 'we' are inclined to say or not to say. In particular, I am not talking about 'persons.' The context of this paper is biology as a scientific discipline. Within biology itself, several different species concepts can also be found. I am concerned only with those doctrines that claim to be based on the nature of *Homo sapiens* as a biological species. Those authors who are not interested in what biologists have to say about biological species, or who are content with conceptual pluralism for the sake of conceptual pluralism, will find nothing of interest in this paper.

UNIVERSALITY AND VARIABILITY

All concepts are to some extent malleable and data can always be massaged, but in some areas both activities are more narrowly constrained than in others. For example, it is much harder to argue for genetic than for cultural universals because the identity of alleles is easier to establish than the identity of cultural practices. However, if biological species are characterized by a particular sort of genetic variability, then one might be justified in exposing claims that cultural traits are immune to a similar variability to closer scrutiny. I certainly do not mean to imply by the preceding statement that I think that cultural variability is in any sense caused by genetic variability. Rather, the reason for introducing the topic of genetic variability is that geneticists have been forced to acknowledge it in the face of considerable resistance, the same sort of resistance that confronts comparable claims about cultural variability. If there are any cultural universals, one of them is surely a persistent distaste for variability. But if genetic variability characterizes species even though everyone is absolutely certain that it does not, then possibly a similar variability characterizes cultures even though the parallel conviction about cultures is, if anything, stronger.

For example, Kaplan and Manners remark that a "number of anthropologists have even attempted to compile lists of universal cultural characteristics. Presumably such cultural universals reflect in some sense the uniform psychological nature of man. But the search for cultural universals has invariably yielded generalizations of a very broad, and sometimes not particularly illuminating, nature—such as, all cultures prefer health to illness; or, all cultures make some institutional provision for feeding their members; or, all cultures have devices for maintaining internal order." (1972, p. 151). Massive evidence can be presented to refute the claim that all human beings have essentially the same blood type. A parallel response to the claim that all cultures prefer health to illness is more difficult because of the plasticity of such terms as 'health' and 'illness.' My argument is analogical. Both population geneticists and anthropologists have been strongly predisposed to discount variability. Genetics is sufficiently well developed that geneticists have been forced to acknowledge how variable both genes and traits are, both within species and between them. The social sciences are not so well developed. Hence, it is easier for them to hold fast to their metaphysical preferences.

One reason for anthropologists searching so assiduously for cultural universals is the mistaken belief that some connection exists between universality and innateness. For example, in a paper on the *human* nature of human nature, Eisenberg states that "one trait common to man everywhere is a language; in the sense that only the human species displays it, the capacity to acquire language must be genetic." (1972, p. 126). In the space of a very few words, Eisenberg elides from language being common to man everywhere (universality), to the capacity to acquire language being unique to the human species (species specificity), to its being genetic. Human language is not universally distributed among human beings. Some human beings neither speak nor understand anything that might be termed a 'language.' In some sense such people might not be 'truly' human, but they still belong to the same biological species as the rest of us. Among these people, some may be incapable of acquiring language because they lack the necessary neural equipment, and in some cases this state of affairs is straightforwardly genetic. They are potential language users in the sense that if they had a different genetic make-up and were exposed to the appropriate sequences of environments, then they would have been able to acquire language skills similar to those possessed by the rest of us. But this same contrary-to-fact conditional can be applied to other species as well. In this same sense, chimpanzees possess the capacity to acquire language.

Conversely, any attempt to define language use in such a way as to exclude the abilities of other species results in even a larger percentage of the human race being denied this capacity as well. But regardless of the actual distribution of language use or the capacity for language use, nothing is implied about any genetic basis for language capacity. Blood type in human beings is about as genetic as any trait can be, and yet it is extremely variable. Blood type can be made universal among human beings only by defining it in terms of having some blood type or other — a disjunctive character. For example, at the ABO locus, four different types exist: A, B, AB, and O. Hence, all people have the same blood type at this locus just in case they have one of these types. If one of these alleles were to be lost or another to crop up, the disjunction need only be contracted or expanded accordingly. This strategy is universality made easy. However, it should be noted that even if this all-purpose stragegy were adopted, these disjunctively characterized traits have a temporal dimension.

Except in the preceding vacuous sense, blood type in human beings is anything but universal. Different pople have different blood types, and the combinations of these blood types vary in different populations. An allele which is common in one population may be rare in another, and vice versa. But, one might complain, there must be some blood type which is at least prevalent among the human race. Sometimes certain alleles are widely distributed. In other cases no allele even reaches the fifty percent level. At the ABO locus, the frequencies are A (.447), B (.082), AB (.034) and O (.437) among the white population in England. However, at the MNS locus for this same population, the frequency of the most common genotype is only .260. Of course, these frequencies are quite different in other populations, such as Basques and Navahos. Yet blood type is as genetic as any trait can get.

To complicate matters even further, the allelic frequencies at the dozen or so loci known to influence blood type vary independently of each other. Given the most common genotype at each of these loci, only one-fifth of one percent of the world's population is likely to possess the most common genotype at all of these loci (Lewontin 1982). In short, if blood type has anything to do with human nature, only one person in 500 is truly human. However, blood type is hardly the sort of character which advocates of human nature are likely to emphasize. In order to be human, people must be capable of rationality, lying, feeling guilty, laughing, etc.

And *these* characters are both unique to and universally distributed among human beings. Once again, our application of these terms tends to be so selective that it is impossible to say. Those who insist on the uniqueness of humankind dismiss anything that organisms belonging to other species do or do not do with considerable ease. Although an ape might succeed in solving problems that many human beings cannot solve, in no way can these primates be said to 'think.' The traits (and genes) that characterize all species save our own vary statistically. For some reason those characters that make us what we truly are happen to be universally distributed among all members of our species (at least potentially among normal human beings) and absent in all other species. I find this coincidence highly suspicious.

One reason for insisting on the existence of cultural universals is the mistaken belief that universally distributed characters are liable to have a more determinate genetic basis than those that are distributed in more complex patterns. Another is the desire to formulate laws using these cultural universals. Kinds are easy enough to come by. The difficult task is to discover kinds that function in natural regularities. Even if we grant anthropologists their cultural universals, nothing yet has come of them. In response to the preceding sorts of considerations, Gould complains of "our relentless seach for human universals and our excitement at the prospect that we may thereby unlock something at the core of our being." (1986, p. 68). If evolutionary theory has anything to teach us it is that variability is at the core of our being. Because we are a biological species and variability is essential to biological species, the traits which characterize us are likely to vary, our own essentialist compulsions notwithstanding (see also Dupré 1986).

To repeat, some properties may characterize all human beings throughout the existence of our species. After all, we all have some mass or other, but possessing mass can hardly fulfill the traditional functions assigned to human nature because it characterizes all species, not just our own. Some traits may also be unique to our species at the moment, though possibly not universal. For example, we can successfully mate only with other human beings, although a surprisingly high percentage of human beings are sterile. They cannot mate with other members of our own species. But for several million years, no one has been able to mate successfully with an organism belonging to another species. Some combination or combinations of traits must be responsible for this reproductive gap. But once again, these traits are not likely to fulfill the traditional functions of human nature. If all and only human beings were able to digest Nutrasweet, this ability would still not be a very good candidate for the property which makes us peculiarly human.

POTENTIALITY AND NORMALITY

Most phenotypic traits are highly variable both within and between species. In some species, there is more intraspecific variation than interspecific variation. Reverting to the genetic level does not help. In fact, it only reaffirms the preceding observations. Zebras and horses look very much alike, but genetically they are quite different. Human beings and chimpanzees look quite different, but genetically we are almost identical. On one estimate, thirty percent of the genes at loci that code for structural genes in human beings are polymorphic, and in any one individual, roughly seven percent of the loci are heterozygous, while human beings differ from chimpanzees at only three percent of loci. The usual response to these and other observations about patterns of phenotypic and genetic variability within and between species is to discount them. What do biologists know about biology? Organisms that lack a particular trait actually possess it potentially or else are abnormal for not possessing it.

Sometimes the claim that an organism that lacks a trait nevertheless possesses the capacity for such a trait makes sense. Reaction norms are frequently quite broad. In a variety of environments, organisms with a particular genotype exhibit character C; in others, C'; in others, C", and so on. They have what it takes to exhibit any one of these character states depending on the environments they confront. For example, on rare occasions, children are raised in near total social isolation until adulthood. As a result they cannot speak or understand any human language, nor can they at this late date be taught one. At one time they had the potential for language use but now lack it. On equally rare occasions, babies are born with little in the way of a cerebrum. If there is a significant sense in which they nevertheless retain the potential for language use, it eludes me. Perhaps such unfortunates are not persons, but they belong unproblematically to *Homo sapiens* as a biological species. Similar observations hold for every other characteristic suggested for distinguishing human beings from other species, whether that characteristic be biochemical, morphological, psychological, social, or cultural. In this respect, rationality is no different from opposable thumbs.

The more usual way to discount the sort of variation so central to the evolutionary process is to dismiss it as abnormal. Normality is a very slippery notion. It also has had a long history of abuse. Responsible authorities in the past have argued in all sincerity that other races are degenerate forms of the Caucasian race, that women are just incompletely formed men, and that homosexuals are merely deviant forms of heterosexuals. The normal state for human beings is to be white, male heterosexuals. All others do not participate fully in human nature. That white, male heterosexuals make up only a small minority of the human race did not give these authorities pause. But the failings of past generations are always easier to see than our own. Few responsible people today are willing to argue in print that blacks are abnormal whites or that women are abnormal men, but it seems quite natural to most of us to consider homosexuals abnormal heterosexuals. Heterosexuality is the normal state programmed into our genes. It needs no special explanation. Normal genes in a wide variety of normal environments lead most children quite naturally to prefer members of the opposite sex for sexual and emotional partners. Homosexuality, to the contrary, is an abnormal deviation that needs to be explained in terms of some combination of defective genes and/or undesirable environments. Such a view is central to several present-day psychological theories. Certainly nothing that a biologist might say about reaction norms, heterozygote superiority, or kin selection is liable to dislodge the deeply held intuitions on which these theories are based—and this is precisely what is wrong with deeply held intuitions.

However, just because a particular notion has been abused in the past, it does not follow that it totally lacks substance. As much of a curse as racism has been and continues to be, biologists are unable to characterize the human species as a homogeneous whole. As a biological species, we are seamless but not homogeneous. Various groups of people at a variety of levels of generality exhibit statistical differences. *Homo sapiens* is polytypic. Even so, perhaps one or more biologically respectable notions of normality and abnormality might be discoverable. The three most common areas of biology in which one might find a significant sense of these notions are embryology, evolutionary biology, and functional morphology.

From conception until death, organisms are exposed to sequences of highly variable environments. The phenotype exhibited by an organism is the result of successive interactions between its genes, current phenotypic make up and successive environments. The reaction norm for a particular genotype is all possible phenotypes that would result given all possible sequences of environments in which the organism might survive. Needless to say, biologists know very little about the reaction norms for most species, our own included. To estimate reaction norms, biologists must have access to numerous genetically identical zygotes and be able to raise these zygotes in a variety of environments. When they do, the results are endlessly fascinating. Some reaction norms are very narrow, that is, in any environment in which the organism can develop, it exhibits a particular trait and only that trait. Sometimes reaction norms turn out to be extremely broad. A particular trait can be exhibited in a wide variety of states depending on the environments to which the organism is exposed. Sometimes a reaction norm starts off broad but rapidly becomes quite narrow. Some reaction norms are continuous; others disjunctive. Sometimes most organisms occupy the center of the reaction norm; sometimes they are clustered at either extreme, and so on. Everything that could happen, in some organism or other does happen.

In spite of all the preceding, the conviction is sure to remain that in most cases there must be some normal developmental pathway through which most organisms develop or would develop if presented with the appropriate environment, or something. But inherent in the notion of a reaction norm is alternative pathways. Because environments are so variable in both the short and long term, developmental plasticity is absolutely necessary if organisms are to survive to reproduce. Any organism that can fulfill a need in only one way in only a narrowly circumscribed environment is not likely to survive for long. Although there are a few cases in which particular species can fulfill one or two functions in only highly specialized ways, both these species and their specialized functions are relatively rare.

But, one might complain, there *must* be some significant sense of "normal development." There is a fairly clear sense of normal development, but it is not very significant. As far as I can see, all it denotes is that developmental pathway with which the speaker is familiar in recent, locally prevalent environments. We find it very difficult to acknowledge that a particular environment that has been common in the recent past may be quite new and aberrant given the duration of the species under investigation. Throughout most of its existence, a species may have persisted in very low numbers and only recently boomed to produce a high population density, and high population density might well switch increasing numbers of organisms to quite different developmental pathways. During this transition period, we are likely to look back on the old pathway as normal and decry the new pathway as abnormal, but as we get used to the new alternative, just the opposite intuition is likely to prevail. Although the nuclear family existing outside a kinship group is a relatively new social innovation and is rapidly disappearing, to most of us it seems normal. Any deviation from it is sure to produce humanoids at best.

From the evolutionary perspective, all alleles that we now possess were once more than just rare: they were unique. Evolution is the process by which rare alleles become common, possibly universal, and universally distributed alleles becomes totally eliminated. If a particular allele must be universally distributed among the organisms belonging to a particular species (or at least widespread) in order to be part of its 'nature,' then natures are very temporary, variable things. From the human perspective, evolutionary change might seem quite slow. For example, blue eyes have existed in the human species from the earliest recorded times, and yet fewer than one percent of the people who belong to the human species have blue eyes. Because people with blue eyes can see no better than people with brown eyes, one plausible explanation for the increase of blue eyes in the human population is sexual selection. It might well take thousands of generations for a mutation to replace what was once termed the 'wild-type' and become the new 'wild type.' Early on one allele will surely be considered natural, while later on its replacement will be held with equal certainty to be natural. Human memory is short. From the evolutionary perspective, claims about normal genes tend to be sheer prejudice arising from limited experience.

If by 'human nature' all one means is a trait that happens to be prevalent and important for the moment, then human nature surely exists. Each species exhibits adaptations, and these adaptations are important for its continued existence. One of our most important adaptations is our ability to play the knowledge game. It is important that enough of us play this game well enough because our species is not very good at anything else. But this adaptation may not have characterized us throughout our existence and may not continue to characterize us in the future. Biologically we will remain the same species, the same lineage, even though we lose our essence. It should also be kept in mind that some nonhumans play the knowledge game better than some humans. If those organisms that are smarter than some people are to be excluded from our species while those people who are not all that capable are kept in, something must be more basic than mental ability in the individuation of our species. Once again, I am discussing *Homo sapiens* as a biological species, not personhood. Although in a higher and more sophisticated sense of 'human being' retardates are not human beings, from the crude and pedestrian biological perspective, they are unproblematically human.

The central notion of normality relative to human nature, however, seems to be functional. When people dismiss variation in connection with human nature, they usually resort to functional notions of normality and abnormality. Perhaps someone has produced a minimally adequate analysis of 'normal function,' but I have yet to see it. As the huge literature on the subject clearly attests, it is difficult enough to give an adequate analysis of 'function,' let alone 'normal function.' In general, structures and functions do not map neatly onto each other, nor can they be made to do so. A single structure commonly performs more than one function, and conversely, a single function can be fulfilled by more than one structure. If one individuates structures in terms of functions and function in terms of structures, then the complex mapping of structures and functions can be reduced, possibly eliminated, but only at considerable cost. For example, no matter how one subdivides the human urogenital system, there is no way to work it out so that a particular structure is used for excretion and another structure is used for reproduction. No amount of gerrymandering succeeds without extreme artificiality. Nor has anyone been able to redefine functional limits so that excretion and reproduction turn out to count as a single function.

Like it or not, a single structure can perform more than one function, and one and the same function can be performed by more than one structure. Nor is this an accidental feature of organisms. In evolution, organisms must make do with what they've got. An organ evolved to perform one function might be commandeered to perform another. For example, what is the normal function of the hand? We can do many things with our hands. We can drive cars, play the violin, type on electronic computers, scratch itches, masturbate, and strangle one another. Some of these actions may seem normal; others not, but there is no correlation between common-sense notions of normal functions and the functions which hands were able to fulfill throughout our existence. Any notion of the function of the hand which is sufficiently general to capture all the things that we can do with our hands is likely to be all but vacuous and surely will make no cut between normal and abnormal uses. About all a biologist can say about the function of the human hand is that anything that we can do with it is normal. A more restricted sense of normality must be imported from common sense, society, deeply held intuitions, or systems of morals. Some might argue that this fact merely indicates the poverty of the biological perspective. If so, so be it, but this is the topic of my paper.

A few additional examples might help to see the huge gap that exists between biological senses of function and the various senses of this term as it is used in other contexts. A major topic in the biological literature is the function of sexual reproduction. What is the function of sex? The commonsense answer is reproduction, but this is not the answer given by biologists. Biologically, first and foremost, the primary function of sex is to increase genetic heterogeneity. "But that is not what I mean! When I say that the biological function of sex is reproduction, I do not mean 'biological' in the sense that biologists use this term but in some other, more basic sense." Is being sexually neuter functionally normal? Well, it is certainly normal among honey bees. Most honey bees are neuter females. Many species, especially social species, exhibit reproductive strategies that involve some organisms becoming non-reproductives. What counts in biological evolution is inclusive fitness. It is both possible and quite common for organisms to increase their inclusive fitness by not reproducing themselves. "But I am talking about human beings, not honey bees." From the perspective of commonsense biology, human nonreproductives such as old maids and priests may be biologically abnormal, but from the perspective of professional biology, they need not be.

Finally, having blue eyes is abnormal in about every sense one cares to mention. Blue-eyed people are very rare. The inability to produce brown pigment is the result of a defective gene. The alleles which code for the structure of the enzyme which completes the synthesis of the brown pigment found on the surface of the human iris produce an enzyme which cannot perform this function. As far as we know, the enzyme product performs no other function either. However, as far as sight is concerned, blue eyes are perfectly functional, and as far as sexual selection is concerned downright advantageous. What common sense has to say on these topics, I do not know. My own commonsense estimates about what 'we' mean when 'we' make judgments on such topics depart so drastically from what analytic philosophers publish on these topics that I hesitate to venture an opinion lest I mark myself as being linguistically abnormal.

CONCLUSION

Because I have argued so persistently for so long that particulr species lack anything that might be termed an "essence," I have gotten the reputation of being totally opposed to essentialism. To the contrary, I am rather old fashioned on this topic (see Dupré 1986 for a more contemporary view). In fact, I think that natural kinds do exist and that they exhibit characters which are severally necessary and jointly sufficient for membership. More than this, I think that it is extremely important for our understanding of the natural world that such kinds exist. All I want to argue is that natural kinds of this sort are very rare, extremely difficult to discover, and that biological species as evolving lineages do not belong in this category. Just because one thinks that species are not natural kinds, it does not follow that one is committed to the view that there are no natural kinds at all. One misplaced example does not totally invalidate a general thesis.

In fact, I think that the species category might very well be a natural kind and that part of its essence is variability. If variability is essential to species, then it follows that the human species should be variable, both genetically and phenotypically, and it is. That *Homo sapiens* exhibits considerable variability is not an accidental feature of our species. Which particular variations we exhibit is largely a function of evolutionary happenstance; the presence of variability itself is not. Nor does it help to switch from traditional essences to statistically characterized essences. If the history of phenetic taxonomy has shown anything, it is that organisms can be subdivided into species as Operational Taxonomic Units in indefinitely many ways if all one looks at is character covariation. Compared to many species, our species is relatively isolated in character space. Perhaps a unimodal distribution of characters might be found which succeeds in placing all human beings in a single species and in keeping all nonhumans out. If so, this too would be an evolutionary happenstance and might well change in time.

But why is it so important for the human species to have a nature? One likely answer is to provide a foundation for ethics and morals. If one wants to found ethics on human nature and human nature is to be at least consistent with current biological knowledge, then it follows that the resulting ethical system will be composed largely of contingent claims. The only authors of whom I am aware who acknowledge this state of affairs and are still willing to embrace the consequences that flow from it are Michael Ruse and E. O. Wilson. Ruse and Wilson propose to base ethics on the epigenetic rules of mental development in human beings. They acknowledge that these rules are the "idiosyncractic products of the genetic history of the species and as such were shaped by particular regimes of natural selection. . . . It follows that the ethical code of one species cannot be translated into that of another. No abstract moral principles exist outside the particular nature of individual species." (1986, p. 186).

Although Ruse and Wilson are willing to grant that morality is "rooted in contingent human nature, through and through," they argue that morals are not relative to the individual human being because human cultures "tend to converge in their morality in the manner expected when a largely similar array of epigenetic rules meet a largely similar array of behavioural choices. This would not be the case if human beings differed greatly from one another in the genetic basis of their mental development." (1986, pp. 186, 188). The numbers of genes that influence our mental development have to be at least as large as those that determine blood type. Unless there is evidence to the contrary, the most reasonable hypothesis is that the same sort of variability and multiplicity that characterizes the genes that code for blood type also characterize those genes that code for our mental development. However, perhaps the genetic basis for mental development is a happy exception. Perhaps we all do possess a largely similar array of epigenetic rules based on largely similar genetic makeups. If so, this too is an accident of our recent evolutionary history, and once again ethics is being based on an evolutionary contingency. Ruse and Wilson agree. Because their view is empirical, they "do not exclude the possibility that some differences might exist between large groups in the epigenetic rules governing moral awareness." (1986, p. 188).

Although I feel uneasy about founding something as important as ethics and morality on evolutionary contingencies, I must admit that none of the other foundations suggested for morality provides much in the way of a legitimate sense of security either. But my main problem is that I do not see the close connection which everyone else sees between character distributions, admission to the human species, and such things as human rights. Depending on what clustering technique one uses, the human species can be subdivided into a variety of 'races.' Roughly fifty percent of human beings are male and fifty percent female. The number of intersexes is quite small. Estimates of the percentage of human beings who engage in sexual activity and pair bond exclusively or primarily with members of their own sex vary from five to ten percent. These percentages may vary from society to society and from time to time. I do not see that it matters. All the ingenuity which has been exercised trying to show that all human beings are essentially the same might be better used trying to explain why we must all be essentially the same in order to have such things as human rights. Why must we all be essentially the same in order to have rights? Why cannot people who are essentially different nevertheless have the same rights? Until this question is answered, I remain suspicious of continued claims about the existence and importance of human nature.

Part II

Darwin and Modern Science

Chapter 2

Charles Darwin and
Nineteenth-Century
Philosophies of Science*

To the extent that it can be distinguished from epistemology, philosophy of science as a separate discipline began in England with the publication of the works of John Herschel (1792-1871), William Whewell (1794-1866) and John Stuart Mill (1806-1873). Herschel and Mill carried on in the empiricist tradition that had preceded them, while Whewell was strongly influenced by the writings of Immanuel Kant.[1] But when these philosophers addressed themselves more directly to questions concerning science, they wrote under the twin spectres of Francis Bacon and Isaac Newton. Everyone knew what science was. Science was Kepler's laws, Newton's theory of universal gravitation, William Herschel's extension of physical astronomy to the sidereal regions, and W. C. Well's "Essay on Dew" (1818). Everyone was equally sure of the general character of scientific method. It was not the deductive method of Aristotle and the scholastics but the inductive method expounded by Bacon and practiced by these scientific giants. The task to which Herschel, Whewell and Mill set themselves was to provide an explicit and detailed analysis of science consonant with the great achievements in physics that had preceded them.

The classic works in nineteenth-century philosophy of science were all published prior to the appearance of Charles Darwin's *Origin of Species* in 1859—Herschel's *Preliminary Discourse on the Study of Natural History* (1830), Whewell's massive volumes on the *History of the Inductive Sciences* (1837) and *The Philosophy of the Inductive Sciences, Founded Upon Their History* (1840), and finally Mill's *System of Logic* (1843). Although Mill learned what little he knew of science from reading Whewell's *History of the Inductive Sciences*, his *System of Logic* was in large part an empiricist attack on Whewell's idealist and rationalist views. Whewell refrained from replying to Mill for six years, then published his *On Induction, with especial reference to Mr. J. Stuart Mill's System of*

---

*Reprinted with permission from *Foundations of Scientific Method: The Nineteenth Century*. © 1972 by the Indiana University Press.

Logic (1849), just in time for Mill to insert numerous lengthy footnotes in the third edition of his *System of Logic* answering Whewell's objections. Was induction a process of discovering empirical laws in the facts, or does the mind superinduce concepts on the facts? Were the axioms of geometry, especially the parallel line postulate, inductions from experience, whose truth could be decided by scientific investigation, or were they self-evident truths, whose formulation might be initiated by experience but once conceived, were known to be true *a priori?* In this debate, Herschel placed his great influence largely on the side of Mill, going so far as to concur in Mill's analysis of deduction as proceeding from particulars through general propositions to particulars.[2]

One would think that Darwin could not have chosen a better time to develop and eventually publish his theory of evolution. Earlier scientists had to produce their theories without any explicitly formulated body of methodological principles to guide them. These theories in turn were judged by tacit, or at best, half-articulated standards. At last a scientist could develop a scientific theory in full knowledge of the proper methods of science, and when his theory was published, it could be evaluated according to the explicitly stated criteria set out by the most sophisticated minds of his day.

In point of fact, Darwin did read Herschel's *Discourse* in his last year at Cambridge. Along with Humboldt's *Personal Narrative* (1818), it stirred in him "a burning zeal to add even the most humble contribution to the noble structure of Natural Science."[3] While at Cambridge, Darwin knew Whewell for a short time and found him a great converser on grave subjects. Darwin was also impressed by the breadth of knowledge exhibited by Whewell in his *History of the Inductive Sciences*.[4] and eventually prefaced the *Origin of Species* with a quotation from Whewell's Bridgewater Treatise (1833). But Darwin was indignant that someone might find Whewell profound "because he says length of days adapted to duration of sleep in man !!! whole universe so adapted !!! and not men to Planets. —instance of arrogance!!!"[5] Probably Darwin was not overly displeased when Robert Brown, the botanist, responded to praise of Whewell's *History* by sneering, "Yes, I suppose that he has read the prefaces of very many books."[6] Finally, there is no evidence that Darwin read Mill's *System of Logic* prior to publishing his *Origin of Species*, but afterwards he could hardly have helped being influenced indirectly through his colleague T. H. Huxley, who was very much impressed by Mill.[7]

The effect that Darwin's reading in philosophy of science had on him seems to have been mixed. Herschel's *Discourse* was certainly inspirational. Scientists and men of God were marching arm in arm to produce a better world. The reference in the opening paragraph of the *Origin* to "one of our greatest philosophers" was to Herschel. Darwin's care in recording exceptions to his own views[8] stemmed from Herschel's admonitions.[9] In general, however, the confusions and contradictions that pervaded early works in the philosophy of science were merely duplicated in Darwin's utterancs on the subject. On the one hand, Darwin looked upon "a strong tendency to generalize as an entire evil"[10] and yet admitted that "I cannot resist forming one on every subject."[11] He distrusted "deductive reasoning in the mixed sciences" and claimed, in the formulation of evolutionary theory, to have "worked on true Baconian principles and without any theory collected facts on a wholesale scale."[12] Yet he objected to the view that "geologists ought only to observe and not to theorize," remarking how "odd it is that anyone should not see that all observation must be for or against some view if it is to be of any service!"[13] Perhaps Darwin had no clearer a conception of science and scientific method than the philosophers of his day, but as we shall see, he was certainly no more confused.

The other side of the coin is even more tarnished. One would think that men who had devoted their lives to an analysis of science would be more adept at evaluating a new and revolutionary theory than the average philosopher or practicing scientist. Whatever justification there might be for this surmise, in this instance it could not have been more mistaken. Whewell rejected the theory out of hand. Herschel and Mill were willing at least to entertain the possibility of species evolving but not by the mechanisms Darwin proposed.

Darwin was so anxious to hear Herschel's opinion of the *Origin of Species* that he wrote to Charles Lyell asking him to pass on any comments that Herschel might make since "I should excessively like to hear whether I had produced any effect on such a mind."[14] It did not take long for Darwin to discover the effect which he had produced on Herschel. Again to Lyell, he wrote, "I have heard, by a roundabout channel, that Herschel says my book 'is the law of higgledy-piggledy.' What this exactly means I do not know, but it is very contemptuous. If true this is a great blow and discouragement."[15] Herschel expanded on his criticism of Darwin's theory in the 1861 edition of his *Physical Geography of the Globe*, concluding, "We can no more accept the principle of arbitrary and casual variation and natural selection as a sufficient account, per se, of the past and present organic world, than we can receive the Laputan method of composing books (pushed *à outrance*) as a sufficient account of Shakespeare and the Principia."[16] If Darwin would just admit the necessity of "intelligent direction" in evolution and include it in the formulae of his theory, then Herschel "with some demur as to the genesis of man" was "far from disposed to repudiate the views taken on this mysterious subject in Mr. Darwin's book."

Whewell's refusal to grant even this much to Darwin's theory was to be expected. Since he had steadfastly opposed uniformitarian principles in geology, it was unlikely that any argument or assemblage of data would rapidly convert him to the evolution of organic species. Miraculous divine creations, catastrophes, and the argument from design were vastly superior to Darwin's speculations. In a letter to a professor of theology, Whewell expressed his opinion of evolutionary theory as follows:

> And I may say that the recent discussions which have taken place in geology and zoology do not appear to me to have materially affected the force of the arguments there delivered.[17] It still appears to me that in tracing the history of the world backwards, so far as the palaetiological sciences enable us to do so, all the lines of connexion stop short of a beginning explicable by natural causes; and the absence of any conceivable natural beginning leaves room for, and requires, a supernatural origin. Nor do Mr. Darwin's speculations alter this result. For when he has accumulated a vast array of hypotheses, still there is an inexplicable gap at the beginning of his series. To which is to be added, that most of his hypotheses are quite unproved by fact. We can no more adduce an example of a new species, generated in the way which his hypotheses suppose, than Cuvier could. He is still obliged to allow that the existing species of domestic animals are the same as they were at the time of man's earliest history. And though the advocates of uniformitarian doctrines in geology go on repeating their assertions, and trying to explain all difficulties by the assumption of additional myriads of ages, I find that the best and most temperate geologists still hold the belief that great catastrophes must have taken place; and I do not think that the state of the controversy on that subject is really affected permanently. I still think that what I have written is a just representation of the question between the two doctrines.[18]

And then, of course, there is also the story that no copy of the *Origin of Species* was allowed on the shelves of the library at Trinity College while Whewell was master.

In the face of such rejection by two of the most eminent philosophers of his day, one can imagine Darwin's elation when he discovered that another great philosopher, John Stuart Mill, thought his reasoning in the *Origin* was "in the most exact accordance with the strict principles of logic."[19] Darwin was prepared for the abuse which the content of his theory, especially its implications for man, was to receive from certain quarters, but he was not prepared for the criticism which his methodology was to receive from the more respected philosophers and scientists of his day. Most contemporary commentators tend to dismiss these criticisms as facile, disingenuous and superficial, suspecting that they stemmed more from a distaste for the content of Darwin's theory than from any shortcomings of his methodology, but this dismissal itself is too facile. Certainly repeated invocations of the Baconian method by many of Darwin's critics and even by Darwin himself indicated no great understanding of the actual nature of this method, but nevertheless there were fundamental conflicts between evolutionary theory and the most sophisticated philosophies of science currently popular.[20]

For example, Mill's endorsement was a two-edged sword, and the sharper edge cut deeply into Darwin's own claims for his book. Darwin looked upon the *Origin of Species* as "one long argument from the beginning to the end, and it has convinced not a few able men."[21] He thought that, to some extent at least, he had proved that contemporary species originated from earlier species by evolution through chance variation and natural selection. According to Mill, Darwin had not violated the rules of induction, since the "rules of Induction are concerned with the conditions of Proof. Mr. Darwin has never pretended that his doctrine was proved. He was not bound by the rules of Induction, but those of Hypothesis."[22] And the method of hypothesis was a method of discovery, not justification. Darwin had admirably fulfilled the requirements of one of the methods of discovery, but he had proved nothing! Newton had provided the necessary inductive proof for his theories; Darwin had not.[23] In his last pronouncements on evolution, Mill agreed with Herschel and Whewell that "in the present state of our knowledge, the adaptations in Nature afford a large balance of probability of creation by intelligence."[24]

Professional philosophers of science played a significant role in the reception of evolutionary theory. Unfortunately, this role was largely negative. The purpose of the remainder of this paper will be to discover what it was about the philosophies of Herschel, Whewell, and Mill that led them to reject evolutionary theory as set out by Darwin when it was making converts on every side among biologists and laymen alike. Part of the explanation is that Darwin was caught in the middle of a great debate over some of the most fundamental issues in the philosophy of science—the difference between deduction and induction and the role of each in science, the difference between concept formation and the discovery of scientific laws, the relation between discovery and justification, the nature of the axioms of geometry and their relation to physics, the distinction between occult qualities and theoretical entities, and the conflict between purely naturalistic science and the role of God's direct intervention in nature. Before philosophers of science had thoroughly sorted out these issues, they were called on to evaluate an original and highly controversial scientific theory. But evolutionary theory was not just another scientific theory. It was a theory that struck at the very foundations of the philosophies of science that were being used to judge it. Of the numerous conflicts between evolutionary theory and nineteenth-century philosophies of science, only two will be discussed here—the conflict between teleology and evolution by the mechanisms proposed by Darwin, and the conflict between essentialism and any evolution at all, as long as it was gradual.

TELEOLOGY, CHANCE VARIATION, AND NATURAL SELECTION

The two major varieties of teleology popular in Darwin's day were the external teleology of the Christian Neoplatonists and the immanent teleology of Aristotle. The conflict between evolutionary theory and immanent teleology has been examined at length elsewhere and will not be discussed here (Hull 1965, 1967). The doctrine of external teleology entails a universal consciousness ordering everything for the best. As Plato put it, "I heard some one reading, as he said, from a book of Anaxagoras, that mind was the disposer and cause of all, and I was delighted at this notion, which appeared quite admirable, and I said to myself: if mind is the disposer, mind will dispose all for the best, and put each particular in the best place."[25] It was the Christian doctrine of God as the disposer and cause of all that Darwin had to combat.

In his Bridgewater Treatise (1833), Whewell updated the arguments for God's existence which Richard Bentley had set forth in his "A confutation of atheism from the origin and frame of the world" (1693). Like Bentley, Whewell argued that Newtonian physics was not only compatible with the existence of God, but also necessitated it. Certain phenomena like the earth traveling in an ellipse around the sun were deducible from Newton's laws. Other phenomena like the sun being luminiferous and the planets opaque, the distances of the various planets from the sun, and the inclination of the earth's axis to the plane of its revolution, were not. As far as Newton's laws were concerned, these latter phenomena were "accidental" features of the universe. Yet they had to be precisely as they were if the earth was to support life. If the earth were further away from the sun, it would be too cold to support life; if it were nearer, too hot. If the earth's axis had not been inclined to its plane of rotation, most of the planet would be either too hot or too cold for habitation. If the earth revolved around the sun more slowly, the seasons would be too long; if more quickly, too short, and so on. Since these phenomena necessary for man's existence did not follow from Newton's laws, either they just happened to coincide or else God was responsible. The chance coincidence of so many beneficial phenomena was extremely implausible.

Hence, God was responsible, and if he was responsible for these phenomena, he must exist. The existence of life, especially man, was good, hence, God was good. Chance was eliminated from physical phenomena indirectly by God instituting divine laws and directly by his production of those phenomena which did not follow from these laws.

Like others before him,[26] Whewell entertained a possible alternative explanation for the existence of such a high correlation between the needs of living creatures (especially man) and their environment—the survival of the fit and the perishing of the unfit. Whewell found such explanations inconceivable:

> If the objector were to suppose that plants were originally fitted to years of various lengths, and that such only have survived to the present time, as had a cycle of a length equal to our present year, or one which could be accommodated to it; we should reply, that the assumption is too gratuitous and extravagant to require much consideration.[27]

Mill concurred in Whewell's preference for the argument from design over the principle of the survival of the fittest, even after the publication of *Origin of Species*. "Of this theory when pushed to this extreme point, all that can now be said is that it is not as absurd as it looks, and that the analogies which have been discovered in experience, favourable to its possibility, far exceed what any one would have supposed beforehand."[28]

The facility with which Hershel, Whewell and Mill could demand the exact verification of scientific hypotheses and the exclusion of occult qualities from science on the one hand while on the other asserting God's direct intervention in natural phenomena is nothing less than schizophrenic. All three men had argued for the elimination of the miraculous intervention of God in the material world and the expansion of scientific law to cover all physical phenomena. As Mill expressed himself on the issue, there were two concepts of theism, one consistent with science, one inconsistent. "The one which is inconsistent is the conception of a God governing the world by acts of variable will. The one which is consistent, is the concept of a God governing the world by invariable laws."[29] The more that empirical phenomena could be shown to be governed by secondary causes acting in accordance with divinely instituted laws, the more powerful and omniscient God was shown to be. In the quotation Darwin had selected to introduce the *Origin of Species*, Whewell urges, "But with regard to the material world, we can at least go so far as this—we can perceive that events are brought about not by insulated interposition of Divine power, exerted in each particular case, but by the establishment of general laws."[30] What these pious men did not perceive was that by removing God as an active agent and relegating him to the position of the divine author of immutable laws, they were preparing the way for his total expulsion from science. Like Kant's *Ding an sich*, he was becoming remote, obscure, unknowable, somehow underlying everything and very important, but of no conceivable consequence for any particular scientific investigation.

All of these authors also recognized limits to natural laws, limits which were conveniently just on the other side of currently accepted laws. For example, Whewell argued that theology had to be assiduously excluded from the dynamic sciences but was a necessary adjunct to the historical sciences. "The mystery of creation is not within the legitimate territory of science."[31] Herschel agreed, "To ascend to the origin of things, and speculate on the creation, is not the business of the natural philosopher."[32]

Nineteenth-century scientists are often belabored for believing in special creation, the miraculous flashing together of elemental atoms to produce fully formed organisms or their eggs, but the other alternative, spontaneous generation, seemed even less plausible. "Spontaneous generation" implied much the same process only through some unknown though natural agency. The introduction of evolutionary theory did not change the situation much. If evolution of some sort is admitted, the problem is reduced in scope and pushed back into the distant past, but it is not eliminated. Either the first members of the original species were specially created or else they were spontaneously generated. By the middle of the nineteenth century, the advocates of spontaneous generation had retreated from the spontaneous generation of mice and such to the spontaneous generation of microbes and green matter, a position similar to that held by Lamarck in the preceding century. In Darwin's day, the spontaneous generation of an elephant or a mouse was thought to be absurd. The spontaneous generation of a microbe or an egg by some unknown laws was not quite so absurd. The major advantage that Darwin's theory had over its rivals in this matter was that it required the spontaneous generation of one or a few very simple beings a long time ago. Coincidentally, just when Pasteur was proving that contemporary microbes were not generated spontaneously, evolutionary theory required the spontaneous generation of ancient microbes.

After the appearance of the *Origin*, Darwin was thoroughly denounced for implying that the flashing together of elemental atoms had been the accepted doctrine among biologists on the origin of species. Biologists such as Richard Owen claimed to have presumed, though not speculated on, a naturalistic explanation for the development of species, a mechanism which in Owen's case was embarrassingly similar to that outlined in the *Vestiges of Creation*. Earlier biologists such as Linnaeus had not been outright special creationists. Rather, they had suggested some special creation and some natural development. Certain species were specially created. Others developed from these original species by hybridism, paedogenesis, or some such mechanism. These bastardizations were somewhat more popular than Tycho Brahe's model for the universe, part geocentric, part heliocentric, but not much. Regardless of what they might have thought on the subject, one thing is certain—most serious British scientists in Darwin's day studiously avoided the question of the origin of species. They were encouraged in this conspiracy of silence by the philosophies propounded by Herschel, Whewell and Mill. Certain questions were beyond the reach of science.

It is often said that evolutionary theory brought an end to the inclusion of God as a causal factor in scientific explanations. A more accurate characterization is that Darwin's theory demonstrated conclusively that this day had already passed. The architects of this demise were not atheistic materialists but pious Christians who thought that they were doing religion good service by interposing invariable laws between God and the empirical world. Everything except the origin of the universe and organic species was governed by natural laws. It was only a matter of time until the boundaries of science were enlarged to include these phenomena as well. Even Herschel and Mill were willing to abandon the limitations which they had previously placed on the reign of natural law. They were willing to entertain naturalistic explanations for the introduction of living species into the world, but not Darwin's explanation! Whewell refused to go even this far. As we will see, Whewell's refusal to accept the gradual evolution of species regardless of the mechanism may well have stemmed from his understanding the issues at stake more thoroughly than Herschel and Mill.

Herschel and Mill found Darwin's mechanism for the evolution of species objectionable on two counts. First, chance variation sounded too much like the absence of law. The introduction of new species might be by law but not the law of higgledy-piggledy. Darwin repeatedly stated that by "chance variation" he did not mean to imply the absence of laws governing these variations. Rather he thought that whatever these laws might be, they were unknown and to the best of his knowledge were not teleological in nature.[33] There appeared to be no correlation between the variations which a species might need and those it might get. When most organisms that are born die without leaving issue and the vast majority of species that evolve become extinct without evolving into new species, it was difficult to argue for much in the way of divine guidance in these matters. As Darwin objected to Lyell,[34] "If you say that God ordained that at some time and place a dozen slight variations should arise, and that one of them alone should be preserved in the struggle for life and the other eleven should perish in the first few generations, then the saying seems to be mere verbiage. It comes to merely saying that everything that is, is ordained."

The second reason that Darwin's theory was objectionable to Christian teleologists was the God that it implied. If God created the universe, then one should be able to infer his character from the order evident in his creation. If the universe is a perfectly running machine with a place for everything and everything in its place, then one type of mind is implied. This was the vision of the universe that motivated Herschel, Whewell and Mill to expand the domain of scientific law. God could have constructed the world so that species evolved by chance variation and natural selection, but that kind of God did not seem especially worthy of love and veneration. The God implied by evolutionary theory and a realistic appraisal of the organic world was capricious, cruel, arbitrary, wasteful, careless and totally unconcerned with the welfare of his creations.

Friends and enemies alike urged Darwin to include a little divine guidance in the laws of evolutionary theory. Darwin replied that there was no more need to mention intelligent direction in the formulae of his theory than there was to include it in Newton's theory. "No astronomer, in showing how the movements of planets are due to gravity, thinks it necessary to say that the law of gravity was designed that the planets should pursue the course which they pursue. I cannot believe that there is a bit more interference by the Creator in the construction of each species than in the course of planets."[35] Reference to God had become as otiose in biology as it had long been in physics.

EVOLUTION, NATURAL KINDS AND SCIENTIFIC LAWS

Alvar Ellegård (1958), in his outstanding book on the reception of evolutionary theory in nineteenth-century England, views the controversy over the evolution of species as a conflict between empiricist and idealist philosophies of science. The empiricists promoted the acceptance of evolutionary theory. The idealists were the obscurantists. Our story would be much neater if this were true. In England, at least, it is not. Empiricists and idealists alike were opposed to species evolving and with good reason. Evolution by chance variation and natural selection conflicted with teleology, but with sufficient modification these philosophies could do without teleology. Any evolution at all, regardless of the mechanisms, if it were gradual, conflicted with the essentialist notion of natural kinds, and none of these philosophies could do without natural kinds. The empiricists and idealists attributed a different ontological status to natural kinds, but both agreed that their existence was absolutely necessary if knowledge was to be possible. Thus Peirce (1877) was correct when he observed, "The Darwinian controversy is, in large part, a question of logic," and Dewey (1910) when he concluded "The real significance of Darwinian evolution was the introduction of new 'mode of thinking,' and thus to transform the 'logic of knowledge.' "

One would expect an idealist like Whewell to presuppose the existence of natural kinds. In fact, as far as species of plants and animals are concerned, he did not even bother to argue the issue. He merely referred to the opinion of the most eminent physiologists of his day that indefinite divergence from original types was impossible. For Whewell,[36] "*Species have a real existence in nature, and a transition from one to another does not exist.*" The impossibility of evolution was not a generalization from experience but a necessary prerequisite for knowledge. "Our persuasion that there must needs be characteristic marks by which things can be defined in words, is founded on the assumption of the *necessary possibility* of reasoning."[37] If species evolved gradually, then no one set of necessary characteristics would exist that was sufficient to divide an evolving lineage into discrete species. On Whewell's philosophy, if Darwin's theory were true, knowledge would be impossible—not a small drawback. (Hull 1965, 1967)

Contrary to Ellegard's belief, the empiricist philosophies of Herschel and Mill equally depended on the existence of discrete natural kinds. Mill, for example, distinguished between two types of uniformities in nature—those of succession in time and those of coexistence. The former were expressed in causal laws; the latter in definitions and classifications. Mill's four (sometimes five) methods of induction were designed to discover successions of kinds of events in time, on the assumption that these kinds of events had already been discovered. But as Whewell was happy to point out, Mill's methods "take for granted the very thing which is most difficult to discover, the reduction of phenomena to formulae."[38] In the last analysis, Mill justified causal laws by reference to the law of universal causation. He had no comparable justification of his uniformities of coexistence. Even so, he still maintained that natural kinds were "distinguishable by unknown multitudes of properties and not solely by a few determinant ones—which are partitioned off from one another by an unfathomable chasm. . . ."[39] The universe, so far as known to us, is so constituted, that whatever is true in any one case, is true in all cases of a certain description; the only difficulty is to find the description.[40] Kinds are classes between which there is an impassible barrier. . . ."[41]

Although the empiricist ontologies of Herschel and Mill did not require the existence of discrete natural kinds, their logic of justification did. Proof was to be supplied by eliminative induction. "Either A, B, or C can cause E. A and B are absent. Hence, C must cause E." In order for this inference to afford absolute certainty, all of the alternative causes for a particular kind of event must be specified and all but one eliminated. It is interesting to note that the one kind of induction that Darwin grew to distrust was in fact exclusive induction. Early in his career, he tried to explain the parallel shelves (or roads) that rimmed the sides of Glen Roy (1839). He reasoned that the parallel roads were the former shores of lakes or arms of the sea. If they were the shores of a series of lakes, then huge barriers had to be erected and removed successively at the mouth of the glen. Since Darwin could not see how such huge barriers could be moved about, he eliminated the lake hypothesis. Hence, the shelves were former shores of the sea produced as the land gradually rose above sea-level. Shortly thereafter Agassiz's glacier theory provided the barriers required by the lake hypothesis. In writing to Lyell, Darwin exclaimed, "I am smashed to atoms about Glen Roy. My paper was one long gigantic blunder from beginning to end. Eheu! Eheu!"[42] Later he observed that "my error has been a good lesson to me never to trust in science to the principle of exclusion."[43]

Here was Darwin refusing to trust the principle of exclusion—the very mode of inference that empiricist philosophers were touting as the only method of proof in the empirical sciences! But perhaps the fault lay not with the principle but with Darwin's application of it. In this instance, there might be some justification for the claim, but when we turn to species of living creatures, evolution necessarily precludes successful application of induction by complete elimination. Eliminative induction requires the existence of a finite number of sharply distinguishable natural kinds. But if Darwin's theory were true, then eliminative induction could never be applied to living species as parts of temporal continua, since they were neither discrete nor denumerable.

The conflict was more serious than it might appear. The chief examples of natural kinds in natural science had always been geometric figures, species of plants and animals and, running a poor third, physical elements. If organic species did not form natural kinds, then doubt was raised about other natural kinds. Perhaps parallel lines could meet. One might even be able to transmute lead into gold. Scientific laws themselves might evolve. If Darwin's theory were true, then living species did not form natural kinds. If living species did not form natural kinds, then "All swans are white," even if true, could not be a scientific law. No wonder empiricists like Huxley were disposed toward saltative evolution.

The preceding inferences, however, do not follow as automatically as nineteenth-century empiricists thought. They believed that scientific laws were necessarily universal in form. Approximations were just stages on the road to something better—true universal generalizations.[44] Anything less implied an indeterministic universe and made experimental verification impossible. Mill admitted that in many instances recourse to approximations was necessary, but only because the phenomena had not been correctly reduced to natural kinds. Once natural kinds had been discerned, universal correlation was guaranteed.[45] If species of plants and animals did not form natural kinds, then biological laws about them might forever remain approximations. Peirce[46] did not find this conclusion so abhorrent. Just as Maxwell had applied the statistical method and the doctrine of probabilities to the theory of gases, "Darwin, while unable to say what the operation of variation and natural selection in every individual case will be, demonstrates that in the long run they will adapt animals to their circumstances." The question posed by Darwin's theory to nineteenth-century philosophies of science was whether statistical laws and classes defined by statistically covarying properties could function in science, not as temporary stopgaps, but as permanent features of science. (For further discussion, see Hull, *Philosophy of Biological Science*, 1972.)

Herschel and Mill did not agree with Whewell on very many issues, but it was those issues on which they did agree that made their acceptance of evolutionary theory impossible. If evolutionary theory was to be accepted, certain basic changes had to be made. From Lyell, Asa Gray, Herschel, Mill, and even Peirce to Teilhard de Chardin, philosophers and biologists have urged a little bit of direction in evolution. From Huxley to de Vries, Goldschmidt, Schindewolf, and Goudge they have hoped that evolution might prove to be saltative. The motivation for the first objection was to salvage some remnant of teleology; for the latter to retain the essentialist mode of definition and all that it entailed. Darwin yielded to neither temptation.

NOTES

1. For an extensive discussion of the metaphysics and epistemologies of such philosophers as Descartes, Locke, Hume, Berkeley, Leibniz, and Kant and their relation to science, see Gerd Buchdahl's *Metaphysics and the Philosophy of Science* (Oxford: Basil Blackwell, 1969).

2. See Herschel's review of Whewell's *History and Philosophy of Science* (1841) and his comments on Mill in his review of Quetelet's essays (1850), both in John Herschel, *Essays from the Edinburgh and Quarterly Review with Addresses and Other Pieces* (London: Longman's, Green, 1857).

3. Charles Darwin, *The Autobiography of Charles Darwin*, 1809-1882, ed. Nora Barlow (London: Collins, 1958), 67.

4. Ibid., 66.

5. Charles Darwin, "Darwin's Notebooks on Transmutation of Species," ed. Gavin De Beer, *Bulletin of the British Museum (Natural History) Historical Series* 2:23-200, Third Notebook, 134.

6. Darwin, *Autobiography*, 104.

7. See Huxley's *Lectures and Essays*, note, and his *Lay Sermons*, both in T. H. Huxley, *Collected Essays* (London: Macmillan, 1893-94; reprinted, New York: George Olms Verlag Hildesheim, 1970), vols. 1, 9, pp. 54 and 95 respectively.

8. Darwin, *Autobiography*, 123.

9. John Herschel, *Preliminary Discourse on the Study of Natural Philosophy* (London: Longman, Rees, Orme, Brown & Green, 1830). A facsimile of the first edition (New York: Johnson Reprint Corporation, 1966), 165.

10. Charles Darwin, *More Letters of Charles Darwin*, ed. Francis Darwin and A.C. Seward (London: Murray, 1903), 1:39.

11. Darwin, *Autobiography*, 141.

12. Ibid., 119.

13. Darwin, *More Letters*, 1:195.

14. Charles Darwin, *The Life and Letters of Charles Darwin, including an autobiographical chapter*, ed. Francis Darwin, 3 vols. (London: Murray, 1887), 2:26.

15. Darwin, *Life and Letters*, 2:37.

16. Von Baer expands on this reference to Swift in his *Zum Streit über den Darwinismus* (1873), *Augsburger Allgemeine Zeitung*, pp. 1986-1988, translated in *Darwin and His Critics*, ed. D. L. Hull (Cambridge: Harvard University Press, 1972).

17. The reference is to his own *Indications of the Creator* (1847), a series of extracts from his *History* and his *Philosophy of the Inductive Sciences*.

18. Isaac Todhunter, *William Whewell, D.D.* (London: Macmillan, 1876), 2:433-4.

19. Darwin, *More Letters*, 1:189-190.

20. For further discussion of these issues, see Hull, *Darwin and His Critics*.

21. Darwin, *Autobiography*, 140.

22. John Stuart Mill, *A System of Logic, Ratiocinative and Inductive, Being a Connected View of the Principles of Evidence, and the Methods of Scientific Investigation* (1843), new impression, 8th ed. (London: Longmans, 1961), 328.

23. Ibid., p. 323 and H. S. R. Elliot, ed., *The Letters of John Stuart Mill* (London: Longman, Green and Company, 1910), 2:181.

24. John Stuart Mill, *Three Essays on Religion* (1874) (New York: The Liberal Arts Press, 1958), 172.

25. Plato, *Phaedo*, trans. Benjamin Jowett (Oxford: The Clarendon Press, 1871), st. 96-99.

26. Aristotle, *Physics*, ed. David Ross (Oxford: Oxford University Press, 1937), bk. II, ch. 8.

27. William Whewell, *Astronomy and General Physics considered with reference to natural theology* (1833) (Reprint, Philadelphia: Carey, Leo & Blanchard, 1936), vol. III of the Bridgewater Treatise, 27.

28. Mill, *Three Essays*, 172; see also, *Letters of John Stuart Mill*, 1:236.

29. Mill, *Three Essays*, 135.

30. Whewell, *Astronomy*, 182.

31. William Whewell, *The Philosophy of the Inductive Sciences, founded upon their history* (1840) 2nd ed. (London: J. W. Parker, 1847), 3:309.

32. Herschel, *Discourse*, 38.

33. Charles Darwin, *On the Origin of Species by Means of Natural Selection, or the Preservation of Favoured Races in the Struggle for Life* (1859). A facsimile of the first edition (Cambridge, Mass.: Harvard University Press, 1966), 74, 170, 364.

34. Darwin, *More Letters*, 1:172.

35. Darwin, *More Letters*, 1:154.

36. Whewell, *Philosophy*, 3:626.

37. Ibid., 1:476.

38. Ibid., 1:263.

39. Mill, *Logic*, 80.

40. Ibid., 201.

41. Ibid., 471; see also 379.

42. Darwin, *More Letters*, 2:188.

43. Darwin, *Autobiography*, 84.

44. Mill, *Logic*, 387.

45. Ibid., 388; and John Stuart Mill, *An Examination of Sir William Hamilton's Philosophy, and the Principal Philosophies and Questions discussed in his writings* (1865) (Boston: W. V. Spencer, 1968), 2:308.

46. C. S. Peirce, "The Fixation of Belief," *Popular Science Monthly* 12:1-15 (1877):94.

Chapter 3

Planck's Principle*

One of the most controversial questions concerning the nature of scientific change is the extent to which it is affected by "internal" versus "external" considerations. At one extreme are those who maintain that new ideas triumph in science primarily because the empirical evidence supports them more strongly than any of their competitors. Particular scientists may be influenced to some extent by peculiarities of their psychological makeup and social milieu, but in the last analysis, all that really matters is reason, argument, and evidence. Somewhere in the middle of this debate are those who maintain that strictly scientific considerations are important in science but so are extrascientific beliefs. For instance, statements of basic metaphysical principles may not be strictly a part of science, yet they have frequently influenced the course of scientific development. Religious, socioeconomic, and other beliefs have also played important roles in science. Even though the line between scientific and extrascientific beliefs is not sharp, as beliefs they are at least cognitive factors. Certain authors, however, argue that extracognitive factors also affect scientific development. In the extreme, they claim that the course of science is determined primarily by socioeconomic causes, such as the French Revolution and the rise of the mercantile middle class. On this view, conceptual development is not a function of beliefs, even socioeconomic beliefs, but of noncognitive causes.[1, 2]

Typically, such disputes are carried on in the abstract. Anecdotes and casual impressions pass for evidence. In fact, the idea that such disputes might actually be settled by recourse to evidence hardly seems to have occurred to those engaged in them.[3] The purpose of this article is to test two widely held opinions about one particular episode in the history of science. The episode is the Darwinian revolution in Great Britain. The opinions are that younger scientists were converted much more quickly than older scientists, and that among scientists, Darwin triumphed rapidly and totally. In 1863 Kingsley[4] remarked that the "state of the scientific world is most curious; Darwin is conquering everywhere, and rushing in like a flood by the mere force of truth and fact." In 1870, Bennett[5] noted

---

*This article was coauthored with Peter D. Tessner and Arthur M. Diamond. Reprinted with permission from *Science* 202:17 November 1978. © 1978 by the AAAS.

that the "fascinating hypothesis of Darwinism has, within the last few years, so completely taken hold of the scientific mind, both in this country and in Germany, that almost the whole of our rising men of science may be classed as belonging to this school of thought." In the first part of this article we show that both of these views were widely held in Darwin's day and continue to be accepted by historians of science to the present. We then proceed to test them by discovering how rapidly scientists actually did come to accept the evolution of species, and whether age actually did make a difference.

At the outset, these two beliefs about the Darwinian revolution pose a certain problem for each other. If scientific change must wait for old scientists to die off and be replaced by a new generation, and if the Darwinian flood was as rapid and as total as its Mosaic counterpart, then soon after 1859 the mortality rate of Victorian scientists must have taken an alarming leap. Needless to say, it did not. Our reliance on data to help resolve the dispute over the relative importance of external and internal considerations in scientific development also poses a problem for us. It commits us to some form of internalism. After all, if we did not think that evidence has some influence, we would not have bothered to gather it. If all beliefs are determined in the long run by socioeconomic beliefs or socioeconomic causes, then beliefs on this particular issue will be determined by the same considerations. Recourse to scientific rigor is just empty show, designed to appeal to the prejudices of those who have deluded themselves into thinking that evidence matters. Thus, the design of our study automatically precludes our accepting extreme externalism. This limitation is not as serious as it might seem because few, if any, authors have openly opted for pure externalism—or pure internalism for that matter. The real issue is which factors have actually been operative in particular cases and how important each has been. Our study is designed to answer this question with respect to one factor—age—for one episode in the history of science—the Darwinian revolution.

The distinction between reasons and causes is not an easy one to make, even in principle. In practice it is often even more difficult. A scientist's age, for example, may function either as a noncognitive factor in scientific change or as an index of a variety of cognitive factors. If hardening of a scientist's arteries precludes understanding and acceptance of a new scientific idea, then age is functioning as a noncognitive cause. Of course, older scientists might simply know much more than their younger colleagues and see more of the ramifications of a new idea. Realizing the extent to which Darwin's views negated the science of one's day might be a function of age, but it nevertheless is exactly the sort of cognitive factor that internalists claim is so important in science. Or possibly the older scientist's own career is more intimately connected to the views being challenged. Rejecting a new idea because it threatens one's position in the scientific community is a reason, but it is not the sort of scientific reason that internalists like to think affects the course of science significantly. If age turns out to be correlated with rapidity of acceptance of new scientific ideas, then the various possible explanations for this correlation must be teased apart and examined. However, if no correlation can be found, then doubt is cast on age both as a noncognitive cause and as an index of something else.

PLANCK'S PRINCIPLE

In his autobiography, Planck[6] remarks that a "new scientific truth does not triumph by convincing its opponents and making them see the light, but rather because its opponents eventually die, and a new generation grows up that is familiar with it." If Planck is right, reason, argument, and evidence do not play a very large role in scientific change. Each generation of scientists is raised in a particular orthodoxy and, once indoctrinated, cannot be converted. The death rate of scientists sets an upper limit to the rate of scientific change. One might think that scientists would find such a view repugnant, but time and again scientists can be found making equally cynical remarks about the inability of other scientists, especially older scientists, to change their minds. For example, Lavoisier[7] ends his *Reflections on Phlogiston* as follows:

> I do not expect my ideas to be adopted all at once. The human mind gets creased into a way of seeing things. Those who have envisaged nature according to a certain point of view during much of their career, rise only with difficulty to new ideas. It is the passage of time, therefore, which must confirm or destroy the opinions I have presented. Meanwhile, I observe with great satisfaction that the young people are beginning to study the science without prejudice, and also the mathematicians and physicists, who come to chemical truths with a fresh mind — all these no longer believe in phlogiston in Stahl's sense.

Near the end of the *Origin of Species*, Darwin[8] makes a similar remark:

> Although I am fully convinced of the truth of the views given in this volume under the form of an abstract, I by no means expect to convince experienced naturalists whose minds are stocked with a multitude of facts all viewed, during a long course of years, from a point of view directly opposite to mine. It is so easy to hide our ignorance under such

expressions as the "plan of creation," "unity of design," &c., and to think that we give an explanation when we only restate a fact. Any one whose disposition leads him to attach more weight to unexplained difficulties than to the explanation of a certain number of facts will certainly reject my theory. A few naturalists, endowed with much flexibility of mind, and who have already begun to doubt on the immutability of species, may be influenced by this volume; but I look with confidence to the future, to young and rising naturalists, who will be able to view both sides of the question with impartiality.

T. H. Huxley was so convinced of the inability of older scientists to change their minds that he declared that men of science ought to be strangled on their sixtieth birthday "lest age should harden them against the reception of new truths, and make them into clogs upon progress, and worse, in proportion to the influence they had deservedly won."[9] Needless to say, Huxley took considerable ribbing when he himself turned sixty.

Numerous present-day philosophers, historians, and sociologists can be found agreeing that age makes a difference in the alacrity with which scientists change their minds. For example, both Kuhn[10] and Feyerabend[11] quote Planck's principle in support of their thesis that scientific revolutions are, at bottom, arational affairs. Although Kuhn notes that facts such as these need further reevaluation, he believes that they are "too commonly known to need further emphasis." J. Cole and S. Cole[12] quote Planck's principle in connection with the "gradual replacement of older elites with younger men who may hold new ideas about the conceptual framework of their discipline." Although Cantor (p. 196) acknowledges counterexamples, he concludes that "incommensurability tends to confirm Planck's statement." Bondi[13] finds Planck's principle an "uncomfortable statement, but perhaps not a wholly incorrect one." In his discussion of the social and cultural sources of resistance to scientific change, Barber[14] mentions Planck's principle but does not pursue it. As balanced as Barber's assessment is, the overall impression it gives is that scientists are not as open-minded as they profess to be. Merton[15] goes one step further. Not only are scientists resistant to change, but also this resistance plays a positive role in scientific change. Without it, science would be inundated with half-baked ideas.

Numerous authors have also commented specifically about the role of young scientists in the success of Darwin's theory and the reticence of older scientists. For example, Gunther[16] states that the "older generation, steeped in the Bible, rejected the theory with a sense of shock." Paul[17, 18] notes how difficult it was for the Italian clerical intelligentsia to hold onto the old scientific dogmas as the "generation of anti-Darwinian scientists died and the new biological community accepted, however critically, more and more Darwinistic dogmas." Loewenberg[19] remarks that "Darwin's characteristic perspicacity is nowhere better illustrated than in his prophesy of the reaction of the world of science." Older scientists were all but impossible to convert. Only younger scientists had sufficient flexibility of mind to understand and accept evolutionary theory. Although Hagstrom[20] warns that it would be "just as unwise to accept the statements by Darwin and Planck without question as it would be to accept the statements of Robespierre and Lenin about their opponents in revolutions of another kind," he thinks there is enough to the phenomenon to suggest an explanation:

> Young scientists may find it easier to accept new views than old scientists, who may be more strongly committed to the earlier views. Although young scientists have been subjected to an education in which they are indoctrinated with accepted theories and seldom given any arguments against them, the commitments they make may be superficial. Firm commitments to a theory may be achieved only by those who have used it to account for things previously inexplicable, who have experienced the range of its power and the difficulties of subjecting it to test. Given a crisis or an innovation, the older generation may firmly believe in the possibility of reconciling it with established theory. Younger scientists, on the other hand, will perceive most clearly the incompatibility of innovations and existing theory.

Certainly the claim that well-stocked minds should be more difficult to change than those that are all but empty sounds plausible enough. Certainly, mature scientists should be more committed to received views than young scientists just starting on their careers. However, little in the way of empirical evidence has been presented to show that the phenomenon even exists. Few claims about noncognitive influences on science lend themselves to empirical testing. The nice thing about Planck's principle is that it does. It is easy to find out when nineteenth-century scientists were born and died—more difficult, although not impossible, to discover when they came to adopt various positions on scientific issues, and then to compare the two. If the authors cited in this section are right, budding young scientists in 1859 should have been the easiest to convert to a belief in the evolution of species, old codgers all but intransigent.

THE DARWINIAN FLOOD

In Darwin's day the general opinion was that within ten years or so after the appearance of the *Origin of Species*, Darwin had triumphed. Thomas's comment[21] in his 1877 presidential address to the British Association for the Advancement of Science was typical. He observed that Darwinism had "secured, in the incredibly short space of ten or twelve years, the general approval of a large portion of the scientific world." The choice of the ten-year period is especially fitting because that was the time alloted for the demise of evolutionary theory by Richard Owen, a prediction that especially rankled Darwin. Owen further irritated Darwin by simultaneously rejecting Darwin's views while claiming priority for them.[22]

The ten-year period is also popular among recent commentators on the Darwinian revolution. For example, Himmelfarb[23] concludes, "It was, in fact, not in his lifetime but in a single decade that Darwin saw his ideas triumph." Darlington[24] agrees: "In about ten years' time, however, the educated world was effectively converted to Darwin's view of what had come to be called evolution and was now called Darwinism." Ellegard[25], one of the rare authors who actually performed the sort of wide sampling necessary to justify such claims, also concludes that in Great Britain, at least, the "establishment of an evolutionary view had been virtually achieved among the educated classes before the end of the first decade after the publication of the *Origin of Species*."

Was evolutionary theory more popular among scientists than the educated public? Among scientists themselves, were scientists in certain disciplines more strongly disposed to it than those in other fields? Were all parts of Darwin's theory equally popular? Was the fate of Darwinism the same throughout the scientific world? Little work has been done in attempting to answer such questions. Ellegard's study of the reactions published in the British popular press is one exception. Another is a volume conceived and edited by Glick[18] in which a dozen or so historians compare the reception of Darwinism around the world. In most countries, these authors found the triumph of Darwinism to be rapid and almost total. For instance, Paul[26] discovered rapid, "nearly universal acceptance of Darwinism by the Italian scientific community." Montgomery[27] observed that the battle against Darwinism in Germany was "essentially lost by the end of the decade," although "some opponents were still active in the 1870s." Bulhof[28] noted, "Especially among the younger scientists, the Darwinian theory of an evolution of the species quickly changed in status from a daring hypothesis to an undisputed fact." The transition to the Darwinian world view proceeded "in a remarkably fast tempo, which cannot be explained by the state of scientific theory in the Netherlands around 1859 alone."

In spite of the religious climate in the United States and the opposition of the formidable Louis Agassiz, the victory of evolution in America was just as total and almost as rapid as it had been in Italy, Germany, and the Netherlands. Although Agassiz remained firmly anti-evolution until his death, J. D. Dana, the second most powerful naturalist in the United

States at the time, capitulated in 1874. Although none of the presidents of the "best schools" in the United States would admit that evolution was being taught in their classrooms, the *Presbyterian Observer*, when challenged in 1880 by the *Popular Science Monthly*, could find only one American naturalist who would publicly repudiate evolutionary theory.[29] In spite of the power exercised by the Catholic Church in Spain, Glick[30] concluded that even in Spain, the "permeation of evolutionary ideas was so pervasive that Catholic revanchism was unable to roll back the tide." Change was not so rapid, nor so total, in tzarist Russia and in France. Well-established scientists in Russia held firm in their old beliefs, and the young advocates of evolution had to seek employment elsewhere.[31] Of all the nations in the world that could claim a scientific tradition at the time, France proved to be the most immune to Darwinism.[32]

SCOPE OF THE STUDY

By investigating the published pronouncements and private correspondence of British scientists who were at least twenty years old in 1859 and lived at least until 1869, we have attempted to assess how successful Darwin was in converting the scientific community in Great Britain to a belief in the evolution of species, and the role that age played in the alacrity with which scientists changed their minds on the subject. Each of the limits in scope of our study calls for some comment. An accurate and extensive sampling of scientists around the world was out of the question. Some narrowing of scope was necessary. Great Britain was the obvious choice. Darwin was British, the reception of evolutionary theory has been documented more completely for Great Britain than for any other country, and the literature was most readily available. Of course, the reaction of British scientists may be peculiar. As we have already noted, Planck's principle seems to apply to the situation in Russia. Few, if any, well-established scientists were converted. It does not apply in France but for the opposite reason. French scientists, young and old alike, seemed impervious to the charms of Darwinism.

Because Planck's principle refers to scientists, we have limited our study to scientists as they were conceived at the time. The distinction between scientists and nonscientists was hazier in Victorian England than it is today. It was also drawn along somewhat different lines. In the middle of the nineteenth century, the professionalization of science was only just getting under way in Great Britain. The best universities did not offer degrees in the natural sciences, few posts were open to professional scientists, and scientific organizations were still open to amateurs and royal patrons. When there was any doubt about the status of a subject as a scientist, we tended to cast our net too broadly rather than too narrowly.[33] Our study also tends to be most heavily weighted toward the sciences that touched most directly on the question of the evolution of species; that is, zoology, botany, paleontology, geology, and anthropology. Because of the conflict between Darwin and Lord Kelvin over the age of the earth, a few physicists also made their views known.

The age limitations are equally important. We selected a lower limit of twenty in 1859 both to guarantee that the scientist would have assimilated at least a little of the special creationist world view before being confronted by Darwin's theory and to exclude scientists who were children at the time. Certainly Edwin Ray Lankester (1847-1929) and Edward B. Poulton (1856-1943) were important Darwinists, but not because they were converted to the view. They were raised Darwinists. Ten years was chosen because of the widespread opinion that by then the battle was over. Anyone who lived through that period and still was not won over can legitimately be counted among those who were difficult to convert.

Intellectually, science is extremely elitist. As sociologists of science have shown time and again, a very few scientists produce most of the major innovations (see notes 3, 12, and 15). If their behavior is any indication, scientists do not seem overly concerned with the opinions of ordinary, run-of-the-mill scientists. Instead, they seem to be most interested in converting the big guns. Darwin was no exception. He consciously set out to persuade important, well-placed scientists both before he published his *Origin of Species* and after. He was interested primarily in the verdict of a dozen or so men of science. If they came around, the rest would follow (22, vol. 1, pp. 521 and 529). This attitude probably explains in part the cynicism expressed in retrospect by scientists who succeeded in revolutionizing the science of their day about the inability of older scientists to change their minds. They are not reacting to the behavior of older scientists in general, but to the behavior of the scientists whose opinions mattered to them.

Although we did not limit ourselves just to "important" scientists in our study, our results are surely biased in that direction because of the availability of evidence. Because Darwinism succeeded, young Darwinists left much more in the way of records than did young anti-Darwinists. Young scientists were successful to some extent because they became Darwinists, and the views of successful scientists are much easier to document than those of the failures. For example, in April 1864, a group of London chemists circulated a "Declaration of Students of the Natural and Physical Sciences" among their fellow scientists for signature. The document declared that scientific investigations could not possibly contradict Holy Scripture. When a scientist finds that "some of his results appear to be in contradiction to the Written Word," he "should not presumptuously affirm that his own conclusions must be right, and the statements of Scripture wrong."[34] The ages of the six authors of this declaration in 1864 were 21, 23, 23, 25, 25, and 55. The authors of this declaration as well as the more than 700 scientists who signed it would seem to be excellent candidates for scientists opposed to the evolution of species. Unfortunately, most of the signators are so obscure that no evidence could be found for them. If any group is underrepresented in our survey, it is surely young scientists opposed to the evolution of species.

TABLE 1. Age in 1859 of scientists who accepted the evolution of species within 10 years of the publication of Darwin's *Origin of Species* compared to their age at acceptance and the age in 1869 of those who did not accept evolution.

Names and dates	Age in 1859	Age at earliest evidence of acceptance	Age in 1869 of continued rejectors
Babington, C. C. (1808-1895)	51		61
Balfour, J. H. (1808-1884)	51		61
Bastian, H. C. (1837-1915)	22	32	
Bates, H. W. (1835-1892)	34	32	
Bell, T. (1792-1880)	67		77
Bennett, A. W. (1833-1902)	26	36	
Bentham, G. (1800-1884)	59	63	
Busk, G. (1807-1886)	52	54	
Butler, A. G. (1831-1909)	28	38	
Carpenter, W. B. (1813-1885)	46	47	
Duncan, P. M. (1821-1891)	38	44	
Fawcett, H. (1833-1884)	26	27	
Flower, W. H. (1831-1899)	28	29	
Frankland, E. (1825-1899)	34	39	
Galton, F. (1822-1911)	37	38	
Geikie, A. (1835-1924)	24	24	
Gosse, P. H. (1810-1888)	49		59
Gray, J. E. (1800-1875)	59		69
Grove, W. R. (1811-1896)	48	55	
Günther, A. C. L. (1830-1914)	29		39
Haughton, S. (1821-1897)	38		48
Herschel, J. F. W. (1792-1871)	67	69	
Hirst, T. A. (1830-1892)	29	34	
Holland, H. (1788-1873)	71	72	
Hooker, J. D. (1817-1911)	42	41	
Humphrey, G. M. (1820-1896)	39	46	

TABLE 1—continued

Names and dates	Age in 1859	Age at earliest evidence of acceptance	Age in 1869 of continued rejectors
Hunt, J. (1833-1869)	26		36
Hutton, F. W. (1836-1905)	23	33	
Huxley, T. H. (1825-1895)	34	34	
Jardine, W. (1800-1874)	59		69
Jeffreys, J. (1809-1885)	50	59	
Jenkin, F. (1833-1885)	26		36
Jenyns, L. (1800-1893)	59	60	
Jevons, W. S. (1835-1882)	24	34	
Jukes, J. B. (1811-1869)	48	49	
Kingsley, C. (1819-1875)	40	44	
Lankester, E. (1814-1874)	45	55	
Lewes, G. H. (1817-1878)	42	51	
Lubbock, J. (1834-1913)	25	26	
Lyell, C. (1797-1875)	62	70	
MacIntosh, W. C. (1838-1931)	21		31
Mivart, G. J. (1827-1900)	32	33	
Mill, J. S. (1806-1873)	53		63
Molesworth, W. N. (1816-1890)	43	46	
Morris, F. O. (1810-1893)	49		59
Murchison, R. I. (1792-1871)	67		77
Murray, A. (1812-1878)	47	56	
Newton, A. (1829-1907)	30	31	
Page, D. (1814-1879)	45	50	
Phillips, J. (1800-1874)	59		69
Ramsey, A. C. (1814-1891)	45	46	
Rolleston, G. (1829-1881)	30	31	
Sclater, P. L. (1829-1913)	30	31	
Scott, J. G. (1838-1880)	21	26	
Sedgwick, A. (1785-1873)	74		84
Spottiswoode, W. (1825-1883)	34	39	
Stokes, G. G. (1819-1903)	40		50
Tegetmeier, W. B. (1816-1912)	43	43	
Thomson, C. W. (1830-1882)	29	38	
Thomson, W. (1824-1907)	35	45	
Thompson, A. (1809-1884)	50	60	
Thwaites, G. H. K. (1811-1882)	48	49	

TABLE 1—concluded

Names and dates	Age in 1859	Age at earliest evidence of acceptance	Age in 1869 of continued rejectors
Tristam, H. B. (1822-1906)	37	37	
Tyndall, J. (1820-1893)	39	44	
Watson, H. C. (1804-1881)	55	56	
Wood, S. V. (1798-1880)	61	62	
Young, John (1835-1902)	24	31	

The greatest difficulty that confronted us in our study was deciding what was to count as Darwinism. Because the Darwinian revolution is named after Charles Darwin and seemed to have begun soon after the publication of the *Origin of Species* in 1859, one is tempted to assume that Darwin and his ideas played a central role in the controversy. To be counted as a convert to Darwinism, one might think that a scientist would have to adopt Darwin's ideas, or most of Darwin's ideas, or at least his essential ideas. However, very few scientists in the second half of the nineteenth century accepted evolutionary theory as Darwin set it out. Darwin believed that evolution occurred gradually. The variations that were operative in the evolutionary process were very small, although not "continuous,"[35] and occurred in "all directions." Although Darwin believed that occasionally an acquired character could be transmitted to an organism's progeny, the chief directive force in evolution was natural selection. (Whether Darwin considered sexual selection a special form of natural selection or a distinct directive force is a moot question.) However, the view of evolution that was popular among scientists in the second half of the nineteenth century was saltative, directed, and progressive. Huxley, for example, opted for saltative evolution, the origin of a new species in the space of a single generation. Asa Gray, another of Darwin's most able supporters, argued for directed, pro-

TABLE 2. Victorian scientists who accepted some form of the evolution of species independently of the work of Darwin and Wallace.

Names and Dates	Date	Age
Chambers, R. (1802-1871)	1844	42
Croll, J. (1821-1890)	1848	27
Grant, R. E. (1793-1874)	1851	58
Matthew, P. (1790-1874)	1831	41
Powell, B. (1796-1860)	1845	49
Spencer, H. (1820-1903)	1840	20

gressive evolution. Some of Darwin's most bitter opponents held precisely the same views as his allies such as Saint George Jackson Mivart.

If a scientist must accept everything that Darwin said with respect to the origin of species to count as a Darwinist, then there were few Darwinists in the nineteenth century.[36] If, on the other hand, all it took to be an advocate of Darwinism was to accept a bit here and there, then nearly everyone was a Darwinist. As Leeds[37] notes with some dismay:

> What appears to me striking is how few of the figures discussed in these pages—with the exception of a small number of the Spanish, the Germans, and the English—held a Darwinian view at all. Mostly they assimilated a phrase or an aspect of Darwin's expression of his thought to their own understanding and thought, then, that they were Darwinians. The most striking case is that of the Russians, discussed in James Allen Rogers' paper, in which *not one* of the protagonists of his drama is remotely near the Darwinian model.

Thus, neither the primary nor the secondary literature can be taken at face value. Two scientists could hold exactly the same views and one term himself a disciple of Darwin and the other a staunch opponent. Of all the elements of Darwinism, we have chosen just one to follow—Darwin's claim that species evolve. Although this element of Darwinism was the least original with Darwin, it was his chief concern and the element that supposedly became most widely accepted in his day.[38] It was this belief that swept across the scientific communities of the world like the flood. Scientists may have come to accept the evolution of species because Darwin set out his views in a scientifically respectable way and because he suggested a naturalistic mechanism for such transformations, but paradoxically, if we are to believe the secondary literature, they did *not* accept natural selection.[39] If we had selected some other element in the Darwinian research program to investigate, the results might have been different. For example, Darwin thought that use and disuse might have some effect on later generations, a belief that was widespread at the time. Darwin would have had few scientists to convert. Conversely, if we had selected natural selection instead of evolution, Darwin would have been much less successful. The fates of the various elements in Darwin's theory differ. The relevant issue for our purposes is, however, whether or not these differences in acceptance covary with differences in the ages of the scientists involved.

METHODS AND RESULTS

We were able to gather sufficient data for sixty-seven British scientists who were at least twenty in 1859 and lived until at least 1869 (Table 1).

Our search began with the members of the Royal Society whom Francis Galton deemed genuine scientists and proceeded to scientists mentioned in the secondary literature dealing with Victorian science.[40] Thereafter, our search was largely a random walk. Scientists such as Herbert Spencer and Robert Chambers, who came to believe in the evolution of species independently of Darwin and Wallace, are not included in our study (Table 2). However, we have included two scientists converted by Wallace and Darwin before 1859. Wallace convinced H. W. Bates in 1857, and Darwin was able to persuade J. D. Hooker a year later. (If evolution was so much in the air, why was Darwin able to convince only one of the dozen or so scientists with whom he discussed his theory before the appearance of the *Origin?*)

In order to be classed among the converted, a scientist had to state explicitly, that he believed in the evolution of species—that is, that species arose by means of one species changing through time into another. Whether he believed that evolution was directed or undirected, progressive or nonprogressive, saltative or gradual is irrelevant, as is the subject's beliefs about spontaneous generation and natural selection. A statement to the effect that the author opposed Darwinism lacks sufficient information to be of any use. It could mean anything. Many anti-Darwinists accepted the evolution of species. However, we found no instance in which someone professed to be a Darwinian and yet did not accept at least the claim that species evolve.

TABLE 3. Specialties of scientists who continued to reject the evolution of species in 1869.

Name	Specialty
Babington, C. C.	Botany
Balfour, J. H.	Botany
Bell, T.	Zoology
Gosse, P. H.	Marine biology
Gray, J. E.	Zoology (Mollusca)
Gunther, A. C. L.	Zoology (reptiles)
Haughton, S.	Mathematics and geology
Hunt, J.	Anthropology
Jardine, W.	Zoology (ornithology)
Jenkin, F.	Engineering
MacIntosh, W. C.	Zoology (marine annelids)
Mill, J. S.	Philosophy and economics
Morris, F. O.	Zoology
Murchison, R. I.	Paleontology
Phillips, J.	Geology
Sedgwick, A.	Geology
Stokes, G. G.	Physics and mathematics

The first feature of our data worth noting is that only fifty of the sixty-seven scientists studied (less than three-quarters) had come to accept the evolution of species by 1869. Thus, although the conversion of the scientific community in Great Britain was certainly extensive, it was neither universal nor nearly so. If only seventy-five percent of the scientists at the time accepted the most widely accepted of all the elements in Darwin's theory, then the conversion of the British scientific community was not nearly as rapid nor as total as we have been led to believe. The question remains why Darwinism seemed at the time and in retrospect to be more successful than it actually was. Although our sample is too small to tell, field of interest also did not seem to have much effect. The same spectrum of fields can be found among those who accepted the evolution of species as those who rejected it (Table 3).

If Planck's principle is correct, scientists who came to accept the evolution of species before 1869 should have been significantly younger than those who continued to hold out. Further, of those who accepted evolution, the younger scientists should have been converted much more quickly than the older scientists. We used two methods to test the merits of Planck's principle: first, a simple comparison of the average age in 1859 of accepters and rejecters, and, second, the logit technique[41] to obtain an unbiased estimate of the coefficient of age when acceptance is regressed on age. Both methods were applied first on the data that excluded those who died between 1859 and 1869 and then on the data that included this information (Table 4). In our basic sample, the average age of accepters was 39.6 and that of rejecters was 48.1, a difference of almost ten years.[42] When a two-tailed t-test was performed, the t-statistic was 2.256, indicating that the difference in mean age is statistically significant at $P < .05$. We obtained similar results when we added to our sample scientists who

TABLE 4. Views on evolution of scientists who died between 1859 and 1869.

Names and dates	Age in 1859	Date of acceptance	Age at acceptance	Age at death
Boott, F. (1792-1863)	67	1860	68	71
Brewster, D. (1781-1868)	78			87
Crawfurd, J. (1783-1868)	76			85
Daubeny, C. G. (1795-1867)	64	1860	65	72
Falconer, H. (1809-1865)	50	1863	54	56
Harvey, W. H. (1811-1866)	48	1860	49	55
Henslow, J. S. (1796-1861)	63			65
Hopkins, W. (1793-1866)	66			73
Horner, L. (1785-1864)	74	1861	76	79
Rogers, H. D. (1809-1866)	51	1860	52	57
Whewell, W. (1794-1866)	65			72

had died between 1859 and 1869. For this larger sample, the mean age of accepters rose to 41.7 and the age of rejecters increased to 53.0. The *t*-statistic was 3.071, significant once again at $P < .05$. Thus, age is a relevant factor in distinguishing between those scientists who accepted the evolution of species before 1869 and those who did not.

Next we used the logit technique to obtain the coefficient on year of birth when acceptance is regressed on year of birth. In the equation

$$A = \alpha + \gamma B$$

A is a dummy variable equal to 1 if the scientist accepted evolution before 1869 and 0 if he did not; α is the estimated constant: *B* is the year of birth of the scientist; and γ is the estimated coefficient that minimizes the error in predicting *A*. Using our basic sample, the estimated value of γ is 0.046 with a *t*-statistic of 2.159. As in the case of our first method, enlarging the basic sample to include scientists who died between 1859 and 1869 does not change the results much. The estimated γ is 0.051 with a *t*-statistic of 2.791. Once again, age makes a difference. In predicting acceptance, year of birth is significant at $P < .05$. However, the R^2 (the square of the correlation coefficient) for the regression on our basic data is .06, which means that less than ten percent of the variation in acceptance is explained by age.

Planck's principle also implies that of scientists who accepted the evolution of species before 1869, younger scientists should have changed their minds more quickly than older scientists. To test this hypothesis, we regressed years of delay on age in 1859. The coefficient obtained was −0.052 with a *t*-statistic of −1.193. When scientists who died between 1859 and 1869 were added to the sample, the coefficient became −0.064 and the *t*-statistic −1.796. Thus, in neither case does age seem to matter. Of the scientists who accepted the evolution of species before 1869, older scientists were as quick to change their minds as younger scientists.

CONCLUSION

The results of this study indicate that our intuitions about the course of science, although not totally faulty, are none too reliable. Darwin and his contemporaries thought that nearly all scientists had come to accept the evolution of species within ten years after the publication of the *Origin*. They also thought that younger scientists with their more "plastic" minds were easier to convert than older scientists. Later commentators, looking back at this period, have gathered this same impression. To be sure, the scientists who still refused after 1869 to admit that species evolve were significantly older than those who jumped on the Darwinian bandwagon. However, age explains less than ten percent of the variation in acceptance. More than ninety percent remains to be explained. The possibility exists that at least some of this variation can be explained in terms of the efficacy of reason, argument, and evidence. It should also be noted that twenty-five percent of the scientists in our study remained unconvinced in 1869, and that when the ages of the scientists who did come to accept the evolution of species in this period were compared to the time it took them to be converted, no significant correlation materialized.

Most scientific theories fail. The issue about the relation between the age of scientists and the spread of new scientific ideas arises only for theories that, in retrospect, we think scientists should have accepted. No one complains that the scientific community remained impervious to phrenology, mesmerism, and the flat earth movement. In the case of successful scientific research programs, a new idea becomes increasingly accepted. During the same period, older scientists are dying off at a higher rate than younger scientists. Because these two processes are taking place at the same time, we are led to suspect a causal connection. Clearly the spread of new scientific ideas rarely causes scientists to die. The question remains whether the death of scientists facilitates the spread of new scientific ideas. If we had studied a theory that gained some converts and then disappeared— that is, if we had studied the usual case—our figures might have been quite different. Our study does not show that Darwin conquered everywhere "by mere force of truth and fact," but it does show that the connection between age and acceptance is not as important as people such as Max Planck have claimed.

NOTES

1. For an example of a debate over the role of cognitive and noncognitive factors in science with special reference to phrenology, see G. N. Cantor (2); *Ann. Sci.* 32 (1975); 245. S. Shapin, *ibid.*, 219.

2. G. N. Cantor, *ibid.*, 195.

3. As early as 1949, N. Pastore [*The Nature-Nurture Controversy* (New York: Columbia Univ. Press, 1949)] compared the views of 24 biologists on the nature-nurture issue with their political persuasion. He found that 11 out of 12 conservatives favored nature while 11 out of 12 liberals and radicals opted for nurture as the major influence. S. Cole [in *The Idea of Social Structure*, L. A. Coser, Ed. (New York: Harcourt Brace Jovanovich, 1975). 175] has actually set about testing some of the claims made by philosophers about science. One of the claims that he lists as needing empirical support is Planck's principle (181).

4. Kingsley, C., *Charles Kingsley, His Letters and Memories of His Life.* London: Macmillan, 1890, 253.

5. Bennett, A. W. *Nature (London)* 3 (1870): 30.

6. Planck, M., *Scientific Autobiography and Other Papers* London: Williams & Norgate, 1950, 33-34.

7. Lavoisier, A. L. in *The Edge of Objectivity.* C. C. Gillispie, ed. Princeton, N.J.: Princeton Univ. Press, 1960, 232.

8 Darwin, C., *On the Origin of Species* (a facsimile of the first edition) (Harvard Univ. Press, Cambridge, Mass., 1966), 481-482.

9. Huxley, L. *Life and Letters of Thomas Henry Huxley* (Appleton, New York, 1901), vol. 2, p. 117.

10. T. Kuhn, *The Structure of Scientific Revolutions* (Univ. of Chicago Press, Chicago, 1970), 151.

11. P. Feyerabend, in *Criticism and the Growth of Knowledge*, I. Lakatos and A. Musgrave, Eds. (Cambridge Univ. Press, Cambridge, 1970), 203.

12. J. Cole and S. Cole, *Social Stratification in Science* (Univ. of Chicago Press, Chicago, 1973), 82.

13. H. Bondi, in *Problems of Scientific Revolution*, R. Harre, Ed. (Clarendon, Oxford, 1975), 7.

14. B. Barber, *Science* 134, 596 (1961).

15. R. K. Merton, *The Sociology of Science* (Univ. of Chicago Press, Chicago, 1973), 497-559.

16. A. E. Gunther, *A Century of Zoology* (Science History, New York, 1975), 458.

17. H. W. Paul, in (18), 412.

18. T. F. Glick, Ed., *The Comparative Reception of Darwinism* (Univ. of Texas Press, Austin, 1974).

19. B. Loewenberg, *Am. Hist. Rev.* 38, 687 (1932).

20. W. O. Hagstrom, *The Scientific Community* (Basic Books, New York, 1965), 283-284.

21. A. Thomas, in *Victorian Science*, G. Basalla, W. Coleman, R. H. Kargon, Eds. (Doubleday, Garden City, N.Y., 1970), 205.

22. F. Darwin, *The Life and Letters of Charles Darwin* (Appleton, New York, 1899), vol. 2, 85 and 117. We omitted Owen's name from our study because we were unable to decide what his views were on the origin of species.

23. G. Himmelfarb, *Darwin and the Darwinian Revolution* (Doubleday, Garden City, N.Y., 1959), 252; see also (16), 453.

24. C. D.Darlington, *Sci. Am.* 200, 60 (May 1959).

25. A. Ellegard, *Darwin and the General Reader* (Gothenburg Univ., Gothenburg, Sweden, 1958), 337.

26. H. W. Paul, in (18), 409.

27. W. Montgomery, in (18), 91; see also (42).

28. I. Bulhof, in (18), 284.

29. E. Pfeifer, in (18),204.

30. T. Glick, in (18), 310.

31. A. Vucinich and J. A. Rogers, in (18), 227-268.

32. R. E. Stebbins, in (18), 117-163.

33. Francis Galton was presented with the same problem when he undertook the first sociological study of scientists in Great Britain. His solution was to restrict his sample to the members of the Royal Society who had distinguished themselves in some way other than just being elected to the Society; for instance, by earning a medal, presiding over a learned society or section of the British Association for the Advancement of Science, or being elected to the council of the Society. Of the 500 or so members in 1872, only 189 qualified. To this number, Galton added Herbert Spencer, John S. Henslow, and Robert H. Greg [F. Falton, *English Men of Science; Their Nature and Nurture* (Macmillan, London, 1874)].

34. W. H. Brock and R. Macleod, *Br. J. Hist. Sci.* 11, 41 (1976). The declaration had been signed by 717 scientists when it was finally published in 1865. Sixty-five of the 673 members of the Royal Society signed. Of these, 48 were considered to be sufficiently important scientists to be labeled as such in the *Dictionary of National Biography*. Of these, only three were especially prominent scientists: Sir David Brewster (1781-1868), James Prescott Joule (1818-1889), and Adam Sedgwick (1785-1873). Of special relevance to our study is Brock and Macleod's conclusion that age seemed to be immaterial in determining who signed and who did not sign the declaration (52).

35. D. L. Hull, *Syst. Zool*, 21, 132 (1972); P. J. Bowler, *Ann. Sci.* 35, 55 (1978).

36. R. W. Burkhardt, Jr., *Isis* 67, 494 (1976).

37. A. Leeds, in (18), 439.

38. As Darwin himself said in the *Athenaeum*, 1854, 617 (1863): "Whether the naturalist believes in the view given by Lamarck, or Geoffrey St. hilaire, by the author of the "Vestiges," by Mr. Wallace and myself, or in any other such view, signifies extremely little in comparison with the admission that species have

descended from other species and have not been created immutable; for he who admits this as a great truth has a wide field opened to him for further inquiry."

39. In this article we show that our intuitions about the role of age in acceptance of the evolution of species and the extent of this acceptance by 1869 are faulty. Hence, we would be foolish to accept at face value the widespread belief that evolution was much more widely accepted than natural selection. For example, in 1913, soon after the fortunes of natural selection were supposed to have reached their lowest ebb, E. R. Lankester [*Science from an Easy Chair* (Books for Libraries Press, Freeport, N.Y., 1913), 391] can be found saying: "I recently read an essay in which the writer is good enough to say that, owing to the work of Darwin, the fact that the differences which we see between organisms have been reached by a gradual evolution, is not now disputed. That, at any rate seems to be a solid achievement. But he went on to declare that when we inquire by what method this evolution was brought about biologists can return no answer. That appears to me to be a most extraordinary perversion of the truth. The reason why the gradual evolution of the various kinds of organisms is not now disputed is that Darwin showed the method by which that evolution can and must be brought about. . . . The assertion that the theory of natural selection as left by Darwin 'is now generally held to be inadequate' is fallacious. Darwin's conclusions on this matter are generally held to be essentially true.

40. F. Galton (33); in addition to the usual Victorian lives and letters, Ellegard (25) and Brock and Macleod (34) were especially useful.

41. H. Theil, *Principles of Econometrics* (Wiley, New York, 1971), 628-636.

42. W. Montgomery [in (18), 115] did a similar study of 34 German scientists in 1860. Although his sample was half as large as ours, his results accord reasonably well with ours. He found the mean age in 1860 of the 20 German scientists who came to accept some form of evolution to be 36.8 and the mean age of the 14 who continued to hold out to be just under 50. In Montgomery's study, only 59 percent of the scientists studied were converted.

43. The research for this article was supported in part by NSF grant Soc 75 03535. We thank A. McHutcheon for help in using the logit technique.

Chapter 4

Darwin and the Nature of Science*

Darwin constructed *The Origin of Species* (1859) as an argument *for* the gradual evolution of species primarily by means of chance variation and natural selection and *against* special creation, the belief that "at innumerable periods in the earth's history certain elemental atoms have been commanded suddenly to flash into living tissues" (Darwin, 1859; 483). Critics both at the time and since agree with Rudwick (1972: 222) that in arguing against the special creationists, Darwin "presented his theory with only a straw man to oppose it: *either* slow trans-specific evolution by means of natural selection, *or* direct divine creation of new species from the inorganic dust of the Earth." Rudwick (1972: 207) goes on to suggest that Darwin was carefully avoiding a third, more viable alternative:

> On the contrary, although Darwin later suggested that the only alternative to his evolutionary theory was a naive creationism, in fact there was another explanation available, with intellectual credentials quite as high as Darwin's, and with considerably more credibility to the mind of the time. This alternative was well developed by one who started as Darwin's collaborator but who later became one of his most implacable opponents — the anatomist and paleontologist Richard Owen (1804-1892).

For want of a better term, I will call this third alternative to evolution and special creation "idealism," and would add a fourth alternative as well—reverent silence. Given the highly inductive philosophies of science current at the time, scientists felt perfectly justified in remaining silent on those issues for which they lacked sufficient data. In the *Origin*, Darwin (1859: 310) lists a dozen or so palaeontologists and geologists who "unanimously, often vehemently, maintained the immutability of species" and in retrospect could not recall coming upon a single person, save R. E. Grant, "who seemed to doubt about the permanence of species" (Darwin, 1899: 1: 71). Lyell (1889: 2: 274) confirms Darwin's recollections and adds his own position to the list. "But, speaking generally, it may be said that all the most influential teachers of geology, palaeontology, zoology, and botany continued till near the middle of this century either

---

*Reprinted with permission from *Evolution From Molecules to Men*, ed. D. S. Bendall. © 1983 by the Cambridge University Press. Printed at the University Press, Cambridge.

to assume the independent creation and immutability of species, or carefully avoided expressing any opinion on this important subject."

It is extremely difficult to gauge the prevalence of a belief at a particular time in history. The barriers confronting the type of statistical analysis necessary are all but immobilizing. Rudwick (1972: 208) rightly maintains that natural history was "not old-fashioned in Owen's time" and goes on to add that "Owen himself was not a kind of living fossil epistemologically: his view of nature was that of most of his contemporaries." Paradis (1978: 120) claims, to the contrary, that the "nature-philosophy" tradition exemplified by Owen's work "had never been strong" in England, while Yeo (1979) argues that the Whewell-Owen concept of science at the time was struggling against great opposition to become accepted. G. H. Lewes (1852: 263), for one, viewed the sort of science that he preferred as a minority position in England: "Although Germany and France have applied Goethe's morphological ideas with great success, yet England— true to her anti-metaphysical instinct, unhappily no more than an instinct with the majority—has been very chary of giving them admission, because the real philosophic method which underlies them is not appreciated."

I have no idea how strong each of these traditions was in Great Britain at the time. I do know, however, that leading Victorian scientists can be found explicitly espousing each of the four alternatives mentioned and that Darwin had the same opinion of all but his own—they were not "scientific."

In the *Origin*, Darwin chose to argue against the creationists. All he had to do was to extend the notion of science exemplified in Lyell's *Principles of Geology* (1830-3) to include the origin of species as well as their extinction. By the very act of publishing the *Origin*, Darwin was breaking the gentlemen's agreement that Chambers (1844) had broken in such an ungentlemanly fashion before him. But idealism was quite another matter. He had no idea of how to confront idealistic explanations in terms of Platonic ideas and polarizing forces. Instead he used the scientist's most potent weapon—silence. Although Lyell was Darwin's implicit opponent in the *Origin*, he never published a rebuttal. Although Owen is hardly mentioned, he published one of the most acrimonious critiques of Darwin and Wallace's theory, while at the same time claiming priority (Owen, 1860). After all, had he not repeatedly referred to the "continuous operation of Creative power, or the ordained becoming of living things" (Owen, 1858: 314, 1860: 258)?

I think that Darwin's different reaction to Lyell and Owen can be explained by differences in their views on the nature of science. Darwin agreed with Lyell about the nature of science and wanted only to extend it a bit further. With respect to Owen, the differences were so profound that Darwin could not find sufficient grounds even for disagreement. To combat Owen, Darwin would have to engage in "philosophy," an indulgence he tended to confine to his personal correspondence and private notebooks (Gruber and Barrett, 1974). The Darwinian revolution was as much concerned with the promotion of a particular view of science as it was with the introduction of a theory on the transmutation of species. However, before embarking on a discussion of the interconnections between philosophy and evolutionary theory, a few words must be said about terminology.

One perennial problem in the history of ideas is that no two people ever mean precisely the same thing by such terms as "creation," "idealism," or "science." The idealists were as mixed a lot as were the evolutionists. One solution is never to use the same term for any two authors, as self-defeating a suggestion as I have ever heard. But as soon as one claims that both Darwin and Huxley came to believe in the evolution of species while Sedgwick and Agassiz did not, one invites the specialist to list the indefinitely many ways in which the views of these workers differed. I think that such careful distinctions are absolutely necessary in the history of ideas, but I think that more general works, attempts to compare views and trace them through time, also have a function. In this paper I contrast evolutionism, creationism, and idealism, and try to explain why Darwin thought that his own concept of the origin of species was scientific while the explanations provided by the creationists and idealists were not. In order to circumvent the difficulties inherent in the use of general terms, I use specific scientists to illustrate general positions—Darwin for evolutionism, Owen for idealism, Whewell for creationism, and Lyell for reverent silence. In doing so, I do not mean to imply that the views of any of these scientists were somehow typical of the general position. As I have argued elsewhere, it is as misleading to think of a particular exposition as being typical of a more general system of ideas as it is to think of a particular organism being typical of its species (Hull, 1976, 1978b, 1983). In some cases, there is a point to such exemplifications; in most cases not. The idealists present a special problem because they did not form a group. Claims about Darwinism in the middle of the nineteenth century sound sensible because the Darwinians formed a fairly cohesive social group at the time. Talk of idealism seems less appropriate because of the absence of such a group.

PHILOSOPHY OF SCIENCE

Darwin had the mixed fortune of attempting to solve the mystery of mysteries at the very time that philosophy of science was becoming a self-conscious discipline in the English-speaking world. John Herschel (1830), William Whewell (1837, 1840, 1849), John Stuart Mill (1843), and Lyell (1830-3) carried on at great length about the nature of science and proper scientific method. Darwin read the works of nearly all of these philosopher-scientists: Herschel before leaving on his voyage, Lyell on route, and Whewell upon his return. Darwin found himself largely in agreement with the ideas of these men and thought of himself as pursuing science in the ways they dictated.

Two problems arise, however. The first is that Herschel, Lyell, and Mill disagreed fundamentally with Whewell over the nature of the human mind and our knowledge of the empirical world. As Cannon (1976) and Hodge (1983) see the issue, one instructive way of viewing the Darwinian revolution is to interpret it as a conflict between Herschel, Mill, Lyell, and Darwin on the one side and people like Whewell, Owen (1846, 1848, 1849, 1851), and Edward Forbes (1854) on the other side—the "empiricists" against the "idealists" (see also Ellegard, 1957, 1958; and Hull, 1972).

The second problem is that the "empiricists" and "idealists," as much as they might disagree with each other about the fundamental nature of science, agreed that in *The Origin of Species* Darwin had failed to meet accepted standards of scientific method. Darwin's reasoning in the *Origin* was too hypothetical, too speculative, not sufficiently inductive. Although all of the philosophers mentioned acknowledged the role of hypotheses in science, they also thought that scientific theories of gravitation and light had been proved. As Hodge (1983) shows, Darwin began by thinking he had presented a *vera causa* in the strong sense exemplified by Newton's gravitational theory, but in the face of the negative reactions of the leading philosophers of science of his day, he retreated to a weaker exemplar— contemporary theories of light.

According to one long list of commentators, the sort of reasoning exhibited by evolutionary biologists from Darwin to the present is sorely deficient (Popper, 1957, 1974; Himmelfarb, 1959). According to another equally long list of commentators, there is nothing whatsoever wrong with the methodology of evolutionary biologists (Ruse, 1971, 1975, 1977, 1979; Hull, 1973). In fact Ghiselin (1969) had argued that Darwin's scientific method is a paradigm of good scientific practice. I do not intend to go over these issues once again here. Instead, I intend to pursue a somewhat more fundamental issue. Too often the content of scientific theories and our beliefs about the nature of science are treated as if they change in relative independence of each other, when in actual fact their development is closely interlaced. Just as our methodological beliefs influence the content of scientific theories, the content of these theories influences what we take to be proper method.

As Cohen (1981) argues, Newton not only transformed the science of mechanics but also changed the way subsequent scientists went about doing science. Similarly, as Rudwick (1972) has documented, Lyell was as concerned to redefine the science of geology as he was to support his own particular view of geological phenomena. As Laudan (1981: 9) puts the general position, "it is shifting *scientific* beliefs which have been chiefly responsible for the major doctrinal shifts within the philosophy of science."

I think that numerous puzzles about the reception of Darwin's *Origin* can be resolved if sufficient attention is paid to the influence that the introduction of such fundamental theories as evolutionary theory have on our understanding of science itself. Darwin thought of himself as continuing in the Herschel-Lyell tradition of "inductive science." Thus, he was bewildered by Herschel's characterizing his theory as the "law of higgledy-piggledy" (Darwin, 1899: 2: 37), Mill's (1874) opting for divine plan over evolution, and Lyell's continued reluctance to come out in favour of his theory. That Whewell would reject Darwin's theory was understandable. Darwin's conception of science departed in significant respects from Whewell's modified Kantian views, but why were Herschel, Mill and Lyell so reluctant?

I propose to argue that Darwin's theory struck at the very foundations of the philosophical views held by these philosopher-scientists as well. As far as I can tell, Darwin was unaware of these implications of his theory. Several of his contemporaries perceived these conflicts through a glass darkly, but these dim perceptions were soon brushed aside, just as the triumph of Newton's theory stilled philosophical doubts about action-at-a-distance. However, just as these doubts were exhumed with the advent of relativity theory, conflicts between evolutionary theory and traditional philosophical concepts have surfaced again (Ghiselin, 1974a; Hull, 1976, 1978; Wiley, 1981; Mayr, 1982; Gould, 1982).

REVERENT SILENCE

Not only did Lyell's *Principles of Geology* (1830-3) present a new theory of the formation of the earth's crust, but also "it will endeavour to establish the *principles of reasoning* in the science" (Lyell, 1881: 1: 234). According to Lyell, geologists should explain past geological phenomena in the same way that they explain present-day phenomena, by means of the same kinds of causes acting at approximately the same rates as they are observed to operate today. Lyell extended his naturalistic view of science to include the extinction of species but not their origin. "Whether new species are substituted from time to time for those which die out, is a point on which no decided opinion is offered; that data hitherto obtained being considered insufficient to determine the question" (Lyell, 1830: xii).

In his private correspondence, Lyell was a good deal less circumspect. In response to a letter from Herschel in 1836 acknowledging that a naturalistic explanation of the origin of species is scientifically permissible, Lyell (1881: 1: 467) agrees, complaining that the "German critics have attacked me vigorously, saying that by the impugning of the doctrine of spontaneous generation, and substituting nothing in its place, I have left them nothing but the direct and miraculous intervention of the First Cause, as often as a new species is introduced, and hence I have overthrown my own doctrine of revolutions, carried on by a regular system of secondary causes."

Lyell's German critics had a point. By arguing in print against Lamarck's theory of the transmutation of species, dismissing spontaneous generation as a "fanciful notion left over from Aristotle" (Lyell, 1830: 1: 59), and couching his own agnosticism in terms of "creation," Lyell could not help but realize the impression that he would have on his readers. It is certainly true that initially Darwin took Lyell's *Principles of Geology* as supporting his own Christian creationist belief. In his 1858 Presidential Address to the British Association for the Advancement of Science, Owen (see Basalla, Coleman and Kargon, 1970: 326) warns his audience that "it may be well to bear in mind that by the word 'creation,' the zoologist means 'a process he knows not what.' Once again, even though "creation" might well have been a code word for unknown natural processes, the use of this word, especially when it was coupled with all sorts of additional theistic references, was guaranteed to give just the opposite impression.

Although Darwin's dilemma—either miracles or evolution—was not fair to many of his contemporaries, it was certainly appropriate for some, including no less an authority than William Whewell. Whewell (1847: 3: 624-5) saw the dilemma in precisely these stark terms:

> ... either we must accept the doctrine of the transmutation of species, and must suppose that the organized species of one geological epoch were transmuted into those of another by some long-continued agency of natural causes; or else, we must believe in many successive acts of creation and extinction of species, out of the common course of nature; acts which, therefore we may properly call miraculous.

For his part, Whewell (1847: 3: 638-9) opts for the second alternative. Huxley, in his contribution to *The Life and Letters of Charles Darwin* (F. Darwin (ed.) 1988, 1, 548), poses Darwin's dilemma once again, while ridiculing Whewell's idealistic 'conceivability' criterion for knowledge, remarking, "No doubt the sudden concurrence of half-a-ton of inorganic molecules into a live rhinoceros is conceivable, and therefore may be possible," but for his own part, he refused "to run the risk of insulting any sane man by supposing that he seriously holds such a notion" (Huxley, 1870: 375).

Special creationists applied a double standard to scientific and theisitc explanations of the origin of species. The standards for scientific explanations were extremely exacting while those for theistic explanations were left unspoken. In 1852, prior to the appearance of the *Origin*, Herbert Spencer (1852: 280) objected to this double standard, complaining that those "who cavalierly reject the Theory of Evolution as not being adequately supported by facts, seem to forget that their own theory is supported by no facts at all." In the *Origin* itself, Darwin (1859: 483) echoed Spencer's complaint: "Although naturalists very properly demand a full explanation of every difficulty from those who believe in the mutability of species, on their own side they ignore the whole subject of the first appearance of species in what they consider reverent silence."

After the appearance of the *Origin*, William Hopkins (1860: 87) explicitly defended precisely this asymmetric view of natural and supernatural explanations. Hopkins justifies applying high standards of criticism to Darwin's theory while requiring nothing of its creationist alternative by claiming that the "doctrine of successive creations, any more than that of final causes, does not pretend to be a *physical theory*." To the contrary, it "professes to be a negation of other theories rather than a theory of itself, and therefore cannot be called upon to account for phenomena at all in the physical sense in which we necessarily call upon a definite physical theory to account for them."

Darwin not only shattered the reverent silence of men like Lyell, but also directly confronted the legitimacy of explaining the origin of species by means of supernatural agencies. Darwin scholars are in wide agreement that Lyell posed the species problem that Darwin set about solving. Lyell also provided the general rules of reasoning that Darwin was to employ in solving it. Darwin was willing to push Lyell's line of reasoning into areas that Lyell himself was reluctant even to approach. By including the origin of species within the province of natural science, Darwin threatened the last citadel protecting mind, soul, and morals from the encroachment of science. The conflict continues to the present. In the nineteenth century, however, Darwin played Joshua to Lyell's Moses.

BUT THIS IS NOT A SCIENTIFIC EXPLANATION

Cannon (1976: 382) encourages historians of Victorian science to give "sympathetic attention to various schemes of that period—mostly Ideal Type schemes—which were not then obscurantist but were serious scientific proposals." This is easier to encourage than to accomplish because the Ideal Type world view is so different from our own. To make matters worse, the world view which idealists were combatting is very similar to our own. Hence, even direct quotations have an air of ridicule about them. One thing is certain, however: in the struggle for existence, the Herschel-Lyell-Darwin concept beat the Whewell-Owen-Agassiz concepts hollow. Although these two views of nature, treated this broadly, have wide areas of overlap, where they differed most strongly, the idealists lost out. Should they have lost? Was the resulting science better because they lost? These are the sorts of questions that historians are not supposed to ask and, if asked, are all but impossible to answer.

In 1868 Owen proclaimed that if he were given the alternative, "species by miracle or by law," he for one would opt for the latter (Owen, 1868: 3: 793). Louis Agassiz, in the margins of the copy of the *Origin* that Darwin sent him, wrote, "What is the great difference between supposing that God makes variable species or that he makes laws by which species vary?" Later he asks again, "What does this prove except an ideal unity holding all parts of one plan together?" (Lurie, 1960: 255). The point at issue was the nature of scientific laws and the relation between them and ideal plans. How could an ideal unity hold a plan together?

Because the issues under investigation are metaphysical, they are more than a little difficult to characterize adequately in the space of a few sentences, especially since no two of the authors under discussion held the same views. A good point of entry is the distinction made by Hopkins (1860: 740) between geometrical and physical laws. According to Hopkins, patterns exist out there in nature. Geometrical laws are deduced from the phenomena themselves and are "entirely independent of any theory respecting the *physical causes* to which the phenomena are referable." Physical laws to the contrary present appropriate physical causes. According to Hopkins, Kepler's laws are geometrical while Newton's law of universal gravitation is physical. Mill (1843) designated much the same distinction by his contrast between uniformities of coexistence and causal laws. In biological contexts, the covariation of traits discerned by naturalists and comparative anatomists were examples of geometrical laws or uniformities of co-existence. None of the scientists under discussion doubted that the regularities referred to by the 'unity of type' existed. They differed with respect to their physical or causal explanation.

The preponderance of Owen's work was descriptive. Although his idealistic philosophy might have informed his descriptive work, he tended to raise these issues explicitly only in the beginning or the conclusion of his works, usually in the high-flown theistic language common at the time. Other anatomists might object to the particular patterns that Owen discerned, but no one objected to his searching for them. As geometric laws they were as unproblematic as the relations between conic sections. It was the physical cause that Owen proposed that gave some of his contemporaries pause. Owen's (1848: 172) classic statement of the cause of the interrelationships that seemed so apparent in organic forms runs as follows: "The Platonic *eidos*, or specific organizing principle or force, would seem to be in antagonism with the general polarizing force, and to subdue and mould it in subserviency to the exigencies of the resulting specific form."

I wish I could go on at this juncture to expand on the preceding characterization, but I have been unable to discover such an amplification in Owen's work. He restates the preceding view in a variety of ways but does not present much in the way of detailed explication. What were these polarizing forces? According to what formulae did they vary? Owen never says, but in referring to 'polarizing forces', Owen thought of himself as carrying on in the Newtonian tradition. Just as Whewell (1840: 1: 331) explained the growth of crystals in terms of polarization, Owen explained the repetition of vertebrae in a backbone in these same terms. As Hall (1968) has shown, Newton's work let loose a tidal wave of forces and subtle fluids in science. In most cases, little came of them.

In the first edition of the *Origin* (1859: 435), Darwin mentions Owen's *On the Nature of Limbs* (1849) in connection with the law of the Unity of Type, finding it "interesting." In later editions, once Owen had come out strongly against Darwin's and Wallace's theory, Darwin was more candid, concluding his discussion of Owen with "but this is not a scientific explanation." In retrospect, Huxley recalls sharing Darwin's opinions of Owen's view. Huxley could not see what Agassiz's explanation of the coming and going of species as God thought of them actually explained. "Neither did it help me to be told by an eminent anatomist that species had succeeded one another in time, in virtue of 'a continuously operative creational law' " (Darwin, 1899: 1: 549).

One might complain that these comments by Darwin and Huxley are merely a sign of their partisanship. However, the Darwinians expressed precisely these same views long before the appearance of the *Origin*. The occasion was a paper by Edward Forbes (1854) in which Forbes characterized the distribution of organized beings through time as forming a figure eight with its constriction at the boundary between the Permian and Triassic epochs. As a description of the distribution of fossils, Forbes' claim was straightforward enough. It could be tested by discovering additional fossils. As it turned out, Forbes' distributional claim was soon refuted by J. Barrande's discovery of Cambrian fossils (Darwin, 1903: 2: 230). However, like Owen, Forbes did not stop with stating a geometrical law.

He (Forbes, 1854: 428) went on to explain this distribution as a "manifestation of force of development at opposite poles of an ideal sphere."

Forbes' paper hardly went unnoticed by future evolutionists. Wallace was so incensed by Forbes' "ideal absurdity" that he was led to write his 1855 paper (Marchant, 1916: 54). Darwin was just as irate. In a letter to Hooker in 1854, he remarks, "It is very strange, but I think Forbes is often rather fanciful; his 'Polarity' makes me sick—it is like 'magnetism' turning a table" (Darwin, 1903: 1: 77). Wallace and Darwin were hardly disinterested observers, but Hopkins (1860: 749) raises exactly the same objections to Forbes' reference to polarity, and he can hardly be accused of being biased in favour of evolutionary theory. Hopkins does not object to Forbes' distributional claim as a geometrical law: "If, however, the term *polarity* is intended, on the contrary, to convey the idea of some particular physical cause to which the phenomena are due, the theory becomes a physical theory, which we estimate, as such, at the lowest value, since so far from tracing the action of some definite physical cause, it does not even assign such causes in any comprehensible terms."

Huxley's views on these issues are a good deal more equivocal. In his early writings, Huxley referred to such things as plans and archetypes as freely as Owen did. As Huxley (1893: 1: 7) recalls these early years, "species work was always a burden to me; what I cared for was the architectural and engineering part of the business, the working out the wonderful unity of plan in the thousands and thousands of diverse living constructions, and the modifications of similar apparatuses to serve diverse ends." However, Huxley (1853: 50) claims that for his part, all he means by the "plan" of a particular invertebrate is a "conception of a form embodying the most general propositions that can be affirmed respecting the Cephalus Mollusca, standing in the same relation to them as the diagram to a geometrical theorem, and like it, at once, imaginary and true."

In one of his first letters to Huxley, Darwin (1903: 1: 73) applauds Huxley's work in comparative anatomy: "The discovery of the type or 'idea' (in your sense, for I detest the word as used by Owen, Agassiz & Co.) of each great class, I cannot doubt, is one of the very highest ends of Natural History . . ." Exactly how candid Darwin is being is difficult to judge because Huxley's views on the nature and role of archetypes in science are anything but transparent. For instance, in his review of the tenth edition of Chambers' *Vestiges of the Natural History of Creation* (1853), Huxley argues that he has nothing against archetypes as long as they are not supposed to *do* anything, as long as they are not supposed to be active agents. According to Huxley (1854: 427), the main message of the *Vestiges* is simply "in all its naked crudeness, the belief *that a law is an entity*—a Logos intermediate between the

Creator and his works;" (see also Huxley, 1871): for further discussion see Di Gregorio, 1981).

A very similar objection was to be made of Darwin's use of the notion of natural selection in analogy to artificial selection, as if he intended natural selection "as an agent" (Darwin, 1903: 1: 126). He explained that he used "natural selection" only as shorthand for the "tendency to the preservation (owing to the severe struggle for life to which all organic beings at some time or generation are exposed) of any, the slightest, variation in any part, which is of the slightest use or favourable to the life of the individual which has thus varied; together with the tendency to its inheritance." As misleading as the phrase "natural selection" has been to many (Young, 1971), one can only be thankful that Darwin used it instead of his more exacting description. The point of the description is, however, that natural selection is not an agent over and above the natural processes to which Darwin refers.

Darwin (1859: 206) calls the Unity of Type one of the two commonly acknowledged "great laws" upon which all organic beings have been formed, but he explains the unity of type in terms of unity of descent, not in terms of the action of some force or "idea." Neither sort of explanation can be ruled out *a priori*. The claim that certain limitations of structure inherent in nature explain the relatively few basic patterns that anatomists find in the structure of living organisms was far from implausible at the time. Explanations in terms of common descent were also plausible. And of course nothing prevents an anatomist from combining the two (Gould, 1977a). However, explanations in terms of structural constraints are not of the same sort as those in terms of common descent. The former are characteristics of the inherent make-up of the universe; the latter are the result of historical contingencies. Unless one postulates a "historical law" in the sense of a programmed sequence of events inherent in nature, explanations in terms of common descent are highly contingent. According to Darwin, the patterns so apparent in the living world do not reflect the workings of any underlying *Baupläne* but common history.

A METAPHYSICAL HEAD

In reaction to a paper by James Dwight Dana (1857), Darwin remarked in a letter to Lyell, "I could make nothing of Dana's idealistic notions about species; but then, as Wollaston says, I have not a metaphysical head." The reason is that neither side fully understood the other's position on issues that can only be termed "metaphysical." For over two thousand years, species had been considered paradigm examples of natural kinds, like geometric figures and the physical elements. The point of Dana's paper was to show that all three could be treated in parallel ways. Throughout most of the history of Western thought, natural kinds were viewed as being eternal, immutable, and discrete. All Darwin claimed was that species are not eternal but temporary, not immutable but quite changeable, and not discrete but gradating imperceptibly through time one into another. Nevertheless, Darwin and his fellow Darwinians continued to treat species as natural kinds albeit very peculiar ones. Continuing to view species as akin to geometric figures and the physical elements even though they lack *all* the defining characteristics of this metaphysical category is akin to claiming that something is a triangle even though it has neither three sides, nor three angles, and is not a geometric figure anyway.

In response to the *Origin*, Louis Agassiz (1860: 143) objected:

> It seems to me that there is much confusion of ideas in the general statement of the variability of species so often repeated lately. If species do not exist at all, as the supporters of the transmutation theory maintain, how can they vary? And if individuals alone exist, how can the differences which may be observed among them prove the variability of species?

As Beatty (1982b) has argued, in part, all Darwin is doing is redefining a theoretical term, the sort of activity that goes on all the time in science. Just as the gene concept has varied throughout the history of genetics, as new theories of the gene were introduced and accepted, the species concept has varied. Darwin (1899: 2: 123) dismissed Agassiz's "weak metaphysical and theological attack," but Agassiz had a point. Darwin was not merely redefining a term but redefining it in such a way that it could no longer belong to the traditional metaphysical category in which it had always been placed. It is one thing to redefine species in terms of reproductive gaps, morphological gaps, and so on. It was quite another thing to redefine species so that species could no longer be the *sort* of thing that they had always been viewed as. Dana (1857) wrote his paper to show that natural kinds or species in the generic sense are not the sort of thing that can evolve. According to Dana, the physical elements *qua* elements cannot possibly blend into each other. Either a substance is a multiple of a fixed number, or it is not. If it is, it is an element; if not, not. The same can be said for geometric figures. Conic sections can vary continuously, but triangularity cannot evolve into rectilinearity. Either a geometric figure has three sides, or it does not. Nothing in between can possibly exist (see Rudwick, 1972; Winsor, 1976; Manier, 1978; Ruse, 1979; Ospovat, 1981; Ridley, 1982).

According to such idealists as Agassiz and Dana, structural plans belong in the category "unchangeable kind," not temporary manifestation. As Agassiz (1860: 143) expressed this conviction "I have attempted to show that branches of the animal kingdom are founded upon different plans of structure, and for that very reason have embraced from the beginning representatives between which there could be no community of origin." One cannot legitimately argue that species are immutable because that is how "species" is defined. Definitions are themselves far from immutable. However, one can legitimately object to the assertion that species are mutable *and* that they are instances of a metaphysical category that is defined in terms of immutability. If species evolve *and* ar instances of natural kinds, then both "species" and "natural kind" must be redefined. Perhaps someone could set out a notion of "archetype" or "plan" in which these entities can change through time, but to my knowledge, no one in Darwin's day attempted such a reformulation of traditional metaphysics.

In this regard, the metaphysics implicit in Darwin's theory conflicted with idealistic metaphysics, but it also conflicted with the metaphysics implicit in the Herschel-Lyell philosophy of science. According to these philosopher-scientists, statements of the covariation of the traits that characterize organisms are laws of nature—*geometric* laws, but laws nonetheless. If species evolve, then it follows that laws of nature are evolving, the very state of affairs that Lyell was so concerned to avoid. Although early in his theorizing Darwin toyed with the idea that species might be very much like organisms with a definite life span somehow built into their makeup, by the time he published the *Origin*, he had abandoned this idea (Hodge, 1983). As far as I can tell, no matter how much various Darwinians and anti-Darwinians might disagree with each other, none of them suggested that species belong in the metaphysical category "individual." A detailed discussion of this issue had to await the work of Michael Ghiselin (1969, 1974).

I have no intention of reading Ghiselin's conclusion back into the past. To the contrary, I do not think that anyone at the time saw the conflict in these terms. It is for this very reason that the issues were never joined, and such Darwinians as Huxley were able to remain "pre-Darwinian" as long as they lived (see also Bartholomew, 1975). This state of affairs persists to the present. Even though comparative anatomists clearly acknowledge that species evolve, they insist that they can go about their business as if they did not (Huxley, 1874; Zangerl, 1948; Jardine, 1969; Nelson and Platnick, 1981).

The implications of moving species from the metaphysical category that can appropriately be characterized in terms of "natures" to a category for which such characterizations are inappropriate are extensive and fundamental. If species evolve in anything like the way that Darwin thought they did, then they cannot possibly have the sort of natures that traditional philosophers claimed they did. If species in general lack natures, then so does *Homo sapiens* as a biological species. If *Homo sapiens* lacks a nature, then no reference to biology can be made to support one's claims about "human nature." Perhaps all people are "persons," share the same "personhood," etc., but such claims must be explicated and defended *with no reference to biology*. Because so many moral, ethical, and political theories depend on some notion or other of human nature, Darwin's theory brought into question all these theories. The implications are not entailments. One can always dissociate *"Homo sapiens"* from "human being," but the result is a much less plausible position.

Dana (1857: 488) echoed a common view when he claimed that the kingdoms of life are made up of units properly termed "species." "Were these units capable of blending with one another indefinitely, they would no longer be units, and species could not be recognized. The system of life would be a maze of complexities; and whatever its grandeur to a being that could comprehend the infinite, it would be unintelligible chaos to man." Darwin (1859: 490) concluded his *Origin of Species* with the observation that there is a grandeur to his view of life, and I personally can attest to the fact that one need not be an infinite being to appreciate the grandeur of this view. Darwin (1859: 485) thought that his theory entailed that species must be treated in the same way as naturalists had treated genera, as "merely artificial combinations made for convenience." Ghiselin (1969, 1974a), building on the work of Mayr (1942, 1969), has shown that this inference does not necessarily follow. Just as Darwin carried Lyell's views somewhat deeper into the Promised Land, Ghiselin has played Joshua to Moses.

Part III

Evolution and Individuality

Chapter 5

The Ontological Status of Species As Evolutionary Units*

THE NATURE OF THE SPECIES PROBLEM

Reference to the species problem today might sound quaint and vaguely anachronistic. Perhaps the species problem was of some importance ages ago in the philosophical dispute between nominalists and essentialists, or a century ago in biology when Darwin introduced his theory of organic evolution, but it certainly is of no contemporary interest. But "species," like the terms "gene," "electron," "non-local simultaneity," and "element," is a theoretical term embedded in a significant scientific theory. At one time, the nature of the physical elements was an important issue in physics. The transition from the elements being defined in terms of gross traits, to specific density, to molecular weight to atomic number was important in the development of atomic theory. The transition in biology from genes being defined in terms of unit characters, to production of enzymes, to coding for specific polypeptides, to structurally defined segments of nucleic acid was equally important in the growth of modern genetics. A comparable transition is taking place with respect to the species concept and is equally important.

It is easy enough to say that species evolve; it is not so easy to explain in detail the exact nature of these evolutionary units. Evolutionary theory is currently undergoing a period of rapid and fundamental reformulation, and our conception of biological species as evolutionary units is being modified accordingly. There is nothing unusual about a theoretical term changing its meaning as the theory in which it is embedded changes, but sometimes such development has an added dimension. Not only is the meaning of the theoretical term altered, but the ontological status of the entities to which it refers is also modified. For centuries, philosophers and scientists alike have treated species as secondary substances, universals, classes, etc. Nothing has seemed clearer than the relation between particular organisms and their species. In contemporary terminology, this relation is called

---

*Reprinted by permission of Kluwer Academic Publishers, ed. by R. Butts and J. Hintikka, Foundational Problems in Special Sciences, 91-102. Copyright © 1977 by D. Reidel Publishing Company. Dordrecht-Holland. All Rights Reserved.

class membership. Species are classes defined by means of the covariation of the traits which their members possess. On the same interpretation, organisms are individuals and the species category itself is a class of classes.

However, species have proved to be very peculiar classes. Their membership is constantly undergoing change as new organisms are born and old ones die. At any one time, one can rarely discover a set of traits that all the members of a species have and no members of some other species have. In addition, the members of successive generations of the same species are usually characterized by slightly different sets of traits. These facts of life have forced philosophers to view the names of particular biological species (as well as all taxa) as cluster concepts. However, in this paper, I would like to argue for a radically different solution to the species problem. Just as relativity theory necessitated shifting such notions as space and time from one ontological category to another, evolutionary theory necessitates a similar shift in the ontological status of biological species. If species are units of evolution, then they cannot be interpreted as classes; they are individuals. The purpose of this paper is to show why evolutionary theory requires such a change in the ontological status of species.

There are three basic premises to the argument that I will present. Two are quite familiar; one is a variation on a familiar theme; none is totally uncontroversial. In this paper, however, I will not attempt to defend these premises. Instead, I will show the consequences that follow for the nature of biological species if they are accepted.

THREE BASIC PREMISES

My first premise is that the ontological status of theoretical entities is theory-dependent.[1] Does time really flow like a river independent of the existence and distribution of material bodies? Are species really individuals? I don't think that such questions can be answered without reference to a particular scientific theory. A particular atom of gold is an individual and not a property, universal, process, relation, or what have you, because atomic theory requires atoms to be viewed in this way. The ontological status of electrons is equivocal for similar reasons, the theory in this case being quantum mechanics. A segment of DNA bounded by initiation and termination codons is an individual because molecular genetics requires genes to be interpreted in this way. If species are to be viewed as individuals, it will be because current evolutionary theory necessitates such a conceptualization.

The concept of an individual in philosophy is very broad, including such entities as sense data and bare particulars. In this paper, I will limit myself to a narrower use of the term to refer just to those entities which are characterized by unity and continuity, specifically spatiotemporal unity and continuity (see Hull, 1975). This is the sense in which organisms, planets, houses, and atoms are individuals. Such individuals have unique beginnings and endings in time, reasonably discrete boundaries, internal coherence at any one time, and continuity through time. There are individuals for which such spatiotemporal unity and continuity are not required; for example, nations, political parties, ideas. The United States did not become any the less an individual when Alaska and Hawaii became states. In addition, there are situations in which a nation ceases to exist for a time and then the same nation comes into being again later. However, species as units of evolution fulfill the stricter requirements. They are individuals in the same sense that organisms are individuals. Both are localized in space and time.

On the surface, the distinction between a class and an individual could not seem sharper. A class, on the one hand, is the sort of thing that can have members. The name of a class is a class term defined intensionally by means of the properties its members possess. The relation between a member and its class is the intransitive class-membership relation. An individual, on the other hand, is the sort of thing that can have parts. The name of an individual is a proper name possessing ideally no intension at all. The relation between a part and the individual of which it is part is the transitive part-whole relation. However, classes can be construed in ways which make them all but indistinguishable from individuals. Classes are often defined in terms of simple one-place predicates, like the class of atoms with atomic number seventy nine. Classes can also be defined in terms of relations, sometimes a relation between two classes, sometimes a relation that the members of a class have to each other, sometimes a relation that each member of the class has to a specified focus. For example, *planet* can be defined as any relatively large non-luminous body revolving around a star. Although the relation mentioned in this definition is spatiotemporal, the class itself is spatiotemporally unrestricted because planets can revolve around any star whatsoever.

The problematic cases are those classes defined in terms of a spatiotemporal relation which the members have to each other or to a specified individual. For example, *forest* could be defined in terms of a sufficiently large number of trees no further apart than a certain distance from at least one other tree in the complex. On this definition, the term *forest* would be a spatiotemporally unrestricted class, but each particular forest would not be. Similarly, *tributary system* could be defined in terms of those rivers which flow into one main river. On this definition, *tributary system* would be a spatiotemporally unrestricted class, but each particular tributary system would not be. Such complexes as the Black Forest and the Mississippi River tributary system can be treated as classes only at the expense of collapsing the distinction between classes and individuals, an excellent reason for not doing so.[2] The extension of this analysis to species defined in terms of descent and the names of particular species should be obvious.

The final consideration central to my argument concerns the nature of scientific laws. According to the traditional conception, natural laws must be spatiotemporally unrestricted. To the extent that a scientific law is true, it must be true for all entities falling within its domain anywhere and at any time. The regularities in nature that scientific laws are designed to capture cannot vary from place to place or from time to time. I must hasten to add, however, that my acceptance of this traditional notion of a scientific law does not commit me to a raft of other beliefs commonly associated with it. Laws are not all there is to science. Descriptions, for example, are also important. Nor do I think that recourse to scientific laws is the only way in which an event can be explained. The issue of the nature of scientific laws must be raised, however, because evolutionary theory is often cited as evidence against the view that laws must be spatiotemporally unrestricted. But properly construed, the laws that go to make up evolutionary theory are as spatiotemporally unrestricted as any other laws of nature. Species evolve, languages evolve, our understanding of the empirical world evolves, but the laws of nature are eternal and immutable.[3]

EVOLUTIONARY THEORY—IS IT DIFFERENT?

The vague feeling that philosophers have had that evolutionary theory is somehow different from other process theories stems from three sources, two of them clearly mistaken. One source of the belief that the laws of evolutionary theory are spatiotemporally restricted stems from the process-product confusion, from confusing evolutionary processes such as mutation, selection, and evolution with their product—phylogeny. The statement that mammals arose from several species of reptile is clearly historical in the sense that it describes a temporal succession of events, but such descriptions or phylogenetic sequences are no more part of evolutionary theory than a description of the successive stages in an eclipse is part of celestial mechanics.

A second source of the vague feeling that philosophers have had that evolutionary theory is peculiar is their conception of species as classes. In the nineteenth century, philosophers such as John Stuart Mill distinguished between laws of succession and laws of coexistence. They viewed the apparent universal distribution of traits among the organisms which make up biological species as the best example of such laws of coexistence. Thus, for nineteenth century philosophers, the evolution of species meant the evolution of laws. This line of reasoning is still common today, especially among social scientists.[4] But if species are interpreted as individuals, the evolution of species poses no problem for the traditional conception of a scientific law. A description of an individual as it develops through time is hardly a candidate for the status of a scientific law. If individuals are localized in space and time and scientific laws must be spatiotemporally unrestricted, then no law of nature can contain essential reference to a particular individual. If species (as well as all taxa) are interpreted as individuals developing through time, then any statement which contains essential reference to such individuals can no more count as a scientific law than Kepler's laws—if Kepler's laws had been true only for the sun and its planets.[5] In point of fact, evolutionary theory contains no reference to particular taxa, just what one would expect if taxa are actually individuals and not classes. On this view, "All swans are white" could not count as a scientific law even if it were true.

However, there is a sense in which evolutionary theory might turn out to be peculiar. Biological evolution is a selection process. If selection processes are different in kind from other processes, then selection theories such as evolutionary theory might turn out to be different in form from ordinary process theories. To the extent that there is a difference, it seems to be this: selection processes require the existence of at least two partially independent processes operating at different levels of organization on different time scales. Hence, one finds biologists contrasting ecological time with geological time, a strange manner of speaking to say the least. In a selection process, variation and selective retention result in the evolution of some unit of much larger scope. The entities that vary and that are selected come into being, reproduce themselves, and pass away in such a fashion that these larger units gradually change. However, the resolution of this particular problem has no special relevance to the thesis of this paper. Whether or not selection processes turn out to be reducible to ordinary processes, the consequences for the ontological status of biological species remains the same: they must be interpreted as individuals.

SPECIES AS INDIVIDUALS

According to the traditional formula, three levels of organization are involved in organic evolution. Genes mutate, organisms compete and are selected, and species evolve. We now know that this formula is too simple. Mutation can be as slight as the change of a single base pair or as major as the gain or loss of entire chromosomes. Competition and selection can take place at a variety of levels from macromolecules (including genes) and cells (including gametes) to organisms and kin groups. In addition, an important level of organization exists between kin groups and entire species—the population. Populations are the effective units of evolution. There is no question that genes, cells, organisms and kin groups are related by the part-whole relation. Genes are part of cells, cells are part of organisms, and organisms are part of kin groups. The point of the dispute is whether the relation changes abruptly from part-whole to class-membership above the level of organisms and possibly kin groups.

Several issues are involved in this dispute, including the existence of group selection. Organisms and kin groups form units of selection. Can populations and possibly even entire species form units of selection? Populations and species evolve. Can entities at lower levels of organization like colonies also form units of evolution? What kind of organization is required for something to function as a unit of selection? A unit of evolution? How do units of selection differ from units of evolution? Must evolution always occur at levels of organization higher than that at which selection is taking place? What does it mean to say that something is a unit of selection or a unit of evolution? Can such units be classes as well as individuals?

Considerable disagreement exists among biologists over the answers to the preceding questions, increased to some extent by certain unfortunate terminological conventions like using the terms "organism" and "individual" interchangeably. For example, E. O. Wilson (1974, p. 184) argues that the preceding "are not trivial questions. They address a theoretical issue seldom made explicit in biology":

> In zoology the very word colony implies that the members of the society are physically united, or differentiated into reproductive and sterile castes, or both. When both conditions exist to an advanced degree, as they do in many of these animals, the society can equally well be viewed as a superorganism or even an organism. The dilemma can therefore be expressed as follows: At what point does a society become so well integrated that it is no longer a society? On what basis do we distinguish the extremely modified members of an invertebrate colony from the organs of a metazoan animal?

Theodosius Dobzhansky (1970, p. 23) has long argued that:

> A species, like a race or a genus or a family, is a group concept and a category of classification. A species is, however, also something else: a super-individual zoological system, the perpetuation of which from generation to generation depends on the reproductive bonds between its members.

Michael Ghiselin (1974a) objects to terming species "organisms" lest the term imply that species can function as units of selection the way that organisms do. He prefers the generic term "individual." However, the sage for our purposes is the same. There is something about evolutiona processes that requires that the units of mutation, selection, and evolu tion be treated as individuals integrated by the part-whole relation.

All versions of evolutionary theory from Darwin to the present have included a strong principle of heredity. It is not enough for a gene to be able to mutate; it must be able to replicate and pass this change on. It is not enough for an organism to cope more successfully in its environment than its competitors; it must also be able to reproduce itself and pass on these variations to its progeny. But exactly the same observations can be made about populations and species, possibly not as units of selection but certainly as units of evolution.

The role of spatiotemporal unity and continuity in the evolutionary process is easily overlooked, especially when it is being described in terms of populations. The term "population" is systematically ambiguous in the biological literature. In its broadest sense, a population is merely a collection of individuals of any sort characterized by the distribution of one or more traits of these individuals. Although the members of populations in this broad sense could be chosen at random, usually they are selected on the basis of some criterion; for example, people on welfare, herbivorous quadrupeds, stars increasing in brightness. As biologists such as Ernst Mayr (1963) have repeatedly emphasized, the populations that function in the evolutionary process are populations in a much more restricted sense of the term. Descent is required. But descent presupposes replication and reproduction, and these processes in turn presuppose spatiotemporal proximity and continuity. When a single gene undergoes replication to produce two new genes, or a single cell undergoes mitotic division to produce two new cells, the end products are spatiotemporally continuous with the parent entity. In sexual reproduction, the propagules, if not the parent organisms themselves, must come into contact. The end result is the successive modification of the same population.

Populations are made up of successive generations of organisms. These generations may be temporally disjoint or largely overlapping, but a certain degree of genetic continuity is required for a population to function as a population in the evolutionary process. To be sure, new organisms can migrate into a population and others leave, changing the genetic composition of the population. New genes can be introduced by means of mutation. But such changes cannot be too massive or too sudden without disrupting the evolutionary process. Given the differences in time spans required for mutation, selection and evolution, sufficient continuity is required to allow for the cumulation of the adaptive changes neces-

for evolution. Channeling is required, sufficient channeling to warrant onceptualizing such lineages as individuals.

Identity in populations is determined by the same considerations which determine identity in organisms. Constancy of neither substance nor essence is required in either case; spatiotemporal continuity is. Just as all the cells that comprise an organism can be changed while that organism remains the same organism, all the organisms that comprise a population can be changed while that population remains the same population, just so long as such changes are gradual. Just as all the traits that characterize an organism at one stage of its development can change without that organism ceasing to be the same organism, all the distributions of traits which characterize a population at one stage in its evolution can change without that population ceasing to be the same population, just so long as such changes are gradual.[6]

The factors responsible for spatiotemporal continuity in evolution are fairly straightforward; the factors that promote evolutionary unity are not. In order for selection to result in evolutionary change, it must act on successive generations of the same population. But the units of evolution must also be sufficiently cohesive at any one time to evolve as units. Two issues are at stake: the mechanisms that tend to promote evolutionary unity and the degree of unity necessary for an entity to count as an individual. Certain biologists have argued that in order for organisms to form populations or species, they must reproduce sexually. Gene exchange is the only mechanism capable of producing evolutionary unity (see Mayr, 1963; Dobzhansky, 1970; Ghiselin, 1974a). Others have argued that gene exchange is not all that powerful a force in promoting evolutionary unity. The same selection pressures that produce unity in asexual species produce it in sexual species as well. Gene exchange is only of minor significance (see Meglitsch, 1954; Ehrlich and Raven, 1969).

From the discussion so far, it might seem that populations and species are far from paradigm individuals. In most cases, there is no one instant at which a species comes into existence or becomes extinct. Both speciation and phyletic evolution usually take hundreds, if not thousands, of generations. One mechanism that has been suggested for narrowing the borderline between a newly emerging species and its parent species is Mayr's Founder Principle. According to this principle, speciation in sexual species occurs always or usually by means of the isolation of one or a few organisms. Such isolates rarely succeed in forming a population, but when they do, the resulting population tends to be quite different from its parent species and can undergo additional rapid change. The end result is that the transition between two species is reduced both in time and with respect to the number of organisms involved.

Nor are the organisms that go to make up a species always in close proximity, let alone spatially contiguous. However, the exigencies of reproduction require at least periodic proximity of the relevant entities, whether organisms or merely their propagules. But before the notion that species are spatiotemporal individuals is dismissed, it should be noted that exactly the same observations can be made with respect to organisms as individuals, albeit on a reduced scale; and organisms are supposed to be paradigm individuals. Anyone who thinks that the spatiotemporal boundaries of organisms are that much sharper than those of species should read up on slime molds and grasses. Any problem that can be found in the spatiotemporal unity and continuity of species also exists for particular organisms. If organisms can count as individuals in the face of such difficulties, so can species.[7]

CONCLUSION

I think that the preceding considerations give ample support for the conclusion that species are not spatiotemporally unrestricted classes. However, doubt might remain whether or not they should be interpreted as individuals. Perhaps they belong in some hybrid category like individualistic classes, as Leigh Van Valen has suggested, or complex particulars, as Fred Suppe (1974) has proposed, but the evaluation of such suggestions must wait for further elucidation of these notions. For now, species fit as naturally into the idealized category of spatiotemporally localized individual as do particular organisms. Once again, if organisms are individuals, so are species.

NOTES

1. The claim that ontological status of theoretical entities is theory-dependent is not the same thing as the well-known claim that they are theory-laden, though the rationale behind the two claims is much the same.

2. Another reason for not considering complexes defined in terms of a spatiotemporal relation between spatiotemporally localized individuals as genuine classes is the role that class terms play in science. The chief use of class terms in science is to function in scientific laws. A scientific classification is important to the extent that it produces theoretically significant classes. In fact, I think that the class-individual distinction is best made in terms of the contrasting roles played by classes and individuals in scientific laws.

3. If it was discovered that the laws of nature, as we currently conceive them, actually changed through time, our conception of a scientific law would not have to be modified if these changes were themselves regular. Hence, statements characterizing these regular changes would become the new basic laws of nature.

4. The highly touted book by M. D. Sahlins and E. R. Service (1960) relies throughout on confusing evolutionary processes with the products of such processes. They consistently argue that political laws evolve because political systems evolve. See also T. L. Thorson (1970) for the same crude mistake.

5. The distinction assumed in this discussion is between laws of nature and true accidental generalizations. It is only fair to acknowledge, however, that this distinction is currently one of the most problematic in philosophy of science. At the risk of some circularity, I suspect that the only way in which this distinction can be made is by reference to the actual or eventual inclusion in a scientific theory. Any generalization, true though it may be, cannot count as a scientific law if it remains isolated from all other such generalizations.

6. The subject matter of this paragraph deserves a paper of its own. Neither organisms nor species require constancy of substance or essence for individual identity, but as individuals, organisms and species differ in some important respects. Organisms possess a program that directs and circumscribes their development to some extent. The development of species is much more open-ended. One might wish to argue that an organism's genome is its essence. If so, then this essence is an individual essence and an essence of a very peculiar sort, since genomes are neither eternal nor immutable and two organisms can have the same individual essence without becoming the same individual. Finally, rapid change can occur in a single generation in a population without that population ceasing to be the same population under special circumstances; for example, if gene frequencies differ markedly in males and females.

7. Comparable difficulties exist for the philosophical notion of the self. Unlike organisms and species, most of the problem cases for the self as an individual are hypothetical; see Derek Parfit (1971).

Chapter 6

Individuality and Selection*

Evolutionary theory is currently undergoing a period of rapid development, but in the process several problems have cropped up that are proving to be infuriatingly difficult to resolve—for example, the presence of
so much genetic heterogeneity in natural populations, the prevalence of
sexual forms of reproduction in the face of an apparent fifty percent cost
of meiosis, and the difficulty of explaining how selection can operate at
higher levels of organization. In their most recent publications, the leading theoretical biologists of our day seem to have all but given up hope of
making further progress (Lewontin 1974, Maynard Smith 1978, Williams
1975). Comparable stalemates in the history of science have tended to
result from everyone concerned taking for granted something so fundamental that no clear-thinking person would question it. In the present
case, I think two assumptions are at fault: (a) the view that genes and
organisms are individuals while populations and species are classes, and
(b) our traditional way of organizing phenomena into a hierarchy of
genes, cells, organisms, kinship groups, populations, species, and ecosystems or communities.

In his classic paper on units of selection, Lewontin (1970) accepts the
traditional organizational hierarchy and asks at what level selection can
occur. His answer is that it takes place primarily at the lower levels and
becomes rarer and more problematic at the higher levels. However, something peculiar happens as we follow Lewontin up the traditional hierarchy:
We pass from such commonsense individuals as genes and organisms,
through such borderline cases as colonies, to such commonsense groups
as populations and species. It would be truly amazing if a single process
could operate on entities as different as individuals and groups. At least
some of the difficulty in specifying the conditions under which group selection can occur arises from the lack of a sufficiently careful statement of how
individuals differ from groups and of how these differences bear on selection.

From the beginning of the controversy over group selection, two
quite different sorts of groups seem to have been intended: highly organized groups exhibiting group characteristics and organisms that happen

---

*Reproduced with permission, from the *Ann. Rev. Ecol. Syst.* 11 (1980) 311-32. © 1980 by
Annual Reviews Inc. All rights reserved.

to be located in proximity to each other. In his classic statement, Wynne-Edwards (1963) seems to have had the first sort of group in mind. For example, he says, "In developing the theme it soon became apparent that the greatest benefits of sociality arise from its capacity to override the advantage of the individual members in the interests of the survival of the group as a whole. The kind of adaptations which make this possible, as explained more fully here, belong to and characterize social groups as entities, rather than their members individually. This in turn seems to entail that natural selection has occurred between social groups as evolutionary units in their own right. . . ."

The controversy over group selection has taken two unfortunate turns. First, Wynne-Edwards himself chose about the least likely group characteristic to investigate—the regulation of population size by altruistic restraint. That the selection of one sort of group trait is difficult or impossible does not demonstrate that other sorts of group characteristics cannot be selected. Second, both critics and defenders of group selection have tended to ignore the sort of groups Wynne-Edwards had in mind and to concentrate on organisms that form groups only because they happen to live on the same host or in the same pond (Lewontin 1970, Wade 1978, Williams 1966, 1971, Wilson 1980). In this paper, I intend to do just the opposite. Most biologists seem to take for granted that organisms can be selected. In fact, organisms are the primary focus of selection (Ayala 1978, Ghiselin 1974b, Lewontin 1970, Mayr 1963, 1978). Can entities more inclusive than organisms be selected in the same sense that organisms can?

Such critics of group selection as Williams (1966, 1975) assume that organisms can be selected and then argue that more inclusive entities cannot be selected because they lack certain characteristics. Such critics of organism selection as Dawkins (1976, 1978) respond that not even organisms can be selected because they too lack these characteristics. Thus, biologists are presented with a dilemma. If the arguments against the selection of such groups as colonies and populations are cogent, then organisms cannot be selected either. However, any relaxation of standards sufficient to allow organisms to be selected permits entities more inclusive than organisms to be selected as well.

In his treatment of the subject, Lewontin (1970) begins with a brief characterization of the evolutionary process and then proceeds to review evidence for and against the operation of selection at various levels of organization. I propose to do the opposite, to investigate the general characteristics of the evolutionary process at some length and then to discuss only briefly the particular entities that may or may not possess the characteristics necessary to function in this process. I contend that group selection

of the sort Wynne-Edwards had in mind is not just rare, it is impossible
Anything that has the characteristics necessary to be selected in the same
sense in which organisms are selected has the characteristics necessary to
count as an individual and not a group. Not all individuals can function
as units of selection, but only individuals can be selected. However, many
entities commonly treated as groups are actually individuals.

INDIVIDUALS AND GROUPS

The preceding claims sound more extreme than they are because of a
systematic ambiguity in the term "individual." It is used sometimes in a
narrow sense to mean "organism," sometimes in a broader sense to denote
any spatiotemporally localized and well-integrated entity, such as a gene
or a cell (Hull 1976). Thus Wilson (1971) is forced to call colonies
"superorganisms" when he attempts to show that they can function as
units of selection, as is Dobzhansky (1970) when he makes comparable
claims about species. Similarly, both gene selectionists and organism
selectionists call themselves "individual selectionists" and complain that
others consider kin selection an example of group selection when it is
actually an instance of individual selection (Dawkins 1978, Lewontin 1970,
Williams 1966, Wilson 1975). Although the controversy over group selection is not merely terminological, such terminological complexities do
not help. In this paper, I use "individual" as a generic term in contrast
with "group" and "class."

Individuals are spatiotemporally localized entities that have reasonably sharp beginnings and endings in time. Some individuals do not change
much during the course of their existence, others undergo considerable
though limited change, and still others can change indefinitely until they
eventually cease to exist. But regardless of the change that may occur, the
entity must exist continuously through time and maintain its internal
organization. How continuous the development, how sharp the beginnings and endings, and how well-integrated the entity must be are determined by the processes in which these individuals function, not by the
contingencies of human perception. It is only an accident of our relative
size, longevity, and perceptual acuity that we can see the distances between
the organisms that comprise a species but not the even greater relative
distances that separate the atoms that make up an organism (Ghiselin
1974a, Hull 1976, 1978b). For long enough we have remained, to use
Gould's (1977a) phrase, "prisoners of the perceptions of our size."

The elements that comprise an individual do so because of how they
are organized and not because of any shared similarity (Ghiselin 1974a,
Hull 1976, 1978b). For example, the cells that comprise an organism tend

ɔ be genetically identical, but this is not why they all belong to the same organism. At one extreme, the cells of a gynandromorph are genetically quite different yet belong to a single organism, while at the other extreme, the cells of identical twins belong to different organisms even though they are genetically identical. Although many individuals are functionally organized systems, many are not—such as an atom of gold. Nor are the relations that can organize parts into a whole exclusively spatiotemporal. For example, even though its parts may not be contiguous, an operon functions as a whole in the production of proteins. The distinction between structural and functional wholes is important because opponents of group selection tend to recognize only structural wholes.

Philosophers use the term "class" in a very general sense (Marcus 1974). Classes are the sorts of things that can have members, and entities are considered members of a class because they possess certain properties. For example, planets are relatively large, nonluminous bodies revolving around stars. Classes of the sort that function in scientific laws must in addition be spatiotemporally unrestricted (Hull 1976, 1948b). The term "group," as biologists use it, is halfway between individuals and classes. Groups tend to be spatiotemporally localized and their members considered part of the group because of their location and not because of any internal organization. Selection can act only on spatiotemporally localized entities, but if it is to act on entities more inclusive than organisms in the same sense in which it acts on organisms, these entities must be cohesive wholes and not classes or groups. An individual can be selected for the properties it exhibits. A group can be selected only incidentally—for example, because all its members happen to be very close to each other. Finally, a genuine class can be selected only through its members. Wilson (1974) puts the issue as follows: "In zoology the very word colony implies that the members of the society are physically united or differentiated into reproductive and sterile castes, or both. When both conditions exist to an advanced degree, as they do in many of these animals, the society can equally well be viewed as a superorganism or even as an organism. The dilemma can therefore be expressed as follows: At what point does a society become so well integrated that it is no longer a society?"

Thus the first thing a biologist does in arguing that an entity can or cannot function as a unit of selection is to argue that it is or is not an individual. For example, gene selectionists such as Dawkins (1976, 1978) contend that in most cases entire genomes cannot function as units of selection because they are "torn to smithereens" at meiosis. Organism selectionists such as Mayr (1975) disagree. "The genes are not the units of evolution nor are they, as such, the targets of natural selection. Rather, genes are tied together into balanced adaptive complexes." Genes are linked

both structurally on chromosomes and functionally in biosynthetic p
ways. As structural wholes, they are rearranged to some extent at me
sis. Nevertheless, even in the face of such structural rearrangemen.
genomes can remain functional wholes (1974).

Even though biologists disagree about which entities possess the necessary characteristics to be selected, even though they disagree whether
these entities must be structural or functional wholes, they agree that
they must be individuals. For example, Dawkins (1976) and Eldredge and
Gould (1972) occupy opposite poles in the selectionists' controversy. They
agree that organisms, populations, and species are the same sort of thing,
but they disagree about what sort. Dawkins argues that from the point of
view of selection, they are all amorphous aggregates, as ephemeral as
"clouds in the sky or dust-storms in the desert," while Eldredge and Gould
contend that they are all homeostatic systems, "amazingly well-buffered
to resist change and maintain stability in the face of disturbing influences."

In this paper, I am concerned not so much with deciding which entities have the characteristics necessary to function in the evolutionary process as with specifying the precise nature of these general characteristics.
To do this, I distinguish between three distinct but interrelated processes —
replication, interaction, and evolution. Certain entities (replicators) pass
on their structure largely intact from generation to generation. These entities either interact with their environments in such a way as to bias their
distribution in later generations or else produce more inclusive entities
that do . As a result, even more inclusive entities evolve.

LEVELS OF SELECTION

The living world is traditionally divided into a hierarchy of organizational levels: genes, cells, organisms, colonies, populations, species, and
ecosystems or communities. Not all levels are exhibited in every instance.
For example, not all genes exist in cells, nor in unproblematic organisms.
Only a small percentage of organisms form colonies. Depending on how
one defines population and species, some organisms form populations
and species; others do not. If gene exchange is necessary, then the vast
majority of organisms form neither populations nor species, but only
clones. When the organic world is conceptualized traditionally, individuality wanders from level to level, and as it does, so too does the level at
which selection can occur.

Even such enthusiastic gene selectionists as Dawkins (1976, 1978)
admit that the *amount* of genetic material being selected at any one time
can vary. In genetically heterogeneous populations of sexual organisms,
only single genes last long enough to be selected; but in cases of strictly

...al reproduction, the entire genome can function as a unit of selec-
...n. Organism selectionists acknowledge that selection can operate dif-
...rently at different stages in the life cycle of an organism—for example,
the larvae may be pelagic and the adults sessile. But what if an organism
changes from an individual to a group and back to an individual again
during the course of its life cycle the way that certain slime molds do
(Bonner 1967, Van Valen 1978)? Oster and Wilson (1978) reply that, as
the entities change from individuals to groups, the focus of selection shifts.
For example, early in the development of a hive in a particular species of
bee, selection occurs at the organismic level because of the presence of
several queens, but after the number of queens has been reduced to one,
selection operates at the level of the hive. Similarly, advocates of species
selection do not maintain that all species in all circumstances can be
selected, but only that some can in certain circumstances. Finally, when
biologists such as Dunbar (1960) argue that "selection may apply at the
level of the ecosystem as well as at the levels of the individual and the
specific population," they do not contend that all ecosystems can function as units of selection, but only that mature ecosystems in the warmer
latitudes can.

When biologists address the issue of the levels at which selection can
occur, they take the traditional organizational hierarchy as fundamental
and the level at which selection operates as variable. As a result, selection
wanders from one level to the next from time to time and from group to
group, sometimes acting on genes, sometimes organisms, sometimes colonies, etc. As long as the traditional hierarchy is taken as basic and the
levels at which selection can occur as variable, no simple, nomothetic
generalizations are likely to materialize. Rather, the evolutionary process
must be taken as basic and the levels defined in terms of it. Two entities
that perform the same function in the evolutionary process must be classed
as the same sort of entity even if one happens to be an organism and the
other a colony or a population. In his book on insect societies, Wilson
(1971) argues that organisms and colonies should be treated as the same
sort of thing because they play the same role in the evolutionary process.

Hamilton (1975) complains that Ghiselin's (1974b) views on altruism force him to say, "in effect, that a 'family' or 'breeding stock' is the
equivalent of an individual. Maybe in some sense it can be *almost* equivalent; nevertheless, it seems to me both more exact and less 'metaphysical' to stick to common usage." Likewise the reconceptualizations suggested
in this paper may seem too metaphysical, too radical—as radical and
metaphysical as those introduced into physics a half century ago. With
the work of Einstein, physicists were faced with a dilemma: If they insisted
on retaining Euclidean geometry, they would have to be content with

extremely complicated and variable laws; if they wanted laws applicable anywhere in the universe, regardless of velocity, they would have to abandon Euclidean geometry. They opted for the second alternative. Evolutionary biologists are currently confronted by a similar dilemma: If they insist on formulating evolutionary theory in terms of commonsense entities, the resulting laws are likely to remain extremely variable and complicated; if they want simple laws, equally applicable to all entities of a particular sort, they must abandon their traditional ontology. This reconceptualization of the evolutionary process is certainly counter-intuitive; its only justification is the increased scope, consistency, and power of the theory that results. If the terminology suggested in this paper cannot characterize the evolutionary process more accurately and succinctly than the traditional terminology, it should not (and will not) be adopted.

REPLICATORS AND INTERACTORS

As Mayr (1978) emphasizes, "Evolution through natural selection is (I repeat!) a two-step process." He describes the process in terms of genetic variability and the ordering of that variability by selection. Here I will define the units functioning in these two processes in terms of their most general characteristics; I leave open the question of which entities perform these functions. Building on the work of Williams (1966), Dawkins (1978) suggests *replicator* as a general term for the entities that function as units of selection, regardless of what these entities turn out to be. "Why 'replicator selection' rather than 'gene selection'?" Dawkins (1978) asks. Because it does not prejudge the empirical issues. "The term replicator should be understood to *include* genetic replicators, but not to exclude any entity in the universe which qualifies under the criteria listed."

These general criteria are longevity, fecundity, and fidelity. All three characterize individuals functioning in a copying process. Replicators need not last forever. They need only last long enough to produce additional replicators that retain their structure largely intact. The relevant longevity concerns the retention of structure through descent. Some entities, though structurally similar, are not copies because they are not related by descent. For example, although atoms of gold are structurally similar, they are not copies of one another because atoms of gold do not give rise to other atoms of gold. Conversely, a large molecule can break down into successively smaller molecules as its quaternary, tertiary, and secondary bonds are severed. Although descent is present, these successively smaller molecules cannot count as copies because they lack the requisite structural similarity. Replication by itself is sufficient for evolution of sorts, but not evolution through natural selection. In addition, certain entities must interact causally with their environments in such a way as to bias their distribution in later generations. Originally, these two functions may have been performed by the same entities. The original replicators may well have replicated themselves and interacted with their environments in such a way as to bias their distribution in later generations. But because these two processes are inherently such different processes, requiring very different properties, they eventually became separated into different individuals at different levels of organization. Replicators not only replicate themselves but also produce other entities that interact with ever more inclusive environments.

When Dawkins (1978) defines "replicator," he has replicators interacting with their environments in two ways—to produce copies of themselves and to influence their own survival and the survival of their copies. Just as Dawkins coined the term "replicator" for the entities that function in the first process, I (Hull 1980a) have suggested "interactor" for the entities that function in the second process. Why "interactor" rather than "organism?" For the same reason Dawkins substituted "replicator" for "gene." Just as genes are not the only replicators, organisms are not the only interactors. Thus, the two sorts of entities that function in selection processes can be defined as follows:

> *replicator*: an entity that passes on its structure largely intact in successive replications

> *interactor*: an entity that interacts as a cohesive whole with its environment in such a way that this interaction causes replication to be differential

With the aid of these two technical terms, the selection process itself can be defined:

> *selection*: a process in which the differential extinction and proliferation of interactors cause the differential perpetuation of the relevant replicators.

Thus the question of the levels at which selection takes place must be divided into two questions—at what levels does replication occur, and at what levels does interaction occur? If an entity is to function as a replicator, it must have a structure and be able to pass this structure on to successive generations of replicators. As a replicator it need interact with its environment only to the extent necessary to replicate itself. Although replicators may be part of functional systems, they themselves need not be functional systems. The only adaptations they need exhibit are those to

promote replication. For example, a gene as a stretch of DNA is adap
to replicate itself. It may code for other adaptations but does not its
exhibit these adaptations.

Interactaors must exhibit structure but toward quite different ends —
they must be able to cope with their environments. The success of an
interactor is *measured* in terms of differential perpetuation of the replicators it produces, but it can be *defined* in such terms only at the price of
greatly reducing the empirical content of evolutionary theory (Gould
1977a, Lewontin 1978, Williams 1966). To be sure, the desire to insulate
evolutionary theory against falsification by defining "fitness" solely in
terms of differential replication is understandable, as understandable as
the tendency of behavioral psychologists to define "intelligence" solely in
terms of scores on IQ tests, but it must be resisted for exactly the same
reasons. Instead, some sort of reference must be made to various engineering criteria of fitness (Gould 1977a). For example, one way of
maintaining a constant internal temperature in the face of variation in
external temperature is the production of a layer of insulation, whether
fur, feathers, blubber, or something else. As difficult as it is to apply such
engineering criteria of fitness in particular cases, I see no way in which
such difficulties can be circumvented without evolutionary theory degenerating into an empirically empty formalism.

Dawkins (1976, 1978) defines replicator in terms of strict identity in
structure. A change in a single base pair results in a new replicator. According to Dawkins, nothing more inclusive than a genome in asexual organisms and small segments of DNA in sexual organisms can count as
replicators. Certainly organisms cannot. Because of the role of the environment in development, even identical twins are likely to differ. In my
definition, a replicator need only pass on its structure largely intact. Thus
entities more inclusive than genomes might be able to function as replicators. As I argue later, they seldom if ever do. The relevant factor is not
retention of structure but the directness of transmission. Replicators replicate themselves directly but interact with increasingly inclusive environments only indirectly. Interactors interact with their effective environments
directly but usually replicate themselves only indirectly.

As simple as the distinction between replication and interaction is, it
goes a long way toward resolving certain apparent disagreements that
characterize the biological literature. For example, Ayala (1978) notes
that "it must be remembered that each locus is not subject to selection
separate from the others, so that thousands of selective processes would
be summed as if they were individual events. The entire individual
organism, not the chromosomal locus is the unit of selection, and the
alleles at different loci interact in complex ways to yield the final product."

Dawkins (1978) disagrees. "Of course it is true that the phenotypic
.ect of a gene is a meaningless concept outside the context of many, or
even all, of the other genes in the genome. Yet, however complex and
intricate the organism may be, however much we may agree that the
organism is a unit of *function*, I still think it misleading to call it a unit of
selection. Genes may interact, even 'blend,' in their effects on embryonic
development, as much as you please. But they do not blend when it comes
to being passed on to future generations."

At the very least, Ayala claims that organisms are interactors. Maybe
so, Dawkins responds, but they are not replicators. Evolution of sorts
could result from replication alone, but evolution through natural selection requires an interplay between replication and interaction. Both
processes are necessary. Neither process by itself is sufficient. Omitting
reference to replication leaves out the mechanism by which structure is
passed from one generation to the next. Omitting reference to the causal
mechanisms that bias the distribution of replicators reduces the evolutionary process to the "gavotte of the chromosomes," to use Hamilton's
(1975) propitious phrase. The simplicity of a theory of evolution couched
entirely in terms of changes in replicator frequencies is purchased at the
price of drastically reduced empirical content.

LEVELS OF REPLICATION

In order for an entity to function as a replicator, it must have structure and be able to pass on that structure—the more directly the better,
the more intact the better. When replication is described in this way, genes
are obviously the most fundamental replicators. However, biologists sometimes reject other entities as replicators because they lack certain characteristics, characteristics that even genes do not possess. For example, Stern
(1970) complains that the "theory of natural selection offers no conclusion
that could tell us what it means for an individual to be selected. In the
'eyes' of selection, organisms are merely temporary carriers of characteristics. Individuals die, they are neither preserved nor increased in frequency,
and therefore are not selected." Similarly, Williams (1966) claims that his
view of selection "necessitates the immediate rejection of the importance
of certain kinds of selection. The natural selection of phenotypes cannot
in itself produce cumulative change because phenotypes are extremely
temporary manifestations." However, if this line of reasoning were cogent,
it would count just as strongly against genes as against organisms. Neither genes nor organisms are preserved or increased in frequency. The
phenotypic characteristics of organisms are extremely temporarly manifestations—almost as temporary as the "phenotypic" characteristics of genes.

As substantial entities, all replicators come into existence and pass away. Only their structure persists, and that is all that is needed for them to function as replicators.

GENES AND GENOMES

Genes are linked both structurally in chromosomes and functionally in biosynthetic pathways. Can chromosomes or possibly entire genomes function as replicators? If not, can they be considered functional wholes? Lewontin (1970) begins his discussion of individual selection by claiming that the "primary focus of evolution by natural selection is the individual" and then immediately launches into a discussion of the genotype. To be sure, there is a one-to-one correspondence between genotypes and organisms, but the structural unity of the genotype and the functional unity of the genotype in the production of the organism must be kept distinct from each other and from "the unity of the organism."

In asexual reproduction, the structure of the entire genome is transmitted. In sexual reproduction, there is always the danger of recombination. Recombination has no effect on the structure of genomes in genetically homogeneous populations. However, the more heterogeneous a population is, the more likely that the structure of genomes will be altered by crossover during meiosis. How much alteration can occur before a genome must be considered a new replicator depends on the effect the changes have on the organism as an interactor. How similar is similar enough? Similar enough to respond similarly to similar selection pressures (Williams 1966). Before turning to this topic, one consequence of this line of reasoning must be mentioned. Small populations tend toward increased homogeneity, both because a very few organisms cannot possibly incorporate all the genetic heterogeneity of a large population and because of the effect of inbreeding. If speciation occurs always or usually by means of small, peripheral isolates (Eldredge and Gould 1972, Gould and Eldridge 1977, Mayr 1963), then at speciation, when it really counts, entire genomes can function as replicators.

When the "unity of the genotype" is appealed to, functional unity is usually at issue. If genotypes are functionally organized wholes, it is difficult to see how their constituent parts could be rearranged much without significant disruption of function. Surprisingly, the evidence for the expected linkage disequilibrium is currently equivocal (Franklin and Lewontin 1972). However, from the point of view of replication, structural unity is what matters, not functional unity. (Functional unity is discussed in the next section in connection with interaction.)

ORGANISMS AND COLONIES

In asexual reproduction, the entire organism can replicate albeit in conjunction with the genetic material. In such cases, these organisms are as much replicators as are genes. Sexual reproduction is quite another matter. The only structure literally transmitted from parent to offspring is the structure of the genetic material. At the very least, replication at the level of sexual organisms is indirect, one place removed from the genetic material. How much structural similarity is present in organism lineages? Obviously, in genetically homogeneous populations, ancestor-descendant sequences of organisms consist of individuals that are structurally quite similar: variation is introduced only by environmental differences. Even in genetically heterogeneous populations of sexual organisms, organisms need not vary greatly from generation to generation. Much of the genetic heterogeneity present in populations has little or no phenotypic effect. The functional unity of the genotype in the production of organisms promotes the structural similarity of organisms. To the extent that variation in the overall structure of organisms is selectively neutral, organisms can function as replicators, keeping in mind that the transmission of structure is not as direct as in asexual reproduction.

In order for colonies to function as replicators, they must be individuals, possess structure of their own, and be able to pass on this structure largely intact. Although Wilson (1980) admits that the "insect society is a decidedly more open system that the lower units of biological organization such as the organism and the cell," he still maintains that colonies can function as units of selection. The "great innovation" in the evolution of social insects was the "reproductive neuter, which fixed the limits on the amount of caste differentiation that could occur among the colony members." If ants are *part* of their colony, then they need be no more alike than are the cells that make up an organism. Epithelial and liver cells differ as much as do worker and soldier ants.

In some cases at least, colonies seem to have all the gross characteristics of organisms. Their boundaries are frequently distinct. They exhibit internal differentiation and division of labor. They have properties of their own—such as the percentage of organisms in each caste and the distribution of these castes throughout the colony. Colonies are even capable of passing on these properties when they reproduce themselves: Sometimes a single colony splits equitably into two; sometimes only one or several organisms leave the parent colony. However, as Lewontin (1970) has pointed out, all the cells in an organism in most cases contain the same genes, while "sterile diploid workers are not genetically identical with the fertile queen or the fertile haploid males." Thus, sexual reproduction presents the same range of problems for colonies functioning as replicators as it does for organisms.

POPULATIONS AND SPECIES

It is difficult to tell whether any of the biologists who argue for population selection have replication in mind. Because they mention "population structure," they might. In the preceding discussion, I did not bother to argue that genes, organisms, and colonies are individuals that exhibit structures of their own. In the case of populations, these characteristics cannot be taken for granted. For example, Lewontin (1970) distinguishes between kin selection and the differential survival and reproduction of a population: "Survival of such a unit means simply that the entire population has not become extinct, regardless of the numbers of individuals it contains. Reproduction of a population is more difficult to define, but since we are concerned with some property of the population, then reproduction must mean the budding off of new colonies with the same characteristic property whose evolution we are explaining."

If populations are to function as replicators, they must be able to replicate themselves, either by splitting equitably into two or more populations or by sending out a few organisms to start new populations. Most populations are genetically quite heterogeneous. A population might retain its characteristic gene freqencies if splitting occurs, but the populations that result from a few colonizers are likely to be genetically quite different from the parent population. Further, in what sense can populations be said to have structure? As we have seen, organisms and colonies are functional wholes. They also exhibit structural characteristics. Whether or not they can transmit this structure with sufficient regularity and fidelity to function as replicators is less clear. Stehr (1968) argues that populations are both functional and structural wholes: "One of the basic concepts in population biology is obviously the concept of population itself. The term population often evokes a numerical, merely quantitative, image. Too many ecologists still use the term 'population' as if it would refer to a smaller or larger number of similar individuals, the key words being 'number' and 'similar.' But this is false and the opposite is true. Population is a functional and structural term referring to an integrated grouping of dissimilar and, therefore, mutually dependent individuals."

A continuing feud exists between traditional evolutionary biologists and practitioners of what they deride as "beanbag genetics" (Haldane 1964, Mayr 1959, 1963, 1967, 1975, Michod 1981). The main point of contention is the existence and adequate treatment of levels of organization more inclusive than single genes. Can properties of structured wholes be reduced without loss to the properties of their parts (Wimsatt 1974)? Although this question tends to crop up in the context of population selection, it is equally relevant at all levels of organization. The mass of an organism is nothing but a simple summation of the masses of its parts. A certain percentage of cells will be nerve cells, a certain percentage liver cells, etc. But organism selectionists argue that of greater importance is the distribution of these cells throughout the organism. One cannot understand the role organisms play in the evolutionary process if their structure is ignored. Similarly, the mass of a particular hive of bees is nothing but a simple summation of the masses of its parts. A certain percentage of bees will gather food, a certain percentage circulate air in the hive, etc. But colony selectionists argue that of greater importance is the distribution of these organisms throughout the hive.

Gene selectionists seem to think that all this higher level organization can be ignored without loss. The only organization that matters is the order of bases in DNA. But a physicist might argue that the mass of a gene is nothing but a simple summation of the masses of its constituent parts. A certain percentage of these parts contain guanine, a certain percentage adenine, etc. But gene selectionists are sure to complain that of greater importance is the order of bases in the molecule. Hence, one issue that divides biologists is the levels at which organization must be acknowledged in the evolutionary process. One problem they all share, however, is the nature of organization itself and what role it plays. With respect to populations, the chief problem is the locus of population structure. It is certainly true that populations are spatiotemporally localized entites that develop continuously through time. Gene exchange also serves to promote internal cohesion. Thus, populations are reasonably good examples of individuals; but to function as replicators, they must be special sorts of individuals. They must exhibit structure of their own and be able to pass it on. At times population structure is treated as if it followed from the unity of the genotype. Because all organisms that make up a population share the same core elements in their genotypes, the population itself is supposedly in some sense a whole. At the very least, the notion of population structure needs considerable elucidation. As it stands, it remains problematic.

These problems are only magnified at the level of entire species. Although some species of sexual organisms are made up of a single population, most include several populations that are at least periodically disjunct. As long as the constituent populations exchange an occasional organism, such species can be considered a single, integrated individual. However, when populations remain totally disjunct for long periods ("long" in evolutionary terms), some other criterion must be discovered for including them in the same species. That these populations remain potentially interbreeding means that they are potentially a single individual. The commonest objection raised to potential interbreeding as a criterion for species status has concerned its operational applicability. Such operationist objections to one side (Hull 1968), the real problem is its relevance. Two drops of mercury might be potentially one. If they came into contact with each other, they might merge into a single drop. However, until they do, they remain two drops and not one. Comparable observations should hold for populations as parts of a single species. Do claims of reproductive isolation concern the structure of the species as a whole, its constituent populations, or the genomes of the separate organisms? Eldredge and Gould (1972) claim that species are homeostatic systems, but they are not very explicit about the actual mechanisms that produce this homeostasis. However, one point should be noted: If species and populations are structured wholes, genetic heterogeneity is no longer problematic. One expects individuals to be made up of varied parts.

In sum, replication seems concentrated at the lower levels of the organizational hierarchy, occurring usually at the level of the genetic material, sometimes at the level of organisms and possibly colonies, but rarely higher.

LEVELS OF INTERACTION

Genes, cells, and organisms all interact with their respective environments in ways that result in differential replication. They are organized wholes that exhibit properties of their own, and the nature of these properties determines their success as interactors. In most cases when biologists argue that entities more inclusive than single genes function in the evolutionary process, they have interaction in mind, not replication. For example, Emerson (1959) argues that colonies must develop adaptations analogous to the adaptations of individual organisms if colonies are to be the sort of thing that can be selected. Wilson (1971) maintains that the "superficial aspects of caste, communication, and other social phenomena represent adaptations that are fixed by natural selection at the colony level." To be sure, the reproductives that transmit the gametes are the "ultimate focus of selection," but "it remains true that the colony is selected as a whole, and its members contribute to colony fitness rather than individual fitness."

Similarly, Williams (1966) argues that herds of ungulates cannot be selected because they lack any significant specialization. However, if such specializations were present, that "would justify recognizing the herd as an adaptively organized entity." He goes on to argue, "Unlike individual fleetness, such group-related adaptations would require something more than the natural selection of alternative alleles as an explanation." If herds are, as Williams claims, not functionally organized systems, then they would have no adaptations to explain in the first place, whether by alternative alleles of anything else. The issue is whether entities more inclusive than organisms exhibit adaptations and, if so, whether they can be explained by reference solely to alternative alleles. For those biologists who think no reference need be made in evolutionary explanations to organisms as interactors, the question never arises. If organisms need not be mentioned, certainly higher level interactors can be ignored. However, those biologists who believe that the process I have named "interaction" is central to the evolutionary process must address the question, Can entities more inclusive than organisms function as interactors?

Colonies seem clear examples of interactors. They are organized wholes. Individual organisms do not confront their environments in isolation but as parts of larger wholes. Populations and species once again pose special problems. The problem is not genetic heterogeneity, the retention of structure, and the like. These are characteristics of replicatiors, not interactors. The problem is the existence of populational adaptations, properties characteristic of the population as a whole that allow it to interact with its environment as a whole. If populations and/or species are homeostatic systems, then some such properties must exist. If populations and possibly entire species are to function as interactors, it is not enough that they be made up of homeostatic systems; they themselves must exhibit the appropriate characteristics. Once again, a greater specification of these properties is necessary before any reasonable decision can be made on the issue.

Previously, I made the blanket claim that "group selection" is impossible because in order to be selected in the sense investigated in this paper, an entity must be an individual. Anything that can be selected the way an organism can must be the same sort of thing an organism is. Most discussions of group selection concern the selection of groups just because all the members of the group happen to be confined to the same locality, either because of some barrier or because of population viscosity (Wade 1978, Williams 1971, Wilson 1980). Such groups are genuine groups, and this sort of selection is geuine group selection of the sort that requires such special circumstances (Lewontin 1970). More recently, Stanley (1979) has argued for a process he terms "species selection," a process that differs both from interaction at levels more inclusive than organisms and from genuine group selection, because it does not explain the origin of adaptations. Rather, species selection determines the "fate of adaptations, once established." In Stanley's view, species are neither replicators nor interactors (see also Van Valen 1975).

When biologists refer to the occurrence of selection at levels "higher" than species, they usually have in mind not higher taxa, but ecosystems or communities. I did not discuss ecosystems and communities in connection with replication because no one seems to have argued that these systems can function as replicators. If anything, they can function as interactors. According to Hoffman (1979), "The basic assumption of community ecology and paleoecology is that the recurrent species associations which comprise ecological communities or biocenoses represent a distinct level of biotic organization achieved through ecological integration and coevolution among the species. Under this assumption, communities are claimed to be real biological units each of which is defined by its particular taxonomic composition and ecological structure."

Ecological communities certainly give every appearance of being functionally organized systems, much more so than particular species. The major stumbling block in the path of treating such systems as interactors is the independence of their constituent replicators. All of the examples of interactors discussed thus far have contained as part of their own make-up a single set of replicators. Even if higher-level entities can function on occasion as replicators, the most fundamental replicators in every case are genes. The success or failure of an organism in reproducing itself affects the replication of its genes, *all* its genes. The organisms that comprise an ecological community may interact with the environment of the community as a cohesive whole, but the effects of these interactions on their constituent replicators are not unitary. Hoffman (1979) concludes that there is "no intrinsic, biotic mechanism inducing community dynamics that is an inherent trend to maximize a selection value in either ecological, or evolutionary time." At the very least, ecololgical communities are extremely problematic interactors.

In sum, entities function as interactors at higher levels of organization than those at which replication occurs, at least at the level of colonies, possibly at the level of populations, but probably at no higher levels.

LINEAGES

Replicators and interactors are the entities that function *in* the evolutionary process. Other entities evolve *as a result* of this process, entities commonly termed species. However, the main strategy of this paper is to select terms that are neutral with respect to the empirical points at issue and to define these terms so that any entity possessing the appropriate characteristics can count as performing that function. In this instance, there is no need to invent a term. One is already available:

lineage: an entity that changes indefinitely through time either in the same or an altered state as a result of replication

Neither genes nor organisms can function as lineages because neither can change indefinitely without becoming numerically distinct individuals. However, both form lineages that can and do evolve. In asexual organisms the gene lineages are contained wholly within organism lineages and form constantly branching trees. Recombination at meiosis in sexual organisms has two results: Gene lineages do not form trees but networks, and the structure of the genetic material is altered to some extent from generation to generation even in the absence of mutation. Thus, in sexual organisms, the limits of gene-lineages expand to the limits of the gene pool, while the limits of single replicators gradually shrink to the single nucleotide through successive replications.

On the usual view, species change indefinitely through time and hence are paradigm lineages. But according to Eldridge and Gould (1972) and Gould and Eldridge (1977), most species cannot change much during the course of their existence. Thus, they cannot evolve. However, like genes and organisms, they form lineages, and these lineages evolve. In the vast majority of animal species, species (or species-lineages) form constantly branching trees. In plants, they continue to anastomose. Eventually, however, even plant species form trees. An important characteristic of lineages is that each lower-level lineage is included as part of all subsequent higher-lever lineages. Gene-lineages are included physically as part of organism-lineages. Assuming that these organisms in turn form colonies, the relevant organism-lineages are included in colony-lineages, and so on, up to the level of biological species.

Those biologists who attempt to characterize the species category as an evolutionary unit emphasize *coherence* and *continuity*, two of the most important characteristics of individuals (Ghiselin 1974a, Mayr 1969, Simpson 1961, Van Valen 1976, Wiley 1978). As Mayr (1969) summarizes this position, "Uniquely different individuals are organized into interbreeding populations and into species. All the members are 'parts' of the species, since they are derived from and contribute to a single gene pool. The population or species as a whole is itself the 'individual' that undergoes evolution; it is not a class with members" (see also Mayr 1976a). Recent authors who argue that species are individuals do not claim that species are replicators or interactors, though they might be, but that they are the entities that evolve as a result of the interplay betweem replication and interaction. They are lineages. More than that, they are the most inclusive entities that are "actively evolving entities," to use Wiley's (1979) phrase, According to Wiley, "supraspecific taxa are not actively evolving entities and thus cannot 'give rise' to anything. Put briefly, once a species speciates, it is no longer a single evolving lineage but a series of separate and independently evolving groups." Species are certainly part of the sections of the phylogenetic tree commonly designated as higher taxa, but these taxa evolve only as a result of the evolution of their constituent species.

Comparable observations hold for the lineages formed in asexual reproduction. Advocates of the biological species concept (Dobzhansky 1970, Mayr 1969) have long claimed that strictly asexual organisms do not form species, an assertion that has seemed overly chauvinistic to some. However, the point is that strictly asexual organisms form no higher-level entities; organism-lineages are the highest-level lineages produced (Van Valen 1975). They alone evolve as a result of replication and interaction. Just as not all organisms form colonies, there is no reason to expect all organisms to form species (Van Valen 1976). Or put in the opposite way, these organism-lineages *are* the species in asexual organisms.

Cook (1980) makes comparable distinctions with respect to clonal development in plants. He terms each physiological unit a "ramet" and the entire clone a "genet." He then concludes that "it is the genet upon which natural selection operates. In a large, widespread clone the death of a ramet may have as little evolutionary consequence as the pruning of a branch from a large tree or the loss of a leg in an insect." Cook's observations are appropriate to genets that retain physical connections between their parts; they are inappropriate to genets in which early ramets cease to exist as they produce later ramets. Natural selection cannot operate on what no longer exists.

The only other candidate for a lineage is the ecological community. Boucot (1979) does not argue that communities are selected (in either sense of this term), only that they evolve by means of the replacement of one closely related species by another. May (1978) disagrees. The coevolution of species within an ecosystem might give rise to all sorts of interesting patterns, but "ecological systems as such do not evolve." Once again, the problem seems to be the independence of the separate lineages contained within ecological communities. In connection with "arms races" both between and within species, Dawkins and Krebs (1979) remark that "it is important to realize who are the parties that are racing against one another. They are not individuals but lineages." Species can interact, but they are not forced to share their "battle plans" the way orgainsms in the same species must. "In an interspecific arms race like that between predator and prey, two entirely separate 'lineages' coevolve in parallel, mutually countering one another's adaptations, but in the intraspecific arms race the lineages which are racing against each other are not really lineages at all. The genes that programme the development of queen behaviour are present in workers, and the genes that programme the development of worker behaviour are present in the queens."

In sum, genes, organisms, and colonies form lineages. The separate sexes, castes, and so forth within single species do not. If ecological systems evolve, two different sorts of lineages must be distinguished: those in which the constituent lineages form networks and those composed of independent sub-lineages.

THE PREVALENCE OF SEX

The prevalence of sex remains the major roadblock to an entirely individualistic interpretation of evolution. As Maynard Smith (1971) remarks, "there is however one property, that of sexual reproduction, which is almost universal, and for which the generally accepted explanation involves, implicitly or explicitly, a process of group selection" (see also Maynard Smith 1968). Williams (1971) agrees, noting that "if group selection can produce the machinery of sexual reproduction, it ought to be able to do many other things as well." In a more recent work, Williams (1975) sets out several possible individualistic explanations for the prevalence of sex. Each might apply in special circumstances, but none of these explanations taken severally or conjointly, is adequate to explain why the vast majority of species reproduce sexually. In what appears to be near desperation, Williams (1975) appeals to "historical constraints that preserve sexual reproduction when it has ceased to be adaptive." In higher vertebrates, sexuality is a "maladaptive feature, dating from a piscine or even prochordate ancestor, for which they lace the preadaptiations for ridding themselves."

Stanley (1979) suggests an even more innovative explanation for the prevalence of sex. According to his species selectionist view, sexual species "predominate simply because they maintain a high capacity for speciation, while asexual clones do not." Because "almost every species is ephemeral in geologic time, the impact of extinction upon higher organisms is simply too great to be offset by clonal rates of diversification." Thus Stanley (1979) suggests that the "evaluation of sex be elevated to the level of the higher taxon. It is not primarily the species that benefits, but the clade. In effect, sexuality represents a *sine qua non* for success in species selection."

As original — even bizarre — as Williams and Stanleys explanations are, I do not think they go far enough; they remaim imbued with the commonsense notions of genes, organisms, and species. The very statement of the problem assumes that sexual and asexual organisms form comparable species. For example, Stanley cites White's (1978) estimate that about one in a thousand animal species is asexual; but if we take him at his word and agree that asexual organisms neither form species nor are capable of speciating, then clones and species are not comparable. As Stanley (1979) himself remarks, his view might better be called lineage selection. What counts in evolution is the level at which lineages form constantly diverging trees. This occurs at the level of single organisms in asexual reproduction and single species in sexual reproduction. If like is to be compared to like, asexual lineages should be compared to sexual lineages, and in such a comparison, sexual reproduction becomes as rare as it should be. The existence of sexual reproduction still must be explained, but the scope of the problem is greatly reduced, so reduced that one or more of the explanations suggested for it might be adequate.

CONCLUSION

In the introduction to a symposium on sociocultural evolution, Buckley (1979) complains that, while most "anthropologists and sociologists today recognize sociocultural systems as group entities at their own ontological stage of organization with emergent features, . . . most biologists have not been able to recognize any level beyond the individual organism in other than aggregative statistical terms (populations, communities, ecosystems)." If the discussion in this paper has done nothing else, it should show that Buckley is mistaken.

The reader might now be tempted to agree with Hamilton (1975) that common usage is preferable to all these metaphysical ruminations. As understandable as this temptation is, I suspect that sooner or later common usage will have to be sacrificed if we are to understand the evolutionary process.

Chapter 7

Genealogical Actors in Ecological Roles*

> Actually, the question of realism has noth-
> ing to do with the current controversy since
> both individuals and classes can be real.
> (Mayr, 1987, p. 146).

> Now that species are conceived of as indi-
> viduals, they have to be absolutely concrete,
> and must be viewed as no more intellectual
> constructs than organisms are.
> (Ghiselin, 1987, p. 130).

One of the primary goals of intellectual inquiry is unification—the attempt
to group similar phenomena together and to explain what it is that makes
these phenomena similar. One mistake is to group things together that
are actually quite disparate. For example, Mayr (1987, p. 160) complains
that "teleology" has been applied "indiscriminantely to four entirely different kinds of natural phenomena. Obviously, one cannot solve the problem of teleology as long as one treats such a melange as if it were a
uniform entity." The other mistake is to overlook regularities that actually
exist, to opt for multiplicity for the sake of multiplicity. The safest strategy in intellectual pursuits is to point out the endless differences that exist
in nature without venturing any generalizations about them. As Ghiselin
(1987, p. 139) remarks, if one is sufficiently discerning, no two individuals can be identical without becoming one and the same individual. To
the extent that science involves generalization and categorization, the infinite multiplicity alternative is not open to scientists. They must opt even
at the risk of making mistakes.

Of the two main issues that Mayr and Ghiselin discuss, one is largely
philosophical (the class-individual distinction), the other largely scientific (the nature of biological species). Although considerable disagreement exists over details, something like the difference between primary
substances and secondary substances, particulars and universals, individuals and classes, and so on can be found in the writings of nearly all major

---

*Reprinted with permission from *Biology and Philosophy* 2 (1987) 168-184. © 1987 *by*
D. Reidel Publishing Company.

Western philosophers. The terminology is often bewildering, but the general aim is not. It is to distinguish between particular entities (entities that are spatiotemporally localized, well-organized, cohesive at any one time, and continuous through time) and classes (multiplicities of entities grouped together by some means or other, usually the sharing of one or more properties.)

As an idle exercise, one can construct indefinitely many different classes. One strain in the philosophical literature over realism is whether or not there are intellectually reputable ways of pruning these pluralistic excesses. One solution is to consider as real those classes which human beings, given their relative size, duration, and perceptual acuity, tend to find most intuitively obvious. If in society after society, the distinction between trees, bushes, and plants (herbs) is recognized, then these classes are real. I find this solution mistaken in the extreme. In the first place, people in different sorts of societies sometimes agree in their evaluations of kinds, but just as often not. For example, Brown (1985) discovered significant differences in the species recognized by hunter gathering peoples and those engaged in small-scale agriculture. If all people are essentially the same, then we should all have the same intuitions. In point of fact, we do not. Even if we did, whenever our everyday intuitions conflict with the conclusions drawn by scientists, I for one opt for the latter. As natural as the division between trees, bushes and herbs may seem, it plays no role whatsoever in botany. When Brown (1985) surveyed botanical folk taxonomies in seventeen languages spoken by hunters and gatherers, the concordance between the species of plants that they recognized and those recognized by professional botanists varied from 95.7 percent to 52.1 percent. (For difficulties in comparing the taxa recognized by professional systematists and the local inhabitants of a region, see Atran 1985).

Another solution is to consider those classes that function in scientific laws as real. To put it more precisely, the class terms that function in statements of putative laws of nature are putative natural kinds. In set theory, all sets are equally aggregates. The need felt by generations of philosophers of sicence to distinguish between all universal generalizations and putative laws of nature is mirrored in the desire to distinguish between sets as such and a more significant notion. No analysis has proved totally satisfactory. Even so, I do not see how anyone who wants to understand science can dismiss these distinctions as being of no consequence. With very minor exception, all organisms here on Earth use the same genetic code. No one thinks that this regularity is a law of nature. To the contrary, it is a contingent fact of history. It is equally true that all entities that evolve by means of natural selection replicate themselves. At the very least, this regularity is an excellent candidate for a natural law.

One very good candidate for a natural kind in evolutionary theory is peripheral isolates. Peripheral isolates are, of course, composed of organisms. However, the effect that the fates of these organisms have on evolution is a function of their being part of a peripheral isolate. The entities that putative natural kind terms denote function in the regularities to which the putative laws refer, but they do not function in these regularities as bare particulars. To the contrary, they function the way that they do because they belong to the natural kinds that they do, and they belong to these natural kinds because of the characteristics that they exhibit. Organisms do not take on their properties in virtue of the definitions of the names of the natural kinds to which they belong. To the contrary, the terms referring to natural kinds have the definitions that they do because the organisms belonging to them have the properties that they do. If set theoreticians can incorporate such distinctions into set theory, all well and good. If not, then set theory is not good enough.

When Ghiselin, (1966) suggested that species belong in the metaphysical category individual rather than class, he shifted the question of the reality of species from the reality of classes to the reality of individuals. Traditionally, philsophers have treated the reality of individuals as being much less problematic than the reality of classes. Hence, if species are individuals, their reality is much less problematic. One reason for this asymmetry is that commonsense and scientific notions of what count as individuals tend to coincide much more frequently than commonsense and scientific notions of classes. Both ordinary people and professional biologists recognize the existence of organisms. Organisms are intuitively obvious and scientifically important. With respect to classes, much more disagreement exists between how the world *seems* from the perspective of the man or woman on the street and how scientists say it actually is. As intuitively obvious as the distinction between trees, bushes, and herbs may appear, it has no counterpart in any biological classification. Space may not *seem* to be curved, but scientists tell us that it is. Similarly, species may not *seem* to be individuals, but Ghiselin and Mayr insist that this is what they actually are. However, even with respect to individuals, things are not always as they seem to be. Most ordinary citizens think that a Portugese man-of-war is a single organism, while biologists claim that it is a colony. I see no more reason to defer to common conceptions in the case of organisms than in the case of species.

The distinction between kinds in general (classes) and natural kinds turns on the role of certain classes in science. A parallel distinction must be made between all the various things that have been considered individuals by ordinary people around the world and natural individuals — those individuals over which scientific laws range. Natural individuals are those individuals that make up the extension of natural kinds. Natural kinds refer to natural individuals. Because scientists keep reworking their theories, our estimations of which classes and individuals are natural in this sense will also keep changing. For protracted periods in certain areas of science, scientists give every appearance of improving our understanding of both natural kinds and natural individuals. Some realists use this convergence as evidence for their metaphysical position.

Thus, I agree with Mayr that both individuals and classes can be real as well as with Ghiselin that species are no more intellectual constructs than are organisms. On the analysis I prefer, the reality of classes and individuals are different through related issues. In a trivial, obvious sense, all our conceptions are intellectual constructs, but in a very important, though far from obvious sense, some of our conceptions are not just intellectual constructs. If one considers both species and organisms as individuals, then Ghiselin is right that species are no more intellectual constructs than organisms are—and no less. One consequence of this theory-relative view of ontological status is that species and organisms can count as natural individuals only if scientific laws can be found that range over them.

PHILOSOPHICAL ISSUES

When one looks at the three most common examples of natural kinds— geometric figures, physical elements, and biological species—there is a strong temptation to paraphrase Mayr and say that one cannot solve the problem of natural kinds (or classes in general) as long as one treats such a melange as if it were composed of essentially similar sorts of things. Perhaps all natural kinds have something in common, but not if these examples are taken as paradigmatic. One of the implications for philosophy of the recent literature on the species category is that species do not belong in the same metaphysics category with geometric figures and the physical elements. Of course, one common view among philosophers is that no connections exist between factual knowledge and metaphysics. No matter what the world turns out to be like, genuine metaphsics remains untouched. So a particular metaphysician got all his examples wrong. What difference does that make? I suppose that it is possible for a philosopher to misunderstand just about everything in the world in which he lives and yet produce the perfect metaphysical system, but I am highly suspicious. I find it impossible to believe that the examples that we use as paradigms of a metaphysical category have no influence on our characterization of that category.

Parallel conclusions apply to the other major metaphysical category— particulars or individuals. In the early philosophical literature, particular organisms are the most common examples of primary substances along with such household furnishings as tables and chairs. In more recent times, other examples have been added, such as particular atoms, genes, and wrist-watches. Is this list also a melange of diverse entities? Mayr thinks that it is. Organisms are individuals in a sense quite different from inanimate objects. Most organisms are genetically unique, and all go through par-tially programmed life cycles. Some individuals replicate themselves; some do not. Perhaps these distinctions are metaphysically of no consequence, but from the perspective of understanding natural phenomena, they are crucial. In general, I find the alacrity with which metaphysicians insulate their intellectual activities from any and all empirical considerations a guarantee that their work will continue to remain scientifically sterile.

In his writings, Ghiselin has treated the class-individual distinction as being good enough to handle biological species, while Mayr thinks that a third metaphysical category is needed for species—population. According to Mayr, extremely well-organized, spatiotemporally localized, discrete entities such as organisms must be distinguished from less organized, more diffuse, and amorphous entities such as species. The former are individu-als; the latter populations. Although Mayr acknowledges that the term population incorporates much of the same sort of multiplicity of meaning which he finds so dismaying in other philosophical terms, he still thinks that its consistent use can help clarify the species problem. I hope that he is right, but this maneuver is not likely to succeed. From its inception, population has been applied as readily to stars and molecules as to plants and humans, just the sort of indiscriminate usage that Mayr deplores (Neyman 1967).

Terminology to one side, two important distinctions remain: (a) between spatiotemporal restrictedness and unrestrictedness, and (b) between tightly and loosely organized entities. Although not all organi-zation is spatiotemporal (Alaska is part of the United States of America even though the two are not spatiotemporally contiguous), the sort of organization that matters in biological evolution is. Spatiotemporally organized entities can be arrayed along a continuum from the most highly organized to the most diffuse. Organisms tend to cluster near the well-organized end of the continumm while species tend to cluster near the less organized end, but as Mayr (p. 159) notes, there are entities com-monly classed as organisms that are no better organized than are many species. Most species could lose 10,000 or even 100,000 of their constitu-ent organisms without serious disruption of their population structure. An analogous loss for such well-organized organisms as higher verte-brates would lead to death or serious impairment. "However, in the lower vertebrates and in many kinds of plants . . . a seriously mutilated individ-ual can be restored as quickly as a decimated species."

Thus, according to Mayr (p. 161), the difference between organisms as individuals and species as populations is one of degree, not kind. The difference between these two categories and classes, to the contrary, is one of kind. A class might in point of fact have all its members restricted to one part of the universe. If the universe is finite, as physicists currently claim, then all classes will be localized, but this is a vacuous notion of spatiotemporal restrictedness. Yes, all physical bodies are restricted to the physical universe, and some by accident may be confined to some particular corner of the universe. But some entities function the way that they do because of their spatiotemporal characteristics. Species as the things that evolve through natural selection are among these entities. That is why evolutionary biologists include such spatiotemporal properties in their definitions of the species category. Species are not just aggregates. To state the obvious, if genuine laws of nature must be spatiotemporally unrestricted, then they can include no uneliminable reference to particular species if species are treated as being spatiotemporally restricted. It is equally obvious, that spatiotemporal unrestrictedness is only a necessary condition for something to count as a natural law.

I sympathize with Mayr's (1987, pp. 148-9) bewilderment in reading Kitcher's (1984a, 1984b) discussion of species as sets. Kitcher is willing to construe species in the genealogical sense as being sets defined in terms of certain spatiotemporal relations, but he is unwilling to do the same for organisms. Organisms are not just sets. But if species as lineages can be construed as sets defined in terms of organismal descent, I see no reason to preclude the definition of organisms in terms of cellular descent. In fact, Kitcher (1986) finds all these excursions into "muddled metaphysics" distracting from the real issue—causation (see Sober 1984 for a response to Kitcher's early criticisms). However, until Kitcher explains why set theory is so impoverished when it comes to treating organisms, his view remains a mystery to me. If organisms along with everything else in the world can be treated as sets, then we are right back where we started. Now the issue is the distinction between two sorts of sets—those that are spatiotemporally unrestricted, and those that are spatiotemporally restricted in such a way that the terms referring to them cannot function in statements of laws of nature.

Mayr (1987, p. 147) thinks that the applicability of laws to individuals and classes is a side issue. As Ghiselin notes, Mayr has argued elsewhere (Mayr 1982) that there are no laws in biology. I disagree with Mayr on both issues. The reason that the distinction between spatiotemporal restrictedness and unrestrictedness is so important is that one of the major goals of science from its inception has been the discovery of regularities in nature that are independent of place and time—laws of nature.

If a natural law is true, it is true anywhere and at any time in the universe just so long as the appropriate conditions are met. It might be that all the regularities that scientists currently think are lawful are merely due to the contingencies of the formation of the universe. If so, then there are no scientific laws, but to give up the search for lawful regularities in nature is to alter the goals of science radically. Once again, the issue is causation. If we insist on dividing up the living world inappropriately, we will not discover the operative causal regularities.

As Ghiselin points out, Mayr's own claim that, under certain conditions, speciation occurs only allopatrically is an excellent candidate for an important and yet peculiarly biological law of nature. The conditional character of this law in no way precludes its counting as a genuine law of nature. All laws require boundary conditions. Only when these conditions are met must the law hold. All that matters is that these boundary conditions be specifiable and that they do not include reference to particular times and places. All the coins in my pocket may be dimes, but this is hardly a law of nature. Any philosophy of science that does not distinguish between statements about the coins in my pocket and Newton's Laws is sorely deficient. The different roles of terms referring to individuals and classes in statements of laws of nature is far from a side issue because these differences are the reason why viewing species as individuals rather than classes is important in the first place. One should expect to find biological laws about kinds of species but not about particular species. There can be laws about peripheral isolates, cosmopolitan species, polytypic species, etc., but not about the German Dunkers, *Homo sapiens, Canis familiaris,* etc.

Biology tends to look different from physics if one thinks that biological laws must predict the peculiar path that a particular species takes through the course of its evolution. In principle, I suppose that such predictions are possible, just as physicists can in principle trace the path of a particular atom in an enclosed gas as it bounces around its container, but physicists are also wise enough to content themselves with predictions about the gross characteristics of large ensembles of atoms. Biologists are doing the same with respect to evolutionary phenomena. No evolutionary biologist hopes to be able to predict precisely which species will invade a freshly denuded island, but estimates of the number of species that will eventually populate the island and their ecological density are feasible. As in all areas of science, some biological regularities are due to common history, while some are due to the relevant entities functioning similarly in the same natural processes. To the paleontologist who is trying to reconstruct phylogeny, the former is information; the latter noise. To the evolutionary biologist trying to understand the evolutionary process, the latter sort of regularities are information; the former noise. In short, one man's message is another man's noise.

Treating species as natural individuals rather than as natural kinds may seem like a demotion, but it is not. Both individuals and classes are necessary for theoretical science, and it is important for scientists to individuate classes and the individuals to which they refer appropriately. Mayr is one of the founders of the Modern Synthesis in evolutionary biology. He is also one of the founders of the New Systematics. In his role as a systematist, Mayr frequently claims that biological classifications are "theories." By this, he means that a classification constructed by means of a certain suite of characters should be able to serve as a basis for the prediction of the covariation of additional characters. Good classifications must be robust. This feature of good classifications appears to be superficially similar to what the nineteenth century philosopher of science, William Whewell (1840), termed a "consilience of inductions," the surest sign that one has discovered genuine laws of nature and their constituent natural kinds. For example, Newton's doctrine that the attraction of the sun varies according to the inverse square of the distance from it and other bodies in the solar system explained all three of Kepler's laws as well as the apparently dissimilar phenomenon of the precession of the equinoxes. All of these various phenomena behave similarly because they are instances of the same sort of general process.

But not all covariation is of this sort. Some results from common history. Taxa are characterized by clusters of characters. If taxa are construed as natural kinds, these characters cannot be evolutionary homologies; if taxa are viewed as chunks of the genealogical nexus, they must be. The characters used to describe biological taxa as chunks of the phylogenetic tree covary because of common history. Consilience with respect to spatiotemporally unrestricted characteristics (an appendage that enables flight, an organ that enables sight, and so on) indicates lawful regularities and natural kinds. Consilience with respect to spatiotemporally restricted characteristics (as a vertebrate wing, a vertebrate eye, and so forth) indicates accurate descriptions and natural individuals. Anyone who finds the relevant distinction between spatiotemporally restrictedness and unrestrictedness that I am laboring to elucidate incomprehensible or biologically irrelevant is going to have a very difficult time in understanding biological phenomena.

Thus far, I have concentrated on the general distinction between natural kinds and natural individuals. How about species and organisms in particular? Are all species essentially the same? Are all organisms essentially the same? The answers to these questions depend on how much emphasis is placed on commonsense notions and pre-analytic intuitions. If by "species" we mean all the various things that taxonomists consider species, then all species are hardly the same, essentially or otherwise. If ordinary conceptions are included, the situation becomes even more intractable. Even though systematists sometimes agree with each other and members of the general public in their taxonomic judgments (as Berlin, Breedlove, and Raven 1973), just as often they do not (Brown 1985). Although discrepancies with respect to organisms is not as extensive as with respect to species, they nevertheless exist. If the species category and the organism category are to count as natural kinds, they must be construed as technical terms in a particular theoretical context in biology. As long as one confines oneself to a restricted location and a short duration of time, species can be distinguished quite easily. As Mayr (1987, p. 146) remarks, no one has any trouble telling the chickadee from the starling in one's garden. However, when systematists trace a species geographically over great distances, problems arise. Although a species of chickadee might vary geographically so continuously that contiguous geographic races may be all but undistinguishable, more distant races might appear to belong to different species. The problem is only increased when one attempts to follow species through time. Thus, in species' recognition, the nondimensional situation has a certain priority. Similar observations hold for organisms. No one has any trouble telling one Sequoia tree from another, but slime molds, strawberry patches, and dandelions are quite another matter.

Mayr (1987, p. 155) concedes some sort of epistemological priority to characters. "Furthermore, all monophyletic groupings of organisms, from the population to the highest taxon, have of course something in common. How else would we otherwise determine whether a certain organism is a butterfly or a vertebrate?" Ghiselin (1987, p. 132) considers characters to be epiphenomenal. The conviction that species in some univocal sense exist out there in nature to be recognized by highly trained professionals and intelligent ignoramuses alike stems in part from our generalizing from the nondimensional situation. But as the enduring appeal of the phenetic species concept amply demonstrates, human beings also have a deeply held predilection for recognizing similar organisms as belonging to the same species. If they look alike, they are alike. But as the history of phenetic taxonomy also amply demonstrates, this conviction is mistaken. Given any set of organisms, they can be arranged into species in indefinitely many ways, depending on the characters and clustering techniques used. The problem is one of an embarrassment of riches. On the principles of phenetic taxonomy, there are no ways to choose among so many alternatives. Even Sokal and Crovello (1970) insist that males and females, different castes, as well as all stages in the life cycle of an organism, must be included in the same basic Operational Taxonomic Unit, overall similarity be hanged.

The myth of overall similarity is a metaphysical compulsion with an epistemological source. Species do exist out there in nature, but not because they seem to. The justification for this conviction resides in the theoretical role that species play in the evolutionary process. Even though biologists are flying in the face of convention when they refuse to go along with our ordinary conceptions, very frequently they must. Perhaps from an epistemological perspective, species are classes of similar organisms and the Portugese man-of-war is a single organism. If so, then so much the worse for the epistemological perspective. Species may not *seem* like genealogical units, but if they are to evolve by natural selection, this is precisely how they must be construed. A strawberry patch may not *seem* like a single entity, but in selection processes that is precisely how it functions. My general position is that things that function as the same in the evolutionary process are the same. Such construal will do damage to all sorts of commonsense and pre-analytic intuitions, but that cannot be helped.

SCIENTIFIC ISSUES

Literally dozens of definitions have been suggested for the species category through the years. As Mayr and Ghiselin note, several biologists who suggest different definitions of the species category are nevertheless attempting to capture the same sort of entity—species as genealogical lineages. The fact that the extensions of these different definitions tend to coincide so nicely indicates, as Whewell (1840) noted long ago, that perhaps the term being defined denotes a genuine natural kind. (Please note that here the species category is being referred to, not species taxa. Even if species are viewed as genealogical lineages, the species category might still be a natural kind.) However, many of the definitions of the species category that have been proposed, if applied consistently, produce quite different groups. In such a situation, Kitcher (1984a, 1984b) and Ruse (1973a) before him counsel pluralism. Because different biologists have different interests, they might well need different species concepts. Insisting on the primacy of one species concept over all the others might well result in premature closure.

Neither Mayr nor Ghiselin is very enthusiastic about Kitcher's plea for pluralism with respect to the species concept. Although Kitcher thinks that restricting the term "species" to apply just to those things that evolve is too monistic, he is willing to reject two widely-held species concepts— those of Creationists and pheneticists. Kitcher (1982a) rejects the Creationist species concept as a genuine scientific concept because Creationists are not genuine scientists. Creation science waivers between not being science at all and being very bad science. Kitcher (1984a, 1987) also rejects the species concept suggested by phenetic taxonomists but not because they are not genuine scientists. One might disagree with the principles of classification being espoused by such pheneticists as Sneath and Sokal (1973), but no one can deny that they are engaged in the scientific enterprise. Once again muddled metaphysics is the culprit—the theory-neutral stance proposed by the pheneticists. There simply are no such things as phenetic species, or to put the same point differently, there are way too many of them. Kitcher favors conceptual pluralism, but happily it does not extend all the way to the species concepts proposed by Creationists and pheneticists.

Ghiselin (1987, p. 136) objects that Kitcher's arguing from the various senses of "gene" to be found in molecular biology to pluralism with respect to the species concept is inappropriate. I agree. Molecular biologists divide up the genetic material into several different sorts of units: nucleotides, codons, recons, mutons, cistrons, operons, introns, and more. As different as these units are, they are all individuated from the same perspective and are designed to fit into the same functionally organized system. Recons and mutons can be as short as one nucleotide, codons always consist of three nucleotides, while the length of DNA that exhibits the cistrans effect varies tremendously. Cistrons in turn are organized into operons and so on. There is no incommensurability here, no cross purposes. The same cannot be said for the contrast between molecular, Mendelian, and evolutionary gene concepts. The relation between Mendelian genes and the various molecular units is far from neat (Hull 1974, Rosenberg 1985). Adding an evolutionary dimension, as Williams (1966) suggests, only adds further complexities. Evolutionary genes are variable in ways that Mendelian and molecular genes are not. Anyone who thinks that these various ways of defining "gene" all go together neatly to form a single coherent conceptual network needs only read the literature as these new perspectives were introduced. Howls of outrage went up from the wounded parties.

Some of the apparent plurality among species concepts is of the commensurable sort. Although some equivocation exists, such groupings of organisms as colonies, demes, and populations are part of the same conceptual system arising from the same theoretical perspective. The same cannot be said for taxospecies, biospecies, morphospecies, etc. They do not map neatly onto each other. Not infrequently, they would subdivide the organisms under investigation in radically different ways. Of all these incompatible and incommensurable species concepts, Mayr and Ghiselin urge the adoption of one as being primary—the genealogical concept. In doing so, they are carrying on in the best scientific tradition of opting for one perspective and pushing it for all its worth. Perhaps species as genealogical actors in an ecological play may prove ultimately to be inadequate. Science does march on. If so, then monism will have proved to have been only temporary, but the only way to find out how adequate a particular conception happens to be is to give it a run for its money. Remaining content with a variety of slightly or radically different species concepts might be admirably open minded and liberal, but it would be destructive of science, and this is precisely what Ruse and Kitcher seem to propose.

There is no *a priori* way to choose between competing research programs. Only time will tell. The greatest danger of pluralism is that it provides no means or even motivation for reducing conceptual luxuriance. Without such pruning, the integration of scientific knowledge is impossible. There has to be some reasonable middle ground between anything goes and the insistence that there is one and only one way to divide up the world and we know for all time what that way is. Kitcher is upset that Mayr, Ghiselin, myself, and others find one particular species concept superior to all other candidates and are urging others to adopt it. I can't speak for the others, but I do not think I am infallible. I have changed my mind in the past. I might change it in the future. I fail to see why urging a particular solution to a set of problems is somehow committing a philosophical sin. If pluralism is anything more than the reminder that other serious options exist or may crop up in the future, I do not see what it is. However, these alternatives must be serious and not merely the result of fertile imaginations. I for one reject equal time for nonsense. Both sides of this controversy need to say a word or two about what it is that makes an alternative serious. In my reading, I have come up with only one serious alternative to treating species as genealogical units. It comes from ecology.

The major theme of Ghiselin's paper is the difference between genealogical and ecological groupings of organisms and the primacy of the former. Although Ghiselin and Mayr disagree to some extent about the appropriate way to individuate genealogical units, they agree that the actors in the evolutionary play must be genealogical. Only their roles are defined in terms of ecology. Both perspectives are necessary. Selection is an interplay between replication (the genealogical perspective) and interaction (the ecological perspective), but as Eldredge (1985) has emphasized at some length, the genealogical and ecological hierarchies in nature are far from coincident. They do not even mesh in the sense that the entities at one genealogical level all play the same role at any one ecological level. Assuming that one can define "niche" independently of a specification of the organisms that happen to be filling that niche. I doubt that a biologist would be willing to put a butterfly and a bird in the same species even if they turned out to be filling the same niche. I suspect that what would happen is that elements would be added to the niche until the two genealogical units turn out to be filling distinct niches.

According to Ghiselin, the species category is strictly a genealogical unit, while niche is an ecological unit. Mixing the two together is sure to cause problems. With respect to sexually reproducing species, neither Ghiselin nor Mayr is inclined to mix the two together. Both treat species of sexually reproducing organisms as genealogical units. But some organisms rarely if ever reproduce sexually. For example, in one study only one cell in 250,000 in blue-green algae was found to have resulted from any sort of genetic recombination. Such rare events are hardly sufficient to produce an internally cohesive gene pool. Ghiselin's solution is to conclude that asexual organisms do not form entities more inclusive than single organisms. Just as not all organisms belong to colonies or some other form of kinship group, not all organisms belong to species. But from a taxonomic perspective, this conclusion is dissatisfying. Just as every library book must be placed on some shelf somewhere in the library, there is a strong compulsion among systematists to insist that every organism must belong to some species or other.

Although Mayr (1987, pp. 165-6) finds Ghiselin's solution to be the most "honest," he is forced to conclude that it is not perfect because "there are entities in nature that do not qualify as biological species," but which fill the same place in the ecosystem as do biological species. Originally, Mayr (1942:122) was unwilling to water down his biological species concept by adding a supplemental clause to include asexual organisms; now he is. However, he is still not willing to place hybrid swarms in species. In biological classification, these organisms remain books without a shelf. As counter-intuitive as the conclusion may be, I think that some organisms belong to no species whatsoever.

Another counter-intuitive consequence of a consistently genealogical perspective is that groups of organisms commonly treated by taxonomists to be more inclusive that single species must be treated as single species. Ghiselin mentions oaks. In general, gene exchange occurs at much higher levels in the taxonomic hierarchy among plants than among animals. Hence, Mishler and Donoghue (1982) urge pluralism, but a pluralism somewhat more limited than that countenanced by Kitcher. To the suggestion that their view might be interpreted as "anything goes," they respond that species taxa must be "phylogenetically meaningful," and not all of the species concepts suggested through the years by systematists have been phylogenetically meaningful. Although consistency may well be the hobgoblin of small minds, I prefer a consistent treatment of the evolutionary process. For example, Arnold and Fristrup (1982) take branching and persistence to be the fundamental properties that permit a hierarchical application of the principle of natural selection. Whenever splitting with little or no subsequent merger occurs, that is the same level, and the units at that level count as being the same sort of units, common sense notwithstanding.

Once a consistently genealogical perspective has been settled on, the question remains as to its priority. Why the priority of genealogy to ecology? Why must the actors in the evolutionary play be defined genealogically while the roles are defined ecologically? The answer can be found in Darwin's "strong principle of inheritance." Without that principle, evolution by means of natural selection is impossible. Descent is inherently a spatiotemporal relation. There is no mating at a distance. At the very least, propagules must come into contact. Ancestors can give rise to descendants only if they are in proximity to each other. The nondimensional species concept is important not just because it provides our epistemological entree into the living world, but more importantly because species interact with their environments and other species only in the specious present. The only things that matter about a species' past are those things that have left traces in the present. Even so, it is just as important to emphasize that these time-slices must be organized into lineages if differential propagation is to result in cumulative change. The notion of a generation is so central to our understanding of the evolutionary process that it tends to go unmentioned, but it is crucial nonetheless.

If the preceding considerations are accepted, it is difficult to see how any adequate version of evolutionary theory can be formulated that ignores genealogical units. I agree with Ghiselin (1987, p. 138) that some definitions of the species category try to make species be two different things at once. "On the one hand they want species to be individuals—so they can evolve. On the other hand they want them to be classes of 'ecologically similar' organisms." Trying to combine such markedly incommensurable conceptions into a single classification is guaranteed to produce a mess.

However, it does not follow so automatically that ecological generalizations must range over these genealogical units. Perhaps the only way for ecologists to discover ecological laws of sufficient generality is by totally ignoring genealogy and concentrating solely on ecological relations. Once again, if success comes, it will overcome all in-principle arguments. Biologists have a variety of interests. As a result, they are liable to classify natural phenomena quite differently. Eventually, these various perspectives and interests might merge and a single unified view of their subject matter emerge. For now, each discipline is liable to claim priority for its own preferred classifications. It is not up to philosophers to choose among them, but that does not mean that all classifications are equally reputable or promising. However, only a false sense of coherence is produced by terming all the basic units in these different classifications "species." When sociobiologists introduced "altruism" into biology as a technical term, they engendered considerable confusion. Terming a hodgepodge of different units "species" serves no useful purpose as far as I can see. If pluralism entails confusion and ambiguity, I am forced to join with Fodor's (1984: 42) Granny in her crusade to stamp out creeping pluralism.

PRIORITY AND PERCEPTIVENESS

Finally, I cannot conclude without commenting on the concern that Mayr and Ghiselin show for matters of priority and the role of philosophers in this particular dispute. Who first claimed that species are really spatiotemporal particulars instead of classes? A careful search of the biological literature is sure to uncover dozens of candidates from Buffon and Haeckel to Hennig and Mayr. Some of these potential precursors set out the point clearly and coherently. Others sort of hinted at it. Who should be declared the true precursor? I do not see that it matters. Pick a precursor, any precursor, and canonize him. The usefulness of scientific patron saints is not influenced very strongly by matters of intellectual justice. Mendel was chosen as the patron saint for Mendelian genetics, while Patrick Matthew's formulation of natural selection gets at most a footnote in histories of science. Michel Adanson was rescued from the obscurity of history books and touted for a short while as the patron saint of phenetic taxonomy, while Darwin has proved to be almost the universal patron saint. Dozens of research programs claim to trace themselves back to the great Darwin.

As useful as patron saints are in the ongoing process of science, I think that a much deeper point is at issue. Regardless of who first thought of an idea who succeeded in getting others to appreciate it? To pick one example, Hennig (1950) argued extensively for the view that species are connected systems long before Ghiselin did. Why not give Hennig the credit? The answer is that Hennig has been extremely influential on several issues but not this one. Until Ghiselin, cladists paid no attention to this aspect of Hennig's system of phylogenetics. Yes, it was there all the time, but no one noticed. By all indications, Ghiselin thought up the idea of species being individuals as much on his own as is possible in science. No doubt being raised by Mayr did no harm. Although it took a while, Ghiselin succeeded in forcing this view to the consciousness of the scientist who needed to notice it. For this reason, he deserves a lion's share of the credit, long lists of precursors notwithstanding. Lamarck (1809.104) of all people held a similar view, remarking that men "who strive in their works to push back the limits of human knowledge know well that it is not enough to discover and prove a useful truth previously unknown, but

that it is necessary also to be able to propagate it and get it recognize
Darwin (1899:1:72) agreed:

> Hardly any point gave me so much satisfaction when I was at work on
> the 'Origin,' as the explanation of the wide difference in many classes
> between the embryo and the adult animal, and of the close resemblance
> of the embryos within the same class. No notice of this point was taken,
> as far as I remember, in the early reviews of the 'Origin,' and I recollect
> in expressing my surprise on this head in a letter to Asa Gray. Within
> late years several reviewers have given the whole credit to Fritz Müller
> and Häckel, who undoubtedly have worked it out much more fully, and
> in some respects more correctly than I did. I had materials for a whole
> chapter on the subject, and I ought to have made the discussion longer;
> for it is clear that I failed to impress my readers; and he who succeeds in
> doing so deserves, in my opinion, all the credit.

Mayr also complains of the failure of biologists and philosophers to
read each other's works. Indeed, Mayr (p. 153) cannot recall the "writings of a single evolutionary taxonomist in the period from the 1930s to
1970 who did not reject the class concept of the species. But this went
entirely unnoticed by the philosophers. Evidently they did not read the
writings of the biologists and vice versa." In response to Mayr's hypothesis, I can attest only to my own experience. In graduate school and in the
years soon thereafter, I read *all* the works that Mayr mentions and others
as well. In graduate school, I noted Gregg's (1950) reference to the two
taxonomists who had objected to his treating species as classes. I also
read Mayr's (1963) *Animal Species and Evolution* in which he argued
that species are reproductive communities integrated by gene flow and
the 1966 translation of the revised version of Hennig's (1950) *Grundzüge
einer Theorie der Phylogenetischen Systematik*, in which he insisted that
species are as much individuals as are organisms. I even refereed Ghiselin's
1966 paper in which he first argued that species are not classes but individuals. I thought that the paper was quite good except for that last bit.
By 1974, I had changed my mind. Although the specific context was my
confronting Smart's (1963, 1968) arguments against the possibility of
uniquely biological laws, reading Ghiselin couldn't have hurt either.

But there is a difference between reading and understanding. Now
that the point about the ontological status of species has been emphasized with such great force and repeated so often (too often for the tastes
of some), it is obvious. At the time I was reading the works cited it was
not. The ontological status of species was only one issue out of many.
Several other issues seemed equally important and just as problematic;
for example, the criterion that is to be used to include geographically

avid L. Hull

ıated populations in the same genealogical species. Geographic isolates
ıat have not developed reproductive isolating mechanisms have the potential to exchange genes, but what if they do not? Northern and Southern
Ireland were once a single nation. They still retain the potential to become
one nation again, but until that potentiality is realized, they remain two
nations, not one. In the case of species, potentiality alone is apparently
enough. How come?

In any case, very few authors prior to the early 1970s gave any
indication that they saw the point of claiming that species are not classes,
let alone that they are individuals of some sort. Many to this day do not.
I am constantly being asked by practicing systematists and evolutionary
biologists what all the fuss is about. They do not see that such philosophical issues make any difference. Neither does Kitcher (1986). Mayr thinks
that philosophers have proven especially unable to see why species as
genealogical entities cannot be treated as classes. Perhaps so, but I think
that if a poll were taken, a higher percentage of philosophers of biology
than evolutionary biologists now see the point of these discussions, Kitcher
notwithstanding. In a review of Eldredge's (1985) *Unfinished Synthesis*,
Kitcher (1986:649) considers the thesis that species are individuals as
"one of the least promising suggestions in recent philosophy of science."
According to Kitcher, there is nothing worth fighting over. Those of us
who think otherwise are simply confused; more metaphysical muddles.
Needless to say, I think that Kitcher is mistaken. Not only is shifting
species from one traditional metaphysical category to another important
for both biology and philosophy, but also this is one of the rare instances
in which professional philosophers have played a salutory role in promoting an important conceptual shift in science.

Even though I am well aware that the realist boundaries in universities are those between departments, I would prefer not to discuss these
issues in terms of academic disciplines. I think that philosophers of science and scientists are engaged in the same activity. All that distinguishes
us is emphasis and training. Mutual understanding would be enhanced if
we were somewhat more charitable when we ventured into each other's
territories. From my own experience, scientists have been very helpful in
clarifying my understanding of various biological phenomena or in leading me to the latest research note. Mayr has been among the most helpful. Thus, I am somewhat dismayed by how frequently he lays the ills of
biology at the door of the traditional lovers of wisdom. But perhaps he is
reacting quite understandably to the condescension which too often per-
meates the writings of philosophers of science when they write about the
more philosophical efforts of scientists. For what it is worth, we would all
do better not to be so intellectually territorial.

Part IV

Classification and the Nature of Science

Chapter 8

Consistency and Monophyly*

INTRODUCTION

The three factors in phylogenetic taxonomy are phylogeny, the taxonomic schema, and the relation between the two. Of the three factors in the phylogenetic program, only phylogeny is of an empirical nature. The structure of the taxonomic schema is entirely a matter of logic, and the relation that this schema is to have to phylogeny is primarily a concern of the purposes of taxonomy. Too often controversies that have their basis in the formal aspects of taxonomy are argued as if they were empirical questions to be answered by collecting more and better evidence. One such controversy concerns the status of monophyly as a definitional criterion in phylogenetic taxonomy. The purposes of this paper are to show (a) that the relation George G. Simpson chose as the relation that is to hold between classification and phylogeny (which he terms consistency) is so weak that few implications of a type specific enough to contradict a classifier's views concerning phylogeny can be inferred from a classification; (b) that his requirement of minimal monophyly for all higher taxa is instituted in an attempt to assure that in those instances in which specific implications are derivable, a classification will not contradict phylogeny; and (c) that this attempt fails because he does not and cannot extend the requirement to include taxa at the species level. Whether or not a species is minimally monophyletic is an empirical matter. If all species are minimally monophyletic, then classification can at least in principle be consistent with phylogeny. On the other hand, if some species are in fact not minimally monophyletic, then within the confines of the Linnaean hierarchy a classification cannot be consistent with phylogeny—even in principle.

PHYLOGENY

The first factor in the phylogenetic program and the only one that is of an empirical nature is phylogeny, but even phylogeny is not a brute fact to be discovered merely by looking and seeing. Phylogeny, the subject

---

*Reprinted with permission from Systematic Zoology Vol. 13, No. 1, March 18, 1964, pp. 1-11.

atter of phylogenetic taxonomy, is an abstraction. It is an abstraction in two respects. First, it is inferred almost exclusively from morphological, genetical, paleontological, and other types of evidence and is not observed directly. Some critics of the phylogenetic position claim that in too many instances evidence for inferring phylogenetic descent is too sparse. Others criticize the very notion of inferring phylogeny from such indirect evidence regardless of how extensive it might be. These latter criticisms stem from a naive view of what an inductive inference is and of what justifies inductive inferences. Such criticisms, if valid, would annihilate most of what is known as empirical science. As valid as the former criticisms may be and as invalid as the latter certainly are, neither will be discussed in this paper. Phylogeny will be the given of classification.

The second respect in which phylogeny is an abstraction is fundamental to taxonomy and important to this paper. Certainly the most easily discernible unit in phylogeny is the individual organism. It is equally certain that phylogeny is the result of individuals giving rise to other individuals. But the basic unit in phylogeny for taxonomic purposes is not the individual. Some abstraction from the individual, such as a population or a species, is classified. As Simpson puts it, "Classification involves only groups; no entity possible in classification is an individual" (Simpson, 1961). Another way of putting the same point is that names of taxa are not defined extensionally as sets of individuals. The properties of individuals statistically analyzed are the defining properties of names of taxa. Some authors have suggested defining species names extensionally, for example, John R. Gregg (Gregg, 1954). Although such a treatment might have its set-theoretical advantages, not only is it contrary to taxonomic practice but also it has logically untenable consequences for taxonomic theory.

THE LINNAEAN HIERARCHY

The second factor in the phylogenetic program is the taxonomic schema. Traditionally this schema has been the Linnaean hierarchy, a system of mutually exclusive classes and classes of classes. Parker-Rhodes (1957) describes the logical basis of hierarchical classification as follows. "The required mathematics is that of set-theory; the elements of the sets are specimens, and the sets themselves are circumscriptions, such that by a finite series of observations every specimen can be unambiguously included in or excluded from any given circumscription. It is easy to define logically 'descriptions' to serve as operational procedures for doing this. A 'hierarchy' is a system of sets, here called 'taxa,' classified in ranks from one to n inclusive, such that the members of a taxon of rank n are taxa of rank n—one, the specimens being counted as of rank 0; and such that no two taxa of the same rank have any member in common. The 'extension' of a taxon is the join or set-sum of the extensions of its members, the extension of a taxon of rank 1 being the taxon itself; the members of an extension are specimens, whereas those of the corresponding taxon are other taxa."

One peculiarity of the Linnaean hierarchy which logicians find exceedingly nettlesome (for example, Gregg, 1954, and Beckner, 1959) is the practice known as monotypic classification, the failure to subdivide a taxon for one or more category levels. The purpose of monotypic classification is to indicate that a particular undiversified taxon is extremely divergent from other related but highly diversified forms. Gregg derives a logical contradiction from the practice of monotypic classification in his set-theoretical reconstruction, which indicates only that his reconstruction is inadequate.

Two restrictions of the form of the Linnaean hierarchy are crucial to this paper: taxa cannot overlap in membership; and once separated, two taxa cannot be again reunited at a lower level. As Woodger (1937) expressed, the first restriction, taxa "are such that if we take any two of them they either have no members in common or one is wholly contained in the other." As a result of the difficulties to be discussed later in this paper, some taxonomists are prepared to waive the nonoverlapping property of taxa (Parker-Rhodes, 1957). No one has suggested waiving the second restriction. As long as the two restrictions mentioned previously are adhered to, the Linnaean hierarchy will remain a constantly diverging affair.

Everything that has been said thus far concerning the rules for generating a hierarchy has been of a formal nature. None of the restrictions mentioned resulted from phylogenetic considerations. As a pure schema, the structure of the Linnaean hierarchy is entirely a matter of logic. The way the world is makes no difference. Although logical schemata like the Linnaean hierarchy are in principle free from empirical considerations, they are usually constructed with an eye to what they are to represent and how they are to represent it. However, in the case of the Linnaean hierarchy, its logical form was determined *before* evolutionary theory was introduced and without phylogeny in mind. Linnaeus devised his system to classify discrete species especially created by God. It was to represent the relative overall similarity of species, or some divine plan, but *not* phylogeny. With the advent of evolutionary theory, the phylogeneticists adopted the Linnaean hierarchy as the mode of taxonomic representation without investigating the implications of its structure for the purposes of phylogenetic taxonomy. It is not at all surprising that a logical schema constructed for one purpose proved inadequate for a radically different purpose. However, when the two conflicted it was not the form of the hierarchy that was modified, but the purposes of phylogenetic taxonomy. Instead of adding subsidiary devices to the modes of representation permitted by the Linnaean hierarchy, the phylogeneticists successively weakened the relation which was to hold between a classification and phylogeny. First, taxonomy was to *express* phylogeny. Then it was only to be *based upon* phylogeny. Now Simpson has so reduced the relation that at best classification is only to be *consistent* with phylogeny.

CONSISTENCY

The third factor in the phylogenetic program is the relation between phylogeny and the taxonomic hierarchy. This relation provides the correspondence rules for the taxonomic schema. Simpson (1961) discusses classification as a mode of representation in the following quotation:

> It has often been and still is occasionally said that the purpose of evolutionary classification is to express phylogeny. It is, however, true that no form of classification yet devised, certainly not the Linnaean hierarchy, is really able to express phylogeny, at least not in the sense of presenting it fully and unequivocally. . . . Evolutionary taxonomists have always recognized the fact already considered notorious by Darwin, but they have sometimes said that classification expressed phylogeny when they meant that it is *based on* phylogeny or is a *partial* expression of it. . . . The statement that evolutionary classification is based on phylogeny has also been open to misunderstanding. It has been taken to mean that such classification follows entirely from lines of descent and their branching as shown in the usual diagram of a phylogenetic tree. . . . It is preferable to consider evolutionary classification not as expressing phylogeny, not even as based upon it (although in a sufficiently broad sense that is true), but as *consistent* with it.

The relation between mode of representation and what is represented is often a reciprocal one. In part what the mode of representation can represent determines what is considered the subject matter of the science; in part the preestablished subject matter determines what mode of representation is devised. For example, *that* there is an absolute zero on the absolute scale is a result of the adoption of the ideal gas scale of temperature measurement; *what* the precise numerical value of absolute zero is in degrees centigrade is a fact that can be discovered only by investigating the properties of actual gases (Toulmin, 1953). The interplay between the formal and empirical factors is one of the most difficult and controversial aspects of science. The same situation would be expected to prevail in the science of taxonomy and it does. In the preceding quotation from Simpson, what the relation between the taxonomic schema and phylogeny is *called* is of little importance. However, the shift in Simpson's terminology does give an indication of the direction in which he is moving. He is successively weakening the relation between classification and phylogeny. In this paper, the term "represent" will be used in a logical sense. A logical schema can represent its subject matter in several ways. At one extreme, it can be a pictorial representation, as a light-ray diagram represents optical phenomena in geometrical optics or a dendrogram represents phylogeny in taxonomy. At the other extreme it can be a rather abstract representation, as a theory represents a range of phenomena or language represents the world. Classification began at the pictorial extreme. It has now moved to the other.

The word that Simpson chose to characterize the relation between classification and phylogeny was "consistent." Consistency is usually quite a stringent requirement. As Simpson (1961) interprets it in classification, it is anything but stringent. He says, "A consistent evolutionary classification is one whose implications, drawn according to stated criteria of such classification, do not contradict the classifier's views as to the phylogeny of the group." Simpson's definition is notable in two important respects. First, consistency is defined as a relation *from* classification *back* to phylogeny. Second, it is defined in terms of being *non*contradictory.

Although Simpson always treats consistency as a relation between classification and phylogeny, he never directly addresses himself to the problem of what inferences *from* a classification *to* a phylogeny are valid. All of the discussion preceding and following his definition of consistency give criteria for constructing a classification *given* a phylogeny. The omission is not as serious as it might have been because the inferring techniques which were used to construct the classification in the first place determine what inferring techniques can validly be used to reconstruct the original phylogeny. For example, the laws of geometrical optics can be used to determine what images will be projected on the retina of a person's eye when he views a particular scene. Given the retinal image, the same laws can be used to reconstruct the original scene. The odors or sounds which were present in the original scene cannot be reconstructed from the retinal image because they were not constructed as part of the image in the first place. The same situation exists in classification as a mode of representation.

The reciprocal inferences characterized in the preceding example are complicated in taxonomy because neither the relation between phylogeny and classificaton nor the relation between classification and phylogeny is a one-one relation. The inferring techniques as outlined by Simpson are such that from a single phylogeny numerous classifications can be inferred, and that from any one of the numerous classifications numerous phylogenies can be inferred. Simpson's definition of consistency is a direct result of the one—many—very many progression in moving from a phylogeny to a classification and back to phylogeny again.

Simpson says that a classification is consistent if it does not contradict the classifier's views as to the phylogeny of the group. What Simpson means can be put in two different ways. A classification is consistent if at least one of the phylogenies inferable from it is the phylogeny from which the classification was originally constructed. Some of the other phylogenies implied by the classification might happen to contradict the classifier's views concerning the phylogeny of the group, but as long as not *all* possible reconstructions are incorrect, the classification can be held to be consistent. Perhaps a better way to put the same point is that most implications of a classification are neutral with respect to phylogeny. No particular phylogenetic relationship is implied. Only several are definitely denied. A classification is consistent as long as all of the implications validly inferred from it are at least neutral with respect to phylogeny. None specifically contradicts it. The limits of the inferring techniques permitted by Simpson will be discussed in the following sections.

THE DENDROGRAM

The dendrogram is usually (but not always) the intermediary mode of representation between phylogenetic evidence and a classification. Like any mode of representation, it is capable of representing only certain relationships. What it can and cannot represent depends on the limitations of its form. Within these limits, what it does and does not represent depends on the use to which it is to be put. In phylogenetic taxonomy, the dendrogram is intended to represent phylogeny in almost a pictorial way. It represents phylogeny on a two-dimensional surface employing branching and diverging lines. The horizontal axis represents degree of divergence, parallelism, and convergence. The vertical axis represents development in time. Lines splitting and splitting again represent diversification. Thus, a line splitting into two lines represents a species splitting into two descendant species. Two lines splitting at different levels on the vertical axis represent two species splitting at different times. Degree of divergence, parallelism, and convergence cannot always be represented so unequivocally because too many factors are involved. Even a three-dimensional dendrogram would not be adequate to represent all niceties of phylogenetic development in these respects. Nothing in the form of the dendrogram prohibits two lines converging to form a single line. If the basic unit used

in the dendrogram is the species and if a certain species is polyphyletic a
the species level, then the relationship could be represented by the
dendrogram. Of course, if the basic unit was the genus, polyphyletic species could not be represented. Even though the dendrogram is not ideal
for representing phylogeny it can indicate relative antiquity, order of splitting, diversification, and polyphyletic descent at whatever level is chosen
as basic. It is less successful in indicating degree of divergence, parallelism, and convergence. As will be seen, classifications are still less successful in each of these respects.

A classification attempts to represent by an arrangement of words
what a dendrogram attempts to represent by an arrangement of lines. Its
only methods of representation are rank assignment and class inclusion
or exclusion. Such methods of representation are even less adequate for
representing phylogeny. Not only is the indication of degree of divergence, parallelism, and convergence even less accurate, but also the ability to show relative antiquity and order of splitting is lost — unless a price
is paid in simplicity and symmetry. For example, reptiles, birds, and mammals are all classes of the subphylum Vertebrata. Their being classed at the
same category level does not imply that they are all equally ancient; that
is, that the stem reptile, bird, and mammal evolved at about the same
time. Nor does it imply anything about order of splitting except that one
of these classes was not derived from both of the others. All three classes
may be descended from an immediately ancestral taxon, or one or more
of the classes may be descended from one of the others. In reality, mammals and birds are derived from certain ancient reptiles, and mammals
diverged from their reptilian ancestors before birds diverged from their
reptilian ancestors. Such information is not contained in classification.

Phylogeneticists from Darwin (1859) through Julian Huxley (1942)
to G. G. Simpson (1961) have argued that time as such is not crucial in
phylogeny, only degree of divergence and diversification. Thus, they feel
that they need not represent time in a classification — although in a
dendrogram of the same phylogeny they would indicate it. The justification for not indicating relative antiquity in classification may be that
time as such is not phylogenetically important. But even if it were important, it could not be represented in classification using the techniques
of representation permitted in the Linnaean hierarchy without a prohibitively asymmetrical redistribution of the taxa in the hierarchy. Ancient
forms, although they are extinct and undiversified, would have to be
assigned high rank while contemporary highly diversified forms would
often have to be assigned low rank. Coincidently, what *can* be represented by the Linnaean hierarchy is exactly what turns out to be phylogenetically significant.

Within the confines of the Linnaean hierarchy, only very general indications of relative antiquity can be shown. Nothing can be inferred precisely about the specific relative antiquity of a particular taxon. Ancient forms tend to be classified at a higher level than their relative diversification would otherwise warrant. Nevertheless, no arrangement of taxa implies unequivocally that one particular taxon evolved before, at the same time as, or later than another taxon. However, there is no reason why a subsidiary method of representation could not be added to those now permitted in the taxonomic schema. Just as the lengths of lines on a road map are not exact guides to mileage, rank assignment is not an exact guide to relative antiquity. But just as mileage is indicated on road map by numbers printed above the appropriate line segments, the relative antiquity of each taxon could be indicated in brackets after its name in the classification. Whether or not very many taxa would lend themselves to such precise dating and whether or not phylogeneticists would feel that the inclusion of such information in a classification is beneficial, the point to keep in mind is that if time is not indicated in a classification, it is not because of some illusive quality of phylogeny or some necessary deficiency in the purposes of phylogenetic taxonomy. It is a necessary consequence of the form of the Linnaean hierarchy. Incidentally, it may also be phylogenetically insignificant.

ORDER OF SPLITTING

Although the *length* of each line in a dendrogram is not translatable into a classification within the present form of the Linnaean hierarchy, one would think that at least the *order* of branching or splitting would have to be indicated if a classification is to lay any claims to being "phylogenetic." But as in the case of relative antiquity, any attempt at indicating order of splitting by means of rank assignment and class inclusion or exclusion would result in a prohibitively complex and asymmetrical classification. For example, mammals, lizards, crocodiles, and birds probably split from the main reptilian stock in that order. And yet mammals and birds are given class status, whereas the intermediate lizards and crocodiles are classed as reptiles. In general, a classification gives a very rough indication of order of descent, but at no one particular spot in the classification can it be decided exactly which taxon was derived from which. The only arrangement prohibited by the form of the Linnaean hierarchy is the classifying of one taxon parallel to two taxa both of which are immediately ancestral to it. As will be seen in the following section, such a practice is also prohibited by Simpson's canon of monophyly.

Perhaps order of splitting is another relationship which is not impc
tant to phylogeny. Coincidentally, order of splitting is another relationship which the present form of the Linnaean hierarchy cannot represent.
As in the case of relative antiquity, there is no reason why order of splitting could not or should not be indicated in a classification. A subsidiary
device could be appended to those now utilized; for example, subscripts
could be appended to the names of taxa, indicating, when known, which
taxa are descended from which. Thus, appropriate subscripts appended
to "Mammalia" and "Aves" would indicate that both mammals and birds
are descended from certain ancestral reptiles. The fact that classification
as it now stands does not and cannot provide such accurate information
does not mean that order of splitting is phylogenetically unimportant or
that it cannot be represented; it indicates merely a paucity of mode of
representation in the Linnaean hierarchy.

MONOPHYLY AND HIGHER TAXA

Thus far, according to Simpson's definition of consistency, no implications of a classification concerning relative antiquity can contradict
phylogeny because a classification is intended to imply nothing concerning relative antiquity. Nor is anything very precise implied concerning
order of splitting. Of course, a classification taken as a whole does give
some general picture of order of splitting, but at no one point in the
classification can it be determined exactly which taxa are descended from
which. This does not mean that given the rest of a classification a new
species cannot be placed with great precision. For example, given the
classification of the chordates as it now exists, the placing of the species
Homo sapiens in any phylum, class, order, family, and perhaps genus
other than those in which it is now classified would result in a classification that was inconsistent with phylogeny as we know it. However, to the
extent that reclassification of neighboring taxa is permitted, the placing
of a single species is not so definite.

The one thing implied unequivocally by a classification is that a
taxon cannot be classed at the same level with two other taxa if it happens to be derived from both of them. This is exactly Simpson's (1961)
definition of monophyly: "Monophyly is the derivation of a taxon through
one or more lineages (temporal successions of ancestral-descendant populations) from one immediately ancestral taxon of the same or lower rank."
Thus, according to Simpson's definition, a species is minimally monophyletic if it arises from a single species, or even from two or more subspecies in that species; it is not minimally monophyletic if it arises from a
single genus, even if it arises from two or more species in that genus; it is

ot minimally monophyletic if it arises from two or more genera; and so on, for other higher taxa.

In the early days of phylogenetic taxonomy, due in a great degree to Darwin's influence, a taxon was considered monophyletic if and only if it was derived from a single species. If the claim that all taxa are monophyletic in this strict sense is taken as a historical statement about taxa as they were classed in Darwin's day or even today, then it is false. The claim was undoubtedly intended as a dictum to the effect that taxa should be made monophyletic. However, if the dictum is taken literally, then even contemporary classifications would have to be so reorganized that they would cease to perform the primary task of any classification, that of organization and simplification. Phylogeneticists found themselves in a dilemma. Either they had to abandon the requirement of strict monophyly or else phylogenetic taxonomy ceased to be useful as a classification. It never occurred to them that the form of the Linnaean hierarchy was at fault or that a change in this form would resolve the dilemma. Instead, as they had done several times before, they modified the purposes of phylogenetic taxonomy. This time the modification took the form of a redefinition of the requirement of monophyly, weakening it in the way indicated in Simpson's definition.

According to the early strict sense of the word, whether or not any taxon was monophyletic was an empirical matter to be solved by the accumulation of evidence. After the strict definition of monophyly was abandoned, some taxonomists were led to the other extreme, maintaining that monophyly was entirely a matter of convention. Any taxon could be made monophyletic either by splitting it or by combining its ancestral taxa or both. The thesis of this section is that monophyly at the *supraspecific* levels is purely a formal matter, in the sense that all the limitations to the splitting and combining of higher taxa are purely formal constraints. If the evidence indicates that a particular genus is derived from two species that are classed in two separate genera, either it can be divided into two genera or else the two ancestral genera can be combined into one genus. Which of these alternatives is taken depends on the overall symmetry of the classification. No phylogeny is such that it could not be accommodated within the form of the Linnaean hierarchy at higher taxonomic levels.

For example, the species in the genus *Merychippus* are grouped together because their relative similarity and the fossil record indicate that they are closely related. As it turns out, not a single species is immediately ancestral to all of the species in *Merychippus*. They are derived from several species in the genus *Parahippus*. It is no coincidence that all of their ancestral species are grouped together in a single genus. If they weren't, *Merychippus* would not be minimally monophyletic. If all the species immediately ancestral to those in *Merychippus* were so disparate that the taxonomist would not want to group them in a single genus, his only alternative would be to divide *Merychippus* into two genera. No considerations other than the symmetry of the classification limit the taxonomist's reorganization. A taxonomist does not discover that an as yet unclassified higher taxon is monophyletic; he makes it that way.

Simpson's requirement of monophyly for higher taxa is a direct result of the form of the Linnaean hierarchy. It is just weak enough to permit considerable freedom in the arrangement of taxa in the hierarchy; it is just stringent enough to insure that any implications of a classification concerning order of splitting will be at least neutral with respect to phylogeny. In terms of the dendrogram, Simpson's requirement of monophyly states that no matter what higher taxon is chosen as basic, the lines in the dendrogram will be just broad enough to conceal any polyphyly. If the genus is chosen as the basic unit, and if all genera are made minimally monophyletic, then no two lines will ever converge on the dendrogram. Such a restriction is not a requirement of the form of the dendrogram; however, it is required by the form of the Linnaean hierarchy. Here is one more example of a mode of representation impressing its form onto its subject matter. Monophyly for higher taxa is a result of the form of the Linnaean hierarchy and not a result of the purposes of phylogenetic taxonomy or of phylogeny itself.

MONOPHYLY AND THE SPECIES

In the context of phylogenetic taxonomy with its emphasis on the biological definition of species, the significance of monophyly at the species level is quite different from its significance at higher levels. Originally, phylogeneticists held that taxa at all levels had to be monophyletic at the species level; that is, descended from single species. Now, according to Simpson, no taxon at any level—including the species level—has to be so strictly monophyletic. "Species are usually minimally monophyletic, that is, at the specific level, but they may be polyphyletic without thereby violating current taxonomic theory or practice, that is, be partly or fully interspecific hybrid in origin" (Simpson, 1961). Because of the biological definition of species, whether or not a group is a species is an empirical fact. Confronted with the fact that some species are definitely interspecific hybrids, Simpson lifts his formal requirement of minimal monophyly. However, the form of the Linnaean hierarchy has not changed; it still demands monophyly at all levels.

The only way that a species can fail to be minimally monophyletic is by two formerly discrete species converging to the extent that they interbreed and establish a viable hybrid species. The biological definition of species is not applicable to all taxa given species status, but for those species to which it is applicable, whether or not a group of organisms is a species, is an emprical matter. Decisions concerning species status might be difficult decisions to make because of the type and extent of evidence available, but they are decisions that can be made within the limits of precision demanded of an empirical science. Asking whether a group of organisms is a species is a very different kind of question from asking whether the members of a group of geometric figures are all triangles. However, unlike Simpson, some taxonomists make being monophyletic a definitional criterion for species. In this case asking for a clear-cut example of a polyphyletic species is like asking for a clear-cut example of a planet that does not revolve around a star or a triangle that does not have three sides. At worst, an example of a polyphyletic species is a definitional impossibility; at best it will not be a clear-cut example.

If Simpson's definition of monophyly is accepted, and if the biological definition of species is taken seriously, then whether or not a higher taxon is monophyletic is a formal matter; whether or not a species is monophyletic is an empirical matter. It is at least logically possible for a species to be polyphyletic. As it turns out, polyphyletic species are also physically possible because there are several cases of polyphyletic species in the plant kingdom, and there is evidence to indicate that successful hybridization can occur among animal species. In any case, to refute the claim that all species are minimally monophyletic, all that is needed is a single counterexample, and the existence of at least one polyphyletic species is indisputable. As a direct result of its form, the Linnaean hierarchy cannot represent biparental relationships—another reason for not permitting the individual to be the basic unit in either phylogeny or classification. The requirement of minimal monophyly for higher taxa is an insurance that no instance will arise in which this inadequacy will make a classification inconsistent with phylogeny. If a genus is derived from two species, the two species can always be included in a single ancestral genus, making the descendant genus minimally monophyletic. Or else, if not, the descendant genus can be split into two genera, each of which is minimally monophyletic. However, if a species is derived from two species, the two ancestral species cannot be included in a single species because of the biological definition of species. Nor could the hybrid species be split into two species each of which is minimally monophyletic. Thus, the descendant species cannot be *made* monophyletic at the discretion of the taxonomist.

By its very structure the Linnaean hierarchy cannot represent hybrid species. But according to Simpson's definition of consistency, a classification need not imply the correct phylogeny unequivocally. All that is necessary is that at least one of the implied phylogenies is the correct one. Not all the implied phylogenies can be incorrect, yet this is exactly the situation whenever a species is polyphyletic. Because of the form of the Linnaean hierarchy, no matter how a hybrid species is classified, the relation between it and one or the other of its ancestral species is denied. In no case does a classification necessarily imply the exact parentage of any species, but at least in the case of monophyletic species it does not contradict the correct relationship. Whenever a species is polyphyletic, classification will not be consistent with phylogeny.

Here again the form of the Linnaean hierarchy and the purpose of phylogenetic taxonomy conflict. Following the precedent set in similar past conflicts, the relation between classification and phylogeny could be weakened even further. However, any further weakening of the relation would mean that nothing at all would be implied by any species arrangement in a classification. Thus, Simpson's requirement that the implications of a classification must be consistent with a classifier's views concerning phylogeny would become trivial. If a classification implies nothing concerning phylogeny, it cannot conflict with phylogeny. In order for a classification to be able to conflict with phylogeny, at least one specific kind of implication concerning phylogeny must be validly implied by the classification. Any further weakening of the relation between classification and phylogeny would make any precise inferences impossible.

However, as in the case of relative antiquity and order of splitting, a subsidiary method of representation could be devised to indicate the biparental relationship in hybrid species. For example, the system of subscripts mentioned that would indicate order of splitting could be expanded slightly to indicate polyphyletic descent. The name of a polyphyletic species would have two subscripts appended to it. Such devices have not been adopted by any taxonomist and it is doubtful that they ever will be, in spite of Julian Huxley's early recognition that "new methods of denoting relationship are needed when we have to take into account the convergence and union of branches as well as their divergence" and his overly optimistic prophecy that systematics would "invent subsidiary terminologies to cope with the complexity of its data" (Huxley, 1942). Without some radical expanding of the form of the Linnaean hierarchy, however, evolutionary taxonomy is left in the predicament that a classification implies much in general about phylogeny but little that is specific, and that one of the tacitly assumed requirements of the Linnaean hierarchy forces a classification to conflict with phylogeny whenever it is polyphyletic at the species level.

/ *David L. Hull*

SUMMARY

Of the three main factors in phylogenetic taxonomy, only phylogeny is of an empirical nature, but even phylogeny is not just a brute fact. It is an abstraction, both because it is inferred from indirect evidence and because the phylogeny that taxonomists classify is the evolution of constructed entities such as species or populations. The Linnaean hierarchy is the schema tacitly assumed in taxonomy. Its only modes of representation are rank assignment and class inclusion or exclusion. Because all taxa at a particular level must be mutually exclusive and because two taxa once separated cannot be classed together again at a lower level, the Linnaean hierarchy is a constantly diverging affair. G. G. Simpson takes consistency to be the correct relation between the taxonomic schema interpreted in a classification and phylogeny. Consistency is a relation that is to hold from classification to phylogeny; that is, no implications validly drawn from a classification can contradict the classifier's views concerning phylogeny. Because the relation from phylogeny to classification and that from classification back to phylogeny are each one-many relations, few inferences specific enough to contradict phylogenetic views can be validly drawn from classification. Most implications of a classification are completely neutral with respect to specific phylogenetic relationships. This is not to say that nothing in general is implied by a classification concerning phylogeny, or that most implications of phylogenetic relationships are neutral with respect to classification. Within very broad limits, a classification is consistent if at least one of the possible phylogenies implied by it is the original phylogeny from which it was constructed. A classification is inconsistent if and only if all implied phylogenies conflict with the original phylogeny.

The methods of representation of the dendrogram are adequate for representing relative antiquity, order of splitting, diversification, and polyphyletic development on the level chosen as basic; they are less adequate for representing degree of divergence, parallelism, and convergence. The methods of representation permitted by the Linnaean hierarchy are most adequate for indicating diversification. Only a general indication of divergence, parallelism, convergence, and order of splitting are given, and relative antiquity is not shown at all. The form of the Linnaean hierarchy actually prohibits the consistent classification of polyphyletic taxa. Simpson's redefinition of the requirement of monophyly is calculated to make sure that polyphyly at higher levels never exists to the extent that it conflicts with the form of the Linnaean hierarchy. He is able to redefine monophyly so that it conveniently suits his purpose because any empirical situation that occurs can be accommodated by a redistribution of neighboring taxa. Such redistribution is limited only by broad formal restrictions. In the case of the species category, Simpson abandons his requirement of monophyly. Because of the biological definition of species, whether or not a species is monophyletic is an empirical matter; species cannot be made minimally monophyletic at the descretion of the taxonomist. Because of the diverging nature of the Linnaean hierarchy, it cannot represent biparental relationships among taxa. The form of the Linnaean hierarchy necessarily implies that all of its consituent taxa are at least minimally monophyletic. Some species, however, are not. Thus, at those places in the hierarchy where a hybrid species is classified, the classification cannot be consistent with phylongeny?

Using only the methods of representation permitted by the Linnaean hierarchy, the phylogeneticists tried to recast taxonomy into a radically new shape with radically new purposes. They were defeated before they began, not because no schema can express, be based upon, or be consistent with phylogeny, but because the schema they tacitly assumed was inadequate. Perhaps it is an exaggeration to say that the purpose of phylogenetic taxonomy has been to make classification represent the form of the Linnaean heirarchy instead of phylogeny. It is no exaggeration to say that its purpose has been to represent phylogeny whenever the form of the Linnaean hierarchy permitted. It has permitted very little. A classification implies much in general about phylogeny but little that is specific enough actually to contradict phylogeny. What is worse, in the one area in which specific implications are possible, classification actually does contradict phylogeny. One solution to this predicament is a modification of the form of the Linnaean hierarchy. How extensive a modification is made depends on how extensively evolutionary taxonomists wish to represent phylogeny.

Chapter 9

Karl Popper and Plato's Metaphor*

INTRODUCTION

As Thomas Kuhn (1970) has noted, philosophical considerations tend to come to the foreground in science only during scientific revolutions. Since a period in the history of science is considered a "revolution" because of the depth and extent of the changes that are occurring, the role of philosophy in scientific revolutions should come as no surprise. Philosophy is supposed to be about the deepest questions. One issue that has played a prominent role in the controversy over cladistic analysis has been the falsifiablility of scientific theories. A second philosophical issue closely connected to the first has engendered remarkably little heated discussion: whether species are spatiotemporally localized individuals (historical entities) or classes (in particular natural kinds). One explanation for the different responses to these two philosophical issues may well be that systematists can see the implications of falsifiability claims for their own research but fail to see what difference it makes whether species are individuals or classes. If what they are doing is not "science," then they are in real trouble, but whether species are individuals or classes, they can continue to classify as they have in the past.

The purpose of this paper is to explain the central role of theories, natural kinds, and natural individuals in present-day philosophy of science, the connection that these distinctions have to falsifiability, and the relevance that all of this has to the science of biological classification. In the past, too much of the discussion of these issues has been clouded by an intense concern over what Karl Popper did or did not say and/or intend (Bock, 1973; Cracraft, 1978; Kitts, 1977, 1978, 1980; Nelson, 1978a; Patterson, 1978; Platnick, 1977, 1979; Platnick and Gaffney, 1977, 1978a 1978b; Ruse, 1979b; Wiley, 1975). In this paper, I set out a philosophical position that is fairly common among philosophers of science. I also think that it is roughly the same position that Popper holds. If others think that he held quite different views on the subjects treated, fine. If not, then that is fine too. All truth does not reside in the writings of Sir

*Reprinted with permission from *Advances in Cladistics*, vol. 2, ed. N. Platnick & V. Funk
Columbia University Press, 1983.

Karl Popper. A particular thesis about science could be important and true even if Popper never mentioned it. Conversely, even if Popper held a particular view, it still could be trivial or mistaken.

In pointing out that Popper's principle of falsifiability applies to theories and not to methods, Platnick (1979:539) remarks that Popper's writings are "primarily concerned with the justification of particular scientific theories, such as the taxonomic hypothesis that spiders are more closely related to whipspiders than they are to scorpions." I agree with Platnick that Popper was concerned with the justification of scientific theories, but I do not think by "theories" he meant taxonomic claims of the sort Platnick indicates. Instead he was interested primarily in such theories as Newtonian theory and relativity theory (Popper, 1962:34). To make matters worse, in one place where Popper (1957:106107) discusses examples of biological taxa, he explicitly rejects them as the proper subject for his principle of falsifiablility (see also Popper, 1959:65).

Justifying my disagreement with Platnick over what Popper really said would require exegesis of the sort that only a Popper scholar would find interesting. Instead, I intend to discuss the issues—the nature of scientific theories and the possible connections that various sorts of taxonomic "theories" about such things as whipspiders have to such issues as falsifiability. If whipspiders are genuine natural kinds, certain things follow about the falsifiability of any statement containing reference to whipspiders. If this taxon is a numerical universal, with many but a finite set of members, quite different considerations follow. If species are individuals, yet another set of implications follow about the falsifiability of statements that refer to them. I happen to prefer the latter interpretation of species (Hull, 1976, 1978b), but all I do in this paper is examine each of these alternatives, not argue for any one of them.

PROCESS THEORIES

The term "theory" is used in a wide variety of ways in ordinary English. This same variety is reflected in scientific discourse. One common scientific usage is that a hypothesis when it is first suggested and has very little evidence to back it up is a theory. According to this usage, when Darwin thought his Galapagos finches belonged to different varieties of the same species, he had formulated a theory in the same sense as he was to do several years later when he started working on his theory of evolution. One problem with this usage is to find a term to apply to theories when they are reasonably well confirmed. "Fact" does not seem quite right. As it turns out, scientists continue to call theories "theories" even after they are well confirmed. Such complex and variable uses of the term "theory" make for very difficult communication.

Out of this great morass of terminology, philosophers have selected one sense of "theory" that they take to be of prime importance—the notion of a scientific theory as a set of statements attempting to capture some very general *processes* in nature. In most instances, especially in contexts dealing with the testing of scientific theories, this is what philosophers mean when they say "theory." In order to distinguish this usage from others, such theories are sometimes referred to as "process theories." Examples of process theories are relativity theory, evolutionary theory, and behavioral theory. In each case, the scientists who formulated these theories postulate a set of entities, properties of these entities, and processes in which they function. In relativity theory, two previously independent features of nature—space and time—are collapsed into one. According to Einstein, masses are supposed to move relative to each other in certain ways. In evolutionary theory, certain entities are supposed to interact with each other and their environments so that gene replication is differential. As a result, other entities, usually species, evolve. The basic entities of behavioral theories are organisms and their behaviors. In this theory, relationships are postulated between various sorts of conditioning regimens and rates of change in the behavior exhibitied.

Several observations must be made about theories of the preceding sort. They are intended to be completely general. They apply to *all* entities of the specified *sorts*, and part of the specification of these sorts is *never* spatiotemporal location. In the early days of physics, Kepler (1571-1630) postulated his famous laws about the paths that planets take around the sun. Two centuries later, Bode (1747-1826) suggested a comparable law about the relative distances of each planet from the sun. One problem with these laws as elements in a more inclusive theory is that each mentions the sun, and the sun is a spatiotemporal particular. As frequently as this objection is raised to the analysis of process theories as being spatiotemporally unrestricted, it is very easy to handle. We currently consider a modified form of Kepler's laws to be part of Newtonian theory, but not Bode's law. How come? Because Kepler's laws are generalizable; Bode's law is not. Kepler's laws are generalizable not just to all planets orbiting the sun, but also to all planets orbiting any star whatsoever. They also turn out to be special cases of Newton's even more general laws of nature. Bode's law was reasonably accurate for the next planet discovered. However, it soon began to fall behind. Regardless of the opinions of some physicists in Bode's day, his formulation does not refer to a general feature of the universe. It turns out not to be true of the solar planets, but worse yet, it plays no role in any larger system of laws. Even if it had been true of our solar systrm, it would have been nothing but a peculiarity of this system, a result of the contingencies in its formation.

Perhaps philosophers pay too much attention to process theories, but I think the distinction that they recognize in science between these sorts of theories and all the other things that scientists commonly term "theories" is crucial to our understanding of the world in which we live. Eternal, immutable processes need not have existed in our universe, but they seem to. Because such processes exist, process laws and theories are possible. The nice thing about process theories, to the extent that one has them right, is that they allow inferences regardless of where one happens to be or the time at which one makes the inference. If true at all, process theories of the sort under discussion are just as true in Lawrence, Kansas, as in New York City, just as true now as they were 200 years ago. Our *understanding* of these processes changes through time, but a very basic assumption of science as well as philosophy is that these processes *themselves* do not change from place to place and from time to time. We may be wrong about the existence of such processes, but to abandon the search for them is to abandon a central element in science from its inception. It does not matter whether or not we continue to call Kepler's laws or Bode's law "laws." What does matter is the *roles* that such formulations play in scientific theories. Spatiotemporal generalizations can and do play very different roles in science from those of generalizations that are spatiotemporally limited and restricted.

FALSIFIABILITY

Philosophers commonly note a correlation between the *form* of a statement and how easily it can be tested. Universal statements of the form "All A are B" can be falsified quite easily (a single counter-instance will do it), while they can never be completely verified. Of course, all sorts of errors can creep into the process of testing that have nothing to do with the asymmetry between the falsifiability and verifiability of universal statements. For example, in either case, one might have made an observational error. The point is that, everything else being equal, universal statements can be falsified but not verified. This asymmetry explains the emphasis that philosophers put on falsifiability over and above verifiability. However, this asymmetry holds *only* if the sorts of entities referred to are genuinely unrestricted universals. They must refer potentially to indefinitely many exemplifications. For example, "All planets travel in ellipses around a star" refers to planets and stars in general. At any one time, a finite number of planets may exist in the universe, but the preceding statement refers to *all* planets—past, present, and future. If the universe turns out to have a finite duration, then it might well turn out that in retrospect only a finite number of planets existed, but this is the *only* restriction possible without infringing upon the universality of genuinely universal statements of the form under discussion.

Just the opposite state of affairs obtains with respect to particular statements of the form "Some A are B." Philosophers take such claims to be asserting that at least one A exists that is also a B. Such claims are easy to verify but impossible to falsify conclusively. For example, all one need do to verify a statement such as "Some planets rotate in the same direction as they revolve" is to find a single planet that does. Once one has done that, this statement has been verified. Once again, all sorts of errors can enter in from other sources, but they are irrelevant for the point under discussion. Particular statements can never be conclusively falsified for the same reason that universal claims cannot be verified—they refer to indefinitely many entities. Not until *all* planets had been studied could one claim that *no* planets rotate in the same direction as they revolve, and one cannot study all planets because some no longer exist and others have yet to come into existence.

Some statements are universal in form but refer to a determinate and finite number of entities. Such statements are commonly termed numerical universals. The usual way of limiting the extension of the classes to which a numerical universal applies is by appending spatiotemporal requirements. For example, "All the justices of the Supreme Court of the United States of America in 1970 were male" is a numerical universal. Like unrestricted universal claims, numerical universals are relatively easy to falsify. A single counter-instance will do. However, they can also be verified. In this case, the task is quite easy because the number of entities referred to is quite small. The statement that all the stars in our galaxy in 1970 were of a certain brightness is still a numerical universal, even though the numbers involved are very large and in point of fact no one is going to be able to check them all. The contrast between these two sorts of universal statements is between *in-principle* possibility and *in-practice* possibility. I myself have little patience with in-principle claims, but the asymmetry between falsifiability and verifiability as it is set out in the philosophical literature turns on this distinction.

No one pays much attention to the final permutation of the contrast between universal and particular statements—numerical particulars like "Some justices of the Supreme Court of the United States of America in 1970 were Democrats." Such statements can be both falsified and verified. A single confirming instance verifies such a claim; a finite number of observations can falsify it.

Finally, philosophers distinguish statements that are singluar in form. In singular statements, a specified entity is said to have (or lack) a property or to belong to a class. "Mars is a planet" and "Douglas was a Supreme Court justice in 1970" are both singular statements. Singular statements can be verified as readily as falsified. No asymmetry exists.

Several observations can be made about the preceding sorts of statements. One concerns the problem of induction, one of the major problems in the history of philosophy. If scientific theories and their constituent laws refer to indefinitely many entities of a sort, it is difficult to see how we can infer with any justice from our limited set of observations to the universe at large. Out of all the planets that surely must exist in the universe, we have made observations on only a few, and they are limited to one corner of a single galaxy. What right does a physicist have to say that *all* planets travel in elliptical paths on the basis of such a limited and biased sample? In response to the gravity of the problem of induction, some workers have retreated, claiming that scientists really should talk about what they have immediate evidence for and nothing else, stick with the facts and nothing but the facts. The result is such an impoverished notion of science that most workers learn to live with the problem of induction. However, the point I wish to make is that the very statement of the problem of induction depends on the difference between genuine and numerical universals. There is no problem in going from observations on each of the nine Supreme Court justices to a genenalization about them. At the moment, eight are male and one female. If laws of nature can refer to numerical universals, then there is no problem of induction.

Needless to say, both philosophers and scientists value genuinely universal statements more than any of the other sorts. They are very difficult to come by and afford tremendous power once discovered. Statements of all three sorts—universal, particular, and singular—might be true, but we can do very different things with these different sorts of statements. One important function for singular statements is to test those that are universal in form. The first observation of the red shift or paramecia exchanging genetic material was extremely important because of the implications such observations have for our general understanding of the universe. Later observations are not nearly so important.

One final asymmetry between verification and falsification concerns differences in the way that scientists treat universal generalizations that they take to be true and those that they take to be false. One of the most important features of modern science is that laws do not exist in isolation but are organized inferentially into theories. Hence, a confirming instance of one law indirectly supports all the other laws in the theory, while a disconfirming instance of a particular law indirectly threatens these other laws. When a scientist formulates a new law, he tries to fit it into the accepted body of beliefs in his day. To the extent that it is true, it *must* fit even if it means that the entire theoretical edifice accepted to the time must be dismantled and reassembled. Much more is expected of the universal generalizations that we think might be true than of those we take to be hopelessly false. The first sort must fit together to form theories, while the second sort are simply dumped into a heap.

The question now becomes what sort of statements taxonomic statements are. Let's say that spiders are more closely related to whipspiders than they are to scorpions. What sort of statement is this?

CLADISTIC STATEMENTS

Much of the acrimony that has arisen over the application of the principle of falsifiability to taxonomic statements has concerned not this principle, but the nature of taxonomic statements. Advocates of different schools of taxonomy argue for different sorts of classifications. Pheneticists want to reflect various degrees of overall similiarity, cladists want to reflect as clearly and unambiguously as possible cladistic relations, while evolutionists want to include both grades and clades in their classifications. For the purposes of this paper, I will limit myself just to the goals of cladistic taxonomy. In the English-speaking branch of the cladistic research program, an underlying tension has existed right from the start between two different but related notions of "cladistic analysis"—a generic sense and a specific sense. Sometimes the term "cladogram" seems to be used to refer to a branching diagram that reflects only *one* phylogenetic relationship—sister-group relations—while trees attempt to represent several additional sorts of phylogenetic relations, such as common ancestry and degrees of divergence. In this specific use of the term "cladogram," the entities involved are species, the events speciation, and the characters evolutionary homologies.

However, in many, possibly most, discussions of cladograms, a more general notion can be discerned. Cladograms in the generic sense are branching diagrams in general. Cladistic analysis then becomes the science of branching diagrams. The entities under investigation can be biological species, but they might as well be languages, texts, or possibly societies (Platnick and Cameron, 1977). I think such a discipline is certainly worthwhile, as worthwhile as the attempt to produce general analyses of selection processes or functional systems. It helps to know which features of a situation are essential to it and which are merely the results of the particular subject matter. In connection with cladistic analysis in the general sense, I have only two complaints. One is that I am still not sure how spartan cladograms in the generic sense are supposed to be, and frequently I am unable to tell which sense of cladogram is intended or even if the author actually thinks that there are two senses of "cladogram" and related terms and not one. Because these two senses of "cladogram" are related as species to genus, misunderstanding is easy. Everything that is true of cladograms in the generic sense must be true of cladograms in the specific sense, but not vice versa.

As I read Wiley's *Phylogenetics* (1981), he is concerned with cladistics in the specific sense. One possible goal for a classification is to indicate the order in which sister groups split off in their evolutionary development. In Wiley's system, the basic taxa are species, higher taxa must be monophyletic in Hennig's (1966) sense, and the characters used to group species into taxa of greater and greater inclusiveness are evolutionary homologies. According to Wiley (1981:25, 76, 121-122):

> An *evolutionary species* is a single lineage of ancestor-descendant populations which maintains its identity from other such lineages and which has its own evolutionary tendencies and historical fate.
>
> A *monophyletic group* is a group of species that includes an ancestral species (known or hypothesized) and all of its descendants.
>
> A character of two or more taxa is *homologous* if this character is found in the common ancestor of these taxa, or, two characters (or a linear sequence of characters) are homologues if one is directly (or sequentially) derived from the other(s).

As one might expect, Wiley's (1981:97) notion of a cladogram is equally tied to phylogenetic development:

> *Cladogram.* A branching diagram of entities where the branching is based on the inferred historical connections between the entities as evidenced by synapomorphies. That is, a cladogram is a phylogenetic or historical dendrogram.

Wiley uses the term "dendrogram" for "cladogram" in the generic sense. A dendrogram is a "branching diagram containing entities linked by some criterion" (Wiley, 1981:97).

Nelson and Platnick are interested in Wiley's sense of cladistic analysis, but would prefer to consign most of the considerations that Wiley raises to "arboristics." They themselves would also like to develop cladistic analysis in a more general sense and define their terms to have as little connection as possible with any particular subject matter, including phylogeny and the evolutionary process. For example, they state that in "this book, then, species are simply the smallest detected samples of self-perpetuating organisms that have unique sets of characters. As such, they include as species the 'subspecies' of those biologists who use that term"

(Nelson and Platnick, 1981:12). With respect to such terms as "cladogram" and "cladism," they state that these "terms unfortunately were intended to have an explicitly evolutionary significance pertaining to the actual branching or speciation events, of phylogeny" (Nelson and Platnick, 1981:139). They themselves set out a much more general notion. "*Clado-grams* depict structural elements of knowledge" (Nelson and Platnick, 1981:14). The place at which Nelson and Platnick(1981:140-142) discuss the relation of their notion of cladistic analysis to phylogeny and evolutionary theory is important enough to quote in its entirety:

> *Synapomorphy Patterns.* The majority of the monophyletic groups spec-ified by Hennig's type of trees (cladograms) might be considered evolu-tionary in nature, reflecting actual speciation events—branchings of the historical process. And so might the groups specified by phenetic trees. But *all* of Hennig's groups correspond by *definition* to patterns of synapomorphy. Indeed, Hennig's trees are frequently called synapo-morphy schemes. The concept of "patterns within patterns" seems, there-fore, an empirical generalization largely independent of evolutionary theory, but, of course, compatible with, and interpretable with reference to, evolutionary theory. The concept rests on the same empirical basis as all other taxonomic systems (the observed similarities and differences of organisms). But the concept is not wholly independent of evolutionary theory, for one of its basic elements (nature of evidence) is synapamorphy, or shared advanced character. The other basic elements, namely rela-tionship (what is evidenced) and monophyly (what is resolved), are defin-able only with reference to the branching diagram, and carry no neces-sary evolutionary connotation. Indeed, the concept of synapomorphy may be definable purely as an element of pattern—a unit of resolution, so to speak. If so, Hennig's system would be understandable not merely as the "theory" of "phyletic" taxonomy but as the general theory of taxonomy of whatever sort.

As I read the preceding passage, the goal of cladistic analysis in the generic sense is to become as independent of any particular theory of evolution as possible. No matter how the evolutionary process occurs, the principles of cladistic analysis can handle the resulting patterns. Nel-son and Platnick also seem to want to make cladistic analysis as inde-pendent as possible from phylogeny itself. The one term in their vocabulary that seems inextricably connected to phylogeny, and hence to some ver-sion of evolutionary theory, is "synapomorphy." Many sorts of patterns exist in nature. Patterns within patterns is only one of them. The most likely explanation for such patterns is modification through descent. "Synapomorphy" would seem to be definable only in connection with such phenomena. Hence, even "cladistics" in its most general sense is not quite theory free. Nelson and Platnick (1981:151) state that the cladogram satisfies the concern about futile theorizing of Blackweider, Sokal and Sneath, and other taxonomists, for that theorizing, or at least a large part of it, belongs to the three-step process of deriving a tree from a cladogram.

As Nelson and Platnick state, *most* of the theorizing enters into cladistic analysis only in the construction of trees. However, *some* theorizing enters into the construction of cladograms in even their most general form. Some notion of modification through descent seems presupposed by the notion of synapomorphy. The closest Nelson and Platnick (1981:152) come to eliminating this last vestige of "theory" in cladistics is suggesting that an operational notion of homology might be nothing more than common properties that "might possibly serve as a useful basis for discussion;" see also Nelson and Platnick's (1981:162-165) explication of general synapomorphy.

In setting out the views of Nelson and Platnick (1981) and those of Wiley (1981) before them, I intend no criticism. Both programs seem worthwhile to me. My intent is to indicate where these programs differ so that confusion about what each takes to be the import of taxonomic statements can be avoided. Nor do I intend any position on which of these views are really those of Hennig and which "transformed." It might well be the case that Nelson and Platnick's version of cladistic analysis belongs as the derived state of a cladistic transformation series, or it might well be that their views are the underlying character that integrates the cladistic transformation series into a series. All that matters for the purposes of this paper is the character of taxonomic statements. Are they genuinely unrestricted universals, numerical universals, or particulars?

AGGREGATES AND NATURAL KINDS

One of the most characteristic features of systematics from its inception to the present is the desire to produce a natural system of classification—to carve nature at her joints, to use Plato's apt metaphor (Grube, 1958:31). Organisms can be grouped together in a variety of ways, some more clearly natural than others. Vertebrata originally seemed the paradigm example of a natural taxon, Vermes the paradigm hodgepodge. Many criteria have been suggested to mark the distinction between genuine natural kinds and mere aggregates, none of them totally successful. The criterion that I think holds out most promise is figuring in a genuine law of nature. Any kind term that appears in a law of nature is a genuine natural kind. Any putative kind term that does not is suspect. Of course, this criterion merely shifts the problem to distinguishing laws of nature from other sorts of generalizations. Once again, none of the suggested criteria work all that well, but the one I favor is figuring in a scientific theory. A putative law of nature that remains in inferential isolation from all other putative laws is suspect.

One might opt as well for William Whewell's (1840) consilience of inductions. To the extent that a hypothesis formulated to account for one sort of phenomenon can also account for another, it is likely to be part of the framework of the universe, not an accidentally true universal generalization. In many respects, Whewell's criterion supports the one I prefer. I could fault no one for adopting it (as in Ruse, 1976), just so long as the consilience of inductions is distinguished from a similar but quite different sort of consilience. Following Simon (1969), Wimsatt (1974) describes the process of individuating highly organized systems in terms of different principles of decomposition. When these different principles produce spatiotemporal boundaries that are largely coincident, then it is likely that we a have a natural *individual*, not a natural *kind*.

Throughout the history of philosophy, philosophers have viewed species as paradigm examples of natural kinds. However, the laws in which the names of particular species appeared were not thought of as causal or process laws, but as laws of co-existence, laws that express the ways in which characters go together. Just as a sample of gold under certain conditions is always characterized by a certain color, malleability, ductility, and so forth, a member of a biological species under certain conditions is always characterized by a certain type of hoof, body covering, horn, etc. On this view, statements such as "Gold is malleable" and "*Bos bos*" has horns are both laws of nature, laws of coexistence. The point to note is that this view of taxonomic statements was held *before* the wide acceptance of evolutionary theory. When a new theory is introduced into science, not everything changes. However, if species are supposed to be the things that evolve, if the traits that characterize organisms are supposed to be evolutionary homologies, and if taxa must be monophyletic in an evolutionary sense, then it follows that species cannot be spatiotemporally unrestricted. Hence, they cannot be natural kinds.

Because I have argued for the preceding conclusion at great length elsewhere (Hull 1976, 1978b), I will only sketch the relevant considerations here. In the philosophical literature for the past several hundred years and before, natural kinds are held to be eternal, immutable, and discrete. By "eternal," philosophers mean that natural kinds are somehow built into the framework of the universe. At any one time, a particular natural kind might not be exemplified, but when the conditions are right, it will become exemplified. At one stage in the history of the universe, perhaps no gold atoms existed. However, when atoms of the right sort become formed, gold becomes exemplified. Hence, gold can come and go with respect to exemplification, but given the fundamental makeup of the universe, gold is a permanent possibility. I do not see how anyone who thinks species are the things that evolve can maintain that they are in any sense eternal. They come into existence and pass away and, once extinct, can never come into existence again. This last claim does not concern empirical possibilities, but is a comment on how evolutionary biologists conceptualize species. The dodo is now extinct. As unlikely as it might be, perhaps a species of wild turkey might produce a species that is genetically identical to the dodo. The same array of genomes that characterized the dodo at one point in its evolution (if we knew what this array actually was) also characterizes this newly evolved species. Do these organisms belong to one species or two? As I read both Wiley (1981) and Nelson and Platnick(1981), the answer to this question is two. All three of these authors require genealogical connections for species status.

Natural kinds are also supposed to be immutable. Although a sample of lead might be transfromed into a sample of gold, these elements as natural kinds remain unchanged. The immutability claim refers to the kinds, not their exemplifications. Natural kinds are supposed to be things that remain unchanged in the face of change. Perhaps natural kinds do not exist. Perhaps all is flux. My intent at present is to emphasize that both philosophers and scientists for a very large portion of the history of Western thought have considered natural kinds to be immutable. An organism might change its species, but the species itself remains unchanged. I think the conclusion is inescapable: if species evolve, than they are not immutable.

Natural kinds are also supposed to be discrete; that is, the boundaries between them in *conceptual* space must be absolutely sharp. Real objects may not exemplify a particular natural kind perfectly; for example, no sample of gold may be perfectly pure. But the boundaries themselves are perfect. A geometric figure made up of straight lines has a determinate number of sides. If it has three sides, it is a triangle. If it has four sides, it is a quadrilateral. And so on. One can attempt to square a circle, but in the process one is not changing circularity into squareness, or blurring the conceptual boundary between the two. One modification of traditional views of natural kinds popularized by Wittgenstein (1953) is that the conceptual boundaries between certain natural kinds may be inherently fuzzy. They are not thereby, he argued, unreal. Although fuzzy boundaries are not as easy to deal with as sharp boundaries, they do not make knowledge acquisition impossible (for a fuller discussion, see Hull, 1984).

By now it should be apparent that if species are natural kinds and natural kinds are eternal, immutable, and discrete, then species cannot be temporary, mutable, and indefinite. Thus, it would seem that species cannot evolve. Several responses are possible at this juncture. One can merely redefine "natural kind." Just because early workers defined "natural kind" in one way does not mean that we have to be stuck with such a definition forever. My only objection to this response is that one cannot change the definition of a term and expect it still to function the way it did in the past. Definitions occur in *systems*. To the extent that a system is well integrated, any change has ramifications. One of the ramifications of allowing natural kinds to come and go (*really* come and go, not merely being exemplified and ceasing to be exemplified) is that they can no longer function in laws and theories. Well, one might respond, simply change the definitions of *these* terms. Allow descriptions of variable, changeable processes to count as laws of nature. I am not as wedded to laws of nature as some philosophers, but even I want to draw the line somewhere. On the preceding suggestion, statements like "All the screws in my car are rusty" become laws of nature. In fact, it is difficult to see how to refuse the title to *any* statement, no matter how particularized. Nixon *does* have hair, but terming such a statement a law of nature seems to trivialize the notion past any significance.

One might jump at the chance. All these distinctions that philosophers make are just so much scholasticism. At times, usually late at night after a hard day, I sometimes empathize with such a conclusion, but the next morning I'm all right again. Although the distinctions that present-day philosophers are struggling to make are not good enough, I do not think that they can be modified piecemeal or junked altogether. Redefining "natural kind" so that natural kinds are temporary and change into each other, sometimes gradually, sometimes abruptly, and still expecting them to play the same role that they always played in traditional philosophical systems, is as improbable as redefining "triangle" so that the sum of its internal angles is never 180° and expecting geometry to remain unchanged in the process. Nothing stands in the way of a scientists redefining "natural kind," but in doing so, he has cut himself off from the philosophical literature in which this term occurs. He cannot define "natural kind" in terms of the *negation* of *every* characteristic that philosophers have used to define it in the past and then cite these philosophers to back up his own view of natural kinds.

In the past decade or so, a new view has been introduced on the nature of biological species—that species are individuals and neither classes in general nor natural kinds in particular (Ghiselin, 1974a, 1981). Under this new perspective, the goal of systematics is still to produce *natural* classifications, to cut nature at her joints. Plato intended his metaphor to be a metaphor. Just as organisms have their natural joints, so does nature in a more abstract sense. However, under the new perspective that Ghiselin has proposed, Plato's metaphor is not quite so metaphorical. If one views phylogeny as species evolving and splitting to form a tree, then this tree is an individual of sorts. A "natural" place to subdivide such a tree is at one of its joints, at a speciation event. If a species is largely disassembled at speciation, then it ceases to exist, and two new species come into existence. If a species can bud off new species while retaining its own integrity and cohesiveness, then it can continue to exist after speciation events.

According to Wiley (1981:75), species are individuals in the sense that they function in the evolutionary process. If we take a temporal time-slice across the species that constitute a higher taxon (even if these higher taxa are genuine clades), the result lacks any internal cohesion of the sort that characterizes species. The species that make up a higher taxon belong together because of *history*, not *process*. As Wiley (1981:75) puts his position, "Species are units of evolution, and higher taxa containing more than one species are not units of evolution (Wiley, 1978); rather, natural supraspecific taxa are units of history." And units of history are precisely what natural kinds are *not* supposed to be. Of course, if neither the evolutionary process nor phylogeny has anything to do with classification on one's view, then none of the preceding follows.

For Wiley, at least, neither species nor higher taxa are natural kinds because both are spatiotemporally localized. Because the connection between Nelson and Platnick's version of cladistic analysis and evolutionary theory is very tenuous, the nature of taxa in their system is more problematic. If biological taxa for them are natural kinds, in the usual sense of this term, then organisms from all over the phylogenetic tree could well be included in the same taxon. In fact, nothing stands in the way of organisms in different phylogenetic trees (for example, the proverbial life on Mars) belonging to the same taxon. One would think that a group of systematists who find paraphyletic taxa an abomination would not readily accept taxa that have no phyly at all. However, in order to discern taxa as natural kinds, one must discover defining traits. If these traits are synapomorphies and this concept is not wholly independent of evolutionary theory (Nelson and Platnick, 1981:142), then it would seem that the taxa preferred by Nelson and Platnick are as spatiotemporally localized as those of Wiley. One can term monophyletic taxa "natural kinds" if one wishes, but these natural kinds are spatiotemporally localized "natural kinds." Hence, they can play none of the traditional roles that natural kinds have played in past analyses of science. Redefining terms is a perfectly legitimate activity, but it does not change the world. One can call shoe leather a steak, but such linguistic maneuvering does not make the eating any better.

Another possible way of interpreting taxonomic statements that might justify treating them as unrestricted universals depends on the relation between cladograms in the generic sense and the trees compatible with them. Quite a few papers have been written on the number of trees that are implied by and/or are compatible with a particular cladogram. The number depends on the conventions adopted in cladogram construction. For example, if it is permissible to add an infinite number of unknown taxa to any cladogram, then all cladograms imply the same number of trees—an infinite number. Thus, even though any one taxon might have a finite number of organisms as members, cladograms referring to taxa would nevertheless refer to an infinite number of possible taxa.

This particular way of salvaging the universality of cladograms has a slight air of artificiality to it. If this convention is allowed, all statements become transformed into universal claims with an infinite extension. Hence, claiming that a statement is genuinely universal means nothing, because it no longer marks a distinction. "Nixon has hair" can be transformed into a universal claim by a comparable strategem. Such artificialities to one side, no cladogram that is supposed to refer in any way to phylogeny—even by as slender a thread as Nelson and Platnick allow—can be treated in this way. At one time on earth, life did not exist. In the distant future, all life will have gone extinct. Hence, no matter how one defines species, only a finite number of species can actually have existed in the terrestrial phylogenetic tree.

FALSIFIABILITY AGAIN

One might well claim with some justification that Popper (1962:34) designed his principle of falsifiability to apply to scientific theories that refer only to unrestricted universals. But perhaps Popper intended his principle to apply to other statements as well. Or, regardless of what Popper may or may not have intended, perhaps his principle of falsifiability can be extended to other sorts of statements. I find it hard to interpret claims about the cladistic relationships between whipspiders and scorpions to be scientific theories akin to Newtonian and relativity theories. Hence, any use of the principle of falsifiability would have to be an *extension* of this notion, perhaps not falsifiability in a narrow, crabbed sense of this principle but at least falsifiability in the Popperian "spirit" (Settle, 1979).

I have absolutely nothing against such a project. Taxonomic statements should be testable. However, some care must be taken in reasoning from what a philosopher says about the falsifiability of genuinely universal claims and other sorts of claims. If taxa are viewed as numerical universals, then the asymmetry between verifiability and falsifiability disappears. Statements about numerical universals may be difficult to verify completely, but not impossible. Also, falsifiability in this sense has nothing to do with the problem of induction. There is no problem of induction with respect to numerical universals. Similar implications follow if one interprets taxa as individuals. No asymmetry of inference exists in attempting to verify or falsify singular statements, and falsifiability in this sense, again, has nothing to do with the problem of induction. I am not sure Popper would be very pleased with this extended notion of falsifiability, because it lacks the two characteristics of this notion that he found most important (Popper, 1962:41-42). Of course, scientists need not have the same interests as philosophers. For their purposes, an extended notion may be preferable. In this connection, I have only one warning. If one adopts a principle of falsifiability in some extended sense, one is likely to read some peculiar things about falsifiability in the philosophical literature. The same can be said about natural kinds. If one adopts a notion of natural kind that accepts temporary, changeable entities with fuzzy borders as natural kinds, then the philosophical literature on this topic is liable to be very confusing.

THE IMPORTANCE OF PARTICULARS

I think one reason that scientists want to keep species as natural kinds—even if they must transmute this notion into its negation in the process—is that terms like "natural kind," "law," and "theory," have an honorific sound to them, while terms like "aggregate," "particular," and "description do" not. One might be tempted to refer to a *mere* description but not a *mere* law of nature. However, as understandable as the temptation may be, I think it should be resisted. I agree with those philosophers who maintain that the discovery of natural kinds and the theories in which they function is *necessary* for scientific understanding of the world in which we live. However, particulars and descriptions are *just as necessary*. More than necessary, I think that finding appropriate descriptions and significant particulars are *important* steps forward in science. Granted, many more particulars exist in the universe than natural kinds. One might go down in history for discovering a previously unknown natural kind. It is very unlikely that the discovery of yet another particular is likely to be viewed as a comparably momentous occasion. However, coming to understand the nature of the *sorts* of particulars that can function in various sorts of processes is a significant contribution.

For example, if the levels-of-selection controversy ever becomes worked out in a satisfactory way, that will be quite an accomplishment. One element in that resolution will be a specification of the general characteristics of the sorts of things that can be selected. I think that there is good reason to believe that the only things that can be selected are things that have the general charactieristics that organisms have. Perhaps organisms are not the *only* entities that can be selected, but any entity that can be selected will also be a spatiotemporally localized particular (Hull, 1980b). Genes, chromosomes, gametes, and organisms are clearly particulars. They are also prime examples of entities that function in selection processes (Lewontin, 1970). It follows, then, that if other entities, such as colonies and populations, can be selected *in the same sense* as genes, chromosomes, and organisms, then they too must be particulars.

CONCLUSION

Once, before an audience of scientists, I remarked that one should watch out when a scientist starts doing philosophy. I was interpreted by some as saying that scientists should not do philosophy, as if philosophy were the sovereign property of philosophers. Nothing could have been further from my intention. I do not even like distinguishing scientists from philosophers. Academic degrees to one side, the attempt to understand the world in which we live is a unitary process. Varying elements in this activity can be found in the work of any one inquirer, some more empirical, some strictly formal, some methodological, still others so fundamental that they warrant being termed philosophical. The only real differences between people who are officially scientists and those who are officially philosophers is their emphasis and training. Scientists tend to emphasize and have most of their training in dealing with empirical issues; philosophers tend to emphasize and have their training in dealing with terminological and conceptual issues. But these activities are so intertwined that they cannot be separated usefully. It never occurs to me to go through my own papers deciding which sentences are scientific and which philosophical. I could not do it if I tried, and I see no reason to try.

My remark about watching out for scientists when they do philosophy was intended to emphasize that scientists do not always approach philosophy in a totally disinterested, dispassionate way. They usually are engaged in a particular scientific research program and turn to philosophy to aid them in this program. The preceding is *not* intended as a criticism. I think that this is the way in which scientists *should* approach philosophy. If they find a particular philosophical analysis appropriate to their own undertaking, that is one mark in favor of that analysis. However, other scientists with other concerns might disagree. Philosophers are *not* judges empowered to adjuducate scientific disputes. Nor are they weapons to be used by one group of scientists against another. They are as much a part of the process of rational inquiry as are scientists themselves.

One should also watch out when philosophers do philosophy. They too have their research programs.

In this paper, I have attempted to point out the connections between process theories, natural kinds, natural individuals, falsifiability, and biological classifications. According to most present-day philosophers of the sort that concern themselves with science, scientific classifications should be evaluated according to the contributions they make to the construction and improvement of scientific theories (process theories). They can do so either by providing natural kinds of the sort that function in laws of nature, or else by individuating theoretically significant individuals to function in natural processes, or both. In either case, scientists are striving to carve nature at her joints. On this same view, the testing of classificatory statements is intimately connected to the testing of the relevant theories, and testing is not a simple matter. Naive falsificationism, as the name might indicate, is not good enough. But testing remains fundamental to science.

Chapter 10

Cladistic Theory: Hypotheses
That Blur and Grow*

Most empirical investigators simply "do" science. They study stars, continents, species, and hairdressers. A few investigators, however, are engaged in a self-referential activity—investigating empirical investigators. Certain psychologists study the psychological makeup of scientists. They are well aware that anything that they find out must be equally true of them (Mahoney 1979). Sociologists study the social organization characteristic of scientists. Once again, anything that they find about scientists in general should also be true of sociologists, including sociologists of science (Cole 1975). Although historians are not sure that they are scientists, they are engaged in an empirical activity—chronicling the course of human events, including the history of science. Historians dismiss the histories of science written by scientists as hopelessly biased toward the views that eventually prevailed. Historians propose to treat phlogiston, caloric, and oxygen in equal detail, because these concepts were all equally important in the history of what we now term chemistry. To someone living in Rome, all roads may well appear to lead to Rome, but the historian must be truly a man without a contry. Problems arise when historians attempt to write histories of historiography. Self-reference once again rears its ugly head (Hull 1979a).

Most present-day philosophers of science are spared the problem of self-reference because they do not claim to be engaged in an empirical activity. Some claim instead to legislate proper scientific method on the basis of strictly logical considerations. For example, given the logical character of universal laws and deduction, it follows that laws of nature can be falsified but not verified. Other philosophers content themselves with analyzing scientific language. What *do* biologists mean when they use the term "species" or "adaptation"? If philosophers did the sort of empirical research implicit in such an undertaking, they would be engaged in an empirical, albeit linguistic activity. Too often, however, such activities degenerate into the philosopher's telling us what "we" mean by these terms.

---

*Reprinted with permission from *Cladistics: Perspectives on the Reconstruction of Evolutionary History*, ed. T. Duncan and T. Stuessy. New York: Columbia University Press, 1984.

This particular circumlocution is a code phrase for the philosopher setting out a proposal for how scientists *should* use the terms being analyzed. Thus far, scientists have rarely found these proposals worth adopting.

To the extent that commentators on science make empirical claims about science, they are committed to presenting evidence for their views and are open to the self-referential gambit. The obvious response to anyone who claims that all generalizations are false is, How about the generalization you just made? Similarly, if generalizations must be falsifiable in order to be meaningful, can that generalization itself be falsified? One response is that such principles as the principle of falsifiability are meant to be metaphysical, not empirical. They are not scientific but metascientific. This response is fine as far as it goes, but it leaves unanswered the question of how metaphysical claims are to be evaluated. Why should one prefer the philosophy of Kuhn (1970) to the philosophy of Feyerabend (1975) or Popper (1959)? Philosophers have been very free about telling scientists how to choose between competing scientific theories. Their efforts at doing the same for themselves have been embarrassingly jumbled.

In my own research, I have studied the controversies surrounding pheneticism and cladism in theoretical taxonomy as examples of scientific change. I am hoping to make them test cases for claims that commentators on science make about science. For example, Kuhn and Feyerabend are widely interpreted as saying that scientists who hold different paradigms should not be able to communicate with each other. Their paradigms are incommensurable. In my own research, I have found that scientists frequently do have difficulty in communicating with each other, but this difficulty does not covary universally with their holding different paradigms. Sometimes people who share a paradigm have greater difficulty in communicating with each other than particular scientists who hold different paradigms. The preceding is based on my own perceptions derived from studying the reactions of scientists in one school reading and commenting on the papers of scientists in other schools, for example, in the refereeing process. Some people are very good at reading a paper in the context of a paradigm that they do not themselves hold; others are not. In addition, most of the scientists whom I have interviewed over the years share my perceptions. It is reassuring that my view of science from the outside coincides with the views of those on the inside. If these views are mistaken, then either they are biased by some factor that influences scientists and commentators on science alike, or two errors are being produced by an extremely unfortunate and unlikely confluence of independent factors. But what is a commentator on science to do when his views conflict with those of his subjects?

My study of the pheneticists and cladists over the past 15 years or so has led me to two important conclusions about scientific development: first, that self-interest is an extremely important factor in determining the way that science is conducted, and second, that scientific research programs need not and sometimes do not have any changeless essence. I do not take these features of science to be accidental. They are inherent to the scientific process. The problem is that when I have informed my subjects of these conclusions, they (surprisingly) tend to agree with the former and deny with flashing eyes and whitened knuckes the latter. I had expected just the opposite reaction.

Most scientists are lucky in that their subjects cannot object to the conclusions drawn about them. However, my subjects can. In this case, who is right, the investigator or the subjects? In this paper, I cannot begin to set out the data that I have gathered that have led me to the preceding two conclusions about science. That will have to await a much longer work. However, I will attempt here to explain why the scientists whom I have studied do not share my perceptions about their own research programs. These differences in perception have resulted from my considering the questions, What is phenetic taxonomy and what are its basic principles? and What is cladistic taxonomy and what are its basic principles? The answers given to these questions continue to raise heated disputes, not because the particular answers are wrong, but because of the underlying assumption that conceptual systems such as pheneticism and cladism can be characterized by eternal, immutable essences. A common assumption that I have discovered in the scientists whom I have studied is that their research program may have changed as far as incidentals are concerned, but not with respect to its basic goals and axioms. I find this conviction peculiar, especially in the case of evolutionary biologists, who have devoted their lives to showing that the parallel conviction for biological species is false.

ALTRUISM IN SCIENCE

Is science unique or is it like all other human institutions? From my own studies of the recent disputes in theoretical taxonomy, I have come up with the unremarkable conclusion that it is a little bit of both. Many social theorists, on the basis of philosophical considerations, have concluded that by and large people are selfish. They look after themselves and their own first, then worry about humanity at large. Sociobiologists have come to the same conclusion from purely biological considerations. People, like all organisms, should be genetically selfish. Although the social devices for doing so might be complex and obscure, people should devote the vast majority of their efforts to increasing their own inclusive fitness. I happen to think that these global conclusions about the basic selfishness of people in social contexts are not totally accurate. Social institutions can become so involved, and the interconnections so obscure, that people are not infrequently led to behave in ways that are indistinguishable from those commonly thought of as "altruistic." Systems of reciprocal altruism, when practiced by knowledgeable and highly rational people, can easily boil down to reciprocal selfishness. When practiced by people who are easily influenced by appeals to justice and the common good, they can generate genuine altruism.

The question then becomes, What about scientists? Officially, they claim to be altruistic, devoting themselves selflessly to searching after truth for its own sake. One alternative is to conclude that, yes, scientists are unique. While others scramble after the usual rewards in society, scientists are above the fray. Perhaps medical doctors perform twice the number of operations warranted by the circumstances in order to make more money, but scientists would never stoop to such behavior. They are a special breed. A second alternative is that scientists are deceiving themselves and everyone else. They are as interested as everyone else in making money, looking after their families, putting aside a little for a rainy day, and so on. Regardless of how scientists attempt to make it appear, the disinterested quest for truth takes a second seat to their own selfish goals. Elsewhere (Hull 1978a) I have argued for a view that reconciles these two extreme perspectives: Scientists are as self-interested as everyone else but have adopted peculiar goals. The usual rewards of society are secondary to those that are awarded by the scientific community. The primary goal of scientists is to have their ideas accepted by other scientists. In science *use* is the chief form of acceptance. The best thing that one scientist can do for other scientists is to use their work and give them an appropriate citation. The second best thing is simply to use it.

If the mutual cooperation (or exploitation) just described were all there was to science, it would not be especially peculiar. Many other groups are organized in a similar fashion. But in addition, built into the fabric of science is a system of mutual testing. Scientists check their own work, but more importantly, they also check each other's work. Scientific hypotheses must be testable and on occasion actually be tested. If scientific hypotheses existed in isolation, this requirement would be prohibitive. There are simply too many hypotheses. If scientists were required to test hypotheses one by one before they could be incorporated into the body of scientific knowledge, they would still be working on Ptolemaic astronomy. However, scientific hypotheses do not occur in isolation but in inferential systems—scientific theories. Thus, testing one hypothesis in a system serves as an indirect test of the other hypotheses in the system. In point of fact, scientists spend very little time in testing each other's views. They do not have to. The penalties for doing shoddy or deceptive research are so great because it seriously damages the research of other scientists (Zuckerman 1977). Of all self-policing professions, science is genuinely self-policing, because it is in scientists' own self-interest to check the work of their fellow scientists when it bears on their own research. Scientists do not test hypotheses at random. They concentrate on those hypotheses that either support or refute their results. The nice thing about the organization of science is that it does not require scientists to go against their own self-interest. The good of the individual usually coincides with the good of the group.

THE NATURE OF SCIENTIFIC CHANGE

A motto appears beneath a mural in the Zoological Laboratories at the University of Pennsylvania. It reads, Hypotheses That Blur and Grow.[1] A conflict which has characterized evolutionary biology from Darwin and Huxley to the present has been between gradualistic and more saltative (punctuational) forms of evolution. On the one hand, Darwin maintained the traits appear very gradually and change just as imperceptibly in the evolution of a group. Only rarely does a new trait appear fully formed in the space of a single generation. As a result, taxa tend to blur into one another. In speciation a single species becomes subdivided into two large populations, which gradually diverge from each other as minor changes accumulate. In phyletic evolution a single species changes so much through time that organisms from later time-slices might have very little, if anything, in common with organisms from earlier time-slices. On the other hand, saltationists have varied from extreme positions to views so moderate that they blend imperceptibly into gradualism. For example, Schindewolf (1950) maintained that all higher taxa come into existence in the space of a single generation by means of a mechanism similar to Goldschmidt's hopeful monsters (1940). More recently, Eldredge and Gould (1972) have suggested a microsaltationist view. From an ecological perspective, speciation is a continuous, populational affair, but from the paleontological perspective, it is saltative.

Is scientific development saltative (revolutionary) or gradual (evolutionary)? From my own studies, the answer seems to be, once again, a lttle bit of both. The change from pre-Darwinian to post-Darwinian views of species is about as abrupt as any change in the history of science. The development of evolutionary theory in the interval has been largely gradualistic, with spurts of activity soon after the turn-of-the-century rise of Mendelian genetics, in the 1920s when evolutionary theory began to be mathematized, and again in the 1940s with the new synthesis (Mayr and Provine 1980). Currently we seem to be undergoing another flurry of activity. To the extent that speciation is marked by the appearance of a new trait universally distributed among the organisms belonging to this new species and absent from all other species, biological species can be treated "essentialistically." Such essences are neither eternal nor immutable, as Aristotle thought, but at least they are discrete. Certainly the classification of plants and animals would be much easier on a saltationist's view of evolution. The same can be said of scientific development. If each new theory contains a hypothesis distinct from those contained in its competitors, then scientific theories might grow, but they would not blur.

I have tried out both of the preceding hypotheses about science on scientists. My suggestions about the role of self-interest in the growth of scientific knowledge seem to strike a responsive chord. Scientists can clearly see this behavior in others and, on a little reflection, in themselves. Perhaps this is not all there is to science, but it is certainly part of the story. The reaction to my suggestion that scientific development is to some extent gradualistic has been near universal and surprisingly vehement denial. Perhaps biological evolution is gradualistic, but not scientific development. Scientific research programs emerge full blown in the writings of their advocates and remain unchanged thereafter, at least in their essentials. For each research program, a set of fundamental tenets exists that *all* and *only* the advocates of this program hold. Anyone who rejects or modifies one of these basic tenets cannot possibly be a member of the school. The motto implicit in this attitude is that in science nothing less than total allegiance is acceptable. One must hew to the party line or get out.

The preceding view of scientific development may be accurate. I hope not. I find it extremely repugnant. Occasionally, a group of scientists who are attempting to change the direction of science might be fortunate enough to guess right on all issues and never have to change their minds thereafter. Although such happy first guesses are possible, I do not think that they can be as frequent as scientists themselves claim. Besides, I had always thought that one important element of scientific methodology was a mechanism for forcing scientists to change their minds. Perhaps theologians and philosophers doggedly stick with outworn views, but not scientists. Perhaps religious and political groups demand total allegiance, but not groups of scientists. Why then do scientists perceive their own groups in ways antithetical to the very nature of science? I think that the answer to this question is in part sociological. It also depends on how we tend to conceptualize the world.

The first distinction that must be noted is that between groups of scientists and conceptual systems, for example, between the Darwinians and Darwinism. The most common way to define groups and systems is in terms of shared beliefs. The Darwinians are all those scientists who accept the basic tenets of Darwinism. According to Kuhn (1970:176), "A paradigm is what the members of a scientific community share, *and*, conversely, a scientific community consists of men who share a paradigm." If scientific communities are *defined* in terms of shared beliefs, then the preceding claim is a tautology. Kuhn, however, maintains that the two should be and can be defined independently. Scientific communities are to be defined in terms of their social relations, not shared beliefs. Scientific communities, such as the Darwinians, should be defined in terms of cooperation, not agreement. Do all the members of the same scientific community agree with each other, especially about fundamentals? Kuhn claims that yes, they do. The answer that I have discovered in my own research is that no, they do not.

For example, both J. S. Henslow and Richard Owen helped Darwin in his early years. Was either of these men a Darwinian? From a conceptual point of view, Owen was much closer to Darwin than was Henslow. In fact, after the publication of the *Origin*, Owen claimed priority, while Henslow was never able to accept even Darwin's most basic premise that species evolve. Even so, Henslow helped facilitate the reception of Darwin's theory, while Owen worked against it. From a sociological perspective, Henslow was a very important Darwinian, even though he disagreed with Darwin's views. Owen was not. In my own research, I have discovered that scientists can work effectively with other scientists even when they disagree—even over essentials. For example, C. D. Michener was an important member of a group of scientists who, beginning in the late 1950s, investigated ways to make taxonomic judgments more quantitative and explicit—a group that eventually came to be known as the pheneticists, or numerical taxonomists. That Michener belonged to this research group can be documented in a variety of ways, from quantitative measures, such as counting citations, to impressionistic measures, such as asking those concerned. That he never fully shared in the views most commonly and vociferously enunciated by his fellow pheneticists can also be documented. For example, in one of the earliest publications in their emerging research program, Michener and Sokal (1957) explicitly acknowledge differences of opinion—including differences over basics. That Michener's participation in this research program decreased markedly some time prior to 1973 can also be documented. All one needs to do is count references to Michener in Sokal and Sneath (1963) and compare them to references to Michener in Sneath and Sokal (1973). The decline is precipitous.

Defining social groups in terms of social relations is vastly superior to defining them in terms of adherence to shared beliefs. In point of fact, most of the scientists working together to push a particular view of the world will agree with each other, but an important fact about science is that scientists can cooperate even when they disagree. Group membership is extremely important in science. It helps to have fellow workers who will read your papers, comment on them sympathetically, build on your work in their own papers, and so on. It also helps to have sympathetic referees, members on funding panels, and the like. I find such sympathies not in the least shameful. When new research programs are beginning to get underway, they need relatively gentle treatment. Only gradually should more rigorous standards be imposed.

Social groups contain some people who are central, others who are more peripheral. A person who begins as a peripheral member can become more prominent, and vice versa. People can join a group; others leave it. If a group lasts long enough, it is guaranteed to have a total changeover in membership. What is true for social groups in general is true, I think, for groups of scientists. Both Michener and Paul Ehrlich were among the earliest pheneticist. Like Michener, Ehrlich had early reservations, but in Ehrlich's case they were soon overcome, and he became an enthusiastic supporter of the pheneticist viewpoint (Ehrlich 1961). Later he questioned one of the fundamental tenets of phenetic taxonomy—the existence of a general-purpose classification based on some measure of overall similarity. Ehrlich suggested that possibly the most one can hope for is numerous special-purpose classifications (Ehrlich and Ehrlich 1967). Eventually both Michener and Ehrlich ceased active participation in the phenetic school, Michener to work on his bees and to emerge as one of the enemies of cladism, Ehrlich to return to his butterflies and to lobby for ecological sanity.

The question now becomes, were both men pheneticists? When did they cease being pheneticists? From the point of view of shared beliefs, Michener was never very much of a pheneticist. Although he though that this set of beliefs was worth pursuing, he himself accepted very few of the tenets of phenetic taxonomy. Initially, Ehrlich did, but then he came to question one of the most fundamental principles of phenetics. Even though he no longer publishes in taxonomic theory, Ehrlich considers himself a pheneticist, at least in spirit. From a sociological point of view, both Michener and Ehrlich were once pheneticists; at present neither is. As should be obvious by now, the distinction between groups of scientists and the views they may or may not share must be carefully distinguished and kept distinct if confusion is to be avoided. The problem of how to define conceptual systems remains.

CONCEPTUAL DEVELOPMENT

The easiest way to define a conceptual system is in the same way that many taxonomists define the names of taxa—by means of a particular set of tenets that are severally necessary and jointly sufficient for membership. According to this view, certain tenets are essential, others only incidental. One can have reservations about one or more of the incidental tenets and still be counted as accepting this particular conceptual system. However, one may not have reservations about any of the essential tenets. According to this view, conceptual systems are like territories in a Platonic heaven that people enter and leave as they change their minds. As neat as this way of treating conceptual systems may be, it does not lend itself to conceptual change. If one checks, one discovers that no two "Darwinians" held precisely the same view about evolution. Darwin thought that it was gradual, directed primarily by natural selection, and doubtfully progressive. Huxley agreed but opted for more saltative evolution. Gray held out for some sort of directed evolution, and so on. If Darwinism is defined typologically, then the only inhabitant of this Darwinian heaven was Darwin and there is some doubt about him. Conceptual change is possible in this world view, but it is as jerky as an old silent movie.

Another alternative is to view conceptual systems, as many systematists view the names of taxa, as "cluster concepts." In such systems, certain beliefs are more important than others, but none is necessary. In order to accept a conceptual system using this view, all one has to do is to accept enough of the more important tenets. According to this interpretation, some divergence of opinion is allowed. This second definition of conceptual systems allows conceptual change to be more gradual. Even so, only a certain amount of conceptual change is possible without the abandonment of one conceptual system for another. The biological analog is the division of a single lineage into chronospecies as it undergoes phyletic evolution.

Another alternative is to allow the composition of conceptual systems to change through time *without* subdividing it into separate systems, as long as the system remains cohesive and the change is continuous. According to this interpretation, conceptual systems form historical entities (Ghiselin 1974a, 1981; Hull 1976, 1978b; Eldredge and Cracraft 1980; Wiley 1981). This is the alternative that I prefer. According to this view, conceptual systems themselves can evolve. The evolution may be saltative (revolutionary), but it can also be more gradual (evolutionary). Neither mode is ruled out *a priori*. However, this view also has counterintuitive implications, because views that at one time were competitors to a particular conceptual system can later become part of that system. A proposition can "evolve" into its contradictory.

Although this implication may seem counterintuitive, it accords with the actual evolution of conceptual systems. For example, Darwinism in its early years consisted of a certain cluster of beliefs, not all of them mutually consistent: most versions of Darwinian evolution in Darwin's day were progressive, although Darwin's own version was not. In the interim, Darwinism has evolved to exclude this component, as well as others. Two recent challenges to the synthetic theory have been neutralism and punctuational models of speciation. Of course, Darwinism at various stages in its development included the acceptance of some neutral characters and various sorts of saltative evolution, but at the time that the neutralists and, subsequently, the punctuationalists wrote, these positions were viewed as "challenges." However, in a recent paper Stebbins and Ayala (1981) argue that both views belong in the "framework of the synthetic theory of evolution." How is this possible? Are there no limits to the cooptation that is possible in scientific development? The answer to this second question is, not much. Critics of the synthetic theory complain of its malleability, its ability to incorporate new discoveries and transmute challenges into new planks for its own platform. The mistake that these critics are making is thinking that this state of affairs is peculiar to the synthetic theory of evolution. On the contrary, it is the result of treating conceptual systems as historical entities. It is equally true of Mendelism, Newtonianism, and every other research program in science. Perhaps phyletic evolution is rare in biological contexts, but it is common in scientific development.

CLADISM, TRANSFORMED AND UNTRANSFORMED

In my early discussion about the contrast between scientific communities and their conceptual systems, I used pheneticists as an example. It is now the cladists' turn. Several authors have noted that cladism has become "transformed" during the course of its development (Platnick 1979). Have certain tenets remained unchanged in this process or has cladism been completely transformed? If the former, could anyone at the time have predicted which tenets would remain unchanged? If the latter, can a totally transformed cladism still count as the same research program? Early on, Hennig (1966) and Brundin (1966) set out what they took to be the principles of phylogenetics. They included such principles as dichotomy, monophyly, deviation, equal ranking of sister groups, and the extinction of ancestral species at speciation. More than this, both Hennig and Brundin viewed the principles of phylogenetics as being grounded in a particular view of the speciation process. For example, Brundin (1966:23) states quite explicitly:

172 / *David L. Hull*

It is apparent that the rule of deviation and concepts like plesio-
morphy and apomorphy, indeed all the concepts and principles of phylogenetic systematics, are and have to be based on the speciation process, its premises and phylogenetic meaning. The apomorph daughter
species is thus identical with the spatially isolated peripheral population
of the population genetics which, thanks to successful escape from the
rigid system of genetic homeostasis of the mother population, has been
able to benefit by the development of new adjustments and to acquire
reproductive isolation.

Is Brundin's claim about the theoretical foundations of phylogenetic
systematics one of the essential tenets of this school or only a personal
idiosyncracy? Did cladists never hold such views, do they still hold such
views, did they once hold such views and have now changed their minds,
or what? Answering such questions is not easy, but the task is further
complicated by facts about the politics of science. Science is a competitive affair. Scientists set out their views as clearly and comprehensively as
possible, emphasizing certain parts, hardly mentioning others. Critics then
select certain of these beliefs to challenge. Their choice is not entirely a
function of the original authors' intentions. Critics frequently pick what
they take to be the weakest tenets to criticize. They also tend to focus on
those aspects of other scientists' views that conflict most clearly with
their own system of beliefs. The latter must then decide which views to
defend. If they spend too much time defending a peripheral belief, it will
thereby be elevated to greater importance. If they refuse to respond to a
particular criticism, however, their silence is likely to be interpreted as
assent. For example, in a letter to Darwin, Charles Lyell (Wilson 1970:467)
observed that the "grand argument from absence of mammals & batra-
chians in Oceanic islands is probably felt to be strong by Owen as he has
not ventured to impugn it and therefore declined to bring it into notice."
    Did cladists really think that dichotomy was so important? Whether
they did or not, this was one of the tenets that elicited the loudest objections (Darlington 1970; Mayr 1974). As a result of both these objections
and the subsequent defenses, it became elevated in importance. Thus, any
change or abandonment is likely to appear to be a capitulation. Darlington
and Mayr hardly approached the cladistic research program from an
entirely disinterested, dispassionate perspective. The tenets of cladism that
they list as essential need not be taken at face value. They are likely to be
overly impressed by the ways in which cladistic methods differ from their
own, while pheneticists, such as Sokal (1975) and Sneath (1982), are
likely to emphasize quite different weaknesses. For example, Sokal is
unlikely to complain of the skepticism that cladists such as Nelson (1971,

1972, 1973, 1978b) show toward our knowledge of anything about phylogeny except sister-group relations.

For these same reasons, I do not think that the claims made by cladists themselves can always be taken at face value. They too are involved in the ongoing process of science. They too are liable to demote and promote views, depending on later occurrences. At the cutting edge of science, things are not always crystal clear, and degrees of commitment to particular hypotheses change from day to day. In retrospect, one is tempted to remember the doubts about ideas one has since abandoned and forget the periods of strong conviction. Thus, dichotomy does not look as important as it once did. It is a red herring invented by the opponents of cladistic analysis. If I myself had not witnessed and even participated in long debates over various principles of cladistic analysis, I would be more prone to adopt the current weighting of these principles.

I do not mean to imply that cladists are especially peculiar in this respect. All scientists reevaluate their beliefs. Nor do I mean to imply that changing one's mind is somehow bad. On the contrary, it is central to science. Neither do I think that the objective estimations are impossible to make. For example, any reading of the literature on cladistic analysis shows that monophyly was and continues to be much more important to the cladistic program than dichotomy. I can also understand why scientists tend to downplay any internal disagreements that might crop up. Deemphasis of disagreement among the members of a movement helps to maintain internal cohesion in the group.

Does cladism have an essence? If it does, was it always simply there in the works of Hennig, or did later cladists help to create this essence? In a recent paper on the transformation of cladistics, Platnick (1979:538) argues that, in spite of numerous changes, Hennig's "methods for analyzing data and constructing classifications from them, remain essentially unchanged." Using this interpretation, phylogenetics was from the start essentially a methodological program to develop the logic of constructing branching diagrams and classifications, and nothing else. Of course, Hennig's version included several elements, some of them empirical, as did the early pronouncements of other cladists, but these apparently were incidental to the essence of cladistic analysis.

It is difficult to evaluate such a claim. Certainly Hennig's phylogenetics always included a large methodological element, much more than many early critics realized. Many tenets that looked like claims about evolution were not. But I find it difficult to believe that cladistic analysis from the start was nothing but a formal calculus like set theory or matrix algebra. If it is so, I cannot understand the depth of emotion on both sides of the dispute. I can imagine mathematicians and logicians getting all

worked up over competing formal systems, but not scientists. If phylogenetic systematics from the beginning was really nothing but a methodological program, then many of those involved in this program, as well as
their opponents, were confused. If this claim raises the hackles of cladists
and anticladists alike, I feel obligated to add that this confusion was
extremely productive. I think that neither the proponents nor the opponents of the program could have been roused to expend so much effort on
developing the cladist research program if they had fully understood what
its essence actually was.

The extent to which cladism has been transformed has yet to be
appreciated. Initially, cladism had something to do with evolution, if not
the evolutionary process. It dealt with the splitting of branches on phylogenetic trees, the emergence of evolutionary novelties, and so on. In fully
transformed cladistics, all that is at issue is nested characters—regardless
of whether these characters coincide with speciation events or are themselves evolutionary homologies. At least, this seems to be the drift of
recent works in cladistic analysis (Rosen 1978; Patterson 1980; Nelson
and Platnick 1981). If I understand these authors, the argument is that
either characters can be organized into hierarchic patterns or they cannot. If a hierarchic pattern can be discerned by using a certain set of
characters, these characters are to be preferred. These characters may or
may not coincide with evolutionary novelties. It would, however, be quite
a coincidence if they did not.

I do not know whether the preceding interpretation is accurate. If it
is not, I fail to see how cladistic analysis can be simply "methods for
analyzing data and constructing classifications from them." If the elements of the analysis are some sort of biological species and the traits
evolutionary homologies, then cladistics contains at least two empirical
elements. In either case, in order to avoid confusion, two senses of
"cladistics" must be distinguished—a general sense, in which cladistics is
purely formal, a calculus for generating branching diagrams, and a more
special sense, that of the application of this calculus to certain aspects of
phylogeny as a biological phenomenon (Hull 1979b). I think that it is
cladistics in this special sense that has roused the passions of so many
biologists in the recent past, not cladistics in the general sense. Now that
this creative confusion has served its purpose, I suggest that it is time to
retire it.

The preceding discussion serves a second purpose as well. If the
essence of cladism is strictly methodological, the precise nature of this
methodology was not immediately clear to everyone concerned. I find
the desire to claim that the essence of cladism lay buried in the writings of
Hennig (or possibly Brundin) paradoxical. If Hennig set out the essence

of cladistic analysis in the beginning, then what credit can later cladists claim for themselves? As I look back over the past decade, its events do not look like a gradual uncovering of a truth that lay buried in Hennig's early writings. On the contrary, I think that later cladists vastly improved on Hennig's system. Perhaps they did not totally transform it, but transform it they did, and they deserve considerable credit for the improvements they made. If someone were to ask me where to go to learn the principles of cladistic analysis, I would not recommend Hennig's *Phylogenetic Systematics*.

I see no reason to interpret the preceding remarks about the development of cladistic analysis as indictments. On the contrary, I think that the features of cladism I have pointed out are characteristics of scientific research programs in general. Science is essentially a creative process. It is not a process in which scientists go from no knowledge to total knowledge but from less knowledge to more knowledge, and this process is never complete. As powerful as the methods of scientific investigation surely are they never provide final knowledge. If everything essential to the cladistic research program was already at least implicit in the early writings of Hennig, there would have been very little for later workers to do. As it turned out, there was a lot to do. Although there is a strong tendency to claim that all truth resides in the works of some great scientist (was Darwin really a cladist?), I do not think that this belief gives proper credit to later workers. Later cladists did not simply uncover the basic principles of cladistic analysis by a careful reading of Hennig. To some extent, they created those principles.

A FINAL TURN OF THE SCREW

In studying the principles of biological classification over the past two decades, I have not felt the need to opt for one set or the other. I have never classified an organism, although I have written papers arguing the pros and cons of the principles of classification set out by all three schools. For example, in my earliest publication (Hull 1964), I complained that the principles of evolutionary taxonomy suggested by Simpson (1961) were so weak that only the most variable and impressionistic relation could be established between biological classification and phylogeny (see also Hull 1970). Later I wrote several papers arguing against what I took to be an overly empirical, antitheoretical stance in the work of both the pheneticists (Hull 1967, 1968, 1970) and certain cladists (Hull 1979b, 1980). I now feel these papers to be too one-sided. Of course, scientific classifications cannot be theory-neutral, but scientists are also obligated to make science as "operational" as they can. Operational definitions in the strict sense are inadequate, but the time that scientists spend trying to operationalize their concepts is not wasted.[2]. Similarly, it is important to be reminded of the limits of phylogenetic reconstruction. Perhaps claims about past history are falsifiable *in principle*, but *in practice* too often they are not. As is usually the case for philosophers, I have been more interested in in-principle than in-practice issues.

In an indirect way, I am forced to choose between the various principles of classification enunciated by the various schools of taxonomy. Perhaps I do not have to classify organisms, but I do have to classify taxonomists. The rules I use to classify the taxonomists I am studying necessarily reveal my own preferences. I do not think that the history of recent disputes in taxonomy can be understood if taxonomists are classified phenetically. In fact, one of the greatest weaknesses in past histories of science is the classification of scientists in this way. All philosophers and scientists who ever accepted some form of evolution of species, regardless of when and where they lived, are a motley group, a group that played no role whatsoever in the development of evolutionary theory. In conceptual evolution, descent matters. If the history of taxonomy is to make any sense at all, *who* held a view and *where* he got this view is as important as *what* the view actually is. Early on, Nelson (1972, 1973) exhibited extreme doubts about phylogenetic reconstruction. So did the pheneticists. As similar as these doubts may be, in the history of ideas they count as separate and distinct doubts. They exist in different research programs. Like it or not, I am committed to some form of classification in which descent and modification are central.

For anyone following this extended metaphor, the next question naturally becomes, am I willing to accept paraphyletic groups of taxonomists? Although evolutionary and phenetic taxonomists disagreed on many counts, they agreed that taxa are frequently polythetic (Simpson 1961; Sokal and Sneath 1963; Mayr 1969). Platnick (1979) has argued recently that the reason that taxa seem polythetic is that the traits used are being misidentified. If the principles of cladistic analysis are applied consistently, perfectly nested patterns should materialize. If one insists on retaining traits incompatible with the nested set that one has discovered, then of course the resulting taxa will seem polythetic.

For example, if fins and legs are interpreted as different characters, then the relevant groups appear to be polythetic. However, there is a sense in which fins and legs are the same character. They belong to the same transformation series—paired pectoral and pelvic appendages. Neither snakes nor worms have paired pectoral and pelvic appendages. Even so, lacking paired pectoral and pelvic appendages in these two instances are not the same trait. The former must be scored a loss; the latter must be counted as an absence. Just as not all "eyes" are eyes, not all instances of "no limbs" are instances of no limbs. Thus, it is possible for traits to stay essentially the same while undergoing extensive modification. Evolving lineages might seem to undergo a total turnover in characteristics, but only if one ignores their origins.

When these same considerations are applied to scientific development, their implications are startling. For example, neither Ed Wiley nor Peter Ashlock accepts the principle of dichotomy, but Wiley's rejection cannot be scored as the same character as Ashlock's rejection. They belong to different transformation series. At one time Wiley accepted the principle of dichotomy. He later came to reject it for a variety of reasons. Ashlock never accepted the principle of dichotomy, for reasons quite different from those of Wiley. Thus, Wiley's rejection belongs in the cladist transformation series (he is the snake), while Ashlock's rejection belongs in the evolutionist transformation series (he is the worm).

At this stage, readers are likely to throw up their hands in dismay. If *this* sort of thing is required for an evolutionary analysis of conceptual development, the results are not worth the effort. I certainly can understand this reaction. Perhaps the usual way of treating the history of ideas is preferable. Certainly it is easier. However, in my own research I plan to follow the logic of the genealogical line of reasoning to its conclusion even if it is an absurdity. If nothing else, I will have shown why others should not follow this same path. However, those taxonomists who think that genealogy is a necessary element in biological classifications should not complain that I have grouped them the way that they group organisms.

CONCLUSION

What is phenetic taxonomy? Was Paul Ehrlich a pheneticist? Is he still? What is cladistic taxonomy? Was Hennig a cladist? Is Ed Wiley still a cladist? The purpose of this paper has been to show exactly how complicated these apparently straightforward questions actually are and the number of distinctions one must keep in mind to answer them unambiguously. The first is between a scientific group and its conceptual system. If scientific groups are defined in terms of cooperation and not agreement, then it is at least possible for members of the same research group to disagree with each other. Second, if conceptual systems are viewed as historical entities, it is at least possible for them to undergo total change while remaining the same conceptual system. In the process, a particular tenet may evolve into its negation and still belong to the same conceptual transformation series. In this sense, the research program has remained unchanged, and definitions in terms of essential traits once again become feasible. I hardly want to praise vagueness and ambiguity. After all, the main purpose of this paper is to decrease both. However, I think that vagueness, at least, is absolutely essential to science; scientific development would be impossible without it (Rosenberg 1975). I think that it is no accident that highly original scientists do not set out their views with absolute clarity when they first enunciate them. Further refinement is always necessary, and sometimes this refinement is so extensive that the original is all but unrecognizable in the product. In order to grow, scientific hypotheses must blur.

NOTES

1. Hampton Carson chose this motto as the title of his contribution to Mayr and Provine's anthology (1980) on the genesis of the synthetic theory of evolution.

2. For example, the cis-trans test does not literally "define" the gene concept, but it can be used to determine the limits of particular genes in appropriate circumstances.

Part V

The Role of History in Science

Chapter 11

Central Subjects and
Historical Narratives*

> Philosophy of history runs its course between the Scylla of histori-
> ans who have no patience with philosophers and the Charybdis of phi-
> losophers who have no training in or sympathy for history.[1]

> Instead of denying that cultures are entities, one should tackle the
> general problem by asking whether it is in fact possible to write a his-
> tory of something without presupposing that the object of the history is
> an entity of some type that undergoes change.[2]

At first glance, the changes in contemporary philosophy of science necessary to accommodate the intuitions of historians about historiography
are as great as those required in Aristotelian science by Copernicus' suggestion that the sun, not the earth, occupied the center of the universe. If
fire instead of earth resided in the center of the universe, then the entire
Aristotelian system of the four elements, humors, and polar principles
had to be discarded or else modified out of all recognition—and all of
this just to eliminate a few epicycles from predictive astronomy.[3] As might
be expected, contemporary philosophers of science have been no more
anxious to overthrow their entire analysis of science just to accommodate
the intuitions of historians than sixteenth-century scientists were to abandon all of Aristotelian science just to eliminate a few epicycles. Thus,
philosophers have been forced to argue either that historical narratives
do not concern unique sequences of events, or else that they are not explanatory. In this paper, I shall attempt to show that the apparent conflict
between historiography and philosophy of science is not as major as it
might seem. If historical narratives are viewed as descriptions of historical entities as they persist through time, then the currently accepted analysis of science need not be modified in order to account for the unity
evident in historical narratives. This unity is provided not so much by the
connections between the events related as by the unity and continuity of
the historical entities. Each historical entity in and of itself is unique, but
entities of this kind are not peculiar to history.

---

*Reprinted with permission from *History and Theory*, 14 (1975): 253-274.

Though the position I describe in this paper has been expressed most clearly by historians of human history, most of my examples are drawn from other historical disciplines. The explanation for this emphasis is partly inherent in the position that I am urging, partly a matter of expository style. Human history differs from other historical disciplines such as cosmogony, geology, and paleontology in several important respects. For instance, in human history, the goals, ambitions, beliefs, and the like of the subjects are extremely important. In paleontology, they are of no importance except in relation to human evolution. In cosmogony and geology, they are of no consequence whatsoever. Of greater relevance to the purposes of this paper is the fact that our current scientific theories about human actions and the development of societies are relatively weak and poorly formulated when compared with those we have concerning the evolution of biological species, the development of the earth, and the formation of the universe as a whole. The distinctions I set forth in this paper, though applicable to all historical disciplines, can be seen more clearly in those disciplines that possess highly developed scientific theories. But the most important reason I have for letting my exposition range over all historical sciences is that the general applicability of the analysis presented is the strongest argument in its favor. I think that it is no accident that workers in such disparate fields as evolutionary biology, modal logic, and human history have all converged on a common position with respect to the role of historical entities in science.

CENTRAL SUBJECTS AS HISTORICAL ENTITIES

Historians are all but unanimous in the opinion that the production of historical narratives plays a central role in historiography. Of course, historians do much more than just relate unique sequences of events. On occasion, they provide what might be called cross-sectional histories, in which the numerous facets of a single period are interrelated. Some even attempt to formulate and test various historical laws, though this sort of history is currently out of fashion.[4] But as Glenn Morrow has observed: "It is only in narrative that the philosophical problems peculiar to historical enquiry arise." It is only when an event is "considered as one term of a sequence of events, a sequence that is regarded as having some kind of unity through time, that the logical problems peculiar to history arise."[5] The main sort of continuity and unity envisaged so far by philosophers for historical narratives has been causal. Earlier events in historical sequences cause later events. Hence, a historical narrative is adequate to the extent that it provides causes sufficient to produce subsequent events. Because historical narratives rarely come close to providing such sufficient conditions, philosophers consistently view them as being deficient.[6] But philosophers, in passing this judgment, have consistently ignored the role in history of central subjects as historical entities.

The notion of central subjects is crucial to the logical structure of historical narratives.[7] Assuming for the moment that history could be analyzed completely into a single set of atomistic elements, there are indefinitely many ways in which these elements can be organized into historical sequences. The role of the central subject is to form the main strand around which the historical narrative is woven. In the past, numerous different sorts of entities have served as central subjects in history: individual people, lineages, nations, social movements, and even ideas. The important feature of central subjects is that from the point of view of the historical narrative associated with them, they are *individuals*. The identity and continuity of such individuals can be and must be determined independently of the events that make up the narrative. Central subjects afford the basic unity and continuity of the historical narrative. Any additional unity and continuity of such individuals can be and must be determined independently of the events that make up the narrative. Central subjects afford the basic unity and continuity of the historical narrative. Any additional unity and continuity supplied by the narrative is not just secondary to the more fundamental unity and continuity of the central subject, but derivative of it.

"Individual," as the term is used here, is a technical term from philosophy. An individual is a particular, a thing denoted by its name and nothing else. For example, "Moses" denotes a particular man. Though there are a variety of senses in which "Moses" might be said to having meaning, it has no intension the way that terms like "gold," "love," and "picture" do. But central subjects are not just individuals. They are also historical entities. Initially, the notion of a historical entity seems clear enough. A historical entity is not just any entity existing in time. It is a coherent, unitary entity that either persists unchanged or develops continuously through time. At any one moment, the parts of a historical entity are interrelated by a variety of relations, among which must be spatial proximity and at least intermittent contiguity. The parts of a historical entity must also be interrelated in such a way that the entity exists continuously through time. But in any case, for a historical entity to remain the same entity, no degree of similarity between earlier and later stages in its development is required, as long as this development is spatio-temporally continuous. For example, both Moses and Big Ben are clear-cut cases of historical entitites. Few if any traits that characterized Moses when he was discovered by the Pharoah's daughter in the bullrushes also characterized him when he led the Israelites out of Egypt or when he died in sight of the Promised Land. Nevertheless, he remained the same individual throughout all such changes. Big Ben has changed very little since it was first cast, but this lack of change is not the reason it remains the same individual. Like all historical entities, it remains the same individual because of spatio-temporal continuity. Of course, historical entities are also characterized by numerous additional relations, but these relations vary from example to example.

Living organisms are paradigm cases of historical entities. For example, Moses was born, named, lived, died, and was buried. It is the link-on-link continuity of Moses' body (and to some extent his mind) that makes him a *single* individual and the *same* individual through time and not some set of essential traits that he supposedly possesses. Moses has no essence. Over a period of years, all of the cells in his body could be replaced, and still he would remain Moses. (In fact, brain cells are not replaced the way other cells are.) His personality could undergo considerable modification, and still he would be Moses. (Of course, metaphorically speaking, none of us is the person he once was, either physically or mentally.) An advocate of essentialism might argue that it is Moses' genome which supplies his eternal, immutable essence, but the genetic makeup of organisms is neither eternal nor immutable. Errors are always occurring as cells reproduce themselves. Even if a person were to develop radiation sickness and his genome altered extensively, he still would remain the same person and not become someone else.

The notion of a historical entity becomes less intuitively clear when it is extended to include lineages, social movements, and the like. It may seem somewhat strained to treat nations as individuals existing continuously, though perhaps changing gradually, through time. In order to clarify the situation and to show the general applicability of the analysis proposed in this paper, I have chosen an example from a highly structured area of science to explicate in some detail the relation between individual organisms and particular species. From the point of view of human perception, organisms are individuals; species are not. From time immemorial, logicians have treated organisms and species of organisms as two very different sorts of things. With the advent of modern logic, this distinction has been expressed as the class-membership relation. Organisms are individuals and their names are proper names; species are classes and their names are common nouns to be defined in terms of their essential traits. For example "*Cygnus olor*" might be defined as a large white aquatic bird with a long neck and a hoarse, honking call. Any bird existing anywhere at any time that fulfilled these requirements would count as a swan, regardless of its parentage. Conversely, any bird that lacked any one of these characters would not count as a swan, regardless of its parentage.

Since the acceptance of evolutionary theory, biologists have rightly protested the application of this view of definition to the names of biological species, but philosophers have been slow to appreciate their complaints. Biologists have argued that at any one time many perfectly good species exist that cannot be characterized by a single set of essential traits. When species are traced backward through time, the difficulty in distinguishing species by means of sets of essential traits is only increased. If species are viewed as temporally extended lineages, then rarely can a set of traits be found that divides such lineages into species in any reasonable way. In the face of such empirical facts, several philosophers have concluded that the names of species (as well as all taxa) must be treated as cluster concepts, definable by alternative sets of unequally weighted traits. Although this move is a step in the right direction, it still does not do justice to the situation in biology. As early as 1966, Michael Ghiselin suggested that species as evolving lineages be viewed not as classes but as individuals:

> But leaving aside the problem of ranking, we may observe that Darwin had proposed a radical solution to the traditional question of the "reality" of taxonomic groups. What is "real" is the genealogical nexus, and the groups, or taxa, are chunks, so to speak, of this nexus. As a consequence, it became possible for the nominalist (and Darwin was something of a nominalist) to look upon taxa not as universals but as particulars, or individuals.[9]
>
> As species are individuals, there is but one rigorous way to define their names: ostensively, in a manner analogous to a christening. Thus it should now be obvious that even some logicians who have expounded at length on the logic of classification have failed to grasp one of the most fundamental points: a species name is a proper name.[10]

To anyone brought up on either traditional logic or the reformulations which have followed upon the work of Ludwig Wittgenstein, Ghiselin's proposal sounds just this side of insane. According to traditional logic, "Moses" is a proper name lacking any verbal definition. It denotes a particular individual, and that is all. On this same view, "swan" is a common noun, denoting a class of birds and definable by a set of essential characteristics. While maintaining the traditional ontology, Wittgenstein[11] argued that both proper names and common nouns were definable, but only as cluster concepts. Moses was the person who did enough of the most important things that Moses was supposed to have done. Swans are those birds which have enough of the most important traits characteristic of swans. On the face of it, the claim that "Moses" is a cluster concept is implausible. Moses was the individual who was named Moses, and that is that. If Moses had not been found in the bullrushes by the Pharoah's daughter but was her illegitimate son, he would still have been Moses. If he had not led the Israelites out of Egypt or had died after reaching the Promised Land, he would still have been Moses. Shakespeare would remain Shakespeare even if Francis Bacon had done nearly all the things usually attributed to him.

But it sounds equally strange to say that "swan" is a proper name denoting a particular biological species. However, several logicians have come to argue just this.[12] They claim that neither the names of individual organisms nor the names of particular species are cluster concepts; they are proper names introduced by a baptismal act and passed from person to person in a link-to-link reference-preserving chain. As it so happens, the analysis provided by these logicians fits the situation in biology perfectly. Taxonomists describe new species they discover. They do not provide rigid sets of essential traits that all organisms must have in order to belong to a particular species. Any organism could lack one or more of the traits listed in the species-description and still belong to the species. In fact, an organism could even lack one of its generic traits and still belong to a species of that genus.[13] Instead, one organism is selected as a type-specimen. As such, it need not be typical in any way of its species. Rather it is part of its species, and any organism related to it by the appropriate ancestor-descendant nexus is also part of that species.

The important point of the preceding for our purposes is that the traits listed in a species-description do not *define* the species which they characterize. Species are as much spatio-temporal wholes as are individual organisms. It is no accident that the names of organisms and species have been the best examples to date of cluster concepts. Both organisms and species are historical entities. The traits characteristic of them cluster *because* they are characteristics of historical entities. Species may not *seem* like individuals to the man on the street (and for our purposes this includes logicians), but from the point of view of contemporary biology, they are just that. Thus, evolutionary species could serve as central subjects in historical narratives, and they do. Paleontology is the historical science that weaves historical narratives around evolving species. Similarly, many common-sense classes in other areas might profitably be conceptualized as historical entities, specifically the central subjects of human history. Protestantism might not seem much like an individual, but if it is to perform the function of a central subject, it must be interpreted as such. As Herbert Butterfield observes in this criticism of the Whig interpretation of history: "Sometimes it would seem that we regard Protestantism as a Thing; a fixed and definite object that came into existence in 1517 . . . "[14] Protestantism surely has no fixed and definite limits but it *is* a thing, an historical entity.

In the preceding discussions, I have played fast and loose with our ordinary ways of conceptualizing the world of our experience. For the biological examples, the justification is more than ample. It is less so for the examples from human history. But in either case, if the necessary departures from ordinary usage are not noted, serious confusion can result. For instance, we commonly speak of an individual organism being a "member" of its species, when it is not. Rather, it is a part of its species. Further, even though the name of a historical entity applies to it throughout its existence, we usually use such names as if they applied to the entity only in the specious present. For instance, when we say that Moses wandered through the Sinai, we cannot be referring to Moses as a spatio-temporally extended historical entity. As such, Moses cannot be said to move or not to move. As a four-dimensional space-time worm, he just is. The Moses who moves is a momentary segment of this space-time worm. To complicate matters even further, the parts of Moses as a historical entity are themselves historical entities[15] Exactly the same story can be told for the names of species as evolving lineages. *Cygnus olor* applies both to a spatio-temporally extended lineage and to a time-slice of that lineage.

THE ROLE OF CENTRAL SUBJECTS IN HISTORY

Morton White[16] argues that the cause-effect relationship integrates the events associated with a central subject into a historical narrative. Maurice Mandelbaum counters that the part-whole relation also plays a role:

> What I wish to point out, and to insist upon, is the fact that the existence of a central subject constitutes one of the forms of linkage among the events entering into any particular history, and Professor White does not make this fact clear. In his discussion of the explanatory linkage between the various assertions which are present in an historical account, Professor White has stressed the sequential, causal linkage between one asserted fact and the next, but he has not explicitly mentioned another form of linkage: that which binds asserted facts into one history because they have in common the property of being parts or aspects of that which is the central subject of the history.[17]

The message of the preceding paragraph is that two sorts of linkage are involved in historical narratives: one the cause-effect relation connecting the events associated with the historical entity, and the other the part-whole relation integrating the central subject into a single historical entity. But Mandelbaum does not point out the different roles that these two relations play in historical narratives. Anyone who has ever read any history is aware that historical narratives seem to possess a unity far greater than that justified by the causal laws one might have connecting the various incidents mentioned. For example, Napoleon made a whole series of military, political, and personal decisions during the course of his life. All of these events belong to the same narrative, not because successful generals tend to become political leaders or because short men frequently overcompensate for their feelings of inferiority, but because a single person made all these decisions. One need not possess a sophisticated sociological or psychological theory to reidentify Napoleon throughout his existence.

However, in order for central subjects to play the integrating role which they do in historical narratives, one must distinguish carefully between those properties that make an individual an individual and those properties associated with that individual. The distinction is not between essence and accident, between those properties that Napoleon must have to be Napoleon and those properties that he just happens to have. Rather, it is between those relations, including spatio-temporal unity and continuity, that integrate the central subject into a historical entity and the other properties that the individual has and the events in which it participates. One must also carefully distinguish between those criteria by which one decides when an individual is a *single* individual and the *same* individual through time and those criteria by which one decides when two individuals belong to the same *kind* or when one individual *changes* kind. For example, an atom is an atom and not a molecule or ion because it is composed of a single nucleus and the appropriate number of electrons, whatever that number might be. Two atoms are two atoms and not one because they occupy different places at the same time. Two different time-slices of an individual atom are time-slices of the same atom because they can be connected continuously in time. If they cannot, then they are not the same atom. However, two atoms are atoms of the same *kind* because they have the same structure. Genesis is irrelevant. It does not matter that one atom of gold arose from an atom of lead and another from an atom of platinum. If they both have an atomic number of 79, then they are gold. A single atom or sample of gold is an individual; gold as the class of gold atoms is not.[18]

A similar story can be told for individual organisms and the species of which they are part. The mitotic division of cells is the commonest mechanism by which successive stages in the development of an organism are integrated into an individual. The production of offspring is the mechanism by which successive stages in the evolution of a species are integrated into an individual. That a particular swan has feathers or rapes a woman named Leda is irrelevant to its being an individual, a single individual, and the same individual through time. Similarly, the fact that most swans have white feathers and webbed feet is irrelevant to *Cygnus olor* being an evolutionary individual, a single individual, and the same individual through time. An atom of lead which is transmuted into an atom of gold remains the same individual, though not the same kind of individual. An organism as it goes through its life cycle remains the same individual though its total organization, both internal and external, may change considerably. One species that evolves into another remains the same individual, though not the same kind of individual. Such individuals are historical entities because included among their criteria for identity are continuity in space and continuity in time. Classes of such individuals are not historical entities because they lack such a criterion. On this analysis, particular atoms, genes, organisms, biological species, and societies are historical entities; classes such as gold, genes for albinism, neuter organisms, dominant species, and industrial societies are not.

One consequence of this analysis is that the names of historical entities cannot function in scientific laws, because they lack the requisite generality. By counting Moses, Napoleon, Big Ben, *Cygnus olor*, and the United States of America as historical entities, one can use the spatio-temporal unity and continuity inherent in them to aid in the construction of historical narratives. By doing so, one automatically precludes any of these terms appearing in scientific laws, given the traditional analysis of scientific law.[19] If scientific laws have to be spatio-temporally unrestricted, and historical entities are defined in terms of spatio-temporal unity and continuity, then the two notions are clearly incompatible. If the name of a historical entity appears in a scientific law, it must do so only incidentally (as in Kepler's reference to the sun in his laws). Of course, historical entities can be instances of various natural kinds. For example, *Homo sapiens* is an instance of a dominant species, the United States an instance of a world power, and Napoleon an instance of a charismatic leader. Thus, if "dominant species," "world power," and "charismatic leader" function in any significant scientific laws, then statements about particular historical entities can be derived from these laws, but the names of the historical entities themselves will not appear in these laws.

Although this particular way of conceptualizing the role of central subjects in history is compatible with current logical categories and with the intuitions of historians, problems still remain. What kinds of entities can properly serve as central subjects, the narrative units of human history? What are the principles of unity that bind together successive stages of an individual that make them successive stages in the career of one subject? By what criteria can one decide that a given incident belongs to or is required by a given narrative?[20] When the central subject of a historical narrative is an individual human being, the principle of unity that binds together successive stages of that individual is apparent enough but, as Haskell Fain has pointed out,[21] when the central subject is something like France during the French Revolution, deciding on the appropriate narrative units and the principles that integrate them is not so easy.

For what it is worth, the historian can take some solace in the knowledge that he is not alone in being confronted with such difficult questions. These are precisely the same questions biologists are currently asking about their central subjects. What are the units of competition and natural selection? Are they genes, chromosomes, organisms, colonies, or perhaps some more inclusive units? What are the units of evolution? Genes mutate, organisms reproduce themselves, more inclusive units than organisms evolve, but how are these levels of organization interrelated? Normally competition takes place between individual organisms, but when a colony becomes sufficiently well integrated, it becomes a unit of selection.[22] When a society becomes sufficiently well integrated, it "can equally well be viewed as a superorganism or even an organism."[23] "A species, like a race or a genus or a family, is a group concept and a category in classification. A species is, however, also something else: a supraindividual biological system, the perpetuation of which from generation to generation depends on the reproductive bonds between its members."[24]

THE ROLE OF SCIENTIFIC THEORIES IN HISTORIOGRAPHY

The role of scientific theories and laws has been discussed extensively in the historiographic literature, chiefly from the point of view of their role in explanation. But not all possible roles that scientific theories play in science are so closely connected to explanation. Of these, two are relevant to the issues raised in this paper: the use of scientific theories to reconstruct past events, an activity conceptually distinct from the explanation of these events, and the role of theories in defining central subjects. Once again my examples will be drawn from all historical disciplines and not just from human history, in part because human history does not have much in the way of highly developed psychological or sociological theories to draw upon.

The four most important historical disciplines are cosmogony, geology, paleontology, and human history. Cosmogony is the study of the history of the universe as a physical system, geology the study of the history of the earth, paleontology the study of the history of life, and human history the study of the course of human events. Embryology and the study of learning in animals might also be viewed as historical disciplines because of their concern with the developmental history of individual organisms from conception to death, but these two areas of investigation are peculiar among the historical sciences because their phenomena exhibit a degree of repetitiveness not apparent in other historical sciences. The repetitiveness results from the presence in organisms of a historically developed program that places constraints on the possible states of the system and influences the order of these states. Similar constraints for the universe as a whole, the earth, biological species, or human history are considerably less influential, if not totally absent. However, regardless of this difference, I suspect that central subjects play the same role in these two sciences that they do in other historical disciplines. For example, the causal laws that connect successive sequences of conditioning regimens are none too powerful. However, these sequences do share the feature that they were all performed on the same subject.

In all the historical sciences, the distinction must be made between those rough and ready rules of thumb that are used to reconstruct past events on the basis of current records and the scientific theories that are used to explain these events. For example, cosmogonists might use the colors of the stars to hypothesize about their relative ages. Just as heated metals go from blue or white to red as they cool, stars might undergo similar color transformations. If all or most stars are gradually cooling, then their relatives ages could be estimated from their colors. But this rule of thumb is distinct from any theory governing these celestial bodies and could be used in the absence of such a theory. Once the relevant theory is formulated, this rule may turn out to be derivable from it; or perhaps not. In point of fact, changes in color related to the temperature of stars does follow from physical theory, but such changes are an unreliable guide for deciding the relative ages of stars because some stars are heating up, others cooling down.

Similar observations can be made in other historical sciences. Geologists use a principle they term the "law of superposition" to help reconstruct the history of the earth. This principle states that in any sequence of surface-deposited material, each bed tends to be younger than the one below it and older than the one above. This principle cannot be applied uncritically because the earth's crust can buckle, inverting the order of the strata for short distances. Similarly, a minority of geologists have argued that the continents once formed a single land mass which gradually broke up and drifted apart. However, not until the rise of plate tectonics was there a causal theory adequate to explain such phenomena.[25] Bernard Rensch lists an even hundred rules of thumb that paleontologists use to reconstruct phylogenetic sequences.[26] Some of these rules can be shown to be fairly direct consequences of evolutionary theory; others not. All, however, are of some limited use in reconstructing particular phylogenies. For example, E. D. Cope argued that body size tends to increase during the evolutionary development of a group. This rule seems to be especially applicable to North American vertebrates.[27]

Finally, there are numerous rules in historiography that help historians reconstruct the past from present records. For example, if Aristotle mentions his *History of Animals* in his *Metaphysics* but not vice versa, then he probably began his *Metaphysics* after completing his *History*. Because there are no psychological or sociological theories akin to relativity theory in physics, plate tectonics in geology, or evolutionary theory in biology, the relation of such principles in history to any possible theories is at present even more questionable than in other historical disciplines.

Ernest van den Haag sees the relation between historical reconstruction and scientific laws as follows:

> Since historians do not try to establish universal laws, they do not view events as instances of counterinstances of such laws. Thus, to the scientist, historical facts are evidence for (or against) his laws; to the historian, these laws are part of the evidence for (or against) the event actually having happened. The historian, in the first place, is interested in proving the facts; the scientist is interested in what the facts prove.
>
> Yet, in stressing particulars, historians do not renounce science. They use it, as a court of law does when investigating the past actions of an individual. Only the rules of science permit us to infer from present evidence—all the court and the historians have—any past events whatever.[28]

Historians use a variety of techniques to reconstruct the past. One of these is inferring an event from a genuine scientific law and current data. But many of the truisms and rules of thumb used by historians to reconstruct the past certainly do not deserve the exalted title "scientific law," and in many cases these principles are much more helpful in reconstructing the past than current theories. Cosmogony, geology, and paleontology all possess theories from which such derivations can be made, but the degree to which these theories limit the possible historical development of their respective subject matters varies. Both cosmogonists and geologists make fairly direct use of physical laws to reconstruct the past history of the universe and the earth respectively. The cooling of stars and the deposition of gravel in a river bed follow well-known physical laws. But even so, given current theories and available evidence, the histories of neither the universe nor the earth are uniquely determined. Some leeway exists for alternative reconstructions. The resolving power of evolutionary theory is even weaker. Evolutionary theory sets only very general constraints on possible phylogenetic development, so general that it is of little help to paleontologists in reconstructing phylogenetic sequences. To put the matter simply, scientific theories tell us what can happen. Within these limits, certain additional rules help historians decide what actually did happen. At present, considerable slippage exists between these two sets of principles. The relevant theories do not greatly constrain the possible states of the system, and few of the various rules of thumb used to reconstruct the past are inferential consequences of these theories.

The preceding discussion has concerned the role of scientific theories in reconstructing the past. Scientific theories also play a crucial role in defining central subjects. One of the most fundamental tenets of contemporary philosophy of science is that the basic units in any discipline are defined in the context of the theories governing subject matter of that discipline. For example, what is or is not a physical element is determined by atomic theory. The different elements are not distinguished on the basis of their physical properties, such as malleability, specific density, or atomic weight, but purely in terms of their atomic number. Gold is an element because the smallest unit of gold is an atom. Gold is gold and not lead or uranium because it is made up of atoms with seventy nine protons. Similarly, at any one time, a biological species of sexually reproducing organisms is a segment of a species, not a subspecies or genus, because the appropriate organisms comprising the species are actually or potentially interbreeding with each other and reproductively isolated from organisms that comprise other such species. Successive generations of a biological species are parts of the same species because they are related by the ancestor-descendant relationship. The choice of atomic number for physical elements and the choice of gene exchange for biological species are dictated by atomic theory and evolutionary theory respectively. In the context of other theories, other criteria might well be used.

In his discussion of Morton White's paper, Donald C. Williams makes comparable distinctions for human history:

> Mr. White, to be more specific, requires two kinds of connection in the historian's narrative, in traditional terms a unity of substance and also a unity of cause, and these make some difficulty for each other. The first requirement is his prescription that a historical narrative have a single subject, and is so far from being too stringent that it needs a gloss to save it from triviality. This is because, as he would be the first to concede, the world does not afford a complete and aboriginal roster of primary substances or "real" subjects, metaphysically consolidated within and insulated without, and conversely any designable fragment or sum of things, properties, or events is sufficiently a "subject" to meet the

fundamental logical and ontological requirements, but not, I surmise, the requirement which Mr. White intends. If a "subject" is just a logically individual entity, then for any event, A, there are an infinity of subjects in whose histories A is an episode, and for every two events, A and B, there are an infinity of subject-histories to which both belong, and also an infinity of subject-histories to which one belongs but not the other.[29]

The world of our experience can be analyzed into individuals, parts, properties, classes, and so on in indefinitely many ways. Which ways are preferable? Some philosophers, for example, have argued that the preferable ontologies are those that are epistemologically prior. Thus, all analyses must be commensurable with the fundamental classification of our experiences into sense data. This particular program has been singularly unproductive. The current view among philosophers of science is that the empirical world should be and must be analyzed in terms of the best scientific theories available, regardless of epistemological priorities or common-sense ways of looking at things. It just so happens that people can register light of certain wavelengths. This fact is irrelevant to the physics of light. Ordinary people tend to divide plants into trees, bushes, and "plants," but that is of no consequence to the botanist. Theoretical scientists feel no obligation to make their theoretical entities accord with our psychological perceptions or with ordinary conceptions. Just because organisms seem to be extremely apparent individuals to human beings, a theoretical biologist need not treat them as such. What is or is not an individual or natural kind is theory-dependent.

The major difficulty confronting the historian in this respect is that any theory that might conceivably be relevant to his undertaking is at present so weak that it cannot help him much in deciding what sorts of things to count as individuals in his historical narratives and what sorts as natural kinds. From the point of view of the man on the street, individual people are the chief candidates for the central subjects of histories, but this does not mean that all histories must be about particular human beings. The greatest difficulty in writing histories of cultures, institutions, ideas, and the like is that the relevant social and psychological theories do not provide sufficiently well-formulated principles of unity and continuity for such individuals or sufficiently detailed criteria for deciding what is part of such a central subject and what properly belongs in its associated historical narrative. However, the lack of adequate theoretical underpinnings for human history does not automatically preclude recourse to central subjects in human history. If nothing else, historians can borrow their central subjects from other disciplines, such as organisms and lineages from biology. But even so, biologists recognized species long before they possessed a naturalistic theory in which species functioned as theoretically significant units. Historians can do the same.

CENTRAL SUBJECTS AS UNIQUE INDIVIDUALS

Nothing in the historian's view of his discipline causes greater consternation among philosophers than the claim that historical events, sequences of events, and individuals are in some sense "unique." Philosophers reply to this assertion that in the only sense according to which historical events and individuals are unique, all events and individuals are unique. Each time a lead ball rolls down an inclined plane, across a table, and to the floor, that is a unique sequence of events. These particulars because they *are* particulars will never recur. However, this sort of uniqueness does not preclude these particulars from being assimilated to significant classes and derived from scientific laws. Thus, defenders of the uniqueness claim in history are forced into one of two positions. They must argue either that historical sequences of events and individuals are unique under all descriptions or else that a peculiarly historical perspective exists under which such events and entities are unique.

The first alternative seems patently false. Caesar's crossing the Rubicon, to use the traditional example, was a unique event. This particular human being crossed this particular stream at the moment he did, and that is that. It is logically impossible for this individual to perform that particular act again at that moment, just as a man cannot be his own brother. But this event, unique though it may be, can be assimilated to a variety of reference classes, such as people crossing rivers, generals disobeying orders, ambitious individuals making their big moves. Certainly under some of these descriptions, the event is an instance of a significant generalization, though perhaps not a law of nature. Obviously, historians must be attempting to indicate some other feature of historical narratives than those just discussed. As far as I can tell the uniqueness claim stems from the role of central subjects in historigraphy.

Historians frequently describe their task as the identification of a significant strand to follow in the fabric of history. The metaphor is good enough, as long as one recognizes that not all strands in the tapestry are of the same sort. Mink has observed the "actions and events of a story comprehended as a whole are *connected by a network of overlapping descriptions.*"[30] These overlapping descriptions are in part responsible for the unity and continuity of historical narratives, but they are derivative of the more fundamental unity and continuity of central subjects. For example, if T. H. Huxley is taken to be the central subject of a historical narrative, then his physical and/or psychological continuity from birth to death supplies the primary continuity for the historical narrative. The network of overlapping descriptions of Huxley and the events in which he participated are secondary. Of course, Huxley as an individual can be assimilated to a host of reference classes, but from the point of view of the connections described in the historical narratives these classes are irrelevant. Certain theories may play crucial roles in determining that a human being is a historical entity and in supplying the criteria for deciding where one such entity leaves off and another begins, but these theories are not the theories that interrelate the events discussed in the historical narrative. As mentioned earlier, biologists have made comparable observations about evolving species. The traits characteristic of a species "cluster" because they are properties of parts of the same individual.

One of the difficulties in setting out the role of central subjects in historiography is that frequently more than one central subject appears in a single history, and some of them may exist as individuals at different levels of analysis. For example, T. H. Huxley as a central subject is of a different type from the Huxley family. In the latter case, the Huxley lineage would be described by a recitation of who married whom and begot whom. Such a recitation would not, of course, be a historical narrative but the characterization of a central subject. Nor is the history of a lineage merely the summation of the separate biographies of the individuals people making up the lineage; they must be integrated into a single narrative. The situation is directly paralleled in other historical disciplines. Just as T. H. Huxley begot Leonard Huxley, and Leonard Huxley begot Aldous and Julian Huxley, the ostracoderms gave rise to the placoderms and the placoderms gave rise to the sharks and bony fishes. In each case, the names of the individuals mentioned are proper names and the sequences indicated in this way unique. In fact, the whole point of proper names as rigid designators is to denote uniquely. "T. H. Huxley" is supposed to denote T. H. Huxley and no one else. "Placoderm" is supposed to denote the placoderms and no other segment of the phlogenetic tree. If it is this aspect of historiography which historians have been intent on pointing out in their uniqueness claims, then historiography in no way conflicts with traditional philosophical categories.

But historians do more than just mention the continuing existence of an individual in time or list a series of proper names seriatim. They also produce associated historical narratives. The narrative presupposes the continuity of the central subject. It may even mention certain aspects of that continuity. But in general it is a description of the central subject and the events in which this subject participates. An event in such a narrative might be Huxley defending Darwin against Bishop Wilberforce's intemperate remarks or the development of a bony vertebral column. In general, such historical narratives will have a coherence of their own, though they need not. Even if T. H. Huxley had led a double life, or suffered a radical change in personality in middle age, or had been so scatterbrained from birth that his life was nothing but total confusion, a historian could still write his biography. When a historian is unable to do so, then perhaps he has failed to select a genuine central subject.

Two issues remain: the functioning of ideas as central subject and the explanatory nature of historical narratives. But before these issues are discussed, a gesture must be made, futile though it may be, to allay the inevitable operationist objections. Because the relation between central subject and their associated network of overlapping descriptions is so intimately connected, the two are often confused, especially when the central subject is not a common-sense individual. In such cases, the temporal order of the discovery and recognition of the central subject and the associated network of overlapping descriptions is usually opposite to the order of logical priority. We become aware of the central subject through the cohesion and continuity of its properties and the events in which it participates before we discover the principles that integrate the central subject into a historical entity. No one has ever directly observed the house of Tudor or an evolving species, yet both could function as central subjects in historical narratives. Because we come to discern a central subject by means of a cluster of properties associated with it, operationists are deceived into thinking that this cluster of properties is primary, not the central subject. A dispute over precisely this issue has been going on among taxonomists for more than a decade. Phenetic taxonomists argue that taxonomic groups determined by sets of statistically covarying traits are primary. Evolutionary taxonomists, while agreeing that they discern evolutionary lineages with the help of such clusters of traits, insist that the lineages are primary.[31]

IDEAS AS CENTRAL SUBJECTS

Histories of ideas are one of the most interesting and certainly the most problematic type of history produced by historians. The low opinion that many contemporary historians have of histories of ideas, even when such histories are successful, stems from the peculiar nature of ideas as central subjects. A classic example of a history of ideas is Arthur O. Lovejoy's *The Great Chain of Being* (1936). In this work, Lovejoy says that the history of ideas is:

> especially concerned with the manifestation of specific unit-ideas in the collective thought of large groups of persons, not merely in the doctrines

or opinions of a small number of profound thinkers or eminent writers.

These lectures, then, are intended to exemplify in some small measure the sort of philosophical-historical inquiry of which I have been merely sketching the general aims and method. We shall first discriminate, not indeed, a single and simple idea, but three ideas which have throughout the greater part of the history of the West, been so closely and constantly associated that they have often operated as a unit, and have, when thus taken together, produced a conception—one of the major conceptions in Occidental thought—which came to be expressed by a single term: "the Great Chain of Being."[32]

But Lovejoy never tells us how we are to reidentify these units as the *same* units throughout the history of the West. One might justifiably complain that ideas are so malleable that they actually place no constraints on the historian of ideas. The legitimacy of such histories of ideas, however, can be supported to some degree by cases in which the unit-idea lacked sufficient unity and continuity to support a historical narrative. For example, W. Warren Wagar attempted to follow the belief in progress from Darwin to Marcuse in his book *Good Tidings* (1972), but his exposition consists largely in a series of particular views of particular men organized around extraneous criteria. Wagar was unable to discover any appropriate internal principles of integration because the idea of progress in the twentieth century had ceased to be a central subject the way it had been in the nineteenth century.[33]

The greatest problem posed by histories of ideas for the analysis presented in this paper is that they lack any necessary spatio-temporal properties. Previously I introduced three technical terms: individual, historical entity, and central subject. Individuals are the lowest level entities over which the laws of a particular theory range; for example, mass points in Newtonian mechanics, alleles in population genetics, and responses in learning theory. Historical entities are a special kind of individual—individuals integrated by a variety of particular relations including spatio-temporal unity and continuity. A central subject is a historical entity functioning as the core of a historical narrative. The issue is the role of spatio-temporal unity and continuity in defining historical entities. All of the examples of historical entities discussed thus far have been physical systems integrated by relations that presuppose at least intermittent spatio-temporal continuity of their parts. For example, two organisms cannot reproduce themselves unless their gametes come into contact. In reproduction, the offspring arises from its parents. There is no action at a distance. However, not all historical entities can be characterized in this way. For example, the United States of America includes Alaska and Hawaii as parts, even though these two states are separated from the rest of the states by thousands of miles. If such individuals are to count as historical entities, then the requirement of spatio-temporal unity must be relaxed somewhat. Certain historical entities might be integrated by relations that do not presuppose any spatio-temporal contiguity. In certain cases, it might also be necessary to relax the requirement of temporal continuity. A particular theory might justify terming something an individual and the same individual even though it ceased to exist and then came into exsitence again later on. For example, a biologist might want to say that a particular species became extinct and then evolved again from different stock. However, such claims would necessitate the possession of an extremely powerful theory because such entities are hardly commonsense individuals. In addition, it is extremely doubtful that such entities could function adequately as central subjects.

Literally speaking, ideas can be transmitted only by contact. In order for Linnaeus to have been influenced by Aristotle's ideas on classification, he must have read Aristotle, or read someone who did, or talked to someone who had read Aristotle, and so on. As tenuous as these connections may get, they could serve as a justification for treating ideas as historical entities. But historians of ideas frequently write as though ideas give rise to ideas regardless of any system of communication. Precisely this same problem has arisen in the context of the history of science. Is the history of science a history of scientific communities in their social milieux, a history of scientific theories as parts of a broader conceptual outlook, or some combination of both approaches? Scientists need not be in spatio-temporal proximity to each other to be part of the same scientific community, though they usually are. More indirect communication will do. But contact of some sort is necessary. Scientific communities are historical enities and as such can function as central subjects in historical narratives. Whether ideas can be interpreted so that they are legitimate central subjects is a disputed question. I am predisposed to the opinion that they can be.

THE EXPLANATORY NATURE OF HISTORICAL NARRATIVES

Reader's might be willing to grant most of the preceding but, especially if they are philosophers, might retain some reservations about viewing historical narratives as explanatory. Philosophers have raised objections to the ways in which historians reconstruct the past and to the resulting historical narratives, but they have objected most vehemently to the claims that historians make about the explanatory nature of historical narratives. Perhaps philosophers have been unable to discover the essence of beauty, goodness, horses, lemons, and games, but they have discovered the essence of scientific explanation, and it is subsumption under a scientific law. There is one and only one way of explaining a particular natural phenomenon or regularity and that is to derive it from one or more laws of nature and, when necessary, relevant particular circumstances. On this view, historical narratives are explanatory only to the extent that they contain explicit or implicit reference to scientific laws. If these laws turn out to be weak, then the explanatory content of the corresponding narrative is weak. If there are no such laws, then the historical narrative is not explanatory at all. Because the best generalizations which historians have been able to produce are not very powerful, philosophers have concluded that historical narratives are at best explanation sketches.

Explanation by subsumption accords nicely with many of our preanalytic intuitions about what scientific explanations should be like, and many paradigm cases of scientific explanation fit this analysis: but the dogged insistence of so many philosophers that *only* subsumption can count as scientific explanation has seemed overly doctrinaire, not just to historians but to all scientists. From an ordinary language point of view, it seems implausible to suppose that a term like "explanation" should refer to a single rational process, as implausible as supposing that "dishonesty" refers to a single type of human activity. Just as there are more ways than one to be dishonest, there may well be more than one way to explain something scientifically. Of course, such comments about ordinary usage are liable to impress no one but the most ardent ordinary-language philosopher. Most philosophers maintain that philosophy is to some extent normative. This claim may well be justified but until the grounds for such normative power have been made a good deal clearer than they are now, philosophers would be wise to proceed with caution lest they find themselves once again arguing that space is necessarily Euclidean and species necessarily immutable.

In historical narratives, an event is not explained by subsuming it under a generalization. Instead, it is explained by integrating it into an organized whole. Louis Mink has distinguished several modes of comprehension, including one which he terms the "configurational mode." Examples of this mode of comprehension are holding in mind an entire symphony, novel, or deductive proof. As Mink puts it: "In all of these instances, and in indefinitely many more, there thus seems to be a characteristic kind of understanding which consists in thinking together in a single act, or in a cumulative series of acts, the complicated relationships of parts which can be experienced only seriatim."

We are all aware of the psychological satisfaction we feel when we discover that the falling of an apple and the movement of the moon around the earth are both instances of the same general regularity. Similarly, we are also aware of the satisfaction we feel when we succeed in seeing what at first appeared to be a hodgepodge as a single, cohesive unit, or when we fit an element into an already recognized pattern. The integration of an element into an overall pattern can impart as much intellectual satisfaction as the subsumption of a particular under a scientific law—sometimes more. Such intuitions are important to philosophers and scientists alike. Initially that is all anyone has to go on. But intuitions are not enough. Too often they are faulty. It is the task of the psychologist to set out the psychology of pattern recognition, but as Mink himself remarks, it is the "task of the philosopher to make explicit the patterns of rational inference which inform complex thinking of all sorts."[35] Philosophers have set out the logical structure of deductive explanations in considerable detail. Some headway has been made recently in setting out the structure of statistical explanations. Other sorts of explanation have been neglected until relatively recently. If claims about integrative explanations are to be taken seriously, then some effort must be expended in doing for them what philosophers have done for deductive and statistical explanations. There is nothing inherently alogical about integrating parts into wholes. The logic of the part-whole relation has been worked out in great detail. All that remains is for someone to set out the logical structure of integrative explanations.

NOTES

1. Mazlish, Bruce. "On Rational Explanation in History." In *Philosophy and History*, ed. Sidney Hook, New York: New York University Press, 1963, 275.

2. Fain, Haskell. *Between Philosophy and History*. Princeton: Princeton University Press, 1970, 44.

3. To avoid misunderstanding, two clarifications must be made with respect to the preceding analogy. First, both Ptolemy and Copernicus made us of epicycles in their systems, but predictions could be made on the Copernican system with an accuracy equal to that of the Ptolemaic system, but using fewer epicycles. However, this slight increase in simplicity probably did not play a very important role in converting scientists to the Copernican system.

4. Mink, Louis O. "The Divergence of History and Sociology in Recent Philosophy of History." In *Proceedings of the Fourth International Congress for Logic, Methodology and Philosophy of Science*, ed. P. Suppes *et al*. New York: Elsevier Publishing Company, 1973, 725-742.

5. Morrow, Glenn. "Comments on White's 'Logic of Historical Narration.' " In *Philosophy and History*, ed. Hook. New York: New York University Press, 1963, 286.

6. A few philosophers and historians, however, have questioned the usual analysis of causation in terms of sufficient conditions. They argue that sometimes causes are necessary conditions. In other cases, causes are neither necessary nor sufficient conditions for the events that they are said to cause. See W. B. Gallie. "Explanation in History and the Genetic Sciences," *Mind* 64 (1955): 160-180, reprinted in *Theories of History*, ed. P. Gardiner. Glencoe, Ill.: The Free Press, 1959., 386-402; Michael Scriven. "Explanation and the Prediction in Evolutionary Theory." *Science* 130 (1959): 477-481.

7. White, Morton. "The Logic of Historical Narration." In *Philospohy and History*, ed. Hook. New York: New York University Press, 1963, 4.

8. Beckner, Morton. *The Biological Way of Thought*. New York: Columbia University Press, 1959. Hull, David L. "The Effect of Essentialism on Taxonomy." In *The British Journal for the Philosophy of Science* 15 (1965): 314-326; and 16 (1966): 1-18. These essays argue that the names of particular species are cluster concepts definable by the statistical covariation of their morphological properties. Douglas Gasking, "Clusters," *The Australiasian Review of Psychology* 38 (1960): 1-36, argues that the names of particular species should be defined in terms of a serial relation, a notion verging on that suggested in this paper.

9. Ghiselin, Michael. *The Triumph of the Darwinian Method*. Berkeley and Los Angeles: University of California Press, 1969, 85.

10. Ghiselin, Michael. "On Psychologism in the Logic of Taxonomic Principles," *Systematic Zoology* 15 (1966): 209. John R. Gregg interprets species as classes even though two different taxonomists who read an early version of his paper argued that "species are composed of organisms just as organisms are composed of cells; according to this argument a species is just as much a concrete, spatio-temporal thing as is an individual organism"; see his "Taxonomy, Language and Reality," *American Naturalist* 84 (1950): 425. Roger Buck and David L. Hull continue to ignore the possibility of interpreting species as individuals in their "The Structure of the Linnaean Hierarchy," *Systematic Zoology* 15 (1966): 97-111.

11. Wittgenstein, Ludwig. *Philosophical Investigations*. New York: Macmillan, 1953.

12. Kripke, Saul. "Naming and Necessity." In *Semantics and Natural Language*. ed. D. Davidson and G. Harman. Dordrecht: D. Reidel, 1972, 253-355. However, Kripke treats as rigid designators not only the names of common-sense individuals and biological species, but also many other sorts of terms like"gold" and "meter." I believe that the names of historical entities can be treated as rigid designators; I doubt that Kripke's analysis can be extended as far as Kripke stretches it.

13. Stenzel, H. B. "A Generic Character, Can It Be Lacking in Individuals of the Species in a Given Genus?" *Systematic Zoology* 12 (1963): 118-121.

14. Butterfield, H. *The Whig Interpretation of History*. London: G. Bell and Sons, 1931, 51.

15. Wilson, N. L. "Space, Time, and Individuals." *The Journal of Philosophy* 52 (1955): 589-598.

16. White, 8.

17. Mandelbaum, Maurice. "Objectivism in History." In *Philosophy and History*. ed. Hook, New York: New York University Press, 1963, 46.

18. Marcus, Ruth Barcan. "Essential Attribution." *Journal of Philosophy* 68 (1971): 202. Ruth Barcan Marcus blurs the distinction between an individual being the same individual and its being the same kind of individual when she says that we would not reidentify a sample of gold "as the same thing" if it were transmuted into lead. I think not. We would surely reidentify it as the same sample but not the same kind. However, the notion of genidentity presupposed throughout this paper is not without its difficulties; e.g., how many parts of an individual can be replaced and how rapidly before it ceases to be the same individual and in what sense of "same"? If over a period of years a man were to replace worn-out parts of a car, we would tend to say that this was the same car, even if eventually all the parts had been replaced. However, what if the man had saved all his worn parts and reassembled the original car? I happen to think that such questions cannot be answered in the context of ordinary language. However, they can be in the context of well-formulated scientific theories.

19. Of course, there is always the possibility of questioning the traditional analysis of scientific laws as spatio-temporally unrestricted generalizations, an alternative that would radically alter our current conception of science. Conversely, one might also relax the spatio-temporal requirement for historical entities. Perhaps most historical entities are integrated by relations that presuppose spatio-temporal unity and continuity, but possibly some are not. See later discussion in this paper.

20. Morrow, 289; Mink, "Divergence," 735.

21. Fain, 236.

22. Schopf, Thomas J. M. "Ergonomics or Polymorphism: Its Relation to the Colony as the Unit of Natural Selection in Species of the Phylum Ectoprocta." *Animal Colonies*. Stroudsburg, Pa.: Dowden, Hutchens, and Ross, 1973, 247-294. For a general discussion, see Richard Lewontin, "The Units of Selection." *Annual Review of Ecology and Systematics* 1 (1970): 1-18.

23. Wilson, E. O. "Review of *Animal Colonies*." *Science* 184 (1974): 54.

24. Dobzhansky, Theodosius. *Genetics of the Evolutionary Process*. Berkeley and Los Angeles: University of California Press, 1970, 23.

25. Kitts, David. "Physical Theory and Geological Knowledge." *The Journal of Geology* 82 (1974): 1-23. "Continental Drift and Scientific Revolution." *The American Association of Petroleum Geologists Bulletin* 58 (1974): 2490-96.

26. Rensch, Bernard. *Biophilosophy*. New York: Columbia University Press, 1971, 214. Leigh Van Valen makes the same distinction in his "Laws in Biology and History: Structural Similarities of Academic Disciplines." *New Literary History* 3 (1972): 409-419 .

27. For the connections between Cope's Rule and current biological theory, see S. M. Stanley. "An Explanation for Cope's Rule." *Evolution* 27 (1973): 1-26.

28. van den Haag, Ernest. "History as Factualized Fiction." In *Philosophy and History*, ed. Hook, New York: New York University Press, 1963, 214.

29. Williams, Donald C. "Essentials in History." In *Philosophy and History*, ed. Hook, New York: New York University Press, 1963, 374.

30. Mink, Louis O. "History and Fiction as Modes of Comprehension." *New Literary History* 1 (1969): 556.

31. Mayr, Ernst. *Principles of Systematic Zoology*. New York: McGraw-Hill, 1969 *versus* Sneath, Peter H. A. and Robert R. Sokal. *Numerical Taxonomy*. San Francisco: 1973.

32. Lovejoy, A. O. *The Great Chain of Being*. New York: Harper & Row, 1936, 19, 20.

33. Wagar, W. Warren. *Good Tidings The Belief in Progress from Darwin to Marcuse*, Bloomington, Ind.: Indiana University Press, 1972.

34. Mink. "History and Fiction." 552.

35. *Ibid.*, 543.

Chapter 12

In Defense of Presentism*

L. Pearce Williams was so irate over Joseph Agassi's book on Michael Faraday and the section on Faraday in a book by William Berkson that he was moved to entitle his review "Should Philosophers Be Allowed to Write History?"[1] Williams answers the question posed in the title of his review with a resounding "No!" He complains that philosophers are prone to scandalous carelessness in transcribing quotations and to inaccurate descriptions, not to mention some highly questionable interpretations. They are more interested in plausible connections between ideas than in actual connections, in what *they* would have thought in the circumstances rather than in what the people concerned *actually* thought. But worst of all, philosophers tend to use history of science to illustrate their own views on the nature of science, rather than treating it inductively. Popperians such as Agassi and Berkson view histories of science as good places to introduce conjectures to be refuted by later workers. Imre Lakatos has even gone so far as to state that history of science should be written as it *should* have taken place, given a particular philosophy of science, rather than as it actually did take place: "One way to indicate discrepancies between history and its rational reconstruction is to relate the internal history *in the text*, and indicate *in the footnotes* how actual history 'misbehaved' in the light of its rational reconstruction."[2]

Once Lakatos' position is translated out of the controversial idiom which he invariably prefers, it does not sound so radical and ahistorical. Even so, Williams would surely object. "History," according to Williams, "is an inductive science."[3] I happen to agree with most of Williams' historiographical preferences. I too value accurate quotations, citations, and descriptions even when I myself fall short. However, an inductivist philosophy of history is no less a philosophy of history because it is inductivist and widely shared by other historians. Williams is caught up in the sort of self-referential snarl so dear to the hearts of philosophers. It is unlikely that Williams himself gathered his principles of historiography inductively from an extensive examination of past histories of science; rather, he brings his preferences to his study of past science. His historical work will be influenced as surely by his principles of good historiography

---

*Reprinted with permission from *History and Theory*, 18 (1979): 1-15.

as the works of the Popperians are by theirs. Williams may have no general philosophy of science. He certainly does not recommend an inductivist philosophy to physicists and biologists. But he does hold an inductivist philosophy of history.

Should philosphers be allowed to write history? Should *historians*? In spite of excesses on both sides, I am forced to answer both questions with a resounding "YES!" If the philosophical views that a historian holds have any influence on the history he writes, and I cannot see how such influence can be avoided, then philosophers have something to contribute to history. Conversely, if the subject matter of philosophy of science is science, then historians surely have much to contribute to philosophy of science. Further, for any philosopher attempting to develop an evolutionary analysis of science, the temporal dimension to the units of conceptual evolution becomes crucial. Historians have more to contribute to philosophy than just examples. In conceptual evolution, actual connections between ideas are what count, not "logical" connections.[4] In general, I find the academic divisions characteristic of universities all too real. Scientists, historians, sociologists, and even philosophers help to increase our understanding of science. Each of these fields has its own goals, techniques, and standards. Some consideration must be shown by people trying to work in more than one field to the indigenous mores of the different disciplines. But sympathy is also called for. Allowing or not allowing someone to write history is incompatible with free inquiry.

PRESENTISM

Present-day historians frequently criticize their predecessors for a variety of poor historiographic practices, especially for a cluster of interrelated faults commonly labeled "presentism." In an early criticism of what he termed the Whig interpretation of history, Herbert Butterfield complained of "the tendency in many historians to write on the side of Protestants and Whigs, to praise revolutions provided they have been successful, to emphasize certain principles of progress in the past and to produce a story which is the ratification if not the glorification of the present."[5] Comparable observations apply to history of science. For example, Stephen G. Brush points out the tendency of early historians of science to "judge every scientist by the extent of his contribution toward the establishment of modern theories. Such an interpretation looks at the past in terms of present ideas and values, rather than trying to understand the complete context of problems and preconceptions with which the earlier scientist himself had to work."[6]

In this chapter, I intend to argue that certain forms of presentism are both undesirable and eliminable. It is certainly a mistake to think that by "gemmule" Darwin meant the same thing that present-day geneticists mean by "gene," or to criticize him for not holding the modern conception. Nor could anything introduce greater distortion into a historical narrative than assuming that the agents concerned viewed the empirical world the way we do today. However, I also intend to defend certain forms of presentism in history of science as necessary evils and still others as perfectly legitimate. I realize that my defending presentism in any form is likely to prove as popular among historians as my saying a few words at a meeting of the Parent-Teacher Association on behalf of child molesters, but I think that the faults of presentism are not as transparent as they might at first appear.

For example, one of Thomas Kuhn's maxims for the "new internal historiography" is that the "historian should set aside the science that he knows. His science should be learned from the textbooks and journals of the period he studies, and he should master these and the indigenous traditions they display before grappling with innovators whose discoveries or inventions changed the direction of scientific advance."[7] However, Kuhn prefaces the preceding maxim with the remark that the historian should set aside the science that he knows only "insofar as possible" and "it is never entirely so, nor could history be written if it were."[8] Similarly, Murray G. Murphey notes that historians "are now calling for a historicist approach which will seek to understand the past in its own terms, not in terms of its relation to later events which happen to interest certain investigators."[9] He then asks, "But what does it mean to understand the past in its own terms? It means, I think, to seek for an understanding of past phenomena in terms of the system of thought and action of which they were a part. Of course, this system is in part our construction, as is any theory, and it must usually contain recently discovered principles of which the members of past societies were unaware."[10]

If an historian knows no science of his own period, then he certainly cannot read it back into the past or pay undue attention to precursors. In practice, of course, such abject ignorance of the present is impossible, even for historians and philosophers of science, but what of Kuhn's remark that history could not be written if it were, and Murphey's claim that understanding the past in its own terms is compatible with referring to principles unknown at the time? Practicing historians might well reply that historiographers like Kuhn and Murphey are manufacturing problems where none exist. Historians know what they mean when they claim to write of the past in its own terms even if historiographers do not. On occasion an historian might slip, allowing his narrative to be distorted by his own perspective, but the goal is clear.

I am of two minds on this issue. Many of the points I make in this paper might seem too obvious to warrant mentioning. One way to evaluate a philosophical exposition is the extent to which it accords with the practices and intuitions of those actually working in the field under investigation. The more frequently my reader exclaims, "Of course, everyone knows that!" the better I like it. But philosophy is also prescriptive. On occasion, the reader is likely to be moved to exclaim, "Rubbish! Only a philosopher could talk such nonsense." In such circumstances, the only thing that a philosopher can do is to explain his position as best he can and to show how, when one thinks about it, it makes admirably good sense. In this paper, I discuss three sorts of presentism, reading present-day meanings, principles of reasoning, and empirical knowledge back into earlier periods. I argue that in all three cases knowledge of present-day language, logic, and science is necessary not only for investigating the past, but also for communicating the results of these investigations to the historians's contemporaries. I also limit myself to presentism in the history of science. Whether comparable observations apply with equal force to history at large must remain, for the purpose of this paper, a moot question. However, I happen to think that they do.

RECONSTRUCTION VERSUS COMMUNICATION

A distinction which should prove helpful in the succeeding sections of this paper is between the methods that historians use to find out about the past and the means they use to communicate these findings to their contemporaries. In rare cases, the historian can use current scientific theories to infer the occurrence of a past event; for instance the dating of a document that mentions a lunar eclipse of the sun by means of current data and the principles of celestial mechanics. In doing so, he is hardly contravening any principles of historiography. He is not claiming that the people at the time understood eclipses the way we do or possessed our principles of celestial mechanics. He is simply using the science available to him to infer the past. The historian is lodged squarely in the present. He must use the theories, methods, and data available to him in reconstructing the past or use nothing at all. Knowledge of the present becomes even more important when the historian turns from trying to discover what happened in the past to writing up his findings. Histories are written not only *by* people and *about* people but also *for* people. The people about whom a history is written lived in the past, but the historian and his readers live in the present. No purpose is served by pretending otherwise. The very fact that the historian shares knowledge of the present with his readers is what allows him to communicate successfully with them. Any historian completely ignorant of the present could not begin to discover what happened in the past. Afer all, his evidence is all in the present. He would be at an equally grave disadvantage in writing history for people living in the present. As Maurice Mandelbaum has observed: "a historian knows something about the nature of his own society through having grown up in it, and he will have learned through its culture something about its past; furthermore, in any society in which there is *inquiry* into the past, a historian will also know something about societies other than his own, and about their pasts." As erroneous as the historian's knowledge of the present may be, as much distortion as it may introduce into his work, it is also absolutely necessary.

One often hears that history must be rewritten for every generation, as if this observation implied that each generation necessarily reads its own prejudices into the period under investigation. As true (or false) as this assumption may be, the need to rewrite history has other sources as well. Sometimes later historians have access to data which was unavailable to earlier workers, but more importantly they will be writing for a different audience with different life experiences. Communication is a relation. If either partner in the relation changes, the relation itself changes. The two-member relation of a contemporary historian studying the past becomes a three-member relation when the historian attempts to explain an earlier period to people living in the present. Successive histories of the same period may differ markedly, not because the period under investigation has changed, not because historians necessarily introduce their own concerns and prejudices into their work (though they may), but because the readers of these histories are different. A history of the Peloponnesian War written for a Victorian schoolboy must differ markedly from one written for students today. This point does not depend on the audience existing at different times. Differences in culture are what matters. Contemporary cultures can differ as markedly from each other as those that exist serially in time.

THE RELATIVITY OF MEANING

Periodically, philosophers have mused about how nice it would be to have an ideal language in which everything could be said with absolute precision. Historians, however, are presented with real languages in which the same word can mean very many things to different people, and these meanings can change through time. Although natural languages are far from total chaos, they also pose serious problems for anyone who wishes to understand and to be understood. An historian will have been raised in a particular subculture speaking the variant of his language peculiar to that subculture. If one wishes to learn about a contemporary subculture and its language, one can always become part of it and learn through participation. Of course, it might be impossible to eliminate totally one's previous experience. Some immigrants always view their new surroundings through the eyes of their original homes, but at least there are non-linguistic ways of reducing the discrepancies. Such non-linguistic experience is all but unavailable to the historian studying an earlier period. By and large the best he can do is to immerse himself in the records currently available, and the most informative records tend to be linguistic. Whether the historian's subjects speak a foreign language or an earlier version of his own language, the historian begins by translating their utterances into his own idiom. Little by little, however, he may develop the ability to think in the language of the period under investigation. But how can he be sure that he has completely annulled the distortions which his own culture and language are likely to introduce into his understanding? He has caught himself often enough in the past. How can he be sure that anachronisms will not continue to infect his investigations?

One message of recent philosophy for all empirical investigators, including historians, is that absolute certainty is not possible. The only thing that one can hope to do is to decrease the likelihood of error, and there are numerous ways to do that. One is to read the works of other historians, especially historians from other cultures and times. Each historian brings with him his own set of biases, but it is much easier to detect the biases of others than one's own. To the extent that the biases of different historians are themselves different, they tend to be mutually corrective. Another way to decrease the bias that one's own conceptual scheme can introduce is by studying more than one area. I might be so indoctrinated in contemporary evolutionary theory that I dismiss nineteenth-century notions of saltative evolution as supernatural. However, I might not be so totally committed to the conceptual outlook of contemporary geology. Reading the uniformitarian debate in geology might liberate my understanding of biological evolution. That increase in understanding might in turn improve my original understanding of geology. As illogical as the bootstrap effect may be, the resulting increase in understanding is nonetheless real.

The point I wish to emphasize is that one way to eliminate the biases introduced into our understanding of past science by our knowledge of current science is *not* by ignoring the fact that we do understand certain areas of present-day science. If an historian knows anything about the science of his day, and it is difficult to see how that can be avoided, he would be wise to become very clear about his views so that he does not allow them to color his reading of early science. For example, one often hears that Darwin held a "blending" theory of inheritance in contrast to our modern "particulate" theories, and that he thought that the variations operative in the evolutionary process were "continuous" rather than the small, discrete mutations which we now take to be the ultimate source of variation. Such claims are hopelessly misleading, not because Darwin's views are being contrasted with modern ideas, but because the two are being confused. The historian has been taken in by a century of scientific propoganda.

Another problem posed by the relativity of meaning is that the historian may well be able to neutralize his own preconceptions by long years of study, but his readers will not have had the benefit of this same extensive experience. After eliminating as best he can his own misunderstandings of the past, the historian must make sure that his readers do not fall into the same traps. One might be tempted to try to avoid the difficulties posed by translating from one language into another by using the language of the period under investigation; for instance, by writing about classical Greek science in classical Greek. Such a maneuver has all the advantages of publishing a book as its own translation or, as Lewis Carroll remarked, attempting to use a country as its own map:

> "What do you consider the *largest* map that would be really useful?"
> "About six inches to the mile."
> "Only *six inches!*" exclaimed Mein Herr. "We very soon got to six *yards* to the mile. Then we tried a *hundred* yards to the mile. And then came the grandest idea of all! We actually made a map of the country on the scale of *a mile to the mile!*"
> "Have you used it much?" I enquired.
> "It has never been spread out yet," said Mein Herr. "The farmers objected: they said it would cover the whole country, and shut out the sunlight! So we now use the country itself, as its own map, and I assure you it does nearly as well."[12]

I have heard historians complain of calling anyone a biologist prior to Lamarck's coining the term "biologie" in 1802. I can see the point of not confusing the sort of thing Aristotle did with the activities of a Lamarck, Darwin, or Pasteur, but I cannot see how refusing to term Aristotle a "biologist" will help in the least. The gap between Pasteur and Lamarck is even greater than that between Lamarck and Aristotle. Current usage departs even more radically from Lamarck's original usage. To be sure, Darwin did not use the term "evolution" in the *Origin of Species*. At the time it referred roughly to what we now call ontogenetic development. But as Michael Ruse has stated quite forcefully, it now means *evolution*, and "we today have a perfect right to use our own language."[13] If use of one's own language in writing about the past is presentism, then presentism is a necessary element in good historigoraphy.

One way to overcome the difficulties introduced by the relativity of meaning is to use the closest contemporary term while warning the reader of the relevant differences. Another is to introduce the term actually used at the time but with an appropriate explanation. The point to notice is that on both strategies, the same explanation is given and it can be given only in the full knowledge of the differences and similarities between the culture that is being written *about* and the culture being written *for*. For example, it is difficult to see how one could get a present-day reader to understand Darwin's views on inheritance and evolution without introducing such anachronistic terms as "genotype" and "phenotype." Genotypically, Darwin's theory of inheritance was nearly as particulate as Mendel's theory and even more particulate in certain respects than current views. After all, Darwin's gemmules were tiny, discrete particles. On Darwin's view, phenotypic traits tended to blend because of the variable number and kind of gemmules which he believed contributed to the formation of any one trait. Finally, Darwin neither said nor believed that variation was "continuous." He thought that the variations operative in evolution were slight, small, and insensibly fine in contrast to sports. The notion of continuous variation was introduced much later in the dispute between the biometricians and the Mendelians.

Writing history requires translation, whether the languages concerned are two different contemporary languages, such as German and English, or different stages in the development of the same language. I can read *Beowulf* with no greater ease than *Buddenbrooks*. And, as Sir Karl Popper has argued, translation requires interpretation:

> Everybody who has done some translating, and who has thought about it, knows that there is no such thing as a grammatically correct and also almost literal translation of any interesting text. Every good translation is an *interpretation* of the original text; and I would even go so far as to say that every good translation of a nontrivial text must be a theoretical reconstruction. Thus it will even incorporate bits of a commentary. Every good translation must be, at the same time, close *and* free.[14]

THE RELATIVITY OF REASONING

As historians of philosophy have pointed out, our systems of logic, like natural languages, have changed through the years. Certain sorts of arguments that were prohibited in Aristotelian logic are now considered to be perfectly valid, and vice versa. Aristotle's philosophy of science was condemned by Bacon, and we in turn condemn his extreme inductivism. In a review of Adolf Grünbaum's *Philosophical Problems of Space and Time* (1973), Arthur Miller complains that Grünbaum's "analysis is carried out ahistorically, that is, exclusively in terms of the philosophy of science circa 1973."[15]. There is an obvious point to Miller's criticism. If Grünbaum supposes that the scientists under scrutiny accepted the same philosophy of science which he himself accepts, then he is mistaken. If Grünbaum fails to mention differences in the principles of reasoning accepted in the period under investigation and those prevalent today, he is omitting important information. However, Miller also seems to be criticizing Grünbaum for using present-day standards of good reasoning in his own analysis.

When an historian begins to study a period, should he himself use the methods of good reasoning accepted at the time under investigation or his own? Put this bluntly, the answer is painfully obvious. In the initial stages of inquiry, an historian cannot use the standards accepted at the time because he has no way of knowing what they are. More importantly, even as he comes to understand these earlier principles of reasoning, he would be wrong to substitute them for his own. Doing so would mean replacing principles which he and his fellow historians take to be correct with those which we now take to be mistaken. More serious problems arise when historians attempt to *evaluate* the reasoning used by earlier scientists. Many historians maintain that such evaluations have no place in history. Historians should record what happened and nothing else. Such historiographic dicta are easier to enunciate than to defend. Present-day scientists make mistakes, equivocate on the meanings of terms, claim that certain conclusions follow from their premises when they do not, and so on. Their contemporaries feel perfectly free to point out these mistakes. However, once science slips into the past and becomes the province of the historian, all such evaluations must suddenly cease.

As always, there is some point to such prohibitions. Mutual criticism among scientists living at the same time results in the improvement of science. For example, there was some point to William Hopkins' scolding Darwin for his sloppy methodology.[16] It might have forced Darwin to improve his practice or explain why there was nothing wrong with it. This debate, of course, would have taken place in the context of nineteenth-century views on the subject. The same justification does not apply to later criticisms by such historians as Nordenskiöld and Himmelfarb.[17] There is no way that they can hope to improve Darwin's methodology by their criticisms. Instead, the point of their cirticisms seems to cast doubt on contemporary versions of evolutionary theory by attacking Darwin. In doing so, they are using (possibly abusing) history in the service of a scientific cause. They are masquerading science as history.

214 / *David L. Hull*

However, prohibitions about importing present-day principles of good reasoning into the history of science can be carried too far. For example, the explicitly stated philosophies of science in the first half of the nineteenth century in Great Britain were extremely empirical and inductivitist. In this context, many of Darwin's contemporaries claimed that his theory was logically unacceptable. It was one mass of conjectures, unsubstantiated assertions, and leaps of faith. Darwin and his defenders claimed otherwise. Can an historian say nothing more? When Darwin's practice is compared to the inductivist standards of a John Stuart Mill, it comes up wanting. But this is only part of the story. In general, the actual practice of other nineteenth-century scientists fared no better. In addition, then as now, scientists had too much sense to swallow methodological pronouncements without a bit of salt. After studying Mill, Whewell, Newton, and Darwin, an historian is forced to conclude that Mill and Whewell distorted the work of these scientists to fit their own purposes. Does proper historiographic method preclude an historian from *saying* so? I hope not.

The problem of self-reference discussed earlier is only magnified when at issue are the principles of good reasoning. We are not all biologists or historians, but we are all "reasoners." No matter what hat an investigator is wearing at any one moment, there is one hat that he can never take off. No matter what else an historian may be doing, he is using certain principles of reasoning, and his use implies at least tacit acceptance. Although divine revelation was once thought to be a legitimate way to arrive at conclusions about the world in which we live, no historian today would justify his findings in these terms, any more than he would use the "logic" exhibited in the writings of a mystic in his own investigations of that mystic. However, the very fact that a contemporary historian would never cite Scripture in support of his discussion of the debate over evolutionary theory places him squarely in the naturalistic camp, and naturalism was one of the chief points at issue. If an historian actually thinks his principles of investigation are superior to those of the people whom he is studying, if his use of these principles implies that he thinks they are superior, what is the point of his not honestly *saying* so? Of course, Grünbaum uses philosophic principles circa 1973 in his analysis. What other principles should he use?

When we turn from the methods by which an historian attempts to discover what went on in the past to his communicating these findings to his contemporaries, the problem of discrepancies between the principles of reasoning used in the past and today arises once again. If an historian sets out without comment a line of reasoning that on today's standards is clearly fallacious, his readers have every right to feel puzzled. Similarly, presented with a scientist's failing to draw what seems like an extremely obvious conclusion from a set of premises, a modern reader might also be justifiably puzzled. One possible source of the puzzlement is that the scientists concerned did not share with us our current principles of logic. For example, many of the peculiarities of Aristotle's laws of motion make sense once we are told that Aristotle's syllogistic logic is applicable only to existent things—and the void is the absence of everything. Of course, there is always the possibility that the scientist made a mistake, given the standards of his day, or else failed to see the obvious. But in many cases the question arises only because of differences between our principles of reasoning and those accepted in earlier periods. Having noticed such discrepancies, the historian would only increase confusion if all he did was pass over them without comment.

THE RELATIVITY OF TRUTH

One of the chief faults that modern historians find with the histories written by their predecessors, especially those written by scientists emeriti, is the tendency to read current empirical knowledge back into the past, describing, for example, the origin of vaccination as if everyone concerned understood the nature of viruses and contagious diseases. Even worse is the condemnation of early scientists for not knowing what we know today. However, sometimes present-day historians in their historiographical asides sound as if they think that truth is relative. Throughout the history of civilization, most people believed that the earth was flat. Today most people believe that it is roughly spherical. Unlikely though it may be with respect to this overly simple example, we too could be wrong. The problem is how to describe this state of affairs in full recognition of the fallibility of human knowledge and the variability of human discourse.

One solution is to equate truth with belief. Saying that something is true is equivalent on this view with saying that the people in question believed it. On one extreme interpretation, such claims imply that the earth changed its shape as people changed their beliefs on the subject. The earth used to be flat, and now it is roughly spherical. The absurdity of this interpretation can be avoided by refusing to talk about the shape of the earth in the first place and to refer only to people's beliefs. People used to believe that the earth was flat; now they believe that it is roughly spehirical. The actual shape of the earth is irrelevant to the historian. As attractive as this maneuver may seem, it accomplishes nothing because the next question is whether these people actually held the beliefs being attributed to them. Beliefs about the shape of the earth are just as much part of the empirical world as the shape of the earth—and no easier to discover.

David L. Hull

Regardless of what they might say on the subject, the actions of historians belie any belief in the relativity of truth. Did Marx write to Darwin asking to dedicate *Das Kapital* to him? No historian would accept as evidence in this dispute the unsupported beliefs of his fellow historians, regardless of how widely or how deeply they were held. At times historians say things that make it sound as if they believed that truth is relative. To be sure, the beliefs of the people living in a society in some sense "define their reality." But reality has a way of forcing itself on us independent of our beliefs. Whether or not historians are right to do so, they act as if there were more to history than the beliefs of historians. The presentation of relevant data and cogent arguments are what really count. Perhaps historical claims, like all empirical claims, will never attain absolute certainty. Perhaps the relativity of meaning will always interfere with our attempts to describe the empirical world precisely. No doubt our understanding of rationality will continue to change through time. But there is a difference between belief and rationally justified belief. If historians are willing to make this distinction for themselves—and they are—they should be willing to make it for others as well.

Because early historians of science unfairly lampooned such figures as Aristotle, Lamarck, and Gall for holding some of the views they held, modern historians are led to argue that no mention should be made of discrepancies between the empirical beliefs of the scientists under investigation and our own. One should set out a scientist's ideas and leave it at that. Once again, there is considerable point to this maxim. In order to understand Aristotle's physiological system, it is important to know that he thought that the brain cooled the blood. That we now take this belief to be mistaken is not very important. However, this maxim itself can be carried too far. We can learn a great deal about a scientist by the mistakes he makes. For example, Aristotle himself seems to have dissected many of the organisms which he described. In general, he was a very good observer. When his descriptions depart too radically from the organisms as we now know them, the historian has the right to suspect that Aristotle did not make these dissections but is passing on second-hand information. Similarly, we know today that several of the physical differences Aristotle notes between men and women do not exist. That Aristotle thought they did tells us something of the attitudes in his society about the sexes.

Historians use our knowledge of the present to reconstruct the past. They could not do otherwise. All the evidence they have available to them exists in the present. Historians are also well aware that certain features of the world in which we live change through time. The earth has cooled, continents have drifted, mountain ranges have worn away, jungles have come and gone, species have become extinct, human societies have arisen and disappeared. One task of the historian is to chronicle these changes. But he also believes, and must believe if he is to reconstruct the past on the basis of the records surviving to the present, that the processes producing these changes are sufficiently stable through time. Darwin, for example, believed that certain traits could be explained only in terms of the inheritance of acquired characteristics. That is no surprise. The belief was common at the time. The evidence seemed to support it, and it fit nicely into his theory of inheritance. That we now take such beliefs to be mistaken is irrelevant. However, what if Darwin had mentioned that snow is black? Instead of mindlessly registering that Darwin believed that snow is black, the historian would surely try to find out if Darwin actually held such a belief and if so, why. Darwin was not prone to make such patent observational mistakes. The source of the historian's puzzlement is that he knows that snow is white now and that we have every reason to believe that it was just as white in Darwin's day—regardless of the beliefs of the people at the time. Similarly, Christians have traditionally maintained that Mary was a virgin when she gave birth to Jesus. The historian must surely take note of these beliefs, but he is also warranted in looking for the biological father. He has every right to believe that virgin births were no more common two thousand years ago than they are today.[18]

Historians use their knowledge of the present in reconstructing the past. They also use it in writing for readers who are likely to share this knowledge with them. A modern reader is just as likely to be shocked at Darwin's claiming that snow is black as the historian. Some explanation is surely called for. Present-day readers are likely to view a belief in Lamarckian modes of inheritance as not only mistaken but also unscientific. Mistaken, though justified, it surely was. Unscientific it was not. Which of Darwin's beliefs the historian decides to expand in this connection is not determined by which turned out to be correct and which faulty, given current knowledge, but by which are likely to puzzle the modern reader and which not. Because the only science a present-day reader is likely to know is the science contained in contemporary textbooks, the historian is well advised to pay attention to similarities and differences between this science and the science under discussion. For example, the first time that a person reads Darwin commenting on three-to-one ratios in inheritance, he is likely to jump to the conclusion that Darwin had just stumbled on the key to Mendelian genetics. Why this conclusion is mistaken takes some explaining. Ignoring the likelihood that this is exactly the sort of mistake that someone knowing modern Mendelian genetics is prone to make can hardly be good historiography.

CONCLUSION

In this paper, I have been concerned to show that knowledge of the present is absolutely crucial for the historian, both in reconstructing the past and in explaining it to his readers. From his position in the present, the historian must use all evidence and tools available to him in reconstructing the past even if this knowledge was unavailable to the people in the period under investigation. He then must communicate these findings to his contemporaries. Even the most compulsive historian is likely to know more about his own age than the one he is studying. His reader is sure to. Warnings about "presentism" are designed to prevent our knowledge of the present from distorting our knowledge of the past. Perhaps the possible abuses of prohibitions against presentism detailed in this paper are exaggerated. I am afraid they are not. The two commonest responses which I have received to this paper are that no historian has ever held the historiographic principles which I discuss—they are straw men—and that every right-thinking historian does.

NOTES

1. Williams, L. Pearce. "Should Philosophers Be Allowed to Write History?" *The British Journal for the Philosophy of Science* 26 (1975): 241-253. Agassi, Joseph. *Faraday as a Natural Philosopher*. Chicago and London: University of Chicago Press 1972. Berkson, William. *Fields of Force*. London: Routledge & Kegan Paul 1974. Williams has since tempered his condemnation of Berkson but not Agassi, "Reply to Agassi and Berkson." *The British Journal for the Philosophy of Science* 29 (1978): 252.

2. Lakatos, Imre. "History of Science and Its Rational Reconstruction." in *PSA 1970*, ed. R. Buck and R. Cohen. Dordrecht, Holland: D. Reidel 1971, 107.

3. Williams, 253.

4. Popper, Karl. *Objective Knowledge*. Oxford: Clarendon Press 1972. Toulmin, Stephen. *Human Understanding*. Princeton, N. J.: Princeton University Press 1972. Laudan, Larry. *Progress and Its Problems*. Berkeley: University of California Press 1977.

5. Butterfield, Herbert. *The Whig Interpretation of History*. London: G. Bell and Sons 1931, v.

6. Brush, Stephen G. "Should the History of Science Be Rated X?" *Science* 183 (1974): 1169.

7. Kuhn, Thomas. "The History of Science." *International Encyclopedia of the Social Sciences* 14 (1968): 76.

8. *Idem.*

9. Murphey, Murray G. *Our Knowledge of the Historical Past.* Indianapolis and New York: Bubbs-Merrill 1973, 120.

10. *Idem.*

11. Mandelbaum, Maurice. *The Anatomy of Historical Knowledge.* Baltimore and London: Johns Hopkins University Press 1977, 113.

12. Dodgson, Charles Lutwidge. *Sylvie and Bruno Concluded* In *The Complete Works of Lewis Carroll.* London: Macmillan 1939, 556-557.

13. Ruse, Michael. *The Darwinian Revolution.* Chicago and London: Chicago: University of Chicago Press, 1979a, preface.

14. Popper, Karl. *Unended Quest.* La Salle, Ill.:Open Court Press 1976, 23.

15. Miller, Arthur I. "Review of Adolf Grünbaum, 'Philosophical Problems of Space and Time' (Dordrecht, Holland, 1973)." *Isis* 66 (1975): 590-594. Grünbaum, Adolf. "Remarks on Miller's Review of 'Philosophical Problems of Space and Time'." *Isis* 68 (1977): 447-448. Miller, Arthur I. "Reply by Arthur I. Miller." *Isis* 68 (1977): 449-450.

16. Hopkins, William. "Physical Theories of the Phenomena of Life." *Fraser's Magazine* 61 (1860): 739-752; 62 (1860): 74-90. Reprinted in Hull, D. L. *Darwin and His Critics: The Reception of Darwin's Theory of Evolution by the Scientific Community.* Cambridge, Mass.: Harvard University Press 1973, 229-272.

17. Nordenskiöld, Erick. *The History of Biology* [1920-1924], transl. Leonard Bucknall Eyre. New York: Tudor Publishing Company 1928. Himmelfarb, Gertrude. *Darwin and the Darwinain Revolution.* Garden City: Doubleday 1959.

18. In his review of Joe D. Burchfield's *Lord Kelvin and the Age of the Earth* (New York: Science History Publications 1975), Edward Bullard discusses the story which Burchfield tells and then concludes:
In spite of the careful account of all these things some readers may feel a little deprived. An historian must study the past in its own terms. He must not ask 'What was Henry VIII's attitude to women's lib?' This viewpoint has been adopted also by historians of science, and in some degree, is clearly necessary. But should one go the whole way? The author of this book consistently refrains from saying that anything is right or wrong, silly or unjustified. If Kelvin assumes that the Earth was initially at 1,500°C, the author reports that he said it and that it was a more or less arbitrary choice, but he does not add that it matters very little what figure is taken. On the other hand no one would guess that Kelvin's assumption of the absence of convection within the Earth was crucial and that the attacks on it were well based. The history of science is different from other kinds of history; there is the additional fact that some things are correct and some wrong *sub specie aeternitatis.*

I share Bullard's feelings of deprivation, but I do not think that these feelings are limited just to readers of histories of science.

19. The major sort of relativity that I do not discuss in this paper is the relativity of morals. Strangely enough, historians who would never dream of criticizing an early scientist for not having present-day conceptions, for failing to adhere to those principles of good reasoning which we now hold, or for making what we take to be factual errors feel perfectly free to sneer at early scientists for not living up to the historian's own moral standards. Denigrating Darwin for believing that a previous insemination of a mare can affect later pregnancies is bad historiography; condemning him as a racist is somehow perfectly all right. But Darwin's attitudes on racial matters were as "enlightened" by nineteenth-century standards as were his ideas on heredity.

Chapter 13

Conceptual Evolution and
The Eye of the Octopus*

The major reason for evolutionary analyses of conceptual change being so unsatisfactory is that they are modeled on an inadequate understanding of biological evolution. Genes are not in the least like beads on a string, an entire meadow can function as a single organism in the evolutionary process, and species are not classes of similar organisms, regardless of the dictates of common sense and ordinary usage. To make matters worse, even when such biological concepts as genes, organisms and species are adequately understood, they are still not general enough to function in a truly general theory of evolution (Hull 1980). In order for evolution to occur by variation and selection, certain entities (replicators) must pass on their structure largely intact. In biological evolution, replication occurs primarily at the level of the genetic material. Certain entities must also interact with their environments in such a way that this replication is differential. Entities at a wide variety of levels, including genes, chromosomes, cells, organisms, kinship groups, and possibly even populations and entire species can perform this function. As a result of these two processes, other entities (lineages) change indefinitely through time—they evolve. For our purposes, the most important feature of the preceding process is that at all levels it is spatiotemporally localized. Evolution is a local, not global phenomenon. Both the entities that function in selection processes and the entities that evolve as a result are spatiotemporally localized entities. They are individuated in terms of location, internal cohesiveness and continuity through time. They are historical entities. The sort of identity that is fundamental is genidentity.

Neither biologists nor philosophers of biology are unanimous in their acceptance of the preceding characterization of the evolutionary process. In general, opponents consider the things that evolve (species) as spatiotemporally unrestricted classes such that sufficiently similar organisms, living at different times and widely separated places, can be interpreted

---

*Reprinted with permission from Barcan Marcus et al., eds. *Logic, Methodology and Philosophy of Science VII.* © Elsevier Science Publishers B. V. (1986) 643-665.

as belonging to the same species (Kitts and Kitts, 1979; Caplan 1980, 1981: Kitcher, 1984a). Defenders maintain that such a conception of species might have some warrant, but whatever the use these classes may have in other contexts, they cannot evolve (Ghiselin, 1974a; Hull, 1976a, 1978b; Wiley, 1981; Sober, 1984). In this paper, I can present only the briefest sketch of the reasons for treating both the entities that function in selection processes and the entities that evolve as a consequence of them as historical entities. My main purpose is to extend this line of reasoning to conceptual evolution, especially the sorts of conceptual change that occur in science. Concepts are traditionally treated as classes of similar (or identical) tokens. For example, in this paper thus far, five tokens of the term-type "evolution" have appeared. Clearly, there are many contexts in which concepts can and should be viewed as tokens of the same type, but the evolutionary context is not one of them. If concepts are to evolve, then they can no more be construed as similar tokens of the same type than can species be interpreted as classes of similar organisms. Both must be construed as lineages. Just as not all eyes are "eyes," not every set of axioms with the same assertive content can count as the same theory. Not all instances of Darwin's theory count as "Darwin's theory."

In this paper, I begin with a brief justification of treating biological phenomena the way I do, using the eye of the octopus as an example. I then proceed to present parallel arguments for treating concepts in the same way. Objections are likely to arise at three junctures. First, certain readers may disagree with my understanding of the evolutionary process; for example, it is not necessarily localized in space and time. Second, they might object to any attempt to treat conceptual evolution as analogous to biological evolution, regardless of the nature of the biological analogy. Finally, they might be willing to accept my analysis of biological evolution and the attempt to present an analogous treatment of conceptual evolution but disagree with my particular attempt. I have dealt with the first two sorts of objections elsewhere (Hull, 1981, 1982) and cannot go over this same ground here. In this paper, I must confine myself to objections of the third sort.

WHEN IS AN EYE NOT AN EYE?

The structure/function distinction runs throughout biology. Should anything that functions as an eye count as an eye, or must eyes exhibit a certain structure, or both? When de Voe (1981, 433) states that eyes are "sensory organs that direct onto thin layers of neural tissues—retinas— whatever of the external world can be conveyed by emitted, refracted, scattered, or reflected quanta of light," he is defining eyes in terms of a combination of structural and functional criteria. On this definition, many organs that organisms use to see don't count as eyes, including some vertebrate eyes. I am not about to address the tangle of problems surrounding the relative primacy of functional and structural criteria in defining classes of organs in biology. Instead, I propose to add yet another dimension to the problem — descent. Evolutionary biologists are unwilling to consider two organs the "same" organ, no matter how similar they are in structure and/or function, if they lack the requisite ancestor-descendant connections (Wiley, 1981). The eye of the octopus is the usual example.

Because nearly all organisms living here on Earth use exactly the same genetic code and those that do not depart in only minor ways, biologists conclude that all terrestrial life had a single origin. Thus, if present-day cephalopods and vertebrates are traced far enough back in time, they have common ancestors. When organs in present-day organisms that are structurally and/or functionally the same are traced back in this tree of life, they do not always converge on a common ancestral organ. They are not evolutionarily the "same." They are not evolutionary homologies. Conversely, when organs in present-day organisms that are structurally and/or functionally quite different are traced back in time, sometimes they rapidly converge on the same organ in a common ancestor. Similarity to one side, they are instances of the same organ. For example, no matter how similar the eyes of the octopus are to vertebrate eyes, they are not homologous. Conversely, no matter how different the spiracle in sharks may seem to the eustachian tube in human beings, they are evolutionary homologies.

Similarities and differences in structure are certainly part of the evidence that biologists use to decide which structures are or are not evolutionary homologies, but any degree of similarity in structure and/or function that excludes cephalopod eyes is likely to exclude certain vertebrate eyes as well. If one looks closely enough, systematic differences between vertebrate eyes and the eye of the octopus can be discerned, but the only reason to look that closely is that differences in overall structure (*Bauplan*), embryonic development, and fossil record imply that these two organs are evolutionarily different. They have different histories. They emerged in different lineages.

The distinction between similar organs and evolutionary homologies is so commonplace, even among non-evolutionary biologists, that it is liable to arouse little resistance. School children are taught that the wings of birds, bats, flying fish and insects are not all "wings" in the same sense. The "forearms" of birds and bats are homologous as "forearms" but not as wings. At no level of analysis are the "wings" of insects and flying fish nomologous to each other or to the "forearms" of bats and birds. Evolutionary biologists begin to meet resistance when they argue that two gene-tokens with exactly the same structure do not necessarily belong to the same gene-type. Population geneticists distinguish between genes with similar structures but only the most distant ancestral connections (independent genes) and those that are identical by descent. Ordinary molecular biologists do not. In their terminology, "homologous" genes need not be evolutionary homologies. CUU is CUU, and that is that.

One common justification for distinguishing evolutionary homologies from analogies and convergences is that failure to do so produces mistakes in historical reconstructions. If one wants to reconstruct phylogeny accurately, similarity due to common descent must be distinguished from similarity due to common functional and/or sructural requirements, responses to common selection pressures, and so forth. The scope of the problem can be seen by comparing the organisms that inhabit the Mohave and Sahara Deserts (Cody, 1974). Although the niches in these two deserts are very similar and the organisms that occupy these niches are comparably similar, the organisms living in these widely separated deserts are just as distantly related phylogenetically. A niche occupied in the Mohave Desert by a lizard might be occupied in the Sahara Desert by a snake. Which sort of similarity should take precedence? From the point of view of accurate historical reconstruction, discerning evolutionary homologies is essential. The story for the evolutionary process is not so straightforward.

The process-product distinction is common in philosophy. Selection, competition, and mutation are all part of the evolutionary process. The product is phylogeny. Because the term "evolution" is frequently used for both, they are easy to confuse. When a scientist entitles a paper "The Evolution of the House Mouse," he might be referring to its phylogenetic development, the processes through which it arose, or both. As it turns out, knowledge of the details of the evolutionary process are not much help in reconstructing phylogeny. Regardless of the resolution of the various controversies currently exercising evolutionary biologists, paleontologists will continue to reconstruct phylogeny as they have in the past. One exception is the controversy over the tempo of evolution. The more saltative the evolutionary process turns out to be, the less likely paleontologists are to find fossils that are intermediate between related species.

But evolutionary biologists want to do more than reconstruct phylogeny. They want to understand the evolutionary process. To do so, they have to discern regularities in this process and the entities that function in these regularities. For example, if speciation usually occurs by the isolation of peripheral populations, then those species with longer and more convulated peripheries are likely to speciate much more frequently than other species. On this view, species with extensive, convoluted peripheries is a biological "natural kind," and particular species exemplifying these characteristics count as instances of this natural kind. Other possibilities for evolutionary natural kinds are the the continua between monotypic and polytypic species, eurytopic and stenotopic species, r-selection and K-selection, sexual reproduction, asexual reproduction, and various combinations thereof.

It might seem that paleontologists and evolutionary biologists are engaged in incompatible, possibly incommensurable activities. Paleontologists must identify evolutionary homologies in the face of the deceptive similarities introduced by constraints imposed by the evolutionary process, while evolutionary biologists are constantly frustrated by the historical constraints imposed on the evolutionary process by common ancestry. What counts as the message for one is noise for the other. As long as one views biological species and the evolutionary natural kinds listed above equally as kinds, then the two activities do seem at cross-purposes. However, once one distinguishes between genuine kinds (such as polytypic species) and instances of these kinds (for example, *Homo sapiens* as a polytypic species), the two perspectives become totally compatible. The natural kinds of evolutionary theory are spatiotemporally unrestricted in the traditional sense; for instance, sexual reproduction can occur anywhere in the universe at any time just so long as the conditions are right. Particular instances of sexual reproduction require physical contact. There is no fertilization at a distance. At least propagules must come into contact. It is the distinction between kinds and instances of kinds that Kitts (1983) ignores in his otherwise perfectly cogent criticisms of treating species as individuals and their names as proper.

Another example might help. Haplodiploidy is a particular mode of reproduction and sex determination. One sex has a particular complement of chromosomes; the other has double this complement. One is haploid; the other diploid. Haplodiploidy is especially interesting because it is one way for sociality to evolve. However, it has arisen numerous times in the course of evolution. As it is used by evolutionary biologists, haplodiploidy is a natural kind, not an evolutionary homology. It can function in evolutionary theory because it is in no way spatiotemporally localized or restricted. This same distinction applies to the eye example. Eyes as any structure capable of seeing might well function as a natural kind in biological theory; eyes as evolutionary homologies cannot. One can explain vertebrate eyes as functional eyes by reference to the relevant process theories but not their peculiar status as *vertebrate* eyes. To explain this, one must make recourse to the contingencies of their place and conditions of origin. As long as different names are given to natural kinds and evolutionary homologies, little confusion is likely to arise, but in biology the two are frequently given the same or very similar names. Not all carnivores belong to Carnivora, and not all organisms that belong to Carnivora are carnivorous. "Carnivorous" and "functional eyes" might function in laws of nature: Carnivora as a monophyletic taxon and vertebrate eyes as an evolutionary homology cannot.

As simple as the preceding distinction is, it is sufficient to resolve the apparent conflict between the historical and process perspectives in biology. But of greater importance is the fact that built into the processes of biological evolution are spatiotemporal requirements. In crucial instances, the formulae of population genetics range over entities that are not just similar in structure but *identical by descent*; in particular, the entire apparatus of kin selection. In this context, the coefficient of relationship concerns the likelihood that one allele rather than another gets passed on. To be sure, any two organisms picked at random from a population are likely to have similar alleles at the vast majority of their loci, but kin selection requires that this similarity in structure be acquired by immediate reproduction, these descendant alleles will be similar to the ancestor alleles that gave rise to them, but the converse is not true. Many alelles with the same structure, when traced back in time, do not converge on the same ancestral allele.

At the lower levels in the evolutionary process, spatiotemporal localization is essential. No one is likely to object to evolutionary biologists treating genes (introns, etc. notwithstanding) or particular organisms (tillers and tussocks notwithstanding) as historical entities. Replication is itself clearly a spatiotemporally localized process. Replicators also produce more inclusive entities that intercede for them with increasingly more inclusive environments. Particular instances of the interplay between replication and environmental interaction are somewhat less obviously spatiotemporally localized. Resistance begins in earnest when one insists that the results of these processes—lineages—are themselves spatiotemporally localized, but anyone who insists on treating lineages as types of similar tokens is going to make hash of the evolutionary process. However, once the immediate effects of selection have left their mark, nothing about selection processes entails that these same decisions be made with respect to more macro-phenomena. The insistence of evolutionary biologists on recognizing evolutionary homologies (such as the vertebrate eye) and monophyletic taxa (like Vertebrata) is an extrapolation from decisions that are absolutely necessary at the microlevel to higher level phenomena. The entities that evolve must be treated as lineages. Arguments to the effect that higher taxa must be treated in the same way are not so conclusive. Not all biologists are willing to treat higher taxa strictly as clades. Some biologists prefer to intercalate "paraphyletic" groups into a phylogenetic classification. The primacy of the lineage perspective can be seen, however, both in the fact that phylogenetic relationships set limits to the introduction of paraphyletic taxa and in the need to justify departures from strict monophyly.[1]

In summary, evolutionary natural kinds are absolutely necessary if we are ever to have an adequate theory of biological evolution. Neither evolutionary homologies nor monophyletic taxa are candidates for these natural kinds because they are inherently spatiotemporally restricted. There can be no "laws of the vertebrate eye." Vertebrata might well be an *instance* of a natural kind, but it itself cannot *be* one. Neither single lineages nor monophyletic chunks of the phylogenetic tree are candidates for spatiotemporally unrestricted classes. If one finds this distinction difficult to maintain in the context of biological evolution, wait until the same distinctions are introduced into conceptual evolution.

WHEN IS DARWIN'S THEORY NOT DARWIN'S THEORY?

One need not be a Platonist to see a role in language for concepts modeled along the traditional type-token analysis. The type-token distinction in language parallels the individual-class distinction at the level of things. Just as individuals are instances of classes, term-tokens are instances of term-types. In language, proper names denote individuals (or particulars of any sort) while general terms denote classes (as well as such things as properties, processes, etc.). But the type-token distinction applies equally to all terms. Numerous instances (tokens) of a term-type can exist for any term-type, regardless of whether it is proper or more general. Several tokens of the term-type "Darwin" have already appeared in this paper, even though Charles Darwin is a paradigm individual and his name a paradigm proper name.

A minimal requirement for something's being an individual and the same individual through time is genidentity—continuous development through time and internal cohesiveness at any one time. Some authors maintain that this minimal requirement is also sufficient. An individual can change any or all of its properties and still remain numerically the same individual in the process. Other authors are willing to allow individuals to change as much as they please just so long as they do not lose their "essential" characteristics—the characteristics that make them the kind of thing that they are. If a comet captured by a star can become a planet while remaining the same individual, then neither comethood nor planethood is part of its essence. Similarly, if an organism can change from one sex to another during the course of ontogenetic development (as many do) without becoming numerically a new individual, then it follows that gender is not part of an organism's essence. No one is essentially male or essentially female.

A common objection to the more demanding criteria for individuality is that there are no essences. If essences do not exist, then retention of essence can hardly be a requirement for individuality. Although I think that the notion of essential characteristics has been repeatedly abused through the centuries, I also happen to believe that we cannot do without it. Even so, requiring that an individual be considered a new individual when it changes its essence leads to some very peculiar results. Genidentity does not always covary with retention of particular characteristics, no matter what characteristics are chosen. For example, organisms are paradigm individuals, and yet there is nothing about an organism that cannot change during the course of its ontogenic development, including material substance, overall structure and even genetic make-up. On the stronger requirement for individuality, either an entity that is changing continuously through time must be divided sequentially into a series of distinct individuals, or else one must conclude that organisms do not belong to any natural kinds whatsoever. As inconvenient as it may be, organisms that have mated successfully with members of one species can and do proceed to mate successfully with members of other species. On the stronger requirement, it follows that an organism becomes numerically a new individual when it ceases to be part of one genealogical nexus and begins to participate in another.

As a result of the preceding considerations, in this paper I have adopted the weaker, minimal requirement for individuality—genidentity. Thus, a proper name denotes the individual it does, and that is that. For the purposes of naming, nothing more is required of lineages (historical entities of all sorts) than genidentity. Gargantua was named "Gargantua," *Gorilla gorilla* was named "*Gorilla gorilla*," and Darwin's theory was named "Darwin's theory." Each of these historical entities may change very little during the course of their development, or they may change extensively. It does not matter. All that matters is that these changes be continuous and that the entity remain sufficiently cohesive in the process (given the appropriate scale). Before pursuing the implications of this perspective for conceptual historical entities, a few words must be said about general terms. For the sake of simplicity, I will limit myself just to classes of the sort that are at least candidates for the status of natural kinds.

On the traditional type-token analysis, numerous different term-tokens belong to the same term-type if and only if they "mean the same thing" and/or denote the same entities. For example, on this view, every instance of the term "evolution" is a token of the same type if it refers to the same sort of process. In natural languages, applying the type-token analysis is difficult because of the extensive ambiguity, redundancy, and vagueness so characteristic of natural languages, not to mention changes in meaning. For example, in the nineteenth century, the term-type "evolution" meant orderly, cyclical, "programmed" change of the sort that occurs in embryological development. Because in 1859 Darwin thought that the transmutation of species had none of these characteristics, he carefully avoided using the term "evolution" in his *Origin of Species*. However, a pre-*Origin* evolutionist, Herbert Spencer (1852), thought that embryological development and evolutionary change were basically the same sort of process and, hence, used "evolution" for both. His usage caught on. Today most evolutionary biologists agree with Darwin about the nature of the evolutionary process but retain Spencer's term. To make matters worse, "evolution" is also used to mean change of any sort, so that we hear about the "evolution" of galaxies and tail fins in Cadillacs.

In the face of such linguistic facts of life, one can understand why philosophers have toyed with the idea of replacing natural languages with languages that are carefully and consciously constructed to avoid the near chaos of natural languages. In the early years, the task was simplified even further by the widely held assumption that the primary function of language is description. Wittgenstein's (1921) *Tracatatus* is a good case in point. In this highly influential work, Wittgenstein took for granted that the primary task of language is accurate, unambiguous description of the world in which we live. Each atomic sentence refers to one and only one atomic fact. On this perspective, the traditional type-token analysis of concepts appears more than adequate, but even philosophers who favor a more wholistic, less atomic view of language do not always feel the need to question traditional type-token conceptual identity. To be sure, the inter-connections between words in a single language make translating from one language to another more difficult, but they do not raise special problems for a single language mirroring the world. Real difficulties surfaced when philosophers such as Wittgenstein (1953) decided that the fundamental function of language is communication, introducing a social dimension to language. A speaker can still describe the world but only in the context of community-based language games. The reverberations of this change in perspective are still making themselves felt throughout philosophy. One impact has been on the old type-token notion of conceptual identity.

Because of continuing difficulties with the notion of "meaning," contemporary analytic philosophers have attempted to deal with general terms without recourse to it. One such suggestion looks initially like the one I propose in this paper, Kripke's (1972) extremely influential notion of rigid designation. Proper names have commonly been viewed as designating their referents rigidly. Kripke (1972) suggested that at least some kind terms might be treated profitably in much the same way. On his analysis, the reference of a speaker's term-token is fixed by means of an initiating event, a sort of "baptism," and then transmitted in a link-on-link reference-preserving chain. It might seem that, on Kripke's view, "sameness of reference" is a historical notion because these reference-preserving chains look very much like historical entities. However, appearances are deceiving. Because reference is preserved in Kripke's chains, all term-tokens that belong to a single chain refer to the same thing in the old similarity sense. For example, if an early token referred to gold, all subsequent tokens must also refer to gold. However, if Kripke's reference-preserving chains are literally link-on-link, the opposite need not be the case. Term-tokens that "referred to the same thing" in the traditional sense might not be part of the chain that emanated from the initial initiating event for that term-type. Several independent link-on-link chains, each with its own initiating event, are possible. If they all refer to the same thing, I suspect that Kripke would want them to be considered term-tokens of the same type. I fail to see how Kripke's sets of link-on-link chains that refer to the same thing are any advance over sets of independent tokens that all refer to the same thing, whether or not they form link-on-link reference-preserving chains.

A whole generation of philosophers have found Kripke's suggestion about rigid designation intriguing, but as always, discontent has set in, albeit not for the reason I have just presented in the preceding paragraph. For instance, Kitcher (1978, 182) has set out a theory of reference in which link-on-link, reference chains can change their referents, and even when they do not, the ways in which the reference of term-tokens is fixed can change. An example of the first sort of change is the term-type "planet." Initially, the extension of "planet" did not include Earth. After the acceptance of Copernicus's theory, it did. As an example of the way in which the mode of reference for a term-type can change, Kitcher (1982b) notes that early on in the history of genetics, tokens of the term-type "gene" were applied only when Mendelian ratios were discerned. Later, the cis-trans test was added. Kitcher (1982b) proposes to handle both sorts of changes by means of his notion of *reference potential*.

Kitcher's (1982b, 345) basic notion is the reference potential of a term-type for an individual speaker, the "class of events which, given the speech dispositions of the speaker, can initiate productions of the type." A derivative notion for Kitcher (182b, 340) is the reference potential for a community, a "compendium of the ways in which the referents of tokens of the term are fixed for members of the community." Although Kitcher (1982b, 339) rejects "mysterious intensional entities," he does acknowledge a role for the intentions of particular language users, which he summarizes in three maxims—conformity, naturalism, and clarity. As Kitcher sees it, in most cases a language user intends to conform to the usage of his community, although in crucial cases he might not. For example, for Darwin as well as for most of his contemporaries, the term "species" referred to such things as dogs, horses and people, but Darwin's contemporaries were firmly convinced that species are immutable. If one putative species is actually descended from another putative species, then automatically they become one species. If Darwin was right, and all present-day species arose from one or a few original species, then only one or a few species actually exist, appearances notwithstanding.

The preceding example also helps to illustrate Kitcher's second maxim. Sometimes people in general and scientists in particular intend to refer to natural kinds, even though the identifying descriptions that they are using may be abandoned by later workers. On occasion, however, one might decide to stick with the description even if it means admitting that one had not been referring to a natural kind (Kitcher, 1982b, 344). For example, most of Darwin's contemporaries defined the term "species" so that particular species have the traditional characteristics of natural kinds. Species at the time were thought to be, in the appropriate sense, eternal, immutable and discrete. On Darwin's view, particular species have none of these characteristics. *Canis familiaris* is in no sense eternal. At one time it did not exist. At some future date, it is sure to go extinct. All species are the contingent effects of natural forces and not part of the framework of the universe. Nor are species immutable. The only way that species arise is through evolution, and for Darwin, evolution was gradual. The boundaries between species are anything but discrete. Perhaps Darwin and his contemporaries intended for the names of particular species to refer to natural kinds, but it is difficult to see how anyone can reject every traditional characteristic of natural kinds for species and still claim that species are natural kinds (but see Kitcher, 1984a). Of course, one possibility is that the term-type "natural kind" was in the midst of changing its reference. As far as I can tell, it was not. In fact, it still has not.

Kitcher's (1982b) third maxim is that, on occasion, scientists intend to refer to that which they can specify. Philosophers have not had much patience with the emphasis that scientists place on operational definitions. After all, they are not "definitions." But Kitcher sees an important role for the tests which scientists devise to help them to apply their terms. For example, if a *cis-trans* test turns out in a particular way, a geneticist is likely to produce a token of the term-type "gene." Although there is much more to a theoretically significant term-type than the methods scientists use at any one time to apply tokens of it. I do not think that it seriously misrepresents the behavior of scientists to claim that they do intend a referent in such circumstances to be whatever was causally linked to the production of this token or satisfied a particular description.

The chief problem for Kitcher, as I see it, is how his notion of reference potential can actually handle changes in reference as well as changes in mode of fixing reference. If Kitcher's linguistic communities were genuine social groups, then they could be used to integrate "diverse initiating events" so that they can refer to the same entities as scientists renew and extend the connections between their terms and the world. But Kitcher (1982b, 346) defines linguistic communities in terms of agreement on initiating events. "With respect to a particular expression type, two speakers belong to the same linguistic community if they are disposed to count exactly the same events as initiating events for production of tokens of the type." As a result, Kitcher is forced to conclude that scientists who belong to the same research team might well belong to different "linguistic communities" with respect to certain terms and the same community with respect to others. Under such circumstances I fail to see how the "dispositions of the community to use tokens of a particular term to refer to a particular range of ways may vary through time" (Kitcher, 1982b, 340) or how terms can have "heterogeneous reference potentials" (Kitcher, 1982b, 345). If the dispositions of a community to use tokens of a term vary through time, then that is not the same community. To the extent that people accept diverse initiating events for a term, they do not belong to the same community.

Kitcher is having much the same problem as Kuhn (1970, 176) confronted when he attempted to clarify his notion of paradigm by noting that a "paradigm is what the members of a scientific community share, *and*, conversely, a scientific community consists of men who share a paradigm." Kuhn is aware of the apparent circularity in the preceding quotation and proposes to avoid it by delimiting his scientific communities sociologically in terms of their professional relations. However, when scientific communities are delimited in this way, an inconvenient fact arises: members of the same scientific community are not always in agreement even over fundamentals. As strange as it may seem, scientists can cooperate with each other even when they are not in total agreement. I think that Kitcher is on the right track in his analysis of reference, but like Kuhn, I think that he must ground reference potential in sociologically delimited communities. In the rest of this paper, I propose to treat Kitcher's linguistic communities as genuine social groups. This means that not everyone who belongs to a particular linguistic community need agree totally about the initiating events for a particular term. Instead of a person belonging to as many linguistic communities as there are terms in his vocabulary, he is likely to belong to only a very few. There are only so many hours in a day. The time necessary to participate in a social group imposes an upper limit to how many social groups one can belong to.

On my reformulation of Kitcher's theory of reference, actual descent from an actual initiating event is *necessary* for two or more term-tokens to be tokens of the same term-type in the evolutionary sense of "term-type." Conceptual tokens must be organized first and foremost into link-on-link chains—lineages. Conceptual lineages can merge, but *merger* is partially independent of both agreement and similarity in references. For example, in 1831, Patrick Matthew published his version of the principle of natural selection, Darwin formulated his version in 1838, while A. R. Wallace did not stumble upon natural selection until 1855. From the perspective of similarity in assertive content, all three of these conceptual tokens are tokens of the same type. Put differently, "natural selection" was initiated three times. Wallace's initiation was not totally independent of Darwin's initiation, because both men had read Lyell and Malthus. Wallace had read Darwin's early work, and both men had exchanged letters on the species problem prior to Wallace's bolt from the blue. As far as I can tell, neither Darwin nor Wallace had read Matthew's (1831) *Naval Timbre and Arboriculture* prior to their own initiating events; see Eiseley's (1979, 72) contrary claim in his continuing anti-Darwin vendetta. Even though the initiating events for Darwin and Wallace were at least partially independent of each other, they belong in the same conceptual lineage because of the interplay between Darwin and Wallace after Wallace sent Darwin a copy of his species paper. Although the two men were never in total agreement about the nature and impact of natural selection, they developed their theories in consort. Matthew's initiating event remained totally outside this conceptual lineage.

From the point of view of natural selection as a conceptual lineage, Matthew's clear statement does not count as the "same" term-type as that of Darwin and Wallace. In conceptual evolution as elsewhere, similarity does not universally covary with identity by descent. In general, this means that truly unappreciated precursors do not count. They are of antiquarian interest only. "But that is not fair!" Whoever said that natural processes, including conceptual evolution, were fair? Fairness at a local level in science at least does matter. By and large, scientists are given credit by their colleagues for that work that these colleagues find useful. Citations serve three main functions in science: to support the work of the scientist who is publishing the citation, to deflect blame if the work that is being cited turns out to be mistaken, and to give credit where credit is due. Scientists attempt to accrue to themselves as much credit as possible, but they also need support. They cannot gain support without giving credit. The success of this system of use and credit depends on the frequency of blatant stealing not becoming too high. Fairness to one's graduate students, fellow team members, and even distant colleagues is relevant to the ongoing process of science. Fairness to scientists who have long been dead is not (Hull, 1978a).

To the extent that setting the record straight is actually operative, attempts to be fair to scientists in the past is a "misfiring" of an otherwise adaptive mechanism. In point of fact, reference to unappreciated precursors in the ongoing process of science serves quite different functions. For example, one way to counter present-day critics is to rail against the close-minded bigotry of the opponents of earlier scientists who proposed similar views. For evolution, Lamarck is always useful because he suffered so pitifully at Cuvier's hands. That Lamarck's notion of "evolution" was significantly different from that of Darwin and Wallace is conveniently neglected. Rarely are the views of unappreciated precursors all that similar to the later views that initiated the search for precursors. I do not intend to denigrate the usefulness of precursors as patron saints in the ongoing process of science, but misplaced romanticism to one side, they do not belong in conceptual lineages on which they had no influence.

The conceptual lineages initiated by Darwin and Wallace actually merged in the middle years of the nineteenth century. They need not have. If Wallace had become incensed by the treatment of his paper by Darwin and his friends or if Darwin had behaved much more territorially than he did, the two men might have become enemies and developed independent conceptual lineages right from the start. Scientists cooperate and compete with each other, but the character of this cooperation differs markedly within and between communities. Wallace became a (peripheral) member of the Darwinians. Other scientists who were in larger agreement with Darwin about the nature of the evolutionary process became adamant anti-Darwinians. A good example is St. George Jackson Mivart. When his efforts to work his way into the Darwinians failed, he came out as a vehement and very effective critic. In general, no simple relation exists between how much scientists agree with each other and how much they cooperate in forming scientific communities. Significant variation of opinion existed within the Darwinians. Conceptual evolution is impossible without it. But disagreement within a group is treated very differently from disagreement between groups; (for a more detailed discussion of Darwinism as a historical entity, see Hull, 1985).

All of the preceding concerns descent as a necessary requirement for conceptual identity in science. I agree with Gould (1977b) that in the study of science, there is a point to distinguishing between "eternal metaphors" and conceptual lineages, but in the ongoing process of science, lineages are fundamental. Perhaps there is some role in science for every-one who happens on the "same" idea, but such a role has yet to be suggested. The only term-tokens that function in science are replicates. To count as replicate, they must be passed on. Periodically, scientists also test their ideas by confronting them with the non-linguistic world. The chief vehicles for both processes (communication and description) are scientists. To the individual scientist, personal credit is the mechanism that makes the machine work. Scientists are also organized into cooper-ating groups of scientists primarily by means of the use that they make of each other's work. In order to have their research program assessed as being progressive, they must have achievements credited to members of their program (Lakatos, 1970). The interplay between replication and interaction with the world to make replication differential operates in conceptual as well as biological evolution.

As if treating actual replication as a necessary condition for concep-tual identity were not problematic enough, treating it as sufficient is even more strongly counter-intuitive. Darwinism as a complex conceptual lin-eage has undergone many transformations in its long history. Darwin thought that evolution is gradual, undirected, possibly in some obscure sense progressive, and largely under the control of natural selection. I have yet to find a fellow-Darwinian who agreed with Darwin on every one of these tenets. The Darwinism that rushed in like a flood was saltative, directed, progressive, and natural selection was usually thought of as only of minor importance. Later, under the influence of August Weismann, Lamarckism was expelled from Darwinism and natural selection ruled supreme. Prior to the *Origin*, Darwin thought that geographic isolation is necessary for speciation, but by 1859, he had convinced himself that it is not. Later, when Moritz Wagner (1872) urged the importance of geo-graphic isolation, Darwin responded hostilely. Later, still, with the work of Ernst Mayr (1942), the importance of geographic isolation became one of the pillars of Darwinism. When neutralists first argued that many traits become widely distributed even though they had no adaptive significance, they claimed to be either anti-Darwinian or at very last non-Darwinian (King and Jukes, 1969), and the Darwinians agreed (Ayala, 1976). Now, the selectionist and neutralist views are "competing hypotheses within the framework of the synthetic theory of evolution" (Stebbins and Ayala, 1981, 967). In the early years of the new synthesis, Richard Goldschmidt's (1940) saltative view of evolution was anathema to the Darwinians. Now Goldschmidt is the patron saint of those authors who want to take the "final step in the modern synthesis" (Raff and Kaufman, 1983, 24). Darwin was wrong in thinking that gradualness was part of the essence of Darwinism (Gould, 1982).

In the preceding paragraph, I have only sketched the wide variety of views that have gone under the name of "Darwinism." The issue is whether Darwinism as a historical entity should be treated as a historical entity individuated by the minimal requirements of genidentity or whether stronger criteria should be added as well. Must Darwinism retain its "essence" in order to remain a single conceptual lineage, or can it evolve indefinitely just so long as a certain degree of internal coherence is retained and the development continuous? Most participants in the dispute over the essence of Darwinism opt for the first alternative. Darwinism definitely has an essence but no two of these disputants can agree on the precise character of this essence. None too surprisingly, every Darwinian thinks that *his* preferred tenets are essential to Darwinism while those of his opponents are only accidental. Prior to Eldredge and Gould's (1972) pushing a somewhat saltative view of speciation (saltative not at the organismic level, or the level of higher taxa, but at the populational level), no one seems to have doubted that gradualism was of the essence of Darwinism. Gould (1982) is now convinced that it is not. Darwinians have also exaggerated the extent and effect of selection as well. Nevertheless, Gould maintains that his version of evolutionary theory is carrying on in the Darwinian tradition. Stebbins and Ayala (1981) agree. Punctualism is also embraced by the all-encompassing arms of the synthetic theory.

As historians have shown, Darwin changed his mind on numerous issues prior to the appearance of Wallace's paper forcing him to go public. Because of the largely private character of these early versions of his theory and all the attention that was paid to the *Origin of Species*, Darwin's views in 1859 have some priority in determining the essence of Darwinism, but Darwin continued to change his mind about evolution after the *Origins*, and his views as expressed in the *Origin* did not gain wide acceptance until long after his death. "Well, in spite of disagreements about every other aspect of the evolutionary process, at least every Darwinian agrees that species evolve. Any theory that does not include at least this much cannot be considered Darwinian." But according to the model of evolution suggested by Eldredge and Gould (1972), species do not evolve. They come into existence rather abruptly and change very little thereafter until they go extinct. Instead of evolving themselves, species are the elements in species lineages. Species lineages are the things that evolve in a step-by-step fashion. Although there is considerable point to evolutionary biologists defining themselves as Darwinian, non-Darwinian, or anti-Darwinian, what Darwin actually said does not play much of a role in this activity. Any attempt to impose some essence on the Darwinian lineage is sure to elicit howls of indignation no matter which tenets are chosen as essential. I have no strong preferences in the matter just so long as the

Darwinian lineage is recognized initially on the minimal requirements of genidentity and subsequent subdivisions do not obscure these connections.

The traits that characterize organisms change through time. Bones that were originally part of the jaws of ancient reptiles became modified through the years into the middle ear ossicles in mammals. Are they the "same" bones or "different" bones? I do not see that it matters. They are stages in a transformation series. I see no reason not to use different terms to refer to different stages in a transformation series just so long as these same terms are not used either for the entire transformation series or for characters not in the appropriate transformation series. Early structures that gave rise to present-day vertebrate eyes belong in the same transformation series with present-day vertebrate eyes even if they are not called "eyes." Similarly, one is only asking for confusion if one refers to both the entire eye transformation series and one stage in this series as "eyes." Finally, all hope is lost if cephalopod eyes are also termed "eyes." The notion of a transformation series is as fundamental to conceptual evolution as it is in biological evolution. Some biologists are willing to subdivide a gradually evolving lineage into successive chronospecies even in the absence of speciation events if the change is great enough (Simpson, 1961). Others are not (Wiley, 1981). I do not see that it matters much just so long as the criteria one uses are made explicit and names are assigned unambiguously. I see no reason not to subdivide the Darwinian lineage into Darwin's Darwinism, late nineteenth century Darwinism, neo-Darwinian Darwinism, the new synthesis Darwinism, and so on, if one is careful not to assume that these stages in conceptual evolution share some common features—because they may not.

The preceding discussion has concerned complex conceptual lineages. Because they contain so many elements, disagreements about each of the elements ramify. Although some of this complexity is decreased when one focuses on less inclusive conceptual entities, it is not eliminated. Reference potential, on my view, is determined by genuine social groups. No matter how narrowly these groups are defined, there is likely to be some disagreement not only about the referents of particular tokens of a term-type, but even about proper modes of fixing reference. At times, reference may be in transition and usage highly ambiguous. That is the price one pays for a genuinely evolutionary analysis of conceptual change. One cannot insist on greater clarity than actually exists. To repeat, within-group variation is one of the chief mechanisms for evolutionary change. Defining groups to eliminate it purchases ease of expression at the cost of obscuring the processes that are producing the change. "But might not one postulate minimal conceptual atoms such that each denotes uniquely?" I think not, but even if such minimal units were plausible, within-group disagreement is still possible.

CONCLUSION AND A CONSEQUENCE

By now, the reader might understand the particular theory of conceptual identity that I am explicating but fail to see what difference it makes. The ramifications of this shift in perspective are numerous and fundamental. I can discuss only one here. If "Darwin's theory of evolution" is taken to refer to a set of tenets, regardless of their occasion of enunciation, then Darwinism in this sense is at least a candidate for a natural kind. One might expect it to function in a putative "law" of conceptual development. One should expect the same factors to be operative in its genesis and/or acceptance whenever a token of it arises. After all, on this view, the world is the way it is whenever the conditions are right, and Darwin's theory is Darwin's theory whenever tokens of the same term-types are expressed. On this view then, if one is an internalist, one should expect the same reasons, arguments, and evidence to be operative in the genesis, or at least acceptance of Darwin's theory whenever this theory arises. After all, on this view, the world is the way it is whenever the conditions are right, and Darwin's theory is Darwin's theory whenever tokens of the same term-types are expressed. On this view then, if one is an internalist, one should expect the same reasons, arguments, and evidence to be operative in the genesis, or at least acceptance of Darwin's theory whenever this theory arises. If the progress so apparent in the fossil record counted in favor of Darwin's theory in England, it should also count in its favor in Germany, France, and America. If not, then variations must be explained away. If one is an externalist, then one should expect the same socioeconomic factors to contribute to the genesis and/or acceptance of Darwin's theory around the world. If the competitive, individualistic character of British society led Darwin to formulate a competitive, individualistic theory of biological evolution, then only scientists living in such countries should formulate Darwin's theory. Parallel observations hold for acceptance as well. People in competitive, individualistic societies should be more prone to accept Darwin's theory.

However, historians who have studied both the genesis and acceptance of Darwin's theory have found no such correlations (Glick, 1974). Internalists found lots of relevant reasons, arguments and evidence, but they varied from country to country. Externalists found an even greater panoply of external factors, but they too varied irregularly from country to country. Externalists at least, are not deterred by these findings. They are not committed to the principle of same cause/same effect. The operative factors in scientists' formulating and/or accepting the views that they do are primarily such things as class allegiance, socioeconomic conditions, and so on, but they "respond to local social and cultural conditions" (Shapin, 1979, 144). In one country, the rise of the mercantile middle class might contribute to, the acceptance of Darwinism; in another, it might contribute to its rejection. In one country, conservatives might be attracted to Darwin's theory; in another, liberals might find it attractive. But no matter what these external factors turn out to be, *they* are what caused the acceptance or rejection of the theory.

As much as this view begs to be abused, as much as it looks like a game that anyone can play and no one can lose, I think that it is appropriate. It would be inappropriate for conceptual systems as natural kinds, but it is totally appropriate for conceptual systems as lineages. The only conditions that are relevant to them are *local* conditions. The failure to see that the same observations hold for internalist explanations as well has caused considerable confusion in traditional histories. In great Britain, "idealism" was just getting a toehold when Darwin published his *Origin*, while special creation was the most recent widely accepted view. Hence, Darwin argued against special creation and ignored the idealists. According to Darwin, neither sort of explanation of species is "scientific," but he emphasized those features of his theory that made it superior to the views of, say, Adam Sedgwick, but avoided confronting the boundary between his conception of science and the "idealism" preferred by Richard Owen. Darwinism was presented with just the opposite state of affairs in Germany, where idealistic views of science reigned and special creation had never been all that popular. In Great Britain, the Darwinians played down the anti-religious implications of evolution; French Darwinians emphasized them. In Germany, the apparently progressive nature of the fossil record was an important datum in favor of evolution; in Great Britain, its effect was mixed because Lyell and Huxley had both argued against it. Perhaps all these intellectual variations should not have existed and should not have influenced the reception of Darwin's theory, but they did. Perhaps there is something properly termed Darwin's theory such that all possible evidence counts eternally for it or against it, but such theories have yet to play any role in science.

On traditional analyses of "explanation," one cannot explain a particular *qua* that particular but only as an *instance* of some universal. Thus, on the view I am advocating, Darwin's theory *qua* Darwin's theory cannot be explained either. It can be an instance of a natural kind, but it itself is not a natural kind. Hence, anyone who proposes to explain the genesis or acceptance of Darwin's theory must find an appropriate natural kind that it exemplifies. Such natural kinds have been extremely difficult to uncover in biological evolution; comparable natural kinds are likely to be even more difficult to discern in conceptual evolution, but at least the task is clear. The lesson that biological evolution has to teach us is that the tokens that are selected must be organized into lineages and that these lineages are not natural kinds. They are not the place to look for evolutionary regularities. The appropriate locus of evolutionary explanations is *kinds* of lineages.

One might explain the prevalence of one sort of reproduction over another in certain circumstances, the ratio of predators to prey, even the evolution of perceptual organs, but there can be no law of the vertebrate eye *qua* vertebrate eye. Similarly, one might explain the occurrence of highly innovative conceptual shifts, the rise of interfield theories, and so on, but not the evolution of Darwin's theory *qua* Darwin's theory. In the absence of relevant conceptual natural kinds and laws of conceptual change, "new knowledge can neither be predicted in advance nor explained after the fact by historians" (Koertge, 1981, 19). Or to put the point differently, the only sorts of explanations possible are highly particularistic statements of the operative particular circumstances. Cock (1983, 39, 57) apologizes for presenting such a "motley" and "miscellaneous collection" of reasons for William Bateson's reluctance to accept the chromosome theory, but these are the only sorts of explanations that one can present for such particulars in the absence of anything that might count as "laws" of conceptual change.

In conclusion, I cannot pretend to have made a strong case for the plausibility of a theory of conceptual evolution. However, I have shown two things. I have shown the lengths to which a proponent of such a theory must go if he hopes to be successful. I have also pointed out a systematic ambiguity in our conceptualization of conceptual change that has frustrated intelligent discussion of it—the distinction between a term-type as a set of similar tokens, and conceptual lineages as causal sequences of term-tokens. The fact that a consistent treatment of notions such as "evolution" and "Darwin's theory of evolution" from either perspective seems counter-intuitive suggests that in our ordinary way of thinking, we vacillate between the two perspectives. By and large, organisms that belong to the same species are *locally* similar to each other. By and large, term-tokens that belong to the same term-lineages are *locally* similar to each other. The mistake is to extrapolate from local to global similarity.[2]

NOTES

1. According to Hennig (1966) and his followers, monophyletic taxa are those that include all and only the descendants of a particular ancestral species. Evolutionary systematists prefer to term such taxa "holophyletic" and limit the term "monophyly" to those taxa descended from a single ancestral species without requiring that all the descendants of a particular ancestral species be included in the same higher taxon. The results is taxa that Hennig (1966) terms "paraphyletic."

2. Appreciation is owed to Philip Kitcher for reading and commenting on an early version of this paper.

Part VI

Sociobiology and the Nature of Science

Chapter 14

Altruism in Science:
A Sociobiological Model of Cooperative
Behavior Among Scientists

The presence of altruistic behavior in certain species of animals has always posed a serious problem for evolutionary theory. Any genes that lead an organism to risk its life for the benefit of another organism should be eliminated quite rapidly from the population. Organisms should not behave altruistically toward each other, but they do. For example, parents commonly invest considerable energy in their offspring, often to their own personal detriment. After all, what could be purer than a mother's love? Somewhat less frequently, siblings can be found risking their lives for each other. The biological explanation for such behavior depends on a redefinition of "personal gain." The greatest gain in evolution and the one to which all other goals are subordinate is the transmission of replicates of one's genes or their duplicates in some other organism. Thus, it is easy to see why biologists argue that the chief benefactor in the parent-offspring relation is the parent. Children are the means by which parents pass on their genes.

In this chapter, I propose to present an analogous explanation for the peculiar social relations that exist between scientists. Just as ambivalence arises when one organism must cooperate with its sexual competitors, a comparable ambivalence arises when scientists must cooperated with their scientific competitors. In science, however, the ultimate goal is not the transmission of genes but of ideas. Scientists behave as selflessly as they do because it is in their own best self-interest to do so. The best thing that a scientist can do for his own career is to get his ideas accepted as his ideas by his fellow scientists. Scientists acknowledge the contributions made by other scientists, again, because it is in their own best self-interest to do so. Such acknowledgments usually take the form of explicit citations, but at a more fundamental level, use is what really matters. One cannot use the work of another scientist without at least tacitly acknowledging its value. Science works as well as it does because the professed goals of the institution happen to coincide with the selfish motives of individual scientists.

---

*Reprinted with permission from *Animal Behavior* 26 (1978):685-697.

What is good for General Motors is not necessarily good for the country, but curiously what is good for individual scientist is good for science.

THE SOCIAL STRUCTURE OF SCIENCE

Upon receiving his doctorate in 1885, David Hilbert swore to "defend in a manly way true science, extend and embellish it, not for gain's sake or for attaining a vain shine of glory, but in order that the light of God's truth shine bright and expand" (Reid, 1970). Early in the history of science, an image was formed of scientists as disinterested, dispassionate automata, cooperating selflessly with their keenest competitors, giving credit where credit is due, searching after truth for its own sake, possibly for the good of humanity but certainly not for "gain's sake" or for attaining a "vain shine of glory." As effective as such an image may be for propaganda purposes, scientists themselves (usually in private) freely express serious doubts about its accuracy, both because it seems so suspiciously self-serving and because it is at variance with their own personal experiences. If discovering the truth is all that matters, why is it so important who discovers what first? Why have scientists developed such an intricate etiquette of citation? Why do scientists engage in priority disputes, which surpass even divorce proceedings in acrimony? Are scientists actually any less concerned with personal gain and glory than anyone else?

In reaction to the popular image of the selfless scientist, some observers have been tempted to go to the other extreme. Scientists are no different from the members of other elitist groups who have jostled their way into comfortable social niches and want to stay there. If any growth of empirical knowledge results from their efforts, it is only incidental to their overriding concern with self-maintenance. According to this view, scientists are as competitive in their dealings with each other as are politicians, labour organizers, and stockbrokers. The chief goal in science is not the pursuit of truth, but the Nobel Prize and a condominium in Palm Desert. Cooperation, giving credit where credit is due, and objective knowledge, are all illusions. Truth in science is decided the same way it is in every other area, by power politics.

Research scientists, the scientists with whom this paper is concerned, do seem to exist in the best of all possible worlds. They are self-evaluating, self-policing, but not self-supporting. Self-policing professions are infamous for not policing themselves, and those that are self-evaluating are equally infamous for doing so on criteria extraneous to the stated goals of the profession. Scientists, however, seem to police themselves with a cold efficiency according to the manifest goals of the profession. In general, there seems to be a close correlation between the recognition scientists receive and the merit of their scientific work. Low quality work is ignored, and downright cheating is punished by rigid ostracism (Cole and Cole, 1972, 1973).

Scientists are paid and frequently quite well for doing what they want to do more than anything else in the world. Research to the research scientist is not just an occupation; it is a compulsion. To complicate matters even further, the funds for research are provided by people who all too frequently are incapable of understanding the research they are being asked to support, at least that is what scientists claim. If ever there were a social institution begging to be abused, science is it. Scientists have been criticized for squandering public funds on such silly research as studying the genetics of fruit flies. Scientists are often extravagant in the way in which they spend their research money. Not infrequently they have used money awarded for one project to work on something else. Scientists are also not immune to the professional junket to pleasant places. However, even the most hostile critics of the scientific establishment have yet to accuse scientists of the sort of massive diversion of public funds so characteristic of other governmentally financed endeavours. As selfish and self-seeking as scientists may be, research funds are used for research.

Another peculiar feature of science is the amount of cooperation and mutual acknowledgment which takes place. Of course, scientists are far from saints. Actual scientists might not look all that cooperative when compared to the Platonic Ideal Scientist, but they exhibit an amazing degree of altruistic behavior when compared to the members of other occupations and professions. On occasion, a businessman will help a competitor by giving him information he needs or by acknowledging the superiority of his product, but not often. Comparable behavior among scientists at least seems prevalent. Scientists could become just as famous and earn just as much money by getting together and voting in a true democratic fashion on matters of empirical fact. Instead, they insist on going through the tedious ritual of running experiments, recording data, formulating hypotheses and testing them. As competitive and political as science may be, the end result has been a growth of knowledge beyond anyone's most optimistic expectations.

SOCIOLOGY OF SCIENCE

One possible explanation for the peculiar behavior of scientists is that they are made of finer stuff than the rest of us. For example, Sir Peter Medawar (1972) has remarked that "scientists, on the whole, are amiable and well-meaning creatures. There must be very few wicked scientists. There are, however, plenty of wicked philosophers, wicked priests, and wicked politicians." Although sociologists admit that some preselection may occur in the choice of an occupation, they are disinclined to believe that prison guards become brutal and attendants in mental institutions callous because they are inherently inferior human beings. They are equally disinclined to believe that scientists behave the way they do because of any innate superiority to other mortals. Rather, they suspect that any putative difference in the way in which participants in different occupations conduct themselves is a function of the social structure of the relevant social institutions.

One school of sociology, the functionalist school founded by Robert K. Merton, explains the social structure of science in terms of the reciprocal exchange between scientists of knowledge for recognition. Priority disputes arise because most of the recognition goes to the person who succeeds in getting his gift of knowledge accepted by his colleagues first. Merton (1973) argues that competition, priority disputes, and the like are an integral part of the social relations between scientists. Ian I. Mitroff (1974) goes even further. "The problem is how objective knowledge results in science not despite bias and commitment, but because of them." Objective knowledge through bias and commitment sounds every bit as paradoxical as bombs for peace. Is Mitroff merely making a virtue out of a vice, or can the "existence and ultimate rationality of science" be explained in terms of bias, jealousy and irrationality?

Merton (1973) attempts to resolve the preceding paradox by distinguishing between the motives of individual scientists and the institutional norms of science. "The quest for distinctive motives appears to have been misdirected. It is rather a distinctive pattern of institutional control of a wide range of motives which characterizes the behavior of scientists. For once the institution enjoins disinterested activity, it is to the interest of scientists to conform on pain of sanctions and, so far as the norm has been internalized, on the pain of psychological conflict." Cole and Cole (1973) note that the two chief forms of deviant behavior in science, stealing another scientist's work and publishing falsified data, are "rare compared to visible deviant behavior in other institutions. They are rare because they generally are not effective in attaining success and because most scientists seem to have a genuine commitment to the norms (of science)."

The observations that such sociologists have made about science and the explanations that they suggest seem well-taken as far as they go. The norms of science enjoin disinterested activity, but why? All social institutions possess norms, but why does science have the norms it does and why are these norms apparently so much more efficacious than those of other professions such as medicine, law, and teaching? Why is deviant behavior in science so less likely to eventuate in success than in other professions? The purpose of this paper is to attempt to answer the preceding questions by reasoning analogically from the sorts of explanations that biologists are currently presenting for social behavior in general. Recent advances have been made in understanding animal behavior by biologists directing their attention away from the costs and benefits of a particular behavior for the organism itself to its effects on gene transmission. The important distinctions in this literature are selfish versus altruistic behavior, genotypic versus phenotypic effects, individual versus group selection, and biological versus social evolution (Alexander 1961, 1971, 1975; Hamilton 1964; Williams 1966, 1975; Trivers 1971, 1974; Ghiselin 1974b; Wilson 1974).

THE SOCIOBIOLOGICAL ANALOGY

To the extent that "altruism" and "selfishness" have clear-cut meanings in ordinary English, an altruistic act is one designed primarily to aid someone else, possibly at some personal risk. The fact that an altruistic act may also benefit the person performing it does not preclude its being altruistic as long as this reciprocal benefit is incidental. A selfish act, on the other hand, is one designed primarily to aid oneself even at the expense of others, although others might incidentally receive some benefit from the act. According to the biological use of these terms, intent is irrelevant; all that matters is the effect. If the effect of a behavior is to benefit the organism's own personal survival, then it is phenotypically selfish; if it benefits the survival of some other organism, it is phenotypically altruistic. If the effect of a behavior is to increase the likelihood of that organism's passing on replicates of its own genes or their duplicates in other organisms, then it is genetically selfish; if it increases the likelihood of genes different in kind from one's own being passed on, it is genetically altruistic. For example, the care which a mother lavishes on her offspring may be phenotypically quite altruistic; genetically it is selfish (Alexander 1974).

The strategy, then, has been to explain all phenotypically altruistic traits in terms of genotypic selfishness. Various biologists may have been attracted to this strongly individualistic view of evolution for deep-seated psychological reasons. Others may be repulsed by it for comparable reasons. But that is not the point. The problem is to explain how a genetically altruistic trait (whether behavioral or otherwise) can be maintained in a population if it has any genetic basis at all. Conversely, the likelihood that a widely distributed trait could be maintained in a population for long periods of time without any genetic base seems slight. When the organisms involved are genetically related in a rather direct manner, the biological explanations in terms of genetic selfishness seem quite compelling. Parents do seem to behave in ways calculated to enhance the survival of their offspring, the more the better. Certain apparent exceptions, such as the killing of one's offspring under especially harsh conditions, turn out to support rather than refute explanations in terms of genetic selfishness. With the possible and certainly marginal exception of human beings, no organism can predict its future environments on a scale necessary to influence its own evolutionary development. Both over-estimating and underestimating the number of offspring that can attain sexual maturity are evolutionary disadvantageous. One response to this problem in species that invest considerable effort in raising their offspring is to conceive the maximal number of offspring but evolve methods of decreasing brood size in times of stress, for example, by killing excess offspring and feeding them to their siblings, a practice not unknown among human beings (Alexander 1974).

However, parents and their offspring are not the only individuals that tend to share numerous genes in common. In certain cases, siblings can share more genes with each other than with their parents. In general, one would expect to see a fairly close correlation between phenotypic altruistic behavior and the percentage of genes that two organisms happen to share. Beginning with the work of Hamilton (1964), much of the literature in sociobiology has concerned itself with following the ramifications of this line of reasoning in various species of social and eusocial organisms. The fact that predictions based on the biological principles set out above have been born out so consistently has been the chief factor in lending plausibility to the entire programme. For example, striking differences should exist in the behavior exhibited by reproductives and non-reproductives. Non-reproductives should be expected to cooperate with each other quite readily to further the reproductive success of the fertile individuals to which they are most closely related. In species made up predominantly of sexually active individuals, however, cooperation poses a problem because fertile individuals must cooperate with their reproductive competitors. Too much aid to a genetically different individual is liable to give that individual a reproductive edge and lead to the elimination of whatever genes contributed to that behavior. From a strictly genetic point of view, soldier ants should willingly sacrifice themselves for the good of their colony; human soldiers should be more reticent.

Certain biologists have attempted to extend their biological explanations for social behavior to organisms that are not related to each other all that closely. For example, one member of a pack of African dogs can induce another to regurgitate food by exhibiting the appropriate begging behavior. If these individuals are all closely related genetically, then such altruistic behavior can be explained at least in principle by reference to genetic selfishness. However, if such packs commonly include genetically quite distinct individuals, then some other explanation must be sought. Robert Trivers (1971) has suggested that altruistic behavior between genetically unrelated individuals can be explained at the organismal level in terms of reciprocity. Genetically based systems of reciprocal altruism evolve in situations where the reciprocal benefit received by the individual performing the service is likely to be greater than its probable cost. In the regurgitation example, the cost to the gorged animal is minimal; the benefit to the recipient is great. The net benefit to the pack is significant. To the extent that reciprocal altruism exists in species besides *Homo sapiens*, it is rare. It is quite common in human societies. The problem is to explain how systems of reciprocal altruism can first become established in a population and how cooperation between genetically unrelated members of the same species differs from the systems of interdependence that develop between species.

In contrast with the extremely individualistic view of evolution sketched above, some biologists have suggested that selection at the level of individual organisms and kinship groups must be supplemented by selection at higher levels of organization (Lewontin 1970). Even though a society or a species might be genetically quite heterogeneous, it might still function as a unit of selection in biological evolution. In such cases of "group selection," a trait that benefits the group as a whole can be established independently of the benefit that individual organisms receive. However, the conditions under which group selection can be efficacious are so rare that few traits are likely to be explicable in these terms (Levins 1970).

In the face of the difficulties mentioned above, sociologists have tended to argue that biological evolution, whether at the level of individual organisms, kinship groups or genetically heterogeneous groups, must be supplemented by extra-biological social evolution. Just as the processes responsible for biological evolution can reinforce or conflict with each other, biological evolution can reinforce or conflict with the processes of social evolution. Unlike a soldier ant, human soldiers are caught between conflicting drives: to risk one's own life for others in the social group or to flee at the risk of this larger group. Either alternative has its genotypic and phenotypic costs and benefits. A brave soldier may well die and leave no further offspring, but a coward may have no society to return to or be ostracized when he does. Donald Campbell (1972), for example, acknowledges the efficaciousness of social indoctrination in human beings, concluding that "self-sacrificial dispositions, including especially the willingness to risk death in warfare, are in man a product of a social indoctrination, which is counter to, rather than supported by genetically transmitted behavioral dispositions."

If the purpose of this chapter were to extend biological explanations of human behavior to scientists, then the difficulties that revolve around reciprocal altruism and the relation between social and biological evolution would have to be resolved. Instead, however, I intend to use the most uncontroversial part of the biological explanation of animal behavior (parental manipulation and kin selection) as a model for a social theory of the structure of science. Of course, being a successful scientist may be as advantageous to one's offspring as success in any other occupation, but scientists do not pass on their ideas through their genes. Certain aspects of cooperative behavior among scientists may be as explicable in terms of reciprocal altruism as is mutual regurgitation among African dogs, and the human tendency to learn about the world in which we live may be as genetically based as the ease with which we can be indoctrinated (Wilson 1975). However, the truth or falsity of such hypotheses are irrelevant to the purposes of this paper. Societies, languages, scientific theories and biological species may all evolve, but the only genuine theory of evolution that we possess is the theory of biological evolution. Hence, I propose to use its most uncontroversial elements as a model for the evolution of science.

COMPETITION AND COOPERATION IN SCIENCE

Science is both a highly competitive and a highly cooperative affair. In this section, I argue that the peculiar social practices that have been developed in science to facilitate cooperation among competitors are exactly what they should be if the chief goal in science is to have one's own ideas incorporated into the generally accepted body of scientific knowledge. Just as biologists explain the social structure of kinship groups by reference to gene flow, I wish to argue that the best way to understand science is to follow idea flow. The phenomena with which I will deal are the manner in which scientists police themselves and pass out rewards, the coincidence in science between the manifest goals of the institution and the individual goals of particular scientists, the efficacy of goals internal to science versus such external goals as money and prizes, and the role of citations in the social organization of science.

A peculiar feature of science is the stringency with which it polices itself. On occasion, a police department will suspend an officer for taking bribes, without the impetus of massive newspaper publicity and a grand jury hearing, but not often. Occasionally, a doctor is defrocked for incompetence instead of for advertising, but not often. There are even cases in which a university professor has been fired for not teaching. But, in general, such cases are noteworthy for their rarity. If self-maintenance is the primary goal of these professions, then they are well-organized to do just that. But if the police are supposed to enforce the law impartially and efficiently, if doctors are supposed to provide competent medical service to the public at large, and if professors are supposed to devote the greater part of their energies to teaching, for example by returning test papers in less than two or three months' time, then their methods of rewards and punishments are hardly calculated to realize these ends. No one should be surprised that they do not.

If the manifest goal of research science is to increase our knowledge of the empirical world, on the other hand, then the social structure of science is well-calculated to do so. Scientists, like the members of all professions, must expend considerable energy in self-maintenance. New members must be recruited, sources of income exploited, and bases of power within the society at large established. But none of these activities is incompatible with the claims scientists make that in their research they are pursuing truth for its own sake. Until quite recently, the medical profession in the United States has been more successful than any other profession in looking after itself, but it also has succeeded in providing technologically advanced medical care to those who could afford it or obtain third party financing. On the surface, the Hippocratic Oath is no more hypocritical than the one which the young Hilbert took. The difference between science and the professions mentioned is the degree to which it fulfils its stated goals, the time spent looking after itself notwithstanding.

From the sociological point of view, pervasive differences in behavior between people participating in various social institutions must be explained in terms of the social structure of those institutions. The sociobiological analogy adds an additional constraint: sufficiently selfish reasons must be found for scientists behaving as selflessly as they do. These reasons involve the usual rewards of money, position, and fame, but in science there is an even stronger driving force: the incorporation of one's own ideas into the body of generally accepted scientific knowledge. The reason that science works so well is that the pursuit of this selfish goal by individual scientists is well-calculated to realize the manifest goal of science as an institution. The individual policeman gains very little from turning in one of his buddies for taking a bribe or from ticketing the mayor's car. In fact, he pays dearly. No one should be surprised that such behavior is so rare. Similarly, university professors are rewarded primarily for their research, not their teaching. Hence, no one should be surprised that university professors spend so little time teaching. None too surprisingly, professors claim that good researchers are invariably good teachers and vice versa, a self-serving claim backed up by little in the way of empirical evidence (Bresler 1968).

Unlike policemen, doctors, and professors (in their roles as teachers), research workers police themselves coldly, dispassionately, almost cruelly. A scientist no longer able to contribute to the work of his fellow scientists is treated with all the compassion shown to aging movie stars. Of course, positions, committee chairmanships and prizes are passed out in science because of many of the same considerations operative in other professions (Greenberg 1967; Friedlander 1972). The buddy system is as pervasive in science as elsewhere. As Medawar (1972) points out, "The element of camaraderie or mateyness in scientific research is one of the attractions of the scientific life." But mateyness has its limits. It is a rare scientist who would sacrifice his own reputation by seconding a view that he takes to be mistaken no matter how much he might like its author.

University administrators, government officials, and members of various honorary committees have some say in the allocation of grants, medals, and other rewards, but only scientists functioning as scientists can allocate the chief reward in science: the recognition of a new scientific achievement by incorporating it into their own work. The most beneficial thing that a scientist can do for his own career is to produce work that is acknowledged by his peers as a contribution to the growth of knowledge. Other scientists acknowledge his achievements, perhaps in part because it is the moral thing to do, but just as importantly because they themselves receive considerable benefit from the advances made by others if they can use them in their own work. The system that makes science work the way it does is facilitated somewhat by the various external rewards established to honour great scientific achievements, though the frequency with which great scientists and their achievements are ignored indicates that such honours in themselves are far from necessary. The history of science does not coincide with the history of the Royal Society and Nobel laureates. The chief reward in science and the system internal to science that makes it operate the way it does is the adoption of one's ideas by one's closest competitors. Conflict in science arises from the difference between the tacit recognition that using an idea entails and the explicit recognition of an appropriate citation.

In the past, sociologists of science have paid considerable attention to such explicit indications of scientific worth as citations. It does not take much for someone to contribute to the scientific literature. A short paper on some minor bit of empirical data will do, just as long as other scientists come up with the same results if they are inclined to repeat the observation or experiment. However, sociologists have shown that a vast majority of papers published are cited rarely if at all. Most citations are to the work of a small percentage of scientists. If number of citations is a reasonably good measure of scientific worth, then it follows that only a small percentage of working scientists contribute materially to the growth of science. Cole and Cole (1972, 1973) have gone even further to show a high correlation between number of citations and other forms of recognition such as the number of honorific rewards, appointments to prestigious departments in prestigious universities and institutes, and academic rank. They conclude that "quality of published research explains more variance than any other variable on several types of recognition."

Like all measures, of course, just the number of times a paper is cited is an imperfect reflection of its scientific value. Sometimes the intrinsic value of a paper is recognized only long after it is published, Mendel's paper on hereditary transmission being the classic example. Sometimes a notion that turns out to be crudely mistaken will receive considerable attention for a while in the scientific literature; for example, phrenology in the nineteenth century. However, being "right" cannot be equated with being "important." Ideas that turn out to be mistaken or that other scientists take to be mistaken can lead to major scientific advances. For instance, Ernst Mayr wrote his *Systematics and the Origin of Species* (1942) in a fit of white heat after reading Richard Goldschmidt's *The Material Basis of Evolution* (1940). At the very least, citation-analysis must be supplemented with content-analysis in any attempt to assess the actual contribution that a particular scientific work makes to the substantive growth of scientific knowledge. If the work cited for ideas it actually contains? Is the idea cited central to the paper or peripheral? Is it cited as being correct or mistaken? Is the work a contribution to the primary literature or a broad synoptic work? On the basis of just counting references in a half dozen British journals, one would conclude that John Herschel was the most important British scientist in 1865. In a sense, he was. Sociologically he was one of the half dozen or so most influential scientists at the time. In retrospect, his scientific achievements do not look so impressive.

The etiquette of citation is as complex as it is tacit. No one has ever written a manual on when to cite and when not to cite, whom to cite and whom not to cite, and the form that the citation should take. For instance, if an author claims priority for an idea published without citation in one of your papers, you can always acknowledge his contribution by citing him in a later publication in the middle of a long list of other precursors. Citing people who cite you is also an excellent practice. If, however, the model that I have set out in this paper for science is correct, citations should be "primarily for possible support of the author's contentions and only secondarily in recognition of previous work" (Goudsmit 1974). The chief benefit that one scientist receives from the work of another is the use he can make of it in his own research, and he cannot use another scientist's work without giving him at least tacit recognition. The problem is, of course, the importance in science of tacit versus explicit recognition. Just as doctors see their role as providing competent, compassionate medical care for those who need it, scientists view themselves as pursuing objective knowledge of the empirical world, but unlike many other professions, the pursuit by individual scientists of their own selfish goals is well-calculated to bring about the professed goal of the discipline. Science does not have to rely solely on appeals to the general good to further its ends. Instead, science is organized to encourage scientists to practise what they preach. But why is attempted theft not more common in science? Would science retain its self-reinforcing character if explicit recognition were abandoned completely for the tacit recognition that follows upon use, or if scientists consistently received little or no recognition until after their deaths? These and other questions currently cannot be answered with any reasonable degree of certainty. Anyone who has had much experience in science can supply numerous anecdotes bearing on such questions, but anecdotal evidence is not enough. Testing of the sort now being conducted by sociologists of science is necessary.

TESTING THE MODEL

Evolutionary theory has proven infuriatingly difficult to test empirically, so difficult that some scientists have been led to claim that it is unfalsifiable; others that it is false. But all scientific theories, not just evolutionary theory, are difficult to test. The illusion that scientific theories have been conclusively verified or falsified by empirical observations can be dissipated rather quickly by reading a little history of science. Even though empirical science is empirical, scientific theories are grossly under-determined by available evidence. The principles of sociobiology are no exception to the rule. The close correlation between phenotypically altruistic behavior and gene flow in social insects is the best supporting evidence to date. Extensions to human beings have proven more difficult to test, but Alexander (1974) has pointed out one significant difference in family structure explicable in sociobiological terms. In societies in which a husband is likely to be the father of his wife's children, the father should help care for his wife's children; in societies in which there is no significant correlation between marriage and intercourse, a man should exert more effort in looking after his sister's children, since he is likely to have more genes in common with them than with his wife's children. The anthropological literature confirms Alexander's prediction. If the explanation of the social organization of science suggested in this paper is to be taken seriously, similar consequences must be derived from it and checked.

Many of the claims about science basic to an explanation of science on the evolutionary model have some empirical support. For example, if anything is characteristic of contemporary science, it is the prevalence of dominance hierarchies. In comparable situations in nonhuman species, a very few males fertilize most of the females. For example, Watts and Stokes (1971) discovered that of the 170 male turkeys belonging to four display groups, only six males accounted for all the matings. Sociobiologists have found that a comparable situation exists in science. A vast majority of the recognition in science, measured on several scales, goes to a small percentage of scientists (Price 1963; Cole and Cole 1972, 1973; Hagstrom 1974). Both biological evolution and science are highly competitive. One would expect, under such circumstances, for both innovation and differentiation to occur, and it does (Hagstrom 1974). According to one prevalent view among biologists, speciation typically results from the isolation of small, ephemeral founder populations. Most such populations become extinct, but the few that manage to survive and expand are likely to evolve into new species (Mayr 1963). As might be expected, sociologists have discovered that periods of rapid innovation in science are typically associated with small ephemeral groups of scientists working together on interrelated problems (Griffin and Mullins 1972). In biological evolution, genes are selected indirectly via the phenotypic traits they control. Species become adapted to their environments by the gradual accumulation of adaptive traits. To the extent that an organism accurately reflects its environmental pressures, it has a better chance of survival. Similarly, an advantage should accrue to a scientist with each successive recognition, and the accumulative advantage should be strongest where individuals are rewarded according to their merits (Allison and Stewart 1974).

Sociologists of science emphasize the institutional aspects of science most strongly, the role of norms over individual psychological motivations. The sociobiological analogy implies in addition, that certain norms should be honoured more readily and frequently than others, viz., those that increase the likelihood that a scientist's ideas will be passed on as his ideas. Cole and Cole (1973) have noted how comparatively rare such deviant behavior as theft and falsification of data are in the scientific community, but they do not notice that the frequencies of these two sorts of behavior are significantly different. If the explanation for the relatively high level of cooperative behavior among scientists suggested in this paper be correct, the sanctions against passing on doctored data should be greater than those against stealing a fellow scientist's work. A scientist who is suspected of stealing his colleagues' ideas may receive fewer preprints, but if the work that he publishes is good, other scientists will use it. However, once a scientist gets a reputation for producing sloppy, mislead-

ing, or outright falsified work, he is written out of the scientific community. As mentioned earlier, repeatability is the minimum requirement for
contributing to the scientific literature. Stealing a graduate student's works
hurts that individual. If stealing of this sort were to become widespread,
it might undermine the entire institution of science. But all cases of false
or misleading information do immediate and direct harm to anyone who
uses it. That is why, for example, recent accusations that Sir Cyril Burt
had knowingly published imaginary data in his twin studies have raised
so much consternation. Claims that several of his graduate students had
actually done all the work would have hardly raised an eyebrow. Stealing
and lying may be equally immoral outside of science, but in science there
is no comparison as to which is the more damaging, and scientists behave
accordingly. Once again, the use which one scientist can make of the
work of another is the *modus operandi* of science.

Other features of science that should be the case if the evolutionary
analogy is appropriate lack much in the way of empirical support. For
example, in the absence of the evolutionary perspective, one might expect
the vast majority of scientists who make no real contributions to the
substantive content of science to be expendable. Because "most research
is rarely cited by the bulk of the physics community, and even more
sparingly cited by the most eminent scientists who produce the most significant discoveries," Cole and Cole (1972) conclude that maybe the "number of scientists could be reduced without affecting the rate of advance."
One can imagine the howls of outrage elicited by this suggestion from the
bulk of the scientific community. However, in biological evolution, numbers are important. Decreasing the number of organisms in a species
increases the likelihood of rapid evolutionary development almost as much
as it increases the likelihood of extinction. It is always easy to look back
and decide who the really important scientists in a period were; it is not
so easy to decide at the time. Biologists are not now in a position to
decide the optimal number of organisms to allow for maximal evolutionary change without increasing the chances of extinction prohibitively.
Sociologists are even in less of a position to do the same for the scientific
community. For now, the wisest choice is to err on the side of excess. We
tend to take science for granted. It was a long time coming, but now that
it is here, it is here to stay. But science, like any other social institution,
could become extinct.

In biology, the contrast is often drawn between r and K selection. In
density independent regimes with the population below carrying capacity, organisms tend to produce huge numbers of offspring to increase the
likelihood that at least a few will survive. In stable, crowded environments, a more appropriate response is to produce only a few offspring

and invest considerable effort in caring for them. Are comparable responses appropriate under similar situations in science? At the sociological level, certain scientists turn out students wholesale; others nurture a select few. At the conceptual level, some scientists publish everything that comes to mind; others publish only a handful of papers during an entire career. (This example was suggested to me by Jack Hailman and improved upon by Stephen Gould, though I am not sure that either wants credit for it.)

If the small scientific communities associated with scientific innovation are analogous to the founder populations of biological evolution, then one should fine the degree and kind of cooperation and competition that takes place within and between such groups to differ significantly. For instance, the young geneticists working in T. H. Morgan's fly room both cooperated and competed with each other, but how different were these interactions from those that took place between the Columbia group and the Texas group (Carlson 1974)? Are sociobiologists themselves divisible into such competing or cooperating groups? If so, does the fact that they are supposed to be aware of how such groups are structured and interact affect how they themselves behave? In biological evolution, selection can take place simultaneously at several levels of organization. Can the same be said for science? These are the sorts of questions that the evolutionary analogy suggests. The fact that some of them at least have never been asked about science before indicates the fruitfulness of the analogy. The further fact that in those cases in which research has been carried out, the results have been what one might expect on the evolutionary analogy is its strongest justification.

HUMANISTIC OBJECTIONS TO SOCIOBIOLOGICAL EXPLANATIONS

The major objection that has been raised to the extension of evolutionary theory to include human beings has not stemmed from sociobiological explanations being any more problematic than most claims that scientists make about the empirical world. The major objection is that human beings are conscious, moral agents. Perhaps the origins of consciousness and our sense of morality can be explained solely on the basis of biological principles, but the manner in which human beings currently function cannot be. Human beings do things for reasons as well as causes. Biologists need not deny that people are conscious, moral agents. Every mother has her reasons for treating her children the way she does, and some of these reasons may be based on what she takes to be moral considerations. Biologists do not attempt to explain such contingencies. Instead, they explain the prevalence of certain patterns of behavior in certain environments. Of course, mothers tend to love their children and behave the way they do in large measure because of these feelings. The biological issue is the function that love plays in the passing on of genes.

For example, it is no accident that orgasm feels good. We now understand the role that intercourse plays in the production of babies, but our ancestors had to reproduce themselves long before they had such knowledge. If orgasm had not felt good, we would not be here. As usual, the same end might have been attained by some other means, but this is the way it is accomplished in *Homo spaiens*. It is equally true that now that we understand the role of intercourse in reproduction, the human race could persist even if orgasm ceased to feel good. In fact, it may be our only hope. By explaining the function of certain feelings and beliefs, biologists do not "explain them away." Parents are no more likely to stop loving their children once they understand the role that such feelings play in the perpetuation of their genes than they are to cease enjoying orgasm once they understand its evolutionary role.

Biologists are not attempting to explain away consciousness or the efficacy of certain moral beliefs, but to explain their prevalence in terms of the contributions they make to the maintenance of the relevant evolutionary unit. A sociologist might explain the student disruptions in the late sixties in terms of the increased percentage of young people in society, decreased career opportunities in the lower age groups, and so on. A psychologist might explain which people tended to become involved in such causes in terms of parental permissiveness, uncritical acceptance of overly idealistic preachings, etc. These explanations are not necessarily incompatible. Nor do they detract from the merits of the various social causes at issue. The major novelty that biologists have contributed to the story is the notice that they have taken of possible conflicts and mutual reinforcements that the exigencies of passing on one's genes might play in the prevalence of certain social structures and behavioral tendencies.

Sociologists have long noticed the tendency of people to attempt to cheat in the social obligations as well as the compensating social sanctions designed to discourage cheating. All biologists have done in this regard is to show how such tendencies might have a genetic base and to confront social planners with the scope of the problem if they attempt to work in opposition to these genetically influenced behavioral tendencies. If the world's population is to be held in check, people must come to identify with the human species in general more strongly than with any less inclusive group, and the strength of this identification must be sufficient to overcome all the factors that conspire to encourage individuals to reproduce themselves. The process would be much easier if various phenotypically selfish means could be found to promote such genetically altruistic behavior.

Similar observations can be made about the sociology of science and the psychology of individual scientists. I do not mean to denigrate the importance of the wow-feeling of discovery in motivating scientists to continue their devotion to research. No one who has experienced the elation of scientific discovery can ever forget it, or fail to want to experience it again. Many of our greatest scientists have worked in relative isolation for crucial periods during the development of their ideas. They have also had the ability to resist conceptual authority (Ghiselin 1974). But none of this precludes a significant role for social groups in the discovery, development and dissemination of new scientific ideas. As scientists are well aware, the joyful feeling that accompanies discovery does not guarantee truth. Of equal importance, possibly even greater importance, is the testing of these bright ideas and their eventual acceptance by one's fellow scientists. Acceptance too is an enjoyable feeling, albeit more subtle and protracted than the joy of discovery.

ELITIST VERSUS EGALITARIAN SCIENCE

Certain objections that have been raised to the explanation of the prevalence of certain social structures in certain environments must be approached, if at all, gingerly. Science as it currently exists is clearly individualistic, competitive, and elitist. The societies that gave rise to modern science and in which it now flourishes are also relatively individualistic, competitive, and elitist. This similarity might be explicable in various ways. Perhaps science has the characteristics it does because it arose where and when it did. Perhaps both Western societies and science have the structure they do because they are instances of the same type of evolutionary processes. Perhaps the correlation is accidental. Contemporary science is organized in a particular way and serves to further particular goals. We know that societies can be structured in a variety of ways. Perhaps science could be structured differently to further different goals. For example, it might be organized in a more egalitarian, selfless, genuinely cooperative way in order to further the more human needs of people at large. Perhaps personal recognition is only an accidental feature of the process by which we have come to discover what the empirical world is like. For example, Gorovitz and MacIntyre (1976) claim that certain norms of experimental design and theory construction are internal to science while those concerning priority are not.

"Natural science could remain essentially what it is now, even if the norms about priority of publication were somewhat different. Natural science might, for example, if it had had a different cultural history, have adopted the ideals of anonymity and impersonality which informed medi-

eval architecture; who precisely built what is for that architecture relatively unimportnat, vastly unimportant compared with who precisely built
what in modern architecture or who discovered what in modern science.
Modern science is thus a competitive race, although one could have internally impeccable science without the competition."

Is science essentially competitive? Could science perform the same
function it does today while organized very differently? Part of the problem in the dispute between the advocates of egalitarian science and the
apologists for the current elitist orthodoxy is the confusion of social and
conceptual elitism. If the evolutionary analysis of conceptual change
presented in this paper is to be taken seriously, then conceptually, science
is necessarily competitive and elitist. Not all ideas are equally good. But it
does not follow from this that science as a social institution must also be
competitive and elitist. The tacit recognition entailed by the incorporation of certain ideas over others into the body of generally accepted scientific knowledge seems unavoidable. Whether science could function as it
does with no explicit recognition being given to individuals or some particular group is a moot point. In this respect, Gorovitz and MacIntyre's
example is not very appropriate. Perhaps individual artisans did not take
credit for particular medieval churches, but the local religious communities did. I doubt that science would become much less competitive, elitist
and "individualistic" if explicit credit were given to particular research
teams or institutions rather than to particular scientists. Perhaps science
could be structured differently so that it would not be so competitive,
elitist, and individualistic. Such a system might even be superior in various ways to contemporary science, but one thing can be said for science
as it is now organized: it works. If the chief goal in science is to further
our knowledge of the empirical world, it does that quite well. Before we
start tinkering with it, the credentials of suggested alternatives might well
be checked with some care, and so far no one has hinted at even the most
general outlines of these alternatives.

One final point must be made before leaving this topic. Critics of
elitist science frequently argue *ad hominem* against their opponents even
though the argument that they present works equally well in both directions. The author of this paper, needless to say, is a member of a competitive, elitist, individualistic society and has vested interests in that society.
My views are no doubt coloured by my personal station in life. To the
extent that I am a member of one or more favored groups, I might well be
led to argue for the *status quo*. To the extent that I am a member of one or
more persecuted minorities, I might be led to view current institutions
more critically. But this is a universal human predicament. The same could
be said of the advocates of egalitarian science. In this paper I have

attempted to explain certain aspects of science as it is currently practised, not to justify them.

THE EVOLUTION OF IDEAS

When the issue is the connection between a particular type of behavior or social norm and the passing on of genes, the principles of sociobiology can be applied directly. Perhaps current strictly biological explanations of sex ratios and parental investment may be mistaken, but surely they are the right sorts of explanations to suggest for such phenomena. If so, then why cannot they be extended to human beings? After all, there is nothing special about the fifty-fifty sex ratio characteristic of *Homo sapiens*. Of course, the human species is unique; all species are. The issue is whether *Homo sapiens*, in contrast to all other species, is unique in just those ways to preclude the extension of the relevant biological principles to them.

Because we have had such a long history of refusing to acknowledge the implications of science when they seem to endanger the image we have of ourselves, I for one am in favour of pushing sociobiological explanations to their limits to see just how appropriate and adequate they turn out to be. But if a wide variety of human behavior and social organization, from homosexuality to "mother's brother" kin groups, can be explained in terms of gene flow, then why draw the line at scientists? Of course, scientists do not pass on their ideas genetically, but they do form social groups. They have students and disciples, not to mention permanent laboratory assistants, as close to eusocial non-reproductives as people are likely to get. Of course, the flow of scientific ideas is unlikely to correspond very closely to gene flow, but as scientists are quick to admit, their real "children" are their ideas, and the chief means by which scientists pass on their ideas are other scientists, especially "young and rising scientists with plastic minds" (Darwin, 1903).

Some readers might interpret the extension of the principles of sociobiology to include scientists themselves as a reductio ad absurdum of the entire enterprise; others as poetic justice; still others as perfectly legitimate. In this connection, I have only two observations to make. First, if one objects to extending the principles of sociobiology to scientists, then one is obligated either to reject their extension to human beings in general, or else to explain why scientists are peculiarly exempt. Secondly, and more importantly, in this paper I have attempted no such extension. Instead, I have sketched a theory of the social organization of research science in terms of the flow of ideas, modelled on contemporary versions of evolutionary theory. As such, it must stand or fall on its own. The only function of the biological model is to suggest a general orientation and structure for the theory. For example, it leads one to look for ideationally selfish effects of the cooperative and altruistic practices that charcterize science. Whether or not the peculiar features of science can actually be explained in terms of the increased likelihood of passing on one's ideas is another matter.

Some might object to my use of the processes of biological evolution as an analogue to the development of science. If the objection is that I have reasoned analogically, then I have no apologies to make. Reasoning by analogy has been part and parcel of science from its inception. If the objection is that biological evolution might be an inappropriate model for the evolution of ideas, then it might have some substance. For example, the notion of passing on an idea is a good deal more problematic than passing on a gene (Hull 1975). Genes are material bodies; ideas are not. The important feature of a gene is its structure, and it can have the same structure regardless of the organism which produces it. It does no good for one organism to steal another organism's genes. They carry all that is relevant to ownership with them. Ideas carry no such intrinsic mark of ownership. That is why explicit acknowledgment is so important in science. A graduate student whose discovery has been appropriated by his major professor can gain some consolation from knowing that science is advanced as much by a new idea that has been stolen as by one whose true origins are acknowledged, but it is questionable whether science could continue to function as successfully as it does if such injustices were commonplace and permanent.

Perhaps the similarities between the evolution of science and the evolution of species might prove to be superficial and the analogy between the two processes pernicious. Certainly the difficulties inherent in individuating ideas so that the "same" idea can be traced through time has always plagued the history of ideas. Scientific theories, research programs, and disciplines are no easier to individuate. Thus far, however, no one has pursued the analogy in sufficient detail to warrant an assessment of its possible value. Instead, it has been dismissed out of hand. Its opponents know in advance that it cannot be of any benefit. However, the evolutionary analogy is sufficiently fundamental to too many currently popular analyses of science to ignore (Toulmin 1972; Popper 1972; Campbell 1974; Laudan 1977).

Chapter 15

Sociobiology: Scientific Bandwagon or Traveling Medicine Show?*

I was originally asked by the editors of this volume to compare the reception of evolutionary theory in the nineteenth century with the reception of sociobiology today. Hindsight is a powerful tool in the hands of the historian. Because evolutionary theory turned out to be basically correct, anyone who opposed it in the nineteenth century must have been a closed-minded bigot. Hence anyone who opposes sociobiology today is equally obstructing scientific progress. In order to decrease the bias inherent in my investigations, I have added a third theory to the equation—an unsuccessful theory, phrenology. In the first half of the nineteenth century, Franz Josef Gall (1758-1828) suggested that there might be some correlation between the shape of a person's skull and his or her mental abilities. We now know that this view is nonsense. As might be expected, phrenology degenerated into quackery. Hence its early supporters must have been gullible fools. But at the height of the movement, phrenologists claimed among their numbers some of the greatest names of the day: John Quincy Adams, Prince Albert, Alexander Bain, Honoré de Balzac, Paul Broca, Charlotte Bronte, Henry Clay, Auguste Comte, George Elliot, David Ferrier, Karl Marx, Clemens Metternich, Edgar Allan Poe, and Mark Twain, not to mention four early evolutionists: Étienne Geoffroy Saint-Hilaire, Robert Chambers, Herbert Spencer, and Alfred Russel Wallace.

Both phrenology and evolutionary theory started off as genuine scientific theories. Serious scientists could be found arrayed on both sides of both issues. However, from our contemporary point of view, Gall lost and Darwin won. What did the phrenologists do wrong? What did the evolutionists do right? Could anyone at the time have been able to predict that evolutionary theory would succeed and phrenology fail? A strong tendency exists to conclude that Darwin's greatest achievement was to devise a theory that was basically correct and that Gall's failure was to come up with a set of ideas that were crudely mistaken. But what Gall *did* wrong was to *be* wrong. Scientific theories that contain a large element of

---

*Reprinted with permission from *Sociobiology and Human Nature*, cd. M. S. Gregory, A. Silvers, and D. Sutch. San Francisco: Jossey-Bass.

truth continue to prosper, while those that are fundamentally in error either drop out of sight or degenerate into some form of pseudo-science. Hence the message for the sociobiologists is "Be right." If the views now being urged by the sociobiologists are reasonably close to the truth, the sociobiological bandwagon will turn into a victory parade. If not, it will degenerate into a traveling medicine show.

However, if the history of phrenology and evolutionary theory have anything to teach us, it is that the truth of new theories *as they are origi-nally set out* is not all that important. Phrenology in the first half of the nineteenth century was no further from the truth than the theory of evolution, which became widely accepted in the second half. What really determines the success or failure of new scientific theories is how advocates of these views continue to conduct themselves. They must be conceptually flexible, socially cohesive, and terminologically rigid. The role of evidence in science is too obvious to belabor, but evidence never totally constrains the freedom of scientists in formulating their theories. The fudge factor is just as important (Westfall, 1973). Any scientist who is not a "master wriggler," to use Darwin's phrase, will see his views refuted almost immediately. Scientists can succeed only if they are willing to break a few methodological rules—sometimes every rule in the book. However, they cannot finagle at all costs. Falsifiability does matter in science but not the falsifiability of disembodied propositions. What really counts is the falsifiability of scientists. To be successful, a scientist must be able to recognize clear threats to his or her position and respond appropriately. But the proper response to imminent refutation is not admitting defeat; it is changing one's position while retaining one's original terminology. Successful scientists are those who master the art of judicious finagling.

METHODOLOGICAL OBJECTIONS

The phenomenal increase in the number of learned journals has spawned a new literary genre—reviews of reviews. In a recent review of the reviews of E. O. Wilson's *Sociobiology: The New Synthesis* (1975), Arthur Caplan (1976, p. 21) remarks that the critical responses "fall into two general categories. Some biologists have taken exception to Wilson's efforts for purely methodological reasons. Others, however, have objected to the book on moral or ethical grounds." (The accuracy of Caplan's conclusion can be confirmed by reading three recent review symposia devoted to sociobiology in the *American Journal of Sociology*, 82, 1976; *Contemporary Sociology.* 5, 1976; and the *American Psychologist.* 31, 1976.) This same observation is equally true of both phrenology and evolutionary theory in the nineteenth century. Neither was judged to be properly scientific: both were deemed to pose a grave danger to humanity. In this section, I deal with the methodological objections raised to phrenology and evolutionary theory in the nineteenth century, comparing them to those currently being urged against sociobiology. In the next section, I do the same for the moral ethical, and social objections. I conclude by seeing whether the differing fates of phrenology and evolutionary theory might not help us predict the future course of sociobiology.

According to the phrenologists, the brain is the organ of the mind. The brain can be analyzed into organs, the human mind into faculties, and an isomorphism can be established between the two. Further, the relative size of each cerebral organ is a good measure of the power of the associated faculty. Finally, the external shape of the skull is an accurate reflection of the external shape of the brain beneath. Thus, by carefully examining a person's skull, one should be able to diagnose his or her mental capacities.

By now, the basic premises of Darwin's theory are commonplace. More organisms are produced than can possibly survive. A relation exists between the traits that an organism exhibits and the likelihood that it will survive long enough to reproduce itself. These traits vary from one generation to the next, and these variations in turn are heritable. Thus, evolution should take place, one species changing into another or splitting into two or more species. The one place where phrenology and evolutionary theory overlap is in their materialistic implications for mind. Minds cannot consist in separate, independent, immaterial substances.

In spite of the differences between these two theories, the methodological objections raised to them were the same. In the nineteenth century, "inductivism" was the official philosophy of science in Great Britain. In this view, true scientists begin by collecting facts wholesale without any preconceived notions. Gradually, low-level regularities emerge. After enough of these low-level regularities have been collected, more general regularities materialize out of them, and so on. Of course, none of the leading philosophers of the day actually held such views even such empiricist philosophers as John Herschel (1792-1871) and John Stuart Mill (1806-1873), but everyone tried to sound as much as possible like Francis Bacon (1561-1626), while surreptitiously acknowledging roles in science for deduction, theorizing, and even speculation (Hull, 1973; Ruse, 1975a).

The methodological criticisms of phrenology voiced by P. M. Roget (1779-1869), the author of one of the Bridgewater Treatises (1834) and of the famed *Thesaurus* ([1852] 1965), are typical. Although Roget agreed that the brain is the organ of the mind and that several analogies lend an air of plausibility to the existence of some localization of brain function, he could go no further, objecting that "nothing like direct proof has been given that the presence of any particular part of the brain is essentially necessary to the carrying on the operations of the mind" (Roget, 1842, 465). Analogies are fine for "directing and stimulating our inquiries to the discovery of truth by the legitmate road of observation and experiment. But to assume the existence of any such analogy as equivalent to a positive proof resulting from the evidence of direct observation is a gross violation of logic" (Roget, 1842, 466).

Numerous philosophers and scientists raised exactly these same objections to Darwin's theory. Adam Sedgwick (1785-1873) likened it to a "vast pyramid resting on its apex and that apex a mathematical point" (Sedgwick, 1860, 334). Darwin had deserted the "true method of induction," the "tram-road of all solid physical truth" (Darwin, 1899, 2, 43). As critical as Sedgwick was, Darwin still fared better than Robert Chambers (1802-1871), the author in 1844 of the popular *Vestiges of Creation*. Sedgwick (1845, 4) claimed that Chambers "has not so much as a mathematical point to rest his foot upon." The methodological objections to Darwin were set out in greatest detail by William Hopkins (1793-1866). While conceding that Darwin had the right to investigate the origin of species, Hopkins also gave Darwin to understand that "we exact from him in the support of his theories the same logical reasoning and the same kind of general evidence we demand before we yield our assent to more ordinary theories" (Hopkins, 1860, 739). But no one had ever directly observed the birth of a new species (nor has anyone to this day). Of all the experiements performed by animal breeders to produce varieties that were intersterile, "we are not aware of one which affords the slightest positive proof" (Hopkins, 1860, 80). Nor were Darwin's fellow Darwinians less critical. T. H. Huxley (1825-1895), for example, argued that the inductive foundations of evolutionary theory would remain insecure until the evolution of a new species was actually observed.

Needless to say, neither Gall nor Darwin presented much in the way of direct evidence or observational proof for their views. Their opponents objected that the connection between their evidence and their basic premises was extermely tenuous. They also complained of the modification that Gall and Darwin made in their theories in the face of recalcitrant data. Gall originally postulated twenty-seven faculties, then raised the number to thirty-three. By the time his disciples had finished with the theory, they had postulated forty-four faculties and associated organs of the brain. In addition, one region of the brain could compensate somewhat for another. As the phrenologists added new faculties, dropped old ones, subdivided certain faculties, merged others, and remapped the regions of the brain accordingly, opponents such as G. Poulett Scrope (1797-1876) grew impatient, complaining, "Such is the kind of evidence on which is founded one of the most extraordinary theories that ever disgraced the unfortunate science of mental philosophy! By rapidly assuming the truth of his hypothesis, the phrenologist is capable of making a stand by means of that very complication and obscurity of his subject which ought to have been present in his mind at the first step of his progress. Once grant the existence of thirty-six organs, reciprocally acting on each other and influenced by adventitious circumstances, and he is a man of little ingenuity who cannot prove any possible arrangement of them to accord with the character of any given individual or provide a plausible account for the apparent discrepancy" (1836, 181).

Similar complaints were voiced on the "ductility" of the reasoning that Darwin used to defend his theory (for example, Hopkins, 1860). Such criticisms of both theories continue to this day, although the magic word is no longer *induction* but *falsifiability*. For example, Robert M. Young (1968, 254) concludes from studying the large compendium of evidence that Gall accumulated that "the phrenological method is a textbook case in support of a falsificationist view of scientific method, for he sought confirmations and failed to take exceptions seriously enough." Gertrude Himmelfarb (1959, 279) makes similar remarks in connection with Darwin's theory: "Thus when the actual evidence in the case proved to be insufficient for his purpose, Darwin referred back to the theory which he had found adequate in other cases—although it was precisely the adequacy of the theory that was being challenged." Darwin's argument "was too evasive and the reasoning too circular to satisfy all Darwin's champions, let alone his critics."

Throughout the history of science, scientists have claimed that they base their theories on the facts and nothing but the facts. Newton can be found proclaiming *"hypotheses non fingo"* ("I do not feign hypotheses"), the phrenologists claimed to deal only with "observed facts of nature," and Darwin (1899, 1, 68) declared that he proceeded in developing his theory "on true Baconian principles and without any theory collected facts on a wholesale scale." Scientific mythology aside, none of these claims has the slightest foundation. What are the sources of this continued hypocrisy? One is that science as we know it developed in reaction to a research program that had been degenerating for some time. The dangers of building a system safely insulated from refutation by ad hoc hypotheses piled on ad hoc hypotheses were all too apparent to scientists struggling to get out from under scholasticism. Scientists wanted to emphasize the difference between their activities and those of scholastic philosophers. Such fears in the early years of science perhaps were justified. They have little justification today.

Another source for the hypocritical standards imposed on newly emerging sceintific theories that is as relevant today as it was in Newton's time is the conception of theories as timeless sets of axioms, as if there were such a thing as *the* theory of evolution, *the* theory of phrenology, or *the* theory of sociobiology. If the theories that function in the ongoing process of science were such discrete axiomatic systems, then complaints about the ductility and circularity of scientific reasoning would be justified. Given a complete, explicitly formulated scientific theory, any particular observation statement will follow from it, or it will not. But actual scientific theories are much more variable and amorphous. It is not always clear which implications follow from a theory and which do not, because it is not always clear which tenets are central to the theory and which not. Scientists continually change their theories. Improvement of a theory in the face of a newly discovered difficulty can look very much like circular reasoning. In short, scientific theories evolve. Because they evolve the way they do, they have no essences.

From the beginning, evolutionists had to argue that species as units of evolution do not have essences. Species change indefinitely through time. At any one time, certain species might be characterized by sets of traits that are possessed by all the organisms that comprise that species and, collectively, *only* by these organisms. But such a distribution of traits need not be characteristic of all species, and if one follows species back through time even these gaps disappear. Species are not individuated on the basis of sets of essential traits, because typically these traits do not exist. More importantly, species are not even individuated on the basis of sets of statistically covarying traits. They are individuated on the basis of descent and evolutionary unity (Simpson, 1961; Ghiselin, 1974a; Hull, 1976). Organisms that belong to the same species tend to be similar to each other, but they need not be and frequently are not.

The consequences of conceptualizing theories as historical entities are profound. For example, in the traditional view, there is some one set of axioms appropriately termed the "Darwinian theory of evolution." Richard Dawkins (1976, 210), in his highly readable book on sociobiology, expresses the essentialist position on the nature of theories with remarkable candor: "When we say that all bioloists nowadays believe in Darwin's theory, we do not mean that every biologist has, graven in his brain, an identical copy of the exact words of Charles Darwin himself. Each individual has his own way of interpreting Darwin's ideas. He probably learned them not from Darwin's own writings, but from more recent authors. Much of what Darwin said is, in detail, wrong. Darwin, if he read this book, would scarcely recognize his own original theory in it, though I hope he would like the way I put it. Yet, in spite of all this, there is something, some essence of Darwinism, which is present in the head of every individual who understands the theory."

Nothing could be further from the truth. Darwin changed his mind on a variety of issues as he continued to develop his theory. He always maintained that species evolve gradually and that natural selection is the chief directive force, but he wavered on nearly every other issue. And no two Darwinians totally agreed with Darwin or with each other about the basic features of evolution. The evolutionary theory that became widely accepted in the nineteenth century was *not* any of the versions Darwin himself set out. The versions that were popular were typically progressive, saltative, and Lamarckian. If theories are interpreted essentially, then none of Darwin's strongest advocates were Darwinists: Huxley because he opted for saltative evolution; Asa Gray (1810-1888) because he preferred divinely directed progressive evolution. On the traditional view of theories, there was no Darwinian revolution. Darwin failed miserably, as miserably as Gall.

In response to the preceding claims about theories as historical entities, one might object that periodically, scientists do claim that particular propositions are fundamental to their theories and if falsified, would falsify their theory. For example, Darwin ([1859] 1964, 201) states that, if "any part of the structure of any one species had been formed for the exclusive good of another species, it would annihilate my theory, for such could not have been produced through natural selection." If taken at face value, statements such as these certainly make it appear as if theories are made up of essential premises and are easily falsifiable. In spite of Darwin's claim, a single instance of a structure in one species that serves the exclusive good of another would not annihilate "evolutionary theory." Even if it could somehow be shown that a structure contributed nothing to the organisms that possessed it, the legitimate conclusion is that natural selection is not the *sole* directive force in evolution—but Darwin repeatedly claimed that he never thought it was! Of greater importance, in the versions of evolutionary theory that actually became popular in the second half of the nineteenth century, natural selection played an even more subsidiary role.

Claims about essential tenets make theories look more static and falsifiable than they actually are. In reality, such claims serve to insulate thoeries against falsification. For example, William Hamilton (1788-1856) thought that he had decisively refuted phrenology by showing the frequency with which large sinuses exist between the cerebrum and the bones of the forehead, thus casting doubt on inferences from the shape of the forehead to the shape of the brain beneath (Cantor, 1975, 211). In response to objections such as these, Andrew Combe (1797-1847) argued that the only way to overthrow phrenology was to prove the negative of at least one of its basic tenets (Cantor, 1975, 213). But the propositions that are most basic to a theory also tend to be the most difficult to confront with evidence, a nice hedge against falsification. The fact that these tenets themselves can be secretly modified further insulates theories against easy refutation.

Exactly the same methodological objections that were raised against phrenology and evolutionary theory in the nineteenth century are currently being raised against sociobiology: "In order to make their case, determinists construct a selective picture of human history, ethnography, and social relations. They misuse the basic concepts and facts of genetics and evolutionary theory, asserting things to be true that are totally unknown, ignoring whole aspects of the evolutionary process, asserting that conclusions follow from premises when they do not. Finally, they invent ad hoc hypotheses to take care of the contradictions and carry on a form of 'scientific reasoning' that is untestable and leads to unfalsifiable hypotheses" (Allen and others, 1976, 182)

The methodological faults that the opponents of sociobiology find with it are real. Sociobiologists do reason in circles, occasionally taking for granted the very thing that they need to prove. Some of their hypotheses do look extremely suspicious. It is easy to appreciate the frustration of anyone trying to falsify the basic principles of sociobiology. What *are* these basic principles, and what conceivable evidence could possibly refute them? In the preceding pages, I have attempted to show that this state of affairs is common in science. The trouble with the methodological objections raised against sociobiology is that the standards from which they flow are applicable only to theories as finished products, and they are being used to assess a newly emerging theory.

Critics of sociobiology complain that no direct evidence has been presented for any of its basic premises. The notion of "evidence" for or against a view is problematic enough. For example, Marshall Sahlins (1976) cites the very same class of social phenomena as counting against sociobiology that Alexander (1975; 1977) touts as its most persuasive confirmation—mother's-brother forms of kinship systems. The notion of "direct evidence" is even more problematic. In case after case in the history of science, the evidence demanded at the time that theory is introduced either is never forthcoming or else materializes long after the theory has been widely accepted. The appearance of clear, conclusive confirmations and refutations by unequivocal data is a function of our retrospective bias in favor of theories that succeeded (Holton, 1978). At the time both Gall's and Darwin's interspecific comparisons were dismissed as not counting as evidence for anything. Today we agree that Gall's comparison of the heads of proud people and peacocks proves nothing. However, Darwin's comparison of the points that appear on the ears of some people and the pointed ears of other species implies, to some extent, common descent. Numerous nineteenth-century scientists called for the observation of one species giving rise to another. We are still waiting. We are also still waiting for the elimination of the gaps in the fossil record.

Sociobiologists have been accused of salvaging their position through the use of *ad hoc* hypotheses. Unfortunately, today's *ad hoc* hypothesis is tommorrow's law of nature. Numerous explanatory devices were dismissed as being *ad hoc* when they were first introduced: the *punctum aequans* of Ptolemaic astronomy (epicycles were all right), Heinrich Hertz's necessarily hidden bodies, Gall's complementation of cerebral organs, the epistatic genes of Mendelian genetics, and Wilson's "multiplier effect." However, there seems to be no correlation between how *ad hoc* a hypothesis seems when it is originally introduced and its eventual fate. Perhaps Wilson's multiplier effect will go the way of the *punctum aequans*, perhaps the way of epstatic genes. The same can be said for the "threshold effects" of the sociobiologists and the "genetic homeostasis" of their opponents. The survival of one theory over the other will determine which hypotheses were legitimate and which *ad hoc*.

One of the most telling criticisms of the sociobiological research program is the uncritical way in which sociobiologists extend to other species of organisms terms designed to refer to human beings and human societies. In ordinary discourse, we refer to Victoria and the fertile females in termite colonies as "queens," to Vietnam and conflicts between members of different ant hills as "wars," and so on. However, nothing about the scientific equvalence of these entities follows from ordinary usage. For example, the social structures that include human queens may have very little in common with termite societies and their queens. Queens in human societies on occasion have considerable authority; termite queens are hardly more than baby factories. (In this particular case, the contrast between termite queens and Victoria is not as great as one might wish.) Hence, the critics conclude that sociobiology rests on "mere analogies" and "mushy metaphors."

Once again, this situation is common in science. Phrenologists adopted commonsense human faculties such as combativeness, covetousness, and cautiousness and then analyzed the brain into organs accordingly. But in this respect, they are no different from early Mendelian geneticists. They too adopted commonsense divisions of organisms into traits—blue eyes, green seed coat, cleft chin, and so on—and then analyzed the hereditary material into genes accordingly. Phrenologists used the shape of skulls to infer the shape of the brain beneath. Only after death could they inspect the brain itself. Mendelians were in even tighter straits. They had nothing like direct access to genes. Instead, they had to postulate genes as a result of following patterns of inheritance for phenotypic traits. The practice of correlating commonsense, observable traits with theoretical, inferred entities is fundamental to theoretical science. The difference between the phrenologists and the Mendelians is the alacrity with which the Mendelians were willing to abandon their original crude classification of traits into kinds. For example, elliptocytosis in human beings was once considered *a* trait. When two different genes, each capable of producing this effect, were discovered, it was promptly divided into two different traits. A few phrenologists, such as David Ferrier (1843-1928), followed a similar pattern, sacrificing functions to physiological accuracy, but most, such as Gall, allowed his catalogue of functions to dictate the organization of the brain (Young, 1968, 260).

The fate of sociobiology will depend in part on how adept sociobiologists are in redefining their commonsense classifications, turning them into technical scientific classifications. The term *work* in ordinary English has very little to do with *work* in physics. Before the sociobiologists are done, *aggression*, *altruism*, and *dominance* in ordinary English may have little in common with these terms as they are used in sociobiological theory. The process is already well underway. Sociobiology does lean heavily on various analogies. So did Darwin's theory (Young, 1971; Ruse, 1973b, 1975b; S. J. Gould, 1976a). Whether these analogies are dismissed as mere analogies retained as useful, or promoted to literal truths will depend on the success of the sociobiological research program.

ETHICAL OBJECTIONS

At first, one might be surprised to discover a scientific theory being condemned for its moral, ethical, and social implications, but the practice has been common throughout the history of science. In each case, the villains have been mechanistic, materialistic, atomistic, and reductionistic theories, and their sin has been the destruction of the image that human beings had forged of themselves. If we do not live in the center of the universe, if we evolved instead of being specially created, if causes operate in the mental world as well as in the physical, if our actions are totally a function of our environment and our genes—then we are nothing. In discussing these charges, one fact frequently is overlooked: By and large, they are justified. Thus far, the most successful scientific theories have been mechanistic, materialistic, and so on, and the acceptance of these theories has destroyed the image that human beings have had of themselves. In the nineteenth century, evolutionary theory destroyed the faith of millions. It still poses a serious threat to the faith of millions more. Theories that concern the connection between our brains, minds, and behavior have been equally threatening. The cries currently being raised about the doctrines of sociobiology may also be justified. The dangers that science has posed to various systems of belief throughout history have proven time and again to be very real.

However, before the dangers that sociobiology poses to humankind can be discussed, three distinctions must be made: One is *rejection* versus *suppression*, another is the *truth* of a claim in contrast to how *dangerous* it might be, and yet another is the difference between the implications that a scientific theory has for *moral principles* and for *social policy*. The first distinction turns on how publicly and openly the view in question is discussed. In order to reject a view, regardless of the reasons for rejecting it, one must be aware of it. The notion of truth is extremely problematic, but at least it is reasonably distinct from the notion of danger. Both true claims and false claims can be dangerous if they are believed and acted on. However, if one is a realist, the presumption is that believing something that is false is always dangerous. Being mistaken about the world in which we live is always liable to lead to trouble. Finally, if one accepts the traditional philosophical view that 'ought" cannot be derived from "is," then a scientific theory might set constraints on social policy, but it cannot determine which acts are moral and which immoral.

Scientists frequently claim that a hypothesis should be rejected because it is false. When the reasons for rejection are scientific, as I have argued in the previous section, decisions are difficult enough to make. When the reasons given for rejecting a scientific theory are extrascientific, scientists are placed in an even deeper quandary. Can extrascientific considerations legitmately enter into a scientist's decision to accept or reject a scientific theory? Should scientists reject a theory because it is incompatible with the formal logic of its day, because it is too complicated, or because it is ugly or evil? The issue is the proper domain of science and its insulation from the rest of human endeavors.

From the beginning, scientists have attempted to protect themselves by a variety of devices. If their views conflicted with current orthodoxies of one kind or another, they could always claim that they were not trying to explain how the world actually is. Instead, all they have been trying to do is to produce calculation devices that allow for more accurate predictions. In other ages, the insulation was accomplished by asserting that scientific theories properly interpreted could not possibly conflict with Scripture properly interpreted. Or one might claim that natural phenomena as they are taking place now are the proper domain for science, but not the mysteries of creation. Or one might argue that science deals with the physical world, not the living world, or the thinking world, or the world in which souls reside. More recently, the positivists have argued for the exclusion of metaphysics from science. Finally, as contemporary wisdom has it, morals at least are totally separate from matters of fact.

In each case, the protective barricade was abandoned once it had served its purpose. Scientists currently are realists: Scientific theories are supposed to tell us what the world in which we live is like. Any good book that foolishly makes factual claims about the empirical world runs the risk of being contravened by scientific investigations. Scientists now deal as freely with questions of creation as with dynamical issues. The domain of science has been steadily enlarged to include biological, psychological, and social phenomena. Science is even beginning to threaten the few remaining sanctuaries of human endeavor in the form of evolutionary epistemologies, naturalistic ethics, and the like. The defenders of the absolute diremption between science and morality have a right to feel uneasy. Philosophers and, to a lesser extent, scientists now acknowledge the inextricability of science and metaphysics. Perhaps morals are next. Perhaps we will yet see the day when philosophers and scientists alike maintain that a scientific theory should be rejected as false becasue it conflicts with some moral tenet or that some moral tenet should be rejected as evil because it conflicts with a currently accepted scientific theory.

That day, however, has not yet come. Even though one version of Marxism (and Marxism comes in as many versions as Christianity and the synthetic theory of evolution) grounds morality in objective reality, all of the participants in the debate over sociobiology seem to agree that no moral implications can be drawn from a genuine scientific theory, and vice versa. However, certain critics insist that scientific theories can have implications for social policy—implications about how society *can* be, rather than how it *should* be. Perhaps everyone in a society should be educated, but if people with twenty-one trisomy (Mongolian idiots, as they used to be called) are not educable, then there is no point in wasting the resources of a society attempting to educate them. When the issue is moral implications, scientists are protected by the is-ought distinction. When the issue is the application of scientific knowledge, scientists seek the protection of the theory-practice distinction. Their task is to seek knowledge for its own sake. Knowledge, of course, can be used for both good and evil. Either way, theoretical scientists are not responsible. In point of fact, however, this is not how scientists have conducted themselves in the past. They have been happy to take the responsibility for the *good* applications of scientific knowledge, accepting Nobel Prizes, knighthoods, and the like. Consistency would seem to require that they also accept some of the responsibility for the bad applications.

In growing numbers scientists are beginning to acknowledge that they carry more responsibility for the applications of scientific knowledge than do ordinary citizens, but ample disagreement exists about the extent of this responsibility. Should a scientific theory be suppressed because it is dangerous, even though it might be true?—that is the question. The slightest hint of suppression is sure to elicit howls of outrage from the scientific community, and understandably so. From the beginning, scientists have suffered at the hands of those who would determine which scientific views could be made public on extrascientific grounds. Most of us are likely to find such suppression villainous. At the beginning of the nineteenth century, the eccesiastical authorities brought sufficient pressure to bear on the Austrian government to force it to prohibit Gall from presenting his views on phrenology to the local citizens, an action that seems only to have increased the popularity of phrenology. At roughly the same time, William Lawrence was forced to withdraw from circulation two books he had published because of their materialistic implications for the human species (Wells, 1971). However, by the second half of the nineteenth century, the most that William Whewell (1794-1866) could do was to ban Darwin's *On the Origin of Species* ([1859] 1964) from the shelves of Trinity College, where he was Master.

Phrenologists and evolutionsists alike used attempts to suppress their views to their own advantage. Like Galileo, they were victims of religious persecution. Even Roget, one of phrenology's sternest critics, condemned the "senseless clamor" against phrenology by "bigoted priests" (1842, 456). J. D. Hooker (1817-1911), looking back at the early reception of evolutionary theory, was no less bitter: "It is not for us, who repeat *ad nauseam* our contempt for the persecutors of Galileo and the sneers at Franklin, to conceal the fact that our great discoverers met the same fate at the hands of the highest in the land of history and science" (Huxley, 1918, 2, 302-303).

In 1864, a group of young scientists circulated a declaration among their fellow scientists, asserting that science had no business contradicting revealed religion. Science and Scripture, once properly construed, could not possibly conflict. They were able to gather only 717 signatures; of these only a handful were those of especially well-known scientists. Their biggest catches were David Brewster, James Prescott Joule, and Adam Sedgwick. The response of C. G. Daubeny (1705-1867) was typical of the scientists who resfused to sign the declaration: "I am not prepared to declare that conclusions honestly arrived at in the course of scientific investigations, as for instance those relating to the age of the world, the antiquity of the human race or the prevalence of a deluge over parts of the globe not at the time inhabited by man ought, as a matter of Christian duty, to be suppressed and ignored" (Daubeny, 1864, 9).

Current attempts to suppress sociobiology because of the dangers it poses to humanity have met with the same response: "The central issue is whether scientists should have the freedom to explore nature no matter how badly their discoveries may be misused or how sharply they may contradict contemporary orthodoxies. It is an argument at least as old as Galileo's clash with the church, and the evidence of history is that the forces of suppression do not prevail for long" (Panati & Monroe, 1976, 51-52).

However, scientists themselves frequently act in ways that effectively suppress ideas with which they disagree. A conspiracy of silence is the scientific community's most effective weapon. In the case of both phrenology and evolutionary theory, the initial response of the scientific community was silence. The more prestigious a society and its journal, the more impenetrable the silence. As Frederick Burkhardt (1974, 33) notes, "Between 1859 and 1870, no paper in either the *Proceedings* or the *Philosophical Transactions* of the Royal Society has as its subject a discussion of Darwin's theory of the origin of species." From Gall and Darwin to Velikovsky and Wegener, a common response of the scientific community to ideas that they take to be hopelessly mistaken is an attempt to suppress them by ignoring them. Anyone may publish anything he or she pleases, but not in a scientific journal, and scientists are under no obligation to take note of ideas if they choose not to. The end result can be fairly effective suppression. For champions of orthodox views, the best response to an attack is initially no response at all. Only if the attacks begin to attract converts can powerful scientists be smoked out to defend themselves. Not too surprisingly, E. O. Wilson's colleagues advised him that the "best response to a political attack . . . is perhaps no response at all" (Wilson, 1976, 183). No doubt his critics were placed in the same position. Any attack, but especially a political attack, serves only to bring further attention to views that they do not want to see disseminated.

Some of the critics of sociobiology seem to argue for the *permanent* suppression of its doctrines *regardless* of their truth. However, most take a more moderate view. They argue instead for raising the standards of proof when the ideas addressed are socially explosive. For example, S. J. Gould (1976a, 22) states, "I make no attribution of motive in Wilson's or anyone else's case. Neither do I reject determinism because I dislike its political usage. Scientific truth, as we understand it, must be our primary criterion. We live with several unpleasant biological truths, death being the most undeniable and ineluctable. If genetic determinism is true, we will learn to live with it as well. But I reiterate my statement that no evidence exists to support it, that the crude versions of past centuries have been conclusively disproved, and that its continued popularity is a function of social prejudice among those who benefit most from the status quo.

The same observations could have been made against Darwin's work, and they were. In response to Darwin's *The Descent of Man* ([1871] 1969), one writer in the *London Times* (April 8, 1871, p. 5) proclaims, "A man incurs grave responsibility who, with the authority of a well-earned reputation, advances at such a time the disintegrating speculations of this book. He ought to be capable of supporting them by the most conclusive evidence of facts. To put them forward on such incomplete evidence, such cursory investigations, such hypothetical arguments as we have exposed, is more than unscientific—it is reckless."

Thus the two classes of objections to sociobiology with which this chapter deals—methodological and ethical—converge on each other. The opponents of sociobiology apply uncommonly high standards of proof to it, but not because they have unreal views about scientific proof. The higher standards result from the reputed danger of certain sociobiological doctrines. If one admits that scientists have some responsibility for the use and abuse of their ideas, the preceding position has much to recommend it. It is certainly rational to raise one's standards of proof when the probable outcome is serious. Rational people demand more evidence of malignancy before removing a kidney than a mole.

However, this position itself is beset with difficulties. In the first place, when the claim that socially dangerous scientific hypotheses should not be made public is coupled with the prohibition of research on socially dangerous hypotheses, the net effect is the total prohibition of "dangerous ideas." Secondly, there is the problem of deciding which ideas are dangerous. Scientists have proven themselves to be extremely good at making decisions regarding empirical fact. But there is no reason to suppose that they are any better than the rest of us in making moral decisions, and the track record of humanity at large on this score is not impressive. The critics of sociobiology assume that the ideal society would be egalitarian, cooperative, and socialistic. But others see nothing wrong with elitism, individualism, and capitalism. To the rugged individualist, the reputed individualistic implications of sociobiology are not in the least alarming.

The critics also assume that there is some connection between the actual content of a theory and its social implications, both licit and illicit. Phrenologists should have been "hereditarians." They tended to be "moderate environmentalists." In Edinburgh, phrenologists tended to champion liberal causes; so did their opponents. On the continent, phrenologists were more conservative (Young, 1968; Parssinen, 1974; Cantor, 1975; Shapin 1975; Cooter, 1976; Cowan, 1977). By and large, Europeans were racists before the publication of *On the Origin of Species*. They remained racist afterward. It is no more difficult to justify the inherent superiority of Caucasians by reference to evolutionary theory than it is by reference to Scripture (Haller, 1971). In connection with phrenology, Steven Shapin

(1975, 241) concludes, "Pure hereditarian ideas may serve as well as pure environmentalist ideas in legitmating tolerance, liberality, and social justice." Similarly, Noam Chomsky (1975, p. 132) points out that extreme environmentalism can be abused as readily as extreme hereditarianism. And, to round out the story, B. F. Skinner (1974) has repeatedly argued that the prevalent belief in free will has also contributed its share to human misery.

To anyone committed to the efficacy, however slight, of reason, argument, and evidence in the course of human affairs, the ease with which scientific theories can be bent to support almost any social cause whatsoever is discouraging, but the problem is not that the implications are social. The same difficulties arise in deciding which observational consequences follow from scientific theories and have the same source—the evolutionary character of scientific theories. Is sociobiology racist and sexist? It is difficult to say. Would the presence in a society of a high percentage of children being raised by people not related to them genetically refute sociobiology? It is just as difficult to say. Such quandaries are common in science. Were phrenology and evolutionary theory racist and sexist? Did the gaps between the cerebrum and the skull refute phrenology and more conclusively than the even larger gaps in the fossil record refuted evolutionary theory? The distinction between licit and illicit implications of scientific theories is far from sharp.

Finally, those who advocate increased standards of support for scientifically dangerous ideas before they are made public are themselves not immune from this same line of reasoning. The suppression of scientific ideas itself carries considerable risk. In the past, all the wrong people seem to have attempted to suppress new scientific ideas for all the wrong reasons. Those who would suppress scientific ideas for moral reasons today are under some obligation to set out the moral standards on which these decision are based and to justify them. This particular dispute is too important for it to continue on the basis of tacitly held moral principles.

CONCLUSION

I began this chapter with the promise that studying the fates of phrenology and evolutionary theory in the nineteenth century might help us assess the current status of sociobiology and predict its future. It is now time to deliver on that promise. The same methodological objections were raised to phrenology and evolutionary theory. Both were condemned as being subversive to humanity. Yet phrenology lost, and evolutionary theory won. The same methodological objections are now being raised against sociobiology, and it too is being condemned for being inhumane. Are either of these sorts of objections likely to make a difference to its success or failure? T. M. Parssinen (1974) has identified four reasons for the decline of phrenology in nineteenth-century Edinburgh: (1) its popularity with the working classes, (2) the crumbling of its scientific basis because of the experimental investigations it encouraged, (3) the disintegration of its organizational structure over such issues as materialism, and (4) the drifting of its members into the study of mesmerism and phrenomesmerism.

Parssinen's list of reasons for the demise of phrenology is interesting in two respects. First, no mention is made of methodological or humanitarian shortcomings. As large as these objections loomed in the critical literature, Parssinen thinks they had little effect. In the first section of this chapter, I tried to explain why methodological criticisms have been so ineffectual in science. One reason is obvious: At any one time in the history of science, scientists have a set of stock objections that they raise to any new theory, regardless of its content or merits. These stock objections tend to be both extremely empirical and highly hypocritical. They are applicable, if at all, only to scientific theories as finished products. They are totally useless in assessing newly emerging theories.

A more subtle reason for the ineffectiveness of methodological criticisms is that the merits of a particular scientific method are determined in large measure by its success. There is nothing especially "unscientific" about introspection. Its poor reputation results from the fact that its results are highly variable, undependable, and idiosyncratic. Scientists have used all sorts of methods in their investigations: observation, intuition, divination, revelation, analogy, common sense, and so on. Which of these methods are genuinely scientific cannot be determined *a priori*. If the "wow!" feeling of discovery were more dependable, confirmation might be much less important. Or, if divine revelation guaranteed truth, scientists might still be using it. Of course, in such circumstances, the science that would have resulted would not be science as we know it. As I see it, philosophy of science is an empirical, not a linguistic, undertaking. Our task is not to analyze the notion of science as it is currently understood—assuming that such a notion exists—but to reform our understanding of science as we come to learn more about it. Any philosophy of science that makes the great achievements in the history of science ill founded, illogical, and irrational must be seriously in error. Scientists are far from infallible, but they are doing something right. In short, I am arguing for a retrospective legitmization of scientific reasoning on the basis of the success of that reasoning. To the extent that sociobiologists are successful, their modes of reasoning will become part of legitimate scientific method. To use Dudley Shapere's felicitous dictum, "In science, we learn *how* to learn *as* we learn."

The influence of the moral character of scientific theories on their reception is more difficult to assess. Extrascientific considerations have had noticeable effects on the success or failure of scientific ideas. One of evolutionary theory's strongest selling points was that it was naturalistic. No miracles were needed. It is also no accident that the form of evolutionary theory that became popular was progressive. Progressivism was pandemic at the time. How much of a role did the hereditarian implications of phrenology and evolutionary theory play in their receptions? In the second section of this chapter, I have tried to explain why such questions are so difficult to answer. In contrast to the iconic representations assumed by traditional philosophies of science, actual scientific theories are extremely amorphous and variable. At any one time, numerous different versions of the same theory coexist, and these clusters change through time. Although the connection between scientific theories and their environments is not chaos, it is extremely complicated and variable. Given the current state of the art, we are in no position to state with any justification the relative importance of various "external" factors in the reception of newly emerging scientific theories. The only study to date that is sufficiently extensive to provide some basis for judgment can be found in Thomas Glick's *The Comparative Reception of Darwinism* (1974), and the only conclusion that it supports is that such connections are extremely variable.

A second feature of Parssinen's list of reasons for the demise of phrenology in nineteenth-century Edinburgh is that only one—the crumbling of its scientific basis—is the sort of reason that traditional philosophies of science consider legitimate. The others concern the sociology of science. If they are operative, they should not be. Reason, argument, and evidence are supposed to be the determining factors for scientists opting one way or the other on scientific issues. So far no one has presented much in the way of evidence that scientists actually *do* behave the way they *should* behave, but, more importantly, evidential and sociological considerations are not as distinct as philosophers have traditionally supposed.

Parssinen mentions the popularity of phrenology among the operative classes, the implication being that popularity among the wrong sorts of people can hurt the reputation of a scientific theory. It is certainly true that phrenology was popular among the working classes and that phrenologists were anxious to convert the operative classes, as indicated by Johann Caspar Spurzheim's (1776-1832) lectures to the London Mechanics' Institution (Parssinen, 1974). But Darwinism was just as popular among the lower classes. Huxley's lectures to working men were a huge success. The popular press is currently paying considerable attention to sociobiology, and the sociobiologists themselves have gone so far as to prepare a high school textbook (De Vore, Trivers, and Goethak, 1973). But if the fates of phrenology and evolutionary theory imply anything on this score, it is that public popularity is neither necessary nor sufficient to guarantee acceptance by the scientific community. It is not lethal, either. Conducting scientific debates under the public eye is more difficult; it is not impossible.

The effects of the other three factors that Parssinen lists as being relative to the failure of phrenology are clearer. The Darwinians were able to tolerate considerable doctrinal divergence while maintaining sufficient social cohesion. The phrenologists were not. Even though Wallace came to advocate phrenology, spiritualism, and a form of radical socialism and withdrew from extending the principles of evolutionary theory to human beings, he always remained a Darwinian and on good terms with Darwin. Huxley differed strongly over the prevalence of saltative evolution, yet remained firmly in the Darwinian camp. However, at a time when phrenology had few active and influential converts, Spurzheim broke with his master, commenting that thereafter Gall ceased to do any original work. The raising of the materialistic implications of phrenology led to wholesale defections (Parssinen, 1974, 13). Although the Darwinians were just as divided over such issues as materialism, they did not allow these disagreements to destroy the cohesiveness of the movement.

Externalists have claimed that the Darwinian clique won because its members were extremely well placed when the dispute over evolution broke out and remained so. For example, in the early years after the publication of *On the Origin of Species*, the presidency of the British Association for the Advancement of Science (BAAS) alternated between Darwinians and anti-Darwinians (Ellegard, 1958). But several early phrenologists were also reasonably well placed in the scientific community — for example, Étienne Geoffroy Saint-Hilaire (1772-1844) and George S. Mackenzie (1780-1848) — and several other were to become so — Alexander Bain (1818-1903), Herbert Spencer (1820-1903), Alfred Russel Wallace (1823-1913), and Paul Broca (1824-1861). However, phrenology as a scientific movement was unable to integrate itself into the larger power structure of science. For example, in 1834 when the British Association for the Advancement of Science turned down the request of George Combe (1788-1858) for a section on phrenology, Combe was forced to organize the Phrenology Association, which met at the same time and in the same city as the BAAS.

Internalists, on the other hand, emphasize the contributions that the evolutionists made to the substantive content of science. Many Darwinians had produced scientific work of recognized excellence before their conversion and continued to do so afterward, but from an "evolutionary perspective." Several early phrenologists also made substantive contributions to science, not the least of which were those of Saint-Hilaire, Bain, Spencer, Wallace, Broca, and Ferrier. Many of the scientific contributions of phrenologists did not bear directly on the principles of phrenology, but the same can be said for the evolutionists. Advances *were* made in the early years of the nineteenth century in understanding the brain, but they were made by the enemies of phrenology, not by the phrenologists. For example, in 1829, Sir Charles Bell (1774-1842) won the first Royal Medal for his work on the nervous system. Much later, Broca and Ferrier presented evidence for cerebral localization in the name of "scientific phrenology" (Young, 1968), but apparently they were too late. Phrenology's reputation had been fixed. In the ninth edition of the *Encyclopedia Britannica*, Macalister (1888, 847) concedes that the "doctrine that the brain is the organ of the mind is now universally received" and that there "is a large weight of evidence, which cannot be explained away, in favor of the exsitence of some form of localization of function." But he is able to assert that "no phrenologists" contributed any original information on these parts.

The question thus becomes "Why, in retrospect, do we view phrenology as having failed and evolutionary theory as having succeeded?" Both contained basic premises that we now take to be true. Both were modified extensively as they developed. Both attracted adherents, among whom were well-placed scientists, some of whom continued to contribute to the substantive content of science in the name of their respective research programs. Part of the answer is differences in number. For every successful phrenologists, there were hundreds of evolutionists. Another turns on scientific theories and research communities being historical entities developing through time. Like species, they are individuated on the basis of descent and unity, not similarity. If asked why two versions of a scientific theory are versions of the same theory, we are likely to answer in terms of extensive overlap in the claims that these two versions make. However, neither historians of science nor scientists themselves individuate theories in this way. Today a growing number of evolutionists (for example, Eldredge and Gould, 1972) are adopting a view of evolution that in several important respects is much more like the version set out by Richard Goldschmidt (1878-1958) than like that of Darwin, yet they consider themselves neo-Darwinians, not neo-Goldschmidtians. Why? Because they trace their views back through such neo-Darwinians as H. L. Carson and Ernst Mayr to Darwin, not to Richard Goldschmidt.

As a result, two formulations can be extremely similar with respect to substantive assertions and not count as versions of the same theory, while two formulations can be substantively very different and still be considered versions of the same theory. For example, in Darwin's day, Huxley and Gray were considered Darwinians, and their versions of evolutionary theory were considered merely modifications of Darwin's views. Saint George Jackson Mivart (1827-1900) set out a non-Darwinian theory of evolution that did not differ materially from the views of Huxley and Gray. It was saltative, like Huxley's, and progressive, like Gray's. The substantive content of science is, of course, important. Scientists are more explicitly and consciously concerned with it than with anything else. But it does not follow on this account that scientific theories should be individuated in terms of similarity in substantive content (Hull, 1975, 1978b; Burian, 1977).

If future historians and scientists are to look back on sociobiology and conclude that it succeeded, then sociobiologists had best busy themselves on several fronts. They should stay active in science, both sociologically and substantively. The actual connections between the contributions that they make and sociobiology are not all that important as long as these contributions are recognized as coming out of the sociobiological research program. It would also help if they—not their opponents—made advances in understanding the biological bases of social behavior. They must be willing to modify their views, no matter how extensively, in the face of various considerations that threaten to undermine their position, while maintaining that these are *modifications*, not *abandonments*. The results are new *versions* of their theory, not *replacements*.

That selection occurs only at the level of the "individual" is supposedly one of the basic premises of sociobiology. If all adaptations can be explained solely by reference to individual genes, then the sociobiologists are right. If recourse to organisms must be made, then claims about selection operating exclusively at the level of genes are merely idiosyncrasies of particular sociobiologists. If kinship groups can function as units of selection, then kinship groups are individuals. If populations can function as units of selection, that is individual selection too. Populations and possibly entire species form individuals (Ghiselin, 1974a; Hull, 1976). If this fails, then include group selection among the tenets of sociobiology.

Looking back, all the versions of evolutionary theory set out in the nineteenth century were seriously flawed. Darwin thought that evolution was gradual, undirected, and guided primarily by natural selection. Today we agree that it is undirected and that natural selection is the primary mechanism for evolutionary change. However, we disagree with Darwin over the subsidiary mechanisms, and a growing number of evolutionists are opting for nongradualistic forms of evolution. Other versions of nineteenth century evolutionary theory fare no better when compared to contemporary versions. The basic premises of phrenology fare no worse. The chief failing of the phrenologists is that they were not sufficiently adept at finagling. Instead of adapting the principles of associationist psychology to those of phrenology, Bain and Spencer defected. Evolutionists were masters at transmuting refutations into confirmations. Phrenologists allowed themselves to be saddled with the weakest part of their program (the reading of heads) instead of the strongest parts (for example, brain localization). Of course, the reading of heads was also the most original part, but comparable observations can be made with respect to evolutionary theory. The weakest and most original part of Darwin's theory was natural selection. That did not keep Darwin's disciples from saving their program at the expense of Darwin's unique contribution. The only form of evolutionary theory that the scientific community was willing to accept was progressive; evolutionists promptly produced a progressive version of evolutionary theory and labeled it "Darwinian." If current versions of sociobiology sound too inhumane, they can always be made to seem more attractive. There is no reason why a book must be named *The Selfish Gene* (Dawkins, 1976). *The Altruistic Organism* would do as well and be no more misleading.

In the long run, the success of sociobiology will depend more on how adaptable the sociobiologists turn out to be and how tenaciously they fight for the term *sociobiology* than on how close their current views are to the truth. One frequently hears rumblings of discontent over the term *sociobiology* and the attention paid to Wilson, but the sociobiologists are stuck with the term and their titular leader. Abandonment of the term and attacks on the man will register as a repudiation of the entire enterprise. The animosities and disagreements that arise among the members of a scientific movement are frequently far more bitter than those that arise between competing groups. If a research program is to succeed, these disputes had better stay intramural. The social cohesion of a research community contributes as much to the success of a research program as does conceptual unity, especially in times of rapid and fundamental conceptual change. In the end, future sociobiologists may agree with none of the claims made by the founders of the movement. In fact, their position may differ in no important respect from that currently held by its opponents. If they call themselves *sociobiologists* and couch their position in the terminology of sociobiology, however, sociobiology will have won (for further discussion, see Hull, 1982d).

Chapter 16

Sociobiology:
Another New Synthesis*

In the heat of battle, we tend to forget that sociobiology is just one more scientific dispute out of many, just one more attempt by one group of scientists to convert the larger scientific community. Sociobiologists are trying to expand the frontiers of biology to include territory that has traditionally been part of the domain of the social sciences. They are also attempting to some extent to redefine the very notion of empirical science to include considerations normally treated by philosophers and theologians.

Neither activity is unusual. From the point of view of the combatants, the controversy may well look like a battle between the forces of good and evil, between unwitting dupes of a capitalist, sexist conspiracy and the new inquisitors bent on suppressing truth for ideological reasons. Although no one connected with the dispute is likely to be in the least interested, the history of science presents a continuous showing of such scientific morality plays (Hull, 1978b). Time and again one group of scientists attempts to appropriate the territory of another. Time and again new research programs are judged on the basis of "extra-scientific" considerations. The success or failure of these research programs in turn redefines both the internal and the external borders of science.

In the early part of the nineteenth century, for instance, philosophers such as William Whewell (1840) argued that questions concerning first beginnings were not an appropriate subject for scientific investigation. However, before the century was over, cosmologists, geologists and evolutionists had not only delineated their own subject matters but also made them a legitimate part of science.

Today, sociobiologists are engaged in similar, time-honored expansionary activities. They are attempting to explain behavioral and social phenomena biologically and possibly to include issues of morals and ethics within the domain of empirical science. That the intended victims are uneasy should occasion no surprise. Slight as it may be, philosophers and social scientists may gain some consolation from the knowledge that, as

---

*Reprinted with permission from *Sociobiology: Beyond Nature/Nurture?*, ed. George W. Barlow and James Silverberg, AAAS Selected Symposium 35, Boulder, Colorado: Westview Press.

the sociobiologists tuck in their napkins in preparation for their feast on philosophy and the social sciences, physicists and chemists are busily gnawing away at the flanks of biology. Reduction in science gives every appearance of a many-headed hydra attempting to consume itself.

A lack of historical perspective is not the only impediment to understanding the current controversy over sociobiology. Another is the tendency of both sides to accept a hypocritical view of science engendered by generations of scientific propaganda. For example, Sir Peter Medawar (1972, 87), in one of his mellower moods, remarks:

> Scientists, on the whole, are amiable and well-meaning creatures. There must be very few wicked scientists. There are, however, plenty of wicked philosophers, wicked priests, and wicked politicians.

That Nicholas Wade (1976, 1153) shares Medawar's high opinion of scientists is revealed by his dismay over the treatment of Wilson's work by the Sociobiology Study Group:

> In short, the Sociobiology Study Group has systematically distorted Wilson's statements to fit the position it wishes to attack, namely that human social behavior is wholly or almost wholly determined by the genes. Such a degree of distortion, though routine enough in political life, is perhaps surprising from a group composed largely of professional scholars.

One scientist distorting the views of another? Incredible. I see no point in the continuation of such hypocrisy. Perhaps the openly political motivation of the Sociobiology Study Group is somewhat unusual in scientific controversies; the reliance on distortion is not. Distortion is not only routine in science, it is a hallowed method of debate. Darwin's opponents consistently castigated him for claiming that natural selection was all-sufficient when he never did. Darwin in turn argued in the *Origin* (1859) as if the only alternative to his theory was miraculous special creation when it was not.

If scientists throughout history have consistently caricatured the views they oppose and show not the slightest inclination of doing otherwise today, it is about time we admitted it. Of course, the sociobiologists have been misrepresented. Some of the opponents of sociobiology reveal only the haziest understanding of its basic principles. For example, Sahlins (1976) happily cites mother's brother/sister's son forms of social inheritance as refuting sociobiology when Alexander (1977) presents such phenomena as its strongest confirmation. In their turn, sociobiologists propose to reduce sociology to biology while freely admitting that they do not know very much sociology. They plan to read up on it. Such interdisciplinary arrogance is common in science. Molecular biologists were just as ignorant of the Mendelian genetics that they planned to reduce to physics and chemistry.

A common practice in ethics is to compare the behavior of real people to some abstract ideal. People always come up wanting, but that is all right. After all, people are only human, and feelings of guilt are good for the soul. What I find disconcerting is that in many cases it is not just human weakness that keeps us from behaving the way we should. Even if we could, we would not because we have too much sense.

I find myself reaching similar conclusions with respect to traditional ideal standards of proper scientific method. The net effect of the scientific enterprise may well be an increase in objective knowledge. A common goal of individual scientists may well be truth for its own sake. But that does not mean that scientists are selfless, dispassionate calculating machines or that science would be improved if they were.

The emotional character of the dispute over sociobiology is not in the least unusual. Scientists, like all of us, find objectivity harder to maintain in areas that touch them personally. The point that needs emphasizing is that, to scientists, their subject matter is always personal. As difficult as it is to believe, the mating habits of *Escherichia coli* are as important to a bacteriologist as those of her husband, maybe more so.

At the very least, we need to distinguish between real scientists and the Ideal Platonic Scientist. But more importantly, we need to scrutinize this ideal type to find out if possibly the reason that scientists fail even to approach it, let alone attain it, is that they have too much sense. The ideal standard is not only ideal, it is mistaken.

THE SOCIOLOGY OF SCIENCE

The controversy over sociobiology has taken on the character it has for several reasons. First, the participants do not view themselves from a historical perspective, as just one more episode in a continuing saga. As far as they are concerned, this is the first time that scientists have criticized science on the basis of extra-scientific considerations. Second, everyone concerned judges the behavior of their opponents by extremely unrealistic standards. They are adhering to the best scientific standards, while their opponents have all but invented the art of scientific parody. Finally, no one is paying the slightest attention to the social dimension of science—as it applies to themselves.

One of the chief goals of science is to discover as much as possible about the world in which we live. For most research scientists, research is not just an occupation, it is a compulsion. But one area in which scientists have shown surprisingly little curiosity is in their own social organization. When the issue is raised, scientists are quick to admit that science is a social institution like any other, but they are sure that such social considerations have no direct effects on the content of science. Truth will out. More than that, when scientists chance to read something written about themselves by a sociologist of science, they react with all the irate indignation characteristic of other human beings who find themselves under scientific scrutiny. Nor are sociologists of science themselves exempt from these generalizations. For years, the Merton group studied a variety of research communities. Not until quite recently have members of the Merton group got around to studying the Merton group itself, and then only with utmost gentleness (Cole and Zuckerman, 1975). If the same sort of intra-group competition so characteristic of other research communities also characterizes the Society for Social Studies of Science, we do not hear about it.

One would think that sociobiologists, a group of scientists devoted to discovering the biological bases of social organization, might be interested in their own social organization and would be quick to apply their own principles to themselves. People in general, so the sociobiologists claim, are basically selfish. Genuine altruism is a myth. All creatures are devoted almost exclusively to the pursuit of their own selfish gains, all creatures except scientists. They are selflessly devoting their lives to the search for truth. Then why the rush for priority? Why arguments over who thought of what first? Truth is truth regardless of who discovers it. But if scientific disputes are just one more example of competition between totally selfish groups, how can sociobiologists possibly justify their righteous indignation over the vigilantism of some of their opponents (Wilson 1976)? Is it just one more instance of the hypocrisy the sociobiologists find so charcateristic of societies or does it have some genuine moral foundation?

Conversely, if all the views set forth by scientists are basically a product of their socio-economic background, then the same observations should apply equally to the opponents of sociobiology. Strangely enough, the sociobiologists come from the same variety of socio-economic backgrounds as their opponents. In the case of the sociobiologists, the fact that they live in a highly competitive, elitist, male-dominated society has forced them to produce a biological theory possessing these same characteristics. Their opponents, however, have somehow freed themselves from these same influences.

Clearly, both sides are presented with difficulties. The paradoxes of vulgar social determinism are no less intransigent than those of vulgar genetic determinism. The Marxists' claim that my living in a capitalist society makes me hold capitalist beliefs is no more palatable than the sociobiologists' claim that my being male makes me hold male beliefs. Although neither side is likely to admit it, they have narrowed their dispute to the time-honored problem of free will, and any scientist worth his salt knows better than to introduce such a topic into a scientific debate. Although I have serious doubts about the direct connections that Marxists see between socio-economic causes and the content of scientific theories, I also find it impossible to believe that scientists are exempt from the same social determinants that they attribute to everyone else. Perhaps the sociobiologists realize that they are self-serving as bankers and politicians and that their protestations about the unfair treatment they have received at the hands of their opponents are to be viewed as sheer hypocrisy, but they have yet to say so in print. Of course, given their views on the role of hypocrisy in society, they should not.

In any case, a sociobiological analysis of the sociobiologists themselves might prove to be not only instructive but also entertaining (Hull, 1978a). What is good for the goose and all that. How did Wilson become the head honcho? What sorts of submissive behavior do others lower in the sociobiological dominance hierarchy exhibit to deflect his aggressive behavior? Do others in Wilson's research group behave like juveniles, or like females in estrus? What strategies are they employing to depose him?

Wilson is popularly considered to be the father of sociobiology, his term "sociobiology" the appropriate name for the movement, and his book *Sociobiology: The New Synthesis* (1975) its official bible. No matter who presents a paper on sociobiology, the main topic of discussion is inevitably Wilson and his book, or more accurately, the first and last chapters of his book. How come Wilson, his term, and his book?

If one wants to understand sociobiology as a scientific research program, one fact must be kept in the forefront: the sociobiologists do not form a homogeneous group, either conceptually or socially. Sociobiologists in a broad sense all want to extend biological modes of explanation to behavior, including human behavior. They cooperate to the extent necessary to oppose their joint enemies. However, not all sociobiologists belong to the Wilson group.

A year before Wilson's book appeared, Michael Ghiselin published his *The Economy of Nature and the Evolution of Sex* (1974b), a work as ambitious as Wilson's and even more provocative. Who can resist quoting Ghiselin's description of his book as a "cross between the *Kama Sutra* and the *Wealth of Nations*," his Copulatory Imperative, or his departing quip, "Scratch an 'altruist,' and watch a 'hypocrite' bleed"? Yet Ghiselin's book has played almost no role in the controversy. Similarly, Ghiselin (1974a), R. D. Alexander (1974) and Robert Trivers (1974) all produced an analysis of parent-offspring conflict at roughly the same time, yet priority is almost always given to Trivers.

Perhaps these and other features of the sociobiological research program can be explained entirely in terms of the inherent worth of the ideas contributed. Perhaps Wilson's book has received the attention it has because it is so vastly superior to all its competitors. Perhaps Trivers receives all the credit for parent-offspring conflict because he actually thought of it first and his development is scientifically superior to that of Ghiselin and Alexander. Or possibly, sociological factors may have played a role.

Sociologists claim that scientists are organized into small, ephemeral groups which they term "invisible colleges." The scientists in these groups cooperate with each other to push new views, treating each other differently from the members of competing research communities. Within-group competition can be even more brutal than between-group competition, but it is different in kind. Although sociologists call these research groups "invisible colleges," they are anything but invisible. References to the work of sociobiologists outside the Wilson group by the Wilsonians are rarer than within-group citation and a good deal less positive. Correspondingly, sociobiologists outside the Wilson camp tend to cite members of their own research community more frequently than the Wilsonians and avoid using Wilson's term to characterize the movement.

I hasten to add that the preceding observations are not intended to be critical of the Wilson group, other sociobiology research communities, or their anti-sociobiology opponents. The formation of such research communities is highly efficacious, if not absolutely necessary in science. For example, initially Darwin formulated his ideas on evolution in relative isolation. Later, as he developed them, he solicited the aid of numerous other workers, usually without letting them in on his heresy. He also established his reputation firmly among other scientists so that when he announced his theory, he would have to be taken more seriously than Lamarck and Chambers before him. Finally, when it came time to disseminate his views, Darwin carefully and consciously formed a small band of scientists to help him push his theory. Charles Lyell and J. D. Hooker read the joint Darwin-Wallace papers at the Linnaean Society, and both T. H. Huxley and Hooker did battle with Bishop Wilberforce at the famous meeting of the British Association for the Advancement of Science in 1860. As Darwin (1899, 101) remarked in a letter to Hooker,

> One thing I see most plainly, that without Lyell's, yours, Huxley's, and Carpenter's aid, my book would have been a mere flash in the pan,

and later to Asa Gray,

> I can now very plainly see from many later Reviews, that I should have been fairly *annihilated*, had it not been for 4 or 5 men, including yourself.

Other evolutionists attempt to preempt the Darwinians, but with no great success. Few scientists accepted Darwin's theory, but everyone agreed that the Darwinians had won. The opponents of Darwinism were no more successful. Behind nearly all the most effective critiques of evolutionary theory can be found the specter of one man—Lord Kelvin. Although Kelvin himself attacked Darwin only indirectly, others in his invisible college were more open in their opposition (Haughton, 1860; Hopkins, 1860; Jenkin, 1867; Tait, 1869). The Kelvin conspiracy, of course, failed, but if Darwin could legitimately form a group to promote his brainchild, he could hardly complain of Kelvin doing the same in opposition.

Scientific discovery and even development can often be carried on in relative isolation, but conversion of the larger scientific community is a social process. If truth were all that mattered in science, there would be no unsung scientific heroes and heroines. There are plenty, from Mendel to Sister Kenny.

In this paper, I cannot present a detailed analysis of the sociobiologists as an emerging research community. I do not have the necessary empirical data, and proper scientific etiquette precludes my mentioning that which I do have. However, I can make a few general observations about scientific research communities as such. I cannot explain with any justification why Wilson, his book, and his term have become so central to the sociobiological research program, but I can explain why some scientist, some book, and some term had to materialize.

THE ESSENCE OF SOCIOBIOLOGY

Thus far, I have mentioned three factors that tend to frustrate an adequate understanding of the emergence of sociobiology: our failure to view it in its historical context, the unreal standards we use to evaluate science, and inattention to the sociology of science. One final feature of the way in which we conceptualize scientific change that all but precludes coherent discussion is the assumption that sociobiology has an "essence."

Throughout the controversy, people constantly ask, What *is* sociobiology? That this question is answered exclusively in terms of the substantative content of sociobiology is bad enough. Worse yet, everyone concerned also assumes that one set of substantive claims can be found to characterize sociobiology if only we look hard enough. For example, Dawkins (1976, 210) asserts that, in spite of all the change that has taken place in evolutionary theory since Darwin, "there is something, some essence of Darwinism, which is present in the head of every individual who understands the theory."

If evolutionary theory has anything to teach us about evolutionary processes, it is that the entities that evolve have no eternal, immutable essences. Whether evolution takes place as gradually as Darwin and modern gradualists think, or in terms of punctuated equilibria as modern proponents of "saltative" evolution maintain (Eldredge and Gould 1972), heterogeneity in the makeup of the units which are evolving (as distinct from those being selected) is necessary for the evolutionary process. (Incidentaly, modern advocates of saltative evolution are playing the same sort of game all scientists play, and central to it is systematic equivocation over the term "gradualism.") The general absence of universal covariation of morphological traits is well known, but the demise of species specificity for behavioral traits has been slow in coming. For example, Emlin and Orig (1977, 222) remark that:

> Until recently, many field biologists have worked under a preconception that species specificity was a characteristic not only of courtship behavior but of mating systems as well. We are now coming to realize that variability in social organization, including mating systems, is widespread.

In spite of the implications of evolutionary theory, scientists consistently treat species as if they were distinguishable by sets of traits that are severally necessary and jointly sufficient for membership, as if evolving species formed unchangeable discrete entities. This tendency results from our need to identify and individuate species. If everything about a species can change through time, how can we possibly pick it out? Biologists have developed a method of individuating species that does not presuppose the existence of a trait (or set of traits) that all and only the members of a particular species possess—the type specimen method. Regardless of the connotations of the term (left over from pre-evolutionary biology), type specimens need not be typical.

Given the existence of extensive metamorphosis in certain species, sexual dimorphism in others, polymorphic species, and so on, the notion of a "typical" specimen verges on being nonsense. For example, Linnaeus designated himself the type specimen for Homo sapiens, but in what biologically significant sense are males more typical than females, Caucasians more typical than other races, Swedes more typical than other nationalities, and so on? The point is not that Linnaeus is the wrong type specimen, but that the notion of a single organism embodying the essence of any species is nonsense (Mayr, 1976b). According to present-day taxonomic practice, type specimens need not be typical. Instead, they are one node in the genealogical nexus. The type specimen merely facilitates attaching the right name to the right chunk of the genealogical nexus (Ghiselin, 1974a; Hull, 1976; 1978b).

One increasingly popular way to view scientific development is from an evolutionary perspective (Burian, 1977; Hooker, 1975; Laudan, 1977; McMullin, 1976; Popper, 1972; Toulmin, 1972). If evolving species are not counterintuitive enough, evolving concepts, theories, and research programs are even more mystifying. The urge to find something changeless in the midst of scientific change is all but irresistible. Dawkins makes his claim about what is present in the head of every individual who understands evolutionary theory, not on the basis of any empirical research, but because of a philosophical conviction concerning the necessary prerequisites of human understanding. If everything can change, including the very meanings of the words we are using, then rational discussion seems impossible.

Thomas Kuhn (1970, 176) is popularly interpreted as distinguishing between scientific communities and paradigms. "A paradigm is what the members of a scientific community share, *and*, conversely, a scientific community consists of men who share a paradigm." As important as this distinction is, neither communities nor paradigms form discrete natural units. At best, they form temporary clusters. At any one time, the boundaries of research groups seem to be surprisingly sharp, but not all members are equally important, nor does their relative status remain unchanged. New members join the group, old members drop out until eventually the makeup of the group is completely changed. For example, J. S. Henslow was one of the earliest Darwinians. He died soon after Huxley joined. Obviously, none of the earliest Darwinians has survived to the present, yet many biologists still consider themselves "Darwinians."

Similar observations apply to units of conceptual evolution. Not all the elements that comprise a scientific paradigm are equally important. Certain ideas that start off as central become demoted as the paradigm develops. Conceptual evolution can be just as drastic as, and frequently more rapid than, the evolution of research communities. Contrary to the intuitive response of famous scientists from Darwin to Max Planck, new scientific truths do not triumph simply by means of their opponents eventually dying off and being replaced by a new generation raised in the new orthodoxy (Hull et al., 1978). For example, within five years after the rediscovery of the principles of Mendelian genetics, all but one of these principles had been abandoned or modified extensively. The exception, the law of segregation, has been modified since. Yet Mendelian genetics remains "Mendelian genetics" in the face of all this change.

Similar observations hold for every other scientific paradigm I have ever studied. To make matters worse, contrary to Kuhn, the boundaries of scientific communities and paradigms do not always coincide perfectly. A scientist can be sociologically part of a research group even though he does not share its paradigm, and many scientists who share the same paradigm are not part of the same scientific community. In the case of the Darwinians and Darwinism, Henslow is an example of the first sort, St. George Jackson Mivart is an example of the second.

In the midst of all this diversity and change, how can we possibly talk about particular scientific communities and paradigms? The technique which taxonomists have developed for dealing with evolving species turns out to be just as effective in dealing with social and conceptual change. A type specimen need not be "typical" to perform its role. It is merely one node in the genealogical nexus and designates its species accordingly. In his original exposition, Kuhn used the term "paradigm" in a multiply ambiguous fashion. He (1970, 175) has since distinguished between two senses of the term:

> On the one hand, it stands for the entire constellation of beliefs, values, techniques, and so on shared by the members of a given community. On the other hand, it denotes one sort of element in that constellation, the concrete puzzle-solutions which, employed as models or examples, can replace explicit rules as a basis for the solution of the remaining puzzles of normal science.

Kuhn recognizes the need for type specimens, or exemplars as he terms them, in conceptual evolution. However, he does not acknowledge the need for type specimens to individuate scientific communities, and he takes for granted that conceptual exemplars must be in some sense "typical" (Kuhn, 1977, 308-318).

Both conceptual and social evolution are extremely variable and at times amorphous. The habit of picking a particular work as an exemplar for a conceptual system and a particular scientist as the focus for a scientific community facilitates the individuation of both sorts of evolutionary units. What I wish to emphasize is that neither needs to be typical in order to perform its assigned function.

Wilson can serve as the focus for the sociobiologists and his book as the exemplar for sociobiology without either being especially exemplary. Usually the scientist who emerges as the leader of a research group does so because of his ability and contributions, but he need not. Darwin, for instance, was justly the focus for the Darwinians, but T. H. Morgan was just as effective as a focus for the Morganians even though he seems to have been mistaken on every particular of his research program and had to be persuaded slowly and painfully by his students (Bowler, 1977).

Similarly, conceptual type specimens usually are extremely important works, possessing all the virtues of major contributions, but they need not. Once again, Darwin's *Origin of Species* (1859) is justly treated as the exemplar for Darwinism, while Erwin Schroedinger's *What is Life?* (1947) was just as efficacious in catalyzing the molecular biology research program even though in retrospect its content is minimal (Olby, 1971).

As attractive as the use of exemplars in designating both scientific communities and their conceptual correlates may appear, it also brings with it accompanying dangers. Both scientific communities and paradigms encompass considerable internal diversity. Sociobiologists agree that there is an essence to sociobiology, but when they get down to details, no two can agree what this essence is. Each is busily trying to get his version of sociobiology accepted as standard, while not openly breaking with his fellow sociobiologists. Because Wilson has emerged as the type specimen, he has some edge, but it does not follow that his views will necessarily prevail. For example, as central to the Darwinian revolution as Darwin was, his ideas were not the ones that swept across the Western world like the flood. Certainly scientists came to accept the evolution of species, but *not* the sort of gradual, undirected evolution favored by Darwin. Instead, the evolution that was widely accepted at the time was directed, saltative, and progressive. Darwin did not triumph in this respect until this century.

Both scientific communities and their conceptual correlates change through time, sometimes changing so extensively that later stages have little in common with earlier stages. That research communities can undergo total change while remaining the "same" community occasions no surprise. We are used to conceptualizing social groups in this way. But comparable observations about conceptual evolution are likely to produce dismay. The possibility that Darwinism in Darwin's day, at the turn of the century, soon after World War II, and today might have no claims in common seems extremely counterintuitive. But if one attempts to view scientific development from an evolutionary perspective, this conclusion follows necessarily.

Regardless of which version of sociobiology becomes standard, later sociobiologists, if there are any, may hold radically different views from those they hold today. In fact, future sociobiologists may end up holding views indistinguishable from present-day critics of sociobiology. Conversely, the sociobiologists may lose. In a generation or so, people may see sociobiology as being as mistaken and pseudoscientific as nineteenth-century phrenology. That will not preclude all scientists of the day accepting ideas indistinguishable from those currently being enunciated by the sociobiologists.

The insistence of political groups and religious cults that their beliefs are really descended from some great figure, such as Marx, Jesus, or Alexander Hamilton, strikes the unconverted as irrelevant, if not downright irrational. What difference does it make whether Marx in *Das Kapital* anticipated all possible future socio-economic development? Why should it matter today that the authors of the Bible viewed homosexuality as an abomination? Who in his right mind should care what the original version of the Constitution of the United States of America actually said?

But scientists spend just as much time arguing over the views of scientists long dead. Everyone, it seems, needs patron saints. Opponents of present-day Darwinism not only argue against the views of contemporary Darwinians, but also feel obligated to denigrate Darwin's contributions. Diverse Darwinians in their turn are adamant that their ideas are really those intended by Darwin all along. For example, a half dozen or so papers published recently have attempted to show that Darwin had anticipated cladism, a newly emerging view of the proper methods of biological classification. Just as many argue that he had not. He really held the current majority position (Ghiselin and Jaffe, 1973; Nelson, 1971, 1974).

Historians of science hold only scorn for the "histories" written by practicing scientists in which they argue that all truth converges on them. But there is a legitimate point to such undertakings. In their discussions of earlier scientists, contemporary scientists are not attempting to describe history as it actually occured, but to define their own research program, showing it to be a natural outgrowth of previous work.

Defining a research program is in part a creative process. Scientists are not only engaged in adding to the cutting edge of science, but also in reinterpreting past science in the light of later achievements. If the recognition of biological taxa is in part a retrospective exercise, no one should be surprised that comparable observations apply to the units of social and conceptual evolution. In evolution, continuity, integration, and causal influence are what matter, not atemporal, acausal, abstract similarity (Hull, 1975, 1976, 1978b, 1979).

Both the opponents of sociobiology and those sociobiologists outside the Wilson camp have objected to the term "sociobiology." It means too many different things to too many different people, but such elasticity of meaning is one of the most important properties of terms like "sociobiology." In advance, there is no way of knowing what sociobiology is going to turn out to be, anymore than one could know at the turn of the century what people's republics were going to be.

The meaning of "sociobiology" will certainly expand and contract as the occasion demands, the way that terms like "gene," "atom" and "species" have. Requiring that key terms in newly emerging research programs be given fixed meanings at the outset would frustrate the growth of knowledge. Socrates called for us to define our terms! Most people have the good sense to know when to ignore him. What then *is* sociobiology? Although this question is legitimate, one of the purposes of this paper has been to show why an adequate answer to it cannot be given in terms of a fixed set of characteristics.

CONCLUSION

In this paper, I have tried to set out some of the reasons why scientific development does not always appear to be totally a matter of reason, argument, and evidence. Part of the problem is that we concentrate on the substantive content of science to the exclusion of all else, and when we do turn our attention to the sociological side of science, we tend to view it hypocritically.

Of course, the substantive content of science is of fundamental importance to scientists and non-scientists alike. Scientists themselves are so fixated on it that they can hardly be brought to think of anything else. And if scientists did not make substantive advances, the rest of us would lose the slight interest we have in their efforts and would certainly be less anxious to support them financially.

I can understand why certain professions insist on keeping a wall of hypocrisy between themselves and the outside world, but if any group can afford to be honest, research scientists can. Perhaps they investigate things the general public might find silly, perhaps they use the funds obtained to work on one project to investigate something else, but research scientists really do spend most of their time, money, and energy doing what they claim to be doing—research (Shapley, 1977, 804).

Scientists do not have a corner on the use of reason, argument, and evidence in making decisions. Nor are these the only factors that matter in the course of scientific development. But they play as great a role in science as in any other endeavor, usually greater. Once the sociological development of science and its use of particular scientists as reference points in individuating scientific communities is distinguished clearly from conceptual development and the use of certain exemplars as reference points for the individuation of paradigms, the "irrational" aspects of science that recent commentators have emphasized appear more, rather than less, rational (Ghiselin, 1971).

In this paper, I have also been concerned to emphasize those features of the controversy over sociobiology that are common to such disputes. It would not be fair to conclude without mentioning two features that are relatively uncommon. In most cases, scientists are able to carry on their disputes in obscure scientific journals rather than in the glare of popular

298 / David L. Hull

attention. Sociobiology has had the misfortune to capture the popular imagination the way the phrenology, Darwinism, Freudianism, behaviorism, and a few other research programs before it have. Scientists are not used to conducting their business under the public eye and are not very good at it. And, as far as I know, the leaders of these other research programs did not suffer physical abuse at the hands of their opponents the way that Wilson has at the hands of some of his more extreme opponents (Walsh, 1978). To quote a short piece sent to me by Mary Jane West-Eberhard:

> Watching scientists come under the Public Eye, watching the effect of a wave of publicity as it sweeps across a quiet field of science, watching the heads bob in its wake, some gasping, sputtering and bewildered in their dumb fixity on science, others struggling up into the public light, grabbing at the chances for attention and power (were they always so desperate for it?) . . . , watching this glorious dunking, so chilling to some and exhilirating to others, one sees the careful clothing washed away and then the painful comic spectacle of the unwittingly naked, blinking, smiling, bowing to the crowds, forgetting in the glory of the spotlight that it has caught them with their pants down.

References

Agassiz, L. "Prof. Agassiz on the Origin of Species." *American Journal of Science and Arts* 30 (1860): 142-154; also in *Annals and Magazine of Natural History* 6 (1860): 219-232.

Alexander, R. D. "Aggressiveness, Territoriality, and Sexual Behavior in Field Crickets (Orthoptera: Gryllidae)." *Behaviour* 17 (1961): 130-223.

_____ . "The Search for an Evolutionary Philosophy of Man." *Proceedings of the Royal Society of Victoria* 84 (1971): 99-120.

_____ ."The Evolution of Social Behaviour." *Annual Review of Ecology and Systematics* 5 (1974): 325-383.

_____ . "The Search for a General Theory of Behavior." *Behavioral Science* 20 (1975): 77-100.

_____ . "Evolution, Human Behavior, and Determinism." In *PSA 1976*, F. Suppe and P.D. Asquith (eds.), (1977): 3-21.

Allen, E. et al. "Sociobiology — Another Biological Determinism." *BioScience* 26 (1976): 182-186.

Allison, P. D., and J. A. Stewart. "Productivity Differences among Scientists: Evidence for Accumulative Advantage." *American Sociological Review* 39 (1974): 596-606.

Arnold, A. J., and K. Fristrup. "The Theory of Evolution by Natural Selection: A Hierarchical Expansion." *Paleobiology* 8 (1982): 113-129.

Atran, S. "The Nature of Folk-Botanical Life Forms." *American Anthropologist* 87 (1985): 298-315.

Ayala, F. J. *Molecular Evolution*. Sunderland: Sinauer, 1976.

_____ . "The Mechanisms of Evolution." *Scientific American* 239 (1978): 56-68.

Bader, T. S. "Similarity and Recency of Common Ancestry." *Systematic Zoology* 7 (1958): 184-187.

Barash, D. *Sociobiology and Behavior*. New York: Elsevier, 1977.

Bartholomew, M. "Huxley's Defense of Darwin." *Annals of Science* 32 (1975): 525-536.

Basalla, G., W. Coleman, and R. H. Kargon (eds.). *Victorian Science*. New York: Doubleday, 1970.

Beatty, J. "Classes and Cladists." *Systematic Zoology* 31 (1982a): 25-34.

————. "What's in a Word?" In *Nature Animated*, ed. M. Ruse. Dordrecht, Holland: D. Reidel, 1982a.

Beckner, M. *The Biological Way of Thought*. New York: Columbia University Press, 1959.

Berlin, B., D. E. Breedlove, and P. H. Raven. "General Principles of Classification and Nomenclature in Folk Biology." *American Anthropologist* 75 (1973): 214-242.

Bigelow, R. S. "Classification and Phylogen." *Systematic Zoology* 7 (1958): 49-59.

Blackwelder, R. E. "The Present Status of Systematic Zoology." *Systematic Zoology* 8 (1959): 69-75.

————, and A. Boyden. "The Nature of Systematics." *Systematic Zoology* 1 (1952): 26-33.

Bock, W. "Philosophical Foundations of Classical Evolutionary Classification." *Systematic Zoology* 22 (1973): 375-392.

Bonner, J. T. *The Cellular Slime Molds*. Princeton: Princeton University Press, 1967.

Boucot, A. J. "Cladistics: Is It Really Different from Classical Taxonomy?" In *Phylogenetic Analysis and Paleontology.*, ed. J. Cracraft and N. Eldredge. New York: Columbia University Press, 1979, 199-210.

Bowler, P. J. "Hugo DeVries and Thomas Hunt Morgan: The Mutation Theory and the Spirit of Darwinism." *Annals of Science* 35 (1977): 55-73.

Bresler, J. B. "Teaching Effectiveness and Government Awards." *Science* 160 (1968): 164-167.

Brown, C. H. "Mode of Subsistence and Folk Biological Taxonomy." *Current Anthropology* 26 (1985): 43-64.

Brundin, L. "Transantarctic Relationships and Their Significance, as Evidenced by Chironomid Midges." *Kunglica Svenska Vetenskapsakademiens Handlingar* 11 (1966):1-472.

Buckley, W. Introduction. *Behavioral Science* 24 (1979): 1-4.

Burian, R. M. "More than a Marriage of Convenience: On the Inextricability of History and Philosophy of Science." *Philosophy of Science* 44 (1977): 1-42.

Burkhardt, F. "England and Scotland: The Learned Societies." In *The Comparative Reception of Darwinism*, ed. T. Glick. Austin: University of Texas Press, 1974. 2nd ed., Chicago: University of Chicago Press, 1988.

Cain, A. J. *Animal Species and Their Evolution*. London: Hutchinson, 1954.

Campbell, D. T. "On the Genetics of Altruism and the Counter-Hedonic Components in Human Culture." *Journal of Social Issues* 28 (1972): 21-37.

————— . "Evolutionary Epistemology." In *The Philosophy of Karl R. Popper*, ed. P.A. Schilpp. LaSalle, IL: The Open Court Publishing Company, 1974.

Cannon, W. F. "The Whewel-Darwin Controversy." *Journal of the Geological Society of London* 132 (1976): 377-384.

Cantor, G. N. "The Edinburgh Phrenology Debate: 1803-1828." *Annals of Science* 32 (1975): 195-218.

Caplan, A. "Ethics, Evolution, and the Milk of Human Kindness." *Hastings Center Report* 6 (1976): 20-25.

————— . "Have Species Become Declassé?" *PSA 1980*, ed P. D. Asquit and R. N. Giere. Ann Arbor: Philosophy of Science Association, 1980, 71-82.

————— . "Back to Class: A Note on the Ontology of Species." *Philosophy of Science* 48 (1981): 130-140.

Carlson, E. O. "The *Drosophila* Group: The Transition from the Mendelian Unit to the Individual Gene." *Journal of the History of Biology* 7 (1974): 31-48.

Chambers, R. *Vestiges of the Natural History of Creation*. London: John Churchill, 1844.

————— . *Vestiges of the Natural History of Creation*, 10th ed. London: John Churchill, 1853.

Chomsky, N. *Reflections on Language*. New York: Random House, 1975.

Cock, A. G. "William Bateson's Rejection and Eventual Acceptance of Chromosome Theory." *Annals of Science* 40 (1983): 19-60.

Cody, M. L. "Optimization in Ecology." *Science* 183 (1974): 1156-1184.

Cohen, I. B. *The Newtonian Revolution* Cambridge: Cambridge University Press, 1981.

Cole, J. R., and S. Cole. "The Ortega Hypothesis." *Science* 178 (1972): 368-375.

————— , and S. Cole. *Social Stratification in Science*. Chicago: University of Chicago Press, 1973.

————— , and H. Zuckerman. "The Emergence of a Scientific Specialty: The Self-Exemplifying Case of the Sociology of Science." In *The Idea of Social Science*, ed. L.A. Coser. New York: Harcourt Brace Jovanovich, 1975, 139-174.

Cole, S. "The Growth of Scientific Knowledge." In *The Idea of Social Science*, ed. L.A. Coser. New York: Harcourt Brace Jovanovich, 1975.

Cook, R. "Reproduction by Duplication." *Natural History* 89 (3) (1980): 88-93.

Cooter, R. J. "Phrenology: The Provocation of Progress." *History of Science* 14 (1976): 211-234.

Cowan, R. S. "Nature and Nurture: The Interplay of Biology and Politics." *Studies in History of Biology* 1 (1977): 133-208.

Cracraft, J. "Science, Philosophy, and Systematics." *Systematic Zoology* 27 (1978): 213-215.

Dana, J. D. "Thoughts on Species." *Annals and Magazine of Natural History* 20 (1857): 485-497.

Darlington, P. J. "A Practical Criticism of Hennig-Brundin 'Phylogenetic Systematics' and Antarctic Biogeography." *Systematic Zoology* 19 (1970): 1-18.

Darwin, C. *"On the Origin of Species:"* A Facsimile of the First Edition (1966). Cambridge, MA: Harvard University Press, 1859.

————— . *The Descent of Man and Selection in Relation to Sex*. London: Murray, 1871.

Darwin, F. (ed.). *The Life and Letters of Charles Darwin*. New York: D. Appleton, 1899.

————— . (ed.). *More Letters of Charles Darwin* (1972). New York: Johnson Reprint Corporation, 1903.

Dawkins, R. *The Selfish Gene*. New York: Oxford University Press, 1976.

————— . "Replicator Selection and the Extended Phenotype." *Zeitschrift für Tierpsycholgie* 47 (1978): 61-76.

————— , and J. R. Krebs. "Arms Races Between and Within Species." *Proceedings of the Royal Society of London*, Series B 205 (1979): 489-511.

De Voe, R. D. "Review of 'Comparative Physiology and Evolution of Vision in Invertebrates,' " ed. I. H. Autrum. *Science* 214 (1981): 433.

De Vore, I., R. L. Trivers, and G.W. Goethak. *Exploring Human Nature*. Cambridge: Educational Development Corporation, 1973.

Di Gregorio, M. "Order or Process of Nature: Huxley's and Darwin's Different Approaches to Natural Science." *History and Philosophy of the Life Sciences* 2 (1981): 217-241.

Dobzhansky, T. *Genetics and the Origin of Species*. New York: Columbia University Press, 1937.

————— . *Genetics of the Evolutionary Process.* New York: Columbia University Press, 1970.

Dunbar, M. J. "The Evolution of Stability in Marine Environments: Natural Selection at the Level of the Ecosystem." *American Naturalist* 94 (1960): 129-135.

Dupré, J. "Sex, Gender, and Essence." *Midwest Studies in Philosophy* 11 (1986): 441-457.

Ehrlich, P. "Has the Biological Species Concept Outlived Its Usefulness?" *Systematic Zoology* 10 (1961): 167-176.

————— ., and A. H. Ehrlich. "The Phenetic Relationships of the Butterflies." *Systematic Zoology* 16 (1967): 301-327.

————— ., and P. H. Raven. "Differentiation of Populations." *Science* 165 (1969): 1228-1231.

Eiseley, L. *Darwin and the Mysterious Mr. X.* New York: Harcourt Brace Jovanovich, 1979.

Eisenberg, L. "The *Human* Nature of Human Nature." *Science* 176 (1972): 123-128.

Eldredge, N. *Unfinished Synthesis.* New York: Oxford University Press, 1985.

————— ., and J. Cracraft. *Phylogenetic Patterns and the Evolutionary Process: Method and Theory in Comparative Biology.* New York: Columbia University Press, 1980.

————— ., and S. J. Gould. "Punctuated Equilibria: An Alternative to Phyletic Gradualism." In *Models in Paleobiology*, ed. T.J.M. Schopf. San Francisco: Freeman, Copper and Company, 1972.

Ellegard, A. "The Darwinian Theory and Nineteenth Century Philosophies of Science." *Journal of the History of Ideas* 18 (1957): 362-393.

————— . *Darwin and the General Reader.* Göteborg: Göteborgs Universitets Arsskrift, 1958.

Emerson, A. E. "Social Insects." *Encyclopedia Britannica* 20 (1959): 871-878.

Emlin, S. T., and L. W. Orig. "Ecology, Sexual Selection, and the Evolution of Mating Systems." *Science* 197 (1977): 215-223.

Feyerabend, P. *Against Method: Outline of an Anarchist Theory of Knowledge.* London: New Left Books, 1975.

Fodor, J. "Observation Reconsidered." *Philosophy of Science* 51 (1984): 207-215.

Forbes, E. "On the Manifestation of Polarity in the Distribution of Organized Beings in Time." *Royal Institution of Great Britain Proceedings* 1 (1854): 428-433.

Franklin, I., and R. C. Lewontin. "Is the Gene the Unit of Selection?" *Genetics* 65 (1972): 707-734.

Friedlander, M. W. *The Conduct of Science*. Englewood Cliffs: Prentice-Hall, 1972.

Ghiselin, M. "On Psychologism in the Logic of Taxonomic Principles." *Systematic Zoology* 15 (1966): 207-215.

――――― . *The Triumph of the Darwinian Revolution*. Berkeley: University of California Press, 1969.

――――― . "The Individual in the Darwinian Revolution." *New Literary History* 3 (1971): 113-134.

――――― . "A Radical Solution to the Species Problem." *Systematic Zoology* 23 (1974a): 536-544.

――――― . *The Economy of Nature and the Evolution of Sex*. Berkeley: University of California Press, 1974b.

――――― . "Categories, Life, and Thinking." *Behavioral and Brain Science* 4 (1981): 269-313.

――――― . "Species Concepts, Individuality, and Objectivity." *Biology and Philosophy* 2 (1987): 127-145.

――――― ., and L. Jaffe. "Phylogenetic Classification in Darwin's 'Monograph on the Sub-Class Cirripedia.'" *Systematic Zoology* 22 (1973): 132-140.

Glick, T. J. *The Comparative Reception of Darwinism*. Austin: University of Texas Press, 1974. 2nd ed., Chicago: University of Chicago Press, 1988.

Goldschmidt, R. *The Material Basis of Evolution* New Haven: Yale University Press, 1940.

Gorovitz, S., and A. MacIntyre. "Toward a Theory of Medical Fallibility." *Journal of Medical Philosophy* 1 (1976): 51-71.

Goudsmit, S. A. "Citation Analysis." *Science* 183 (1974): 28.

Gould, S .J. "Biological Potential vs. Biological Determinism." *Natural History* 85 (1976a): 12-22.

――――― . "Darwin's Untimely Burial." *Natural History* 85 (4) (1976b): 24-30.

――――― . *Ever Since Darwin*. New York: Norton, 1977a.

――――― . "Eternal Metaphors of Paleontology." In *Patterns of Evolution as Illustrated by the Fossil Record*, ed. A. Hallam. New York: Elsevier, 1977b, 1-26.

――――― . "Darwinism and the Expansion of Evolutionary Theory." *Science* 216 (1982): 380-387.

————— . "Evolution and the Triumph of Homology, or Why History Matters." *American Scientist* 74 (1986): 60-69.

————— ., and N. Eldredge. "Punctuated Equilibria: The Tempo and Mode of Evolution Reconsidered." *Paleobiology* 3 (1977): 115-151.

Greenberg, D. S. *The Politics of Pure Science*. New York: New American Library, 1967.

Gregg, J. R. "Taxonomy, Language, and Reality." *American Naturalist* 84 (1950): 421-433.

————— . *The Language of Taxonomy*. New York: Columbia University Press, 1954.

Griffin, B. C., and N. Mullins. "Coherent Social Groups in Scientific Change." *Science* 177 (1972): 959-964.

Grube, G. M. A. *Plato's Thought*. Boston: Beacon Press, 1958.

Gruber, H. E. and P. H. Barrett. *Darwin on Man*. New York: Dutton, 1974.

Hagstrom, W. O. "Competition in Science." *American Sociological Review* 39 (1974): 1-18.

Haldane, J. B. S. "A Defense of Bean Bag Genetics." *Perspectives in Biology and Medicine* 7 (1964): 343-359.

Hall, T. "On Biological Analogs of Newtonian Paradigms." *Philosophy of Science*. 35 (1968): 6-27.

Haller, J. S. *Outcasts from Evolution*. Urbana: University of Illinois Press, 1971.

Hamilton, W. D. "The Genetical Theory of Social Behavior." *Journal of Theoretical Biology* 7 (1964): 1-51.

————— . "Review of Ghiselin (1974b) and Williams (1975)." *Quarterly Review of Biology* 50 (1975): 175-179.

Haughton, S. "Bioyèveois." *Natural History Review* 7 (1860): 23-32.

Hennig, W. *Grundzüge einer Theorie der Phylogenetischen Systematik*. Berlin: Deutscher Zentralverlag, 1950.

————— . *Phylogenetic Systematics*. Chicago: University of Illinois Press, 1966.

Herschel, J. *Preliminary Discourse on the Study of Natural Philosophy*. Chicago: University of Chicago Press, 1830.

Himmelfarb, G. *Darwin and the Darwinian Revolution*. Garden City, NY: Doubleday, 1959.

Hodge, M. J. S. *Darwin and Natural Selection: His Methods and His Methodology*. Dordrecht, Holland: D. Reidel, 1983.

Hoffman, A. "Community Paleoecology as an Epiphenomenoal Science." *Paleobiology* 5 (1979): 357-379.

Holton, G. *Scientific Imagination: Case Studies.* New York: Cambridge University Press, 1978.

Hooker, C. A. "Philosophy and Meta-Philosophy of Science: Empiricism, Popperianism, and Realism." *Synthese* 32 (1975): 177-231.

Hopkins, W. "Physical Theories and the Phenomena of Life." *Fraser's Magazine* 61 (1860): 739-752; 62 (1860): 74-90.

Hull, D. L. "Consistency and Monophyly." *Systematic Zoology* 13 (1964): 1-11.

———. "Certainty and Circularity in Evolutionary Taxonomy." *Evolution* 21 (1967): 174-189.

———. "The Operational Imperative: Sense and Nonsense in Operationism." *Systematic Zoology* 17 (1968): 438-457.

———. "Contemporary Systematic Philosophies." *Annual Review of Ecology and Systematics* 1 (1970): 19-54.

———. "Charles Darwin and Nineteenth Century Philosophies of Science." In *Foundations of Scientific Method: The Nineteenth Century*, ed. R. N. Giere and R. S. Westfall. Bloomington: Indiana University Press, 1972, 115-132.

———. *Darwin and His Critics: The Reception of Darwin's Theory of Evolution by the Scientific Community.* Chicago: University of Chicago Press, 1973.

———. *Philosophy of Biological Science.* Englewood Cliffs: Prentice-Hall, Inc., 1974.

———. "Central Subjects and Historical Narratives." *History and Theory* 14 (1975): 253-274.

———. "Are Species Really Individuals?" *Systematic Zoology* 25 (1976): 174-191.

———. "Altruism in Science: A Sociobiological Model of Cooperative Behavior among Scientists." *Animal Behaviour* 26 (1978a): 685-697.

———. "A Matter of Individuality." *Philosophy of Science* 45 (1978b): 335-360.

———. "In Defence of Presentism." *History and Theory* 18 (1979a): 1-15.

———. "The Limits of Cladism." *Systematic Zoology* 28 (1979b): 416-440.

———. "The Units of Evolution." In *Studies in The Philosophy of Evolution*, ed. U. J. Jensen and R. Harre. London: The Harvester Press, 1980a, 23-44.

———. "Individuality and Selection." *Annual Review of Ecology and Systematics* 11 (1980b): 311-332.

_____ . "Cladism Gets Sorted Out." *Paleobiology* 6 (1980c): 131-136.

_____ . "Sociobiology: Another New Synthesis." In *Sociobiology: (1980) Beyond Nature/Nurture*, ed. G. W. Barlow and J. Silverberg. Boulder: Westview Press, 1980d, 77-96.

_____ . "Kitts and Kitts and Caplan on Species." *Philosophy of Science* 48 (1981): 141-152.

_____ . "The Naked Meme." In *Learning, Development, and Culture*. ed. H. C. Plokin. New York: John Wiley, 1982, 273-327.

_____ . "Hypotheses that Blur and Grow." In T. Duncan and T. Stuessy (eds.), *Cladistics: Perspectives on the Reconstruction of Evolutionary History*. New York: Columbia University Press, 1984, 5-23.

_____ . "Darwinism as an Historical Entity." In *The Darwinian Heritage*, ed. D. Kohn. Princeton: Princeton University Press, 1985, 773-812.

_____ . *Science as a Process: An Evolutionary Account of the Social and Conceptual Development of Science*. Chicago: University of Chicago Press, 1988.

_____ ., P. Tessner and A. Diamond. "Planck's Principle." *Science* 202 (1978): 717-723.

Huxley, J. S. (ed.) *The New Systematics*. Oxford: Oxford University Press, 1940.

_____ . *Evolution: The Modern Synthesis*. London: Allen and Unwin, 1942.

Huxley, L. *Life and Letters of Sir Joseph Dalton Hooker*. London: Murray, 1918.

Huxley, T. H. "On the Morphology of the Cephalous Mollusca." *Philosophical Transactions of the Royal Society* 143 (1853): 29-66.

_____ . "Review of 'Vestiges of the Natural History of Creation' " (1853). *British and Foreign Medico-Chirurgical Review* 19 (1854): 425-439.

_____ . "Paleontology and the Doctrine of Evolution." In *Collected Essays* (1893), vol. 8, pp. 340-388. London: Murray, 1870.

_____ . "Mr. Darwin's Critics." *Contemporary Review* 18 (1871): 443-476.

_____ . "On the Classification of the Animal Kingdom." *Nature* 11 (1874): 101-102.

Huxley, T. H. *Collected Essays*. London: Macmillan, 1893.

Jardine, N. "The Observational and Theoretical Components of Homology." *Biological Journal of the Linneaen Society* 1 (1969): 327-361.

Jenkin, F. "The Origin of Species." *North British Review* 46 (1867): 149-171.

Kaplan, D., and R. A. Manners. *Culture Theory*. Englewood Cliffs: Prentice-Hall, 1972.

King, J. L., and T. H. Jukes. "Non-Darwinian Evolution." *Science* 164 (1969): 788-798.

Kitcher, P. "Theories, Theorists, and Theoretical Change." *Philosophical Review* 87 (1978): 519-547.

————. *Abusing Science: The Case Against Creationism.* Cambridge: MIT Press, 1982a.

————. "Genes." *British Journal for the Philosophy of Science* 33 (1982b): 337-359.

————. "Species." *Philosophy of Science* 51 (1984a): 308-333.

————. "Against the Monism of the Moment: A Reply to Elliot Sober." *Philosophy of Science* 51 (1984b): 616-630.

————. "Bewitchment of the Biologist." *Nature* 320 (1986): 649-650.

Kitts, D. B. "Karl Popper, Verifiability, and Systematic Zoology." *Systematic Zoology* 26 (1977): 185-194.

————. "Theoretics and Systematics: A Reply to Cracraft, Nelson, and Patterson." *Systematic Zoology* 27 (1978): 222-224.

————. "Theories and Other Scientific Statements: A Reply to Settle." *Systematic Zoology* 29 (1980): 190-192.

————. "Can Baptism Alone Save a Species?" *Systematic Zoology* 32 (1983): 27-33.

————., and D. J. Kitts. "Biological Species as Natural Kinds." *Philosophy of Science* 46 (1979): 613-622.

Koertge, N. "Explaining Scientific Discovery." *PSA 1982*, ed. P. D. Asquith and T. Nickles. Ann Arbor: Philosophy of Science Association, 1982, 14-28.

Kripke, S. A. "Naming and Necessity," In *Semantics and Natural Language*, ed. D. Davidson and G. Harman. Dordrecht, Holland: D. Reidel, 1972.

Kuhn, T. *The Structure of Scientific Revolutions*, 2nd ed. Chicago: University of Chicago Press, 1970.

————. *The Essential Tension.* Chicago: The University of Chicago Press, 1977.

Lakatos, I. "Falsification and the Methodology of Scientific Research Programmes." In *Criticism and the Growth of Knowledge*, ed. I. Lakatos and A. Musgrave. Cambridge: Cambridge University Press, 1970, 91-196.

Lamarck, J. B. *Zoological Philosophy* (1984). Chicago: University of Chicago Press, 1809.

Laudan, L. *Progress and Its Problems: Toward a Theory of Scientific Growth.* Berkeley: University of California Press, 1977.

———— . *Science and Hypothesis*. Dordrecht, Holland: D. Reidel, 1981.

Levins, R. "Extinction." In *Some Mathematical Questions in Biology*, ed. M. Gerstennhaber. Providence: American Mathematical Society, 1970.

Lewes, G. H. "Goethe as a Man of Science." *Westminster Review* 58 (1852): 258-272.

Lewontin, R. C. "The Units of Selection." *Annual Review of Ecology and Systematics* 1 (1970): 1-18.

———— . *The Genetical Basis of Evolutionary Theory*. New York: Columbia University Press, 1974.

———— . "Adaptation." *Scientific American* 239 (1978): 212-230.

Lurie, E. *Louis Agassiz: A Life In Science*. Chicago: University of Chicago Press, 1960.

Lyell, C. *Principles of Geology*. London: Murray, 1830-1833.

———— . *Principles of Geology*, 11th ed. London: Murray, 1889.

Lyell, K., *Life, Letters, and Journals of Sir Charles Lyell, Bart.* London: Murray, 1881.

Macalister, A. "Phrenology." *Encyclopedia Britannica* 18 (1888): 842-849.

Mahoney, M. J. "Psychology of the Scientist: An Evaluative Review." *Social Studies of Science* 9 (1979): 348-375.

Manier, E. *The Young Darwin and His Cultural Circle*. Dordrecht, Holland: D. Reidel, 1978.

Marchant, J. ed. *Alfred Russel Wallace: Letters and Reminiscences*. New York: Harper, 1916.

Marcus, R. B. "Classes, Collections, and Individuals." *American Philosophical Quarterly* 11 (1974): 227-232.

Matthew, P. *On Naval Timbre and Arboriculture*. London: Longman, 1831.

May, R. M. "The Evolution of Ecological Systems." *Scientific American* 239 (1978): 161-175.

Maynard Smith, J. "Evolution in Sexual and Asexual Populations." *American Naturalist* 102 (1968): 469-473.

———— . "The Origin and Maintenance of Sex." In *Group Selection*, ed. G.C. Williams. New York: Aldine-Atherton, 1971, 163-175.

———— . *The Evolution of Sex*. New York: Cambridge University Press, 1978.

Mayr, E. *Systematics and the Origin of Species*. New York, Columbia University Press, 1942.

―――― . "Where Are We?" *Cold Springs Harbor Symposium on Quantitative Biology* 24 (1959): 1-14.

―――― . *Animal Species and Evolution*. Cambridge, MA: Harvard University Press, 1963.

―――― . "Evolutionary Challenges to the Mathematical Interpretation of Evolution." In *Mathematical Challenges to the Neo-Darwinian Interpretation of Evolution*, ed. P. S. Moorehead and M. M. Kaplan. Philadelphia: Wiston, 1967, 47-58.

―――― . *Principles of Systematic Zoology*. New York: McGraw-Hill, 1969.

―――― . "Cladistic Analysis or Cladistic Classifications?" *Zeitschrift für Zoologische Systematik und Evolutionsforschung* 12 (1974): 94-128.

―――― . "The Unity of the Genotype." *Bologisches Zentralblatt* 94 (1975): 377-388.

―――― . "Is the Species a Class or an Individual?" *Systematic Zoology* 25 (1976a): 192.

―――― . *Evolution and the Diversity of Life*. Cambridge, MA: Harvard University Press, 1976b.

―――― . "Evolution." *Scientific American* 239 (1978): 46-55.

―――― . *The Growth of Biological Thought*. Cambridge, MA: Harvard University Press, 1982.

―――― . "The Ontological Status of Species: Scientific Progress and Philosophical Terminology." *Biology and Philosophy* 2 (1987): 145-166.

―――― ., E. G. Linsley, and R. L. Usinger. *Methods and Principles of Systematic Zoology*. New York: McGraw-Hill, 1953.

―――― ., and W. Provine, eds. *The Evolutionary Synthesis*. Cambridge, MA: Harvard University Press, 1980.

McMullin, E. "The Fertility of Theory and the Unit for Appraisal in Science." In *Essays in Memory of Imre Lakatos*, ed. R. S. Cohen et. al. Dordrecht, Holland: D. Reidel, 1976, 395-432.

Medawar, P. B. *The Hope of Progress*. London: Methuen, 1972.

Meglitsch, P. A. "On the Nature of the Species." *Systematic Zoology* 3 (1954): 49-65.

Merton, R. K. *The Sociology of Science*. Chicago: University of Chicago Press, 1973.

Michener, C. D., and R. R. Sokal. "A Quantitative Approach to a Problem in Classification." *Evolution* 11 (1957): 130-162.

Michod, R. E. "Positive Heuristics in Evolutionary Biology." *British Journal for the Philosophy of Science* 32 (1981): 1-36.

Mill, J. S. *A System of Logic*. London: Longmans, 1843.

————. *Three Essays on Religion* (1969). New York: Greenwodd Press, 1874.

Mishler, B. D., and M. J. Donoghue. "Species Concepts: A Case for Pluralism." *Systematic Zoology* 31 (1982): 491-503.

Mitroff, I. "Norms and Counter-Norms in a Select Group of Apollo Moon Scientists: A Case Study of the Ambivalence of Scientists." *American Sociological Review* 39 (1974): 579-595.

Nelson, G. " 'Cladism' as a Philosophy of Classification." *Systematic Zoology* 20 (1971): 373-376.

————. "Phylogenetic Relationships and Classification." *Systematic Zoology* 21 (1972): 227-230.

————. "Classification as an Expression of Phylogenetic Relationship." *Systematic Zoology* 22 (1973): 344-359.

————. "Darwin-Hennig Classification: A Reply to Ernst Mayr." *Systematic Zoology* 23 (1974): 452-458.

————. "Classification and Prediction: A Reply to Kitts." *Systematic Zoology* 27 (1978a): 216-217.

————. "Ontogeny, Phylogeny, Paleontology, and the Biogenetic Law." *Systematic Zoology* 27 (1978b): 324-345.

————. and N. Platnick. *Systematics and Biogeography: Cladistics and Vicariance Biogeography*. New York: Columbia University Press, 1981.

Neyman, J. "R. A. Fisher 1890-1962: An Appreciation" *Science* 156 (1967): 1456-1460.

Olby, R. "Schrödinger's Problem: What is Life?" *Journal of the History of Biology* 4 (1971): 119-148.

Ospovat, D. *The Development of Darwin's Theory*. Cambridge: Cambridge University Press, 1981.

Oster, G. F., and E. O. Wilson. *Caste and Ecology in the Social Insects*. Princeton: Princeton University Press, 1978.

Owen, R. "Report on the Archetype and Homologies of the Vertebrate Skeleton." *Report of the Sixteenth Meeting of the British Association for the Advancement of Science*. London: Murray, 1846 169-340.

Owen, R. On the Archetype and Homologies of the Vertebrate Skeleton. London: Van Voorst, 1848.

———. On the Nature of Limbs. London: Van Voorst, 1849.

———. "Review of 'Principles of Geology' by Sir Charles Lyell." Quarterly Review 89 (1851): 412-451.

———. "Darwin on the Origin of Species." Edinburgh Review 111 (1860): 487-532.

———. Anatomy of the Vertebrates, vol. 3. London: Longmans, 1868.

Panati, C., and S. Monroe. "Shockley Revisited." Newsweek 12 (1976): 51-52.

Paradis, J. C. T. H. Huxley: Man's Place in Nature. London: University of Nebraska Press, 1978.

Parfit, D. "Personal Identity." The Philosophical Review 80 (1971): 3-27.

Parker-Rhodes, A. F. "Review of Gregg's 'The Language of Taxonomy.' " Philosophical Review 66 (1957): 124-125.

Parssinen, T. M. "Popular Science and Society. The Phrenology Movement in Early Victorian Britain." Journal of Social History 8 (1974): 1-20.

Patterson, C. "Verifiability in Systematics." Systematic Zoology 27 (1978): 218-221.

———. "Cladistics." The Biologist 27 (1980): 234-240.

Platnick, N. I. "Cladograms, Phylogenetic Trees, and Hypothesis Testing." Systematic Zoology 26 (1977): 438-442.

———. "Philosophy and the Transformation of Cladistics." Systematic Zoology 28 (1979): 537-546.

———., and H. D. Cameron. "Cladistic Methods in Textual, Linguistic, and Phylogenetic Analysis." Systematic Zoology 26 (1977): 380-385.

———., and E. S. Gaffney. "Systematics: A Popperian Perspective." Systematic Zoology 26 (1977): 360-365.

———., and E. S. Gaffney. "Evolutionary Biology: A Popperian Perspective." Systematic Zoology 27 (1978a): 137-141.

———., and E. S. Gaffney. "Systematics and the Popperian Paradigm." Systematic Zoology 27 (1978b): 381-388.

Popper, K. R. The Poverty of Historicism. London: Routledge and Kegan Paul, 1957.

———. The Logic of Scientific Discovery. New York: Basic Books, 1959.

———— . *Conjectures and Refutations*. New York: Basic Books, 1962.

———— . *Objective Knowledge: An Evolutionary Approach*. Oxford: Clarendon Press, 1972.

———— . "Darwinism as a Metaphysical Research Program." In *The Philosophy of Karl Popper*, vol. 1, ed. P. A. Schillp. La Salle, Ill.: Open Court Publishers, 1974, 133-143.

Price, D. *Little Science, Big Science*. New York: Columbia University Press, 1963.

Raff, R., and T. C. Kaufman. *Embryos, Genes, and Evolution*. New York: Macmillan, 1983.

Reid, C. *Hilbert*. New York: Springer-Verlag, 1970.

Ridley, M. "Coadaptation and the Inadequacy of Natural Selection." *British Journal for the History of Science*. 15 (1982): 45-68.

Roget, P. M. "Phrenology." *Encyclopedia Britannica* 17 (1842): 454-473.

Rosen, D. "Vicariant Patterns and Historical Explanation in Biogeography." *Systematic Zoology* 27 (1978): 159-188.

Rosenberg, A. "The Virtues of Vagueness in the Languages of Science." *Dialogue* 14 (1975): 281-305.

———— . *The Structure of Biological Science*. Cambridge: Cambridge University Press, 1985.

Rudwick, M. J. S. *The Meaning of Fossils*. New York: Science History Publications, 1972. Reprinted in Chicago: University of Chicago Press, 1988.

Ruse, M. "Is the Theory of Evolution Different?" *Scientia* 106 (1971): 765-783.

———— . *The Philosophy of Biology*. London: Hutchinson, 1973.

———— . "The Nature of Scientific Models: Formal vs. Material Analogy." *Philosophy of the Social Sciences*. 3 (1973): 63-80.

———— . "Darwin's Debt to Philosophy." *Studies in the Philosophy of Science* 6 (1975a): 159-181.

———— . "Charles Darwin and Artificial Selection." *Journal of the History of Ideas* 36 (1975b): 339-350.

———— . "The Scientific Methodology of William Whewell." *Centaurus* 20 (1976): 227-257.

———— . "Karl Popper's Philosophy of Biology." *Philosophy of Science* 44 (1977): 638-661.

———— . *The Darwinian Revolution*. Chicago: University of Chicago Press, 1979.

———— . "Falsifiability, Consilience, and Systematics." *Systematic Zoology* 28 (1979): 530-536.

———— . "What Philosophy of Biology Is: David Hull through Two Decades." In M. Ruse, ed. *What Philosophy of Biology Is: Essays for David Hull.* Dordrecht, Holland: D. Reidel, 1989.

———— ., and E. O. Wilson. "Moral Philosophy as Applied Science: A Darwinian Approach to the Foundations of Ethics." *Philosophy* 61 (1986): 173-192.

Sahlins, M. *The Use and Abuse of Biology.* Ann Arbor: University of Michigan Press, 1976.

———— ., and E. R. Service. *Evolution and Culture.* Ann Arbor: University of Michigan Press, 1960.

Schindewolf, O. *Der Zeitfaktor in Geologie und Paläontologie.* Stuttgart: Schweizerbart, 1950.

Schrödinger, E. *What is Life? The Physical Aspect of the Living Cell.* New York: Doubleday, 1947.

Scrope, G. P. "Combe's 'Outlines of Phrenology' (1836)." *Quarterly Review* 57 (1836): 169-182.

Sedgwick, A. "Review of 'The Vestiges of the Natural History of Creation' (1844)." *The Edinburgh Review* 82 (1845): 1-45.

———— . "Objections to Mr. Darwin's Theory of the Origin of Species." *The Spectator* (April 7, 1860) 334-335.

Settle, T. "Popper on 'When Is a Science Not a Science?" *Systematic Zoology* 28 (1979): 521-529.

Shapin, S. "Phrenological Knowledge and the Social Structure of Early 19th-Century Edinburgh." *Annals of Science* 32 (1975): 219-243.

Shapley, D. "Research Management Scandals Provoke Queries in Washington." *Science* 198 (1977): 804-806.

Simon, H. A. *The Science of the Artificial.* Cambridge, MA: MIT Press, 1969.

Simpson, G. G. "The Principles of Classification and Classification of Mammals." *Bulletin of the American Museum of Natural History* 85 (1945): i-xvi, 1-350.

———— . *The Major Features of Evolution.* New York: Columbia University Press, 1953.

———— . *Principles of Animal Taxonomy.* New York: Columbia University Press, 1961.

Skinner, B. F. *About Behaviorism.* New York: Random House, 1974.

Smart, J. J. C. *Philosophy and Scientific Realism*. London: Routledge and Kegan Paul, 1963.

————. *Between Science and Philosophy*. New York: Random House, 1968.

Sneath, P. H. A. "Review of Nelson and Platnick (1981)." *Systematic Zoology* 31 (1982): 208-217.

————., and R. R. Sokal. *Numerical Taxonomy*. San Francisco: W. H. Freeman, 1973.

Sober, E. "Sets, Species, and Evolution: Comments on Philip Kitcher's 'Species' " *Philosophy of Science* 51 (1984): 334-341.

Sokal, R. R. "Mayr on Cladism—and His Critics." *Systematic Zoology* 24 (1975): 257-262

————., and T. Crovello. "The Biological Species Concept: A Critical Evaluation." *American Naturalist* 104 (1970): 127-153.

————., and P. H. A. Sneath. *The Principles of Numerical Taxonomy*. San Francisco: W. H. Freeman, 1963.

Spencer, H. "The Development Hypothesis." *The Saturday Analyst and Leader*, (1852): 280-281; Reprinted in *Essays Scientific, Political, and Speculative*. New York: Appleton, 1891, 1:1-17.

Stanley, S. M. *Macroevolution, Pattern and Process*. San Francisco: W. H. Freeman, 1970.

Stebbins, G. L., and F. J. Ayala. "Is a New Evolutionary Synthesis Necessary?" *Science* 213 (1981): 967-971.

Stehr, G. "On Some Concepts in the Population Biology of the Spruce Budworm." *Proceedings of the Entomological Society of Ontario* 99 (1968): 54-56.

Stern, J. T. "The Meaning of 'Adaptation' and Its Relation to the Phenomenon of Natural Selection." *Evolutionary Biology* 4 (1970): 39-65.

Suppe, F. "Some Philosophical Problems in Biological Speciation and Taxonomy." In J. A. Wojciechowski, ed. *Conceptual Basis of the Classification of Knowledge*. Pullach/München: Verlag Dokumentation, 1974.

Tait, P. "Geological Time." *North British Review* 50 (1869): 215-233.

Thorson, T. L. *Biopolitics*. New York: Holt, Rinehart and Winston, Inc., 1970.

Toulmin, S. *The Philosophy of Science*. New York: Harper, 1953.

————. *Human Understanding*. Princeton: Princeton University Press, 1972.

Trivers, R. L. "The Evolution of Reciprocal Altruism." *Quarterly Review of Biology* 46 (1971): 35-57.

————— . "Parent-Offspring Conflict." *American Zoologist* 14 (1974): 249-264.

Van Valen, L. "Group Selection, Sex, and Fossils." *Evolution* 29 (1975): 87-94.

————— . "Ecological Species, Multispecies, and Oaks." *Taxon* 25 (1976): 235-239.

————— . "Arborescent Animals and Other Colonoids." *Nature* 276 (1978): 318.

Wade, M. "A Critical Review of the Models of Group Selection." *Quarterly Review of Biology* 53 (1978): 101-114.

Wade, N. "Sociobiology: Troubled Birth for a New Discipline." *Science* 191 (1974): 1151-1155.

Wagner, M. *The Darwinian Theory and the Law of the Migration of Organisms.* London: Edward Stanford, 1872.

Walsh, J. "Sociobiology Baptized as Issue in Activists." *Science* 199 (1978): 955.

Watts, C. R., and A. W. Stokes. "The Social Order of Turkeys." *Scientific American* 224 (1971): 112-118.

Wells, K. D. "Sir William Lawrence (1783-1867): A Study of Pre-Darwinian Ideas on Heredity and Variation." *Journal of the History of Biology* 4 (1971): 319-361.

Westfall, R. S. "Newton and the Fudge Factor." *Science* 179 (1973): 751-758.

Whewell, W. *History of the Inductive Sciences.* London: Parker, 1837.

————— . *The Philosophy of the Inductive Sciences, Founded upon their History.* London: Parker, 1840.

————— . *The Philosophy of the Inductive Sciences, Founded upon their History,* 2d ed. London: Parker, 1847.

————— . *Of Induction, With Special Reference to Mr. J. Stuart Mill's System of Logic.* London: Parker, 1849.

White M. J. D. *Modes of Speciation.* San Francisco: W. H. Freeman, 1978.

Wiley, E. O. "Karl R. Popper, Systematics, and Classification: A Reply to Walter Bock and Other Evolutionary Systematists." *Systematic Zoology* 24 (1975): 233-243.

————— . "The Evolutionary Species Concept Reconsidered." *Systematic Zoology* 27 (1978): 17-26.

————— . "Ancestors, Species, and Cladograms." In *Phylogenetic Analysis and Paleontology,* ed. J. Cracraft and N. Eldredge. New York: Columbia University Press, 1979.

————— . *Phylogenetics, the Theory and Practice of Phylogenetic Taxonomy.* New York: Wiley, 1981.

Williams, G. C. *Adaptaton and Natural Selection*. Princeton: Princeton University Press, 1966.

——— ., ed. *Group Selection*. Chicago: Aldine-Atherton, 1971.

——— . *Sex and Evolution*. Princeton: Princeton University Press, 1975.

Wilson, D. S. *The Natural Selection of Populations and Communities*. Menlo Park, CA: Benjamin-Cummings, 1980.

Wilson, E. O. *The Insect Societies*. Cambridge, MA: Harvard University Press, 1971.

——— . "The Perfect Societies." *Science* 184 (1974): 54.

——— . *Sociobiology: The New Synthesis*. Cambridge, MA: Harvard University Press, 1975.

——— . "Academic Vigilantism and the Political Significance of Sociobiology." *BioScience* 26 (1976): 183, 187-190.

Wilson, L. G., ed. *Sir Charles Lyell's Scientific Journals on the Species Question*. New Haven, Yale University Press, 1970.

Wimsatt, W. "Complexity and Organizaton." In *PSA 1972*, ed. K. Schaffner, and R. S. Cohen. Dordrecht, Holland: D. Reidel, 1974, 67-86.

Winsor, M. P. *Starfish, Jellyfish and the Order of Life*. New Haven: Yale University Press, 1976.

Wittgenstein, L. *Tractatus Logico-Philosophicus*. London: Routledge and Kegan Paul, 1921.

——— . *Philosophical Investigations*. Chicago: Macmillan, 1953.

Woodger, J. H. *The Axiomatic Method in Biology*. Cambridge: Cambridge University Press, 1937.

——— . *Biology and Language*. Cambridge: Cambridge University Press, 1952.

Wynne-Edwards, V. C. "Intergroup Selection in the Evolution of Social Insects." *Nature* 200 (1963): 623-626.

Yeo, R. "William Whewell, Natural Theology and the Philosophy of Science in Mid-Nineteenth Century Britain." *Annals of Science* 36 (1979): 493-516.

Young, R. M. "The Functions of the Brain, Gall to Ferrier." *Isis* 59 (1968): 251-268.

——— . "Darwin's Metaphor: Does Nature Select?" *Monist* 55 (1971): 442-503.

Zangerl, R. "The Methods of Comparative Anatomy and Its Contributions to the Study of Evolution." *Evolution* 4 (1948): 351-374.

Zuckerman, H. "Deviant Behavior and Social Control in Science." In *Deviance and Social Change*, ed. E. Sagarin. Beverly Hills: Sage, 1977.

Name Index

Wilson, L. G., 172.
Wilson, N. L., 203n.
Wimsatt, W., 101, 154.
Winsor, M. P., 73.
Wittgenstein, L., 155, 185, 202n, 229.
Wollaston, T. V., 72.
Wood, S. V., 53.
Woodger, J. H., 131.

Wynne-Edwards, V. C., 90, 91.

Yeo, R., 63.
Young, J., 53, 277.
Young, R. M., 72, 267, 272, 279, 282.

Zangerl, R., 74.
Zuckerman, H., 166, 288.

Subject Index

Ad hoc hypothesis, 267, 271.

Age, 3, 43-58.

Altruism, 90, 94, 124, 164-66, 243, 245-49, 254, 258, 272, 284, 288.

Analogy, 6, 14, 33, 247-57, 262, 266, 271-72, 279.

Ancestor-descendant relations, 2, 5, 13, 95, 100, 123, 150, 186, 223.

Archetypes, 71, 74.

Asexuality, 86, 94, 97, 99, 106-9, 122, 225.

Baconian method *See also* Methodology, 29, 31, 267.

Bauplan, 72, 223.

Biometricians, 212.

Blue-green algae, 3, 122.

British Association for the Advancement of Science, 47, 60n, 67, 281, 290.

Capitalism, 277, 285, 289.

Catastrophism, 30.

Central subjects, 181-201.

Chance variation, 2, 29, 32-36, 39, 62.

Character covariation *See* Cluster analysis

Checking *See* Testing

Cis-trans test, 120, 178n.

Citation, 165, 168, 205, 233, 243, 244, 252, 253, 290.

Cladistics, 4, 5, 124, 144, 150-53, 157-58, 162-78, 227, 296
  pattern or transformed, 5, 6, 69, 157-58, 162-78, 171-75
  phylogenetic, 4, 122.

Class, 79-87, 89, 92, 106, 110-26, 130, 144, 153, 189, 223, 227.

Classification *See* Systematics

Clone, 7-9.

Cluster analysis, 11, 12, 18, 22-24, 39, 80, 117, 130, 155, 159, 170, 185, 186, 196, 197, 202n, 268.

Cohesiveness, 3, 64, 81, 86, 91, 92, 102, 114, 122, 170, 173, 183, 228, 285.

Colonial organizaton, 84, 89, 92-4, 100-4, 106, 122, 160, 190, 203n, 248.

Commensurability, 46, 120, 163, 194, 225.

Common sense, 1, 6, 12, 13, 17, 20-22, 89, 111-12, 117, 119, 186, 194, 221, 271-72, 276, 279, 295.

Communication, 7, 103, 163, 208-18, 229, 235.

Competition, 83, 172, 233-35, 243-46, 248-61, 288, 290.

Conceptual change, 1, 5, 6, 7, 13, 74, 162-78, 197-99, 206, 221-40, 243-62, 294.

Conceptual units, 7, 168-69, 171, 197-98, 206.

Consilience, 154, 182.

Consistency, 129-43.

Cooperation, 165, 168-9, 177, 232, 234, 243, 244, 248-61, 289, 290.

Copernican theory, 181, 201n, 230.

Cope's Rule, 192.

Cosmogony (cosmology), 182, 190, 191, 192, 285.

Creationism, 2, 3, 5, 30, 31, 34,